MW00341505

THE
GOSPEL
ACCORDING TO SPIRITISM

THE GOSPEL

ACCORDING TO SPIRITISM

by

ALLAN KARDEC

**UNITED STATES
SPIRITIST FEDERATION**
NEW YORK
2020

THE GOSPEL

GOSPEL

ACCORDING TO SPIRITISM

Copyright © 2020 by the United States Spiritist Council

Unless otherwise indicated, all Scriptures are from the Holy Bible, English Standard Version, copyright © 2001 by Crossway Bibles, a publishing ministry of Good News Publishers. Used by permission. All rights reserved.

Original Title: L'évangile selon le Spiritisme
Translator: H. M. Monteiro
Proofreader: Jussara Korngold
Book Layout: HML
Cover Design: Mauro de Souza Rodrigues

ISBN: 978-1-948109-17-8 (United States Spiritist Council)
LCCN: 2020938727

LIBRARY OF CONGRESS CATALOGING-IN-PUBLICATION DATA

K145gas
Allan Kardec, 1804-1869.
    The Gospel according to Spiritism/Allan Kardec; translated by Helton Mattar Monteiro. – New York, NY: United States Spiritist Council, 2020.
    390 p.; 21.59 cm
    Original title: L'évangile selon le Spiritisme (4th ed., 1868)
    ISBN 978-1-948109-17-8
    1. Spirituality. 2. Spiritism. 3. Christianity. I. Title
    LCCN 2020938727

First print: June 2020

Web site: http://www.spiritist.us   Email: info@spiritist.us
Book portal: https://is.gd/USSF1

Manufactured in the United States of America

All rights reserved. No part of this publication may be reproduced, stored in or introduced into a retrieval system, or transmitted, in any form, or by any means (electronics, mechanical, photocopying, recording or otherwise) without the prior written permission of the publisher, except in the case of brief quotations and if the source and publisher are mentioned.

The name "United States Spiritist Federation" is a trade mark registered of the United States Spiritist Council.

CONTENTS

Preface

The spirits of the Lord, which are the virtues of the heaven, make up an immense army which moves as soon as it has received the command, spread over the whole surface of the Earth. Like stars falling from the sky, they come to illuminate the path and open the eyes of the blind.

Truly I say to you, the time has come when all things must be restored in their true sense to dispel darkness, to confound the proud, and to glorify the righteous.

The great voices of heaven reverberate like the sound of the trumpet, and choruses of angels assemble. O humans, we invite you to the divine concert; let your hands catch the lyre; let your voices unite, and in one sacred hymn spread and vibrate from one end of the universe to the other.

Human beings, siblings whom we love, we are near you; love one another, and say from the bottom of your hearts, doing the will of the supreme Parent which is in heaven: "Lord! O Lord!" and you will be able to enter the realm of heaven.

THE SPIRIT OF TRUTH

NOTE: The message above, mediumistically received, summarizes both the true character of Spiritism and the purpose of this book. That is why it has been placed here as preface.

INTRODUCTION

I. PURPOSE OF THIS BOOK

The material contained in the Gospels can be divided into five parts, namely: *The ordinary events of the life of Christ; the miracles; the predictions; the words which served to restore the dogmas of the Church;*[1] *and moral teachings.* Although the first four parts have been controversial, the last has remained unassailable. To this divine moral code, unbelief itself bows; it is the ground where all beliefs can meet, the flag under which all can take shelter, whatever their creeds, because it has never been the subject of religious disputes, which are always and everywhere raised by issues of dogma. Moreover, in discussing them, the religions and denominations would have found their own condemnation, for most have been more attached to the mystical aspect than to the moral aspect, which requires one's inner transformation. For humans in particular, it is a rule of conduct encompassing all the circumstances of private and public life, the principle of all social relations founded on the most rigorous justice. Finally, and above all, it is the infallible path to be pursued toward happiness, a corner of the veil raised concerning future life. This part constitutes the exclusive object of this book.

Everyone admires the moral code contained in the Gospels. Although each one of them proclaims its sublimity and necessity, many people do so out of trust, on hearsay, or resting their faith on some maxims which have become proverbial. However, few know it thoroughly and still less understand it, let alone know how to deduce its consequences. This is largely due to the difficulty posed by the reading of the Gospel, which is unintelligible to the majority of readers. The allegorical form, the intentional mysticism of language, cause most people to read it just as a way of disobliging and freeing their duty and conscience, just like they recite prayers without understanding them; that is, without yielding any fruit. The precepts of morality, scattered here and there, confounded in the

---

1 [Trans. note] Especially in Europe, "the Church" (with a capital C) was a conventional way of referring to the dominant or official religion of one's country – Roman Catholicism in France, at the time.

mass of other narratives, go unnoticed. Then it becomes impossible for one to grasp the whole, and for it to become the subject of a separate reading and meditation.

Although treatises on Gospel morality have been written, their arrangement in modern literary style deprives them of the primitive naivety which imparts them with both charm and authenticity. It is the same with detached, out of context maxims, reduced to their simplest proverbial expression. In this way, they become only aphorisms which lose part of their value and interest, by the absence of the accessories and circumstances in which they were given.

To obviate these inconveniences, I have assembled herein the articles which may constitute, properly speaking, a code of universal morality, without distinction of worship. In the quotations, I have kept all that was useful for developing one's reasoning, while pruning away only things that were extraneous to the subject. I have scrupulously respected Sacy's French original translation² as well as the verse division. But, instead of attaching myself to a chronological order, which would be impossible and without any real advantage in such a subject, the maxims have been grouped and classified methodically according to their nature, so that they are deduced as much as possible from one another. Recalling the numerical order of the biblical chapters and verses makes it possible to resort to the usual, common classification, if it is deemed appropriate.

But this was only material work, which alone would have been only of secondary utility. The essential point was to make it accessible to everyone, by explaining obscure passages, and developing all the consequences with a view to applying them to different situations of life. This is what I have tried to achieve with the help of good spirits which assist me.

Many points of the Gospel, of the Bible, and of sacred writers in general, are unintelligible. Many even seem irrational only for want of the key to understand their true meaning. This key is entirely in Spiritism, as those who have studied it seriously have already been able to convince themselves; and this will be recognized even better later. Spiritism is found everywhere in antiquity and at all ages of

---

2 [Trans. note] A. KARDEC used the old French translation of the Bible by Louis-Isaac Lemaistre de SACY (1613-1684), whereas this English edition, for consistency of biblical citations, uses the *English Standard Version* (ESV).

humankind. Everywhere traces of it are found in writings, beliefs, and monuments; that is why, if it opens new horizons for the future, it sheds a no less vital light on the mysteries of the past.

As a complement to each precept, I have added some of chosen messages from those dictated by spirits in various countries, through different mediums. If these messages were taken out of a single source, they would have had to undergo a personal or ambience influence, while the diversity of sources proves that the spirits give their teachings everywhere, and that there is no privileged person in this respect.[3]

This book is for everyone's use. Each person can draw from it the means of conforming his or her conduct to Christ's moral code. Spiritists will also be able to find in it the applications pertinent to them more specifically. Thanks to the communications established henceforth, permanently, between human beings and the invisible world, the laws of the Gospel, taught to all nations by the spirits themselves, will no longer be dead letter, because everyone will understand them, and will incessantly be asked to put them into practice by the advice of their own spiritual guides. The messages from the spirits are truly *the voices of heaven* that come to enlighten humans and invite all of us *to practice the Gospel.*

---

3 Undoubtedly, I could have given on every subject a greater number of spirit communications obtained in a multitude of other cities and Spiritist centers than those which were quoted. But I had to avoid, above all, the monotony of useless repetition, and limit my choice to those which, for their substance and form, belonged more particularly in the framework of this book, reserving for later publications those which could not fit in here.

As to mediums, I refrained from naming any of them. For the most part, it was at their request that they were not identified, therefore it was not appropriate to make exceptions. The names of the mediums, moreover, would not have added any value to the work of the spirits; it would have been only to satisfy self-esteem, to which really serious mediums would never abide, as they understand that, since their role is purely passive, the value of the communications in no way enhances their personal merit; and that it would be puerile to take pride in a work of intelligence to which they only gave mechanical assistance.

II. The authority of Spiritism

universal control of spirits' teachings[4]

If Spiritism were a purely human conception, it would only have the guarantee of the enlightenment of the one person who conceived it; but no one here below can pretend to claim to have the whole and absolute truth by oneself. If the spirits that revealed it had manifested themselves to just one person, nothing would guarantee its origin, for everyone would have to rely on this person's word, whoever he or she was, that claimed to have received their teaching. Even admitting of an absolute sincerity on the latter's part, at most this person could convince only those around him or her, who could have followers, yet would never succeed in rallying everyone

God wanted the new revelation to come to human beings by a faster and more authentic way. This is why the Creator has instructed the spirits to carry it to all corners of the world, manifesting themselves everywhere, without giving any one the exclusive privilege of hearing their teachings. One individual can be deluded, can delude himself/herself; but this cannot happen when millions see and hear the same thing: it is a guarantee for each and every one. Besides, one can make a person disappear, whereas no one can make whole masses of people disappear; books can be burned, but spirits cannot be burned. Now, even if all books were burned, the source of Spiritist tenets would remain nonetheless inexhaustible, because it is not down here on Earth, but it arises from everywhere, so that everyone can have access to it. In default of humans to spread it, there will always be spirits, which can reach everyone but are out of reach of anyone,

Therefore, it is actually the spirits which disseminate, with the aid of innumerable mediums whom they awaken everywhere. If Spiritism had only one interpreter, however gifted he/she might have been, it would scarcely be known, since such an interpreter, regardless of his/her social class or rank, would have been the object of prejudice on the part of several people. Furthermore, not all nations would have accepted it, whereas the spirits, communicating everywhere,

---

4 [Trans. note] A. Kardec uses the word *control* as a scientific term meaning *verification* or *checking*.

and to everyone, to all religious denominations and to all walks of society, can be accepted by all. Spiritism has no nationality; it is outside all specific worships; it is not imposed by any social class, since everyone can receive messages from their deceased relatives and friends from beyond the grave. This is how it had to be so that it could call all humans to fraternity, to loving fellowship. If Spiritism had not placed itself on neutral ground, it would have kept dissensions instead of appeasing them.

This universality of the teaching of the spirits is the strength of Spiritism. Therein too lies the cause of its rapid dissemination. While the voice of one individual, even with the aid of the printing press, would have taken centuries to reach the ears of a great many people, there are thousands of voices heard simultaneously in all corners of the world, proclaiming the same principles, and conveying them to the most ignorant as well as to the most learned people, so that no one is left out. This is an advantage which has not been enjoyed by any of the religious and philosophical doctrines that have appeared to this day. If, then, Spiritism is genuinely truthful, it fears neither the human ill-will, nor moral revolutions, nor any physical upheavals of the globe, because none of these things can reach the spirits.

But this is not the sole advantage resulting from this exceptional position. Spiritism finds in it an omnipotent guarantee against any schisms that might be aroused by the ambition of some or the contradictions of certain spirits. These contradictions are certainly a stumbling block, but one which carries in itself the remedy beside the evil.

We know that spirits, by reason of the difference which exists in their respective capabilities, are far from being individually in possession of the whole truth; that it is not given to all of them to penetrate certain mysteries; that their knowledge is proportionate to their purification; that average spirits know no more than incarnate humans, and even less than some of the latter. We also know that, among them as among the latter, there are presumptuous and false scholars who think they know what they actually do not know; systematic individuals that take their personal ideas for the truth. Lastly, we are well aware that only spirits of the highest order – those which are completely dematerialized – have completely stripped away all earthly ideas and prejudices. Yet, we also know that deceiving spirits do not have any scruple to take on illustrious names, so as to make their chimeras acceptable. As a result, for all that is outside exclusively moral teaching, the revelations that each can obtain have an individual character without authenticity. Therefore they must be considered as personal opinions of this or that spirit; and it would be unwise to accept them and to carelessly announce them as absolute truths.

The first control[5] is unquestionably that of reason, to which we must submit, without exception, anything that comes from the spirits. Any theory in manifest contradiction with common sense, with rigorous logic, and with positive data that we may possess, or of any respectable name that may sign the message, must be rejected. But this control is incomplete in many cases, due to the insufficiency of certain people's enlightenment, and the tendency of many to turn their own judgment into the sole arbiter of the truth. In such cases, what do individuals who do not have absolute confidence in themselves do? They consult the opinion of the greatest number, and the opinion of the majority should be their guide. So it must be with regard to the teaching of spirits, which provide us themselves with means to that purpose.

The general agreement in the teaching of the spirits is therefore the best control; but it must still take place under certain conditions. The least sure of all is when a medium interrogates several spirits on a dubious point: it is quite obvious that if he/she is under the influence some spiritual obsession, or if he/she is dealing with a deceiving spirit, that same spirit can tell the medium the same thing using different names to identify itself. Likewise, there is not sufficient guarantee in the conformity of what is obtained by mediums belonging to a single Spiritist center, because they too might undergo the same influence,

The only serious guarantee of the teachings of the spirits is in the general agreement which exists among the revelations made spontaneously, through a large number of mediums unknown to one another, and in various different places.

Let it be clear that there is no question here of communications relating to secondary interests, but rather those connected with the very principles of Spiritist tenets. Experience has shown that when a

---

5 [Trans. note] See footnote 4 above.

new principle ought to receive its solution, it is taught *spontaneously* on different locations at once, and in an identical manner, if not in form, at least in substance. If, then, it pleases a spirit to formulate an eccentric system based on its own ideas and away from the truth, we can rest assured that such a system will remain *circumscribed*, and will fall in view of unanimous messages given everywhere else – as attested by several examples I could witness myself. It is this unanimity which has brought down all the partial systems hatched at the origin of Spiritism, when each one explained the phenomena in its own way, before the laws that govern the relations between the visible world and the invisible world were known.

This is the foundation upon which we Spiritists rely when formulating a principle of philosophical and religious doctrine. It is not because it is according to our ideas that we present it as true; we do not pose as the supreme arbiter of truth, and we never say to anyone "Believe such a thing, because we say it to you." Our opinion is in our own eyes only a personal opinion which may be right or wrong, because we are no more infallible than any other person. Nor is it because a principle is taught to us that it is for us the truth, but because it has received the corroboration of general agreement.

From my position, receiving the communications of nearly a thousand serious Spiritist centers scattered all over the world, I am able to see the principles on which this general agreement is established. It is this observation that has guided me to this day; and it is also the one that will guide me in the new fields that Spiritism is called to explore. Thus, by attentively studying the communications coming from various different locations, both in France and abroad, I recognize, from the very special nature of these revelations, that there is a tendency to enter into a new path, and that the moment has come to take a step forward. Such revelations, sometimes made in words, often went unnoticed by many who obtained them. Many others thought they alone had obtained them. Taken alone, they would be worthless to us. Only agreement gives them solemn importance. Then, when it is time to deliver them to the public, everyone remembers having received messages in the same vein. It is this general movement that I observe and study, with the assistance of my spirit guides, which helps me to judge if it is opportune for me to take some action or to refrain from doing something.

This universal control is a guarantee for the future unity of Spiritism, and will annul all contradictory theories. It is in this method of verification that in future we will seek the criterion of truth. What made the success of the tenets formulated in *The Spirits' Book* and in *The Mediums' Book* is that everywhere, everyone has been able to receive directly from the spirits the confirmation of what they contain. If, on all locations, the spirits had come to contradict them, these books would have long since suffered the fate of all fanciful conceptions. Even the support of the press would not have saved them from sinking, while, deprived of this support, they have nevertheless thrived quickly, because they had the support of the spirits, whose good will has overcome and made up for any human ill will. So will it happen to all ideas emanating from spirits or human beings who cannot bear the test of this control, whose power cannot be denied by anyone.

Suppose then that it pleases certain spirits to dictate, under whatever name, a book in the contrary direction. Let us even suppose that, with hostile intention, and with a view to discrediting Spiritism, some malevolence is aroused by apocryphal communications: what influence might these writings have if they are contradicted everywhere by the spirits? It is the actual adherence to the latter that one should make sure about, before launching a system on their behalf. From the system of one to that of many, there is the same distance that exists from a single unit to limitlessness. What can all the arguments offered by detractors do against the opinion of the masses, when millions of friendly voices from space, come from all corners of the universe, and within the bosom of each family, to defeat them? Has not experience in this respect already confirmed the theory? What has become of all these publications supposedly aimed at annihilating Spiritism? Which one has succeeded to hinder its march? Up to this day this issue had not been considered from this point of view, which is one of the most serious, without contradiction. Each counted on oneself, but without taking into account the intervention of the spirits.

Furthermore, the principle of general agreement acts as a guarantee against occasional alterations which sects or denominations would like to make to Spiritism in order to seize it for their profit and accommodate it to their convenience. Anyone who would attempt to deviate Spiritism from its providential purpose would fail, by the very simple reason that the spirits, by the universality of their teaching, will cause the demise of any change that deviates from the truth.

One of the most important truths which results from this is the fact that anyone who wishes to go against the established and corroborated stream of ideas may well cause a small, momentary local disturbance, but never dominate the whole, even in the current time, and even less in future.

It is further apparent that the messages given by the spirits on points of the Spiritist doctrine not yet elucidated cannot be taken as law, as long as they remain isolated; and that they should be accepted only with reservations and as information.

Hence the necessity of using the greatest prudence before publicizing them; and, in case it is thought necessary to publish them, it is of utmost importance to present them only as individual opinions, more or less probable, but nonetheless requiring further confirmation. It is for this confirmation that one must wait before presenting a principle as an absolute truth, if one does not want to be accused of lightness of judgment or of unthinking credulity.

No matter how high the spirits proceed in their revelations with extreme wisdom, they approach the great questions of Spiritism only gradually, as our intelligence is apt to understand truths of a higher order, and circumstances are propitious for formulating a new idea. This is the reason why, from the beginning, they have not said everything, and have not yet said everything even today, never yielding to the impatience of people who are in too much of a hurry and want to pick the fruit before they are ripe. It would be superfluous to anticipate the time assigned to each thing by Providence, for then the really serious spirits would positively refuse their help. But irresponsible and frivolous spirits, caring little for the truth, will answer to any question posed to them. It is for this reason that, to all premature questions, there are always contradictory answers.

The principles stated above are not the result of a personal theory, but rather the inevitable consequence of the conditions in which spirits manifest themselves. It is quite evident that if a spirit says a thing on one side, while millions of spirits say otherwise to the contrary, the presumption of truth cannot be for the one that is alone or nearly totally alone in its opinion. Anyway, to pretend to hold the only right opinion against all the others would be as illogical on the part of a spirit as it is on the part of an incarnate individual. Truly wise spirits, if they do not feel sufficiently enlightened on an issue, never opine about it in an absolute manner. Instead they state that they are dealing with it only from their own point of view, and advise others to await further confirmation.

No matter how great, beautiful, and just an idea may be, it is impossible for it to rally all opinions behind it from the beginning. The resulting conflicts are the inevitable consequence of the movement taking place; they are even necessary, in order to better bring out the truth, and it is useful for them to take place in the beginning so that the wrong ideas are more quickly exhausted. Those Spiritists who have some apprehension about such matters may rest reassured that there is nothing to cause concern. All isolated pretensions will fall by force of circumstances when faced with the great and powerful criterion of universal control.

It is not behind the opinion of a single individual that we will rally ourselves, but rather with the unanimous voice of the spirits. It is not one person, *no more than any other,* who will found the Spiritist orthodoxy; nor is it any spirit coming to impose itself on anyone: but rather the universality of spirits communicating on the whole Earth by God's command. This is the essential character of Spiritism; therein lies its strength and its authority. God wanted Its law to be erected on an unshakable base; which is why It did not let this law rest on the fragile head of a single individual.

It is before this mighty Areopagus,[6] which knows neither coteries, nor jealous rivalries, nor sects, nor nations, that all oppositions, all ambitions, and all pretensions to individual supremacy will be broken. And *we would break ourselves against it, should we wish to substitute our poor ideas for its sovereign decrees.* It is it alone that will decide all the contentious issues, which will silence dissent; and will give right or wrong to those who deserve it by right. Faced with this imposing agreement of all the heavenly voices, what can the opinion of a single human or spirit? Less than a drop of

---

6 [Trans. note] *Areopagus* was a hill in Ancient Greece on which met the highest governmental council and later a judicial court.

water lost in the ocean, less than the voice of a child suffocated by the storm.

Universal opinion, that is the supreme arbiter, the one which pronounces in the last resort. It is formed of all individual opinions; if one of them is true, it does not reach its relative weight in the balance; if it is false, it cannot prevail over all the others. In this immense contest, individualities are erased, and therein lies another defeat for human pride.

This harmonious whole is already being outlined; but this century will not pass until it shines with all its brilliancy so that it dissipates all uncertainties; for in the meantime powerful voices will have been given the mission to make themselves heard to rally humans under the same banner as soon as the field is sufficiently plowed. Meanwhile, the one that floats between two opposing systems to observe in what sense the general opinion is formed will be the sure indicator of the sense in which the majority of the spirits pronounce themselves about the various issues of which they communicate to one another. It is a no less certain sign of which of the two systems will prevail.

III. Historical data

To understand certain passages of the Gospels well, it is necessary to know the value of several words which are frequently used, and which characterize the state of habits, manners and Jewish society at that time. These words, which no longer have the same meaning for us today, have often been misinterpreted, and as such have created a sort of uncertainty. Getting to know their correct meaning further explains the true meaning of certain maxims that seem strange at first sight.

Samaritans – After the schism of the ten tribes, Samaria became the capital of the dissident kingdom of Israel. Destroyed and rebuilt several times, it was, under the Romans, the chief town of Samaria, one of the four divisions of Palestine. Herod, known as the Great, embellished it with sumptuous monuments, and, in order to flatter Augustus, called it *Augusta*, or *Sebaste* in Greek.

The Samaritans were almost always at war with the kings of Judah; a profound aversion, dating from the separation, was constantly being perpetuated between the two peoples, who refused all reciprocal relations. Moreover, the Samaritans, in order to make the split even deeper and to have no future coming to Jerusalem for the celebration of religious festivals, built a temple for themselves and adopted certain religious reforms. They admitted only the Pentateuch containing the law of Moses, and rejected all the books which were appended thereafter. Their sacred books were written in Hebrew characters of the highest antiquity. In the eyes of Orthodox Jews they were heretics, and by that very fact despised, anathematized, and persecuted. The antagonism of the two nations at that time, had as its sole principle the divergence of religious opinions, although their beliefs had the same origin. They were like Protestants of their time.

Samaritans are still found today in some parts of the Levant, particularly in Nablus and Jaffa. They observe the law of Moses with more rigor than other Jews, and enter into an alliance only among themselves.

NAZARENES – Name given in the old law to the Jews who made a vow, either for life or for a while, to keep themselves in perfect purity. They practiced chastity, abstinence from alcoholic beverages, and the preservation of their hair. Samson, Samuel and John the Baptist were all Nazarenes.

Later the Jews would give this name to the early Christians, referring to Jesus of Nazareth.

It was also the name of a heretical sect in the first centuries of the Christian era, which, like the Ebionites – whose principles it adopted – mixed the practices of Mosaism with Christian dogmas. This sect disappeared in the 4th century AD.

PUBLICANS – In ancient Rome, this is how they called officers responsible for the public finances, in charge of the collection of taxes and revenues of all kinds, either in Rome itself or in other parts of the empire. They were analogous to the general farmers and traders of the old regime in France, and still can be found in certain countries. The risks they were constantly running made authorities turn a blind eye to the riches they often acquired, which in many cases were the product of scandalous abuses and profits. The name of publican extended later to all those who had the handling of the public money and to their subordinate agents. Today this word is taken in a bad sense to designate the financiers and agents of unscrupulous business; it is sometimes said: "Greedy like a publican; rich as a publican," when referring to a fortune obtained by wickedness.

Coming from Roman rule the tax was what the Jews most reluctantly accepted, and which caused most rebellion on their part. Several revolts ensued, and it was turned into a religious issue, because it was regarded as contrary to the Mosaic law. A powerful party was formed at the head of which was a certain Judas the Galonite,[7] who had for principle the refusal of the tax. The Jews, therefore, abhorred the tax, and, consequently, all those who were charged to collecting it; hence their aversion to the publicans of all ranks, among whom could be found very estimable people, but who, by reason of their functions, were despised, as well as those who entertained them, and who were confounded in the same reprobation. Jews of distinction would have thought they were compromising themselves by having close relations with them.

TOLL COLLECTORS – These were low-level tax collectors, mainly charged with collecting tolls at the entrance of towns. Their functions corresponded almost exactly to those of today's customs officers and similar positions. They shared the same disapproval as publicans in general. It is for this reason that, in the Gospel, one frequently finds the term *publican* associated to *people of bad life*. This qualification did not imply debauchees and people without a religious confession; it was a term of contempt synonymous with *people of bad company*, unworthy of associating themselves with *dignified people*.

PHARISEES – (From Aramaic *prišayyā* 'separated ones'; related to Hebrew *pārūš* 'separated'.) Tradition formed an important part of Jewish theology; it consisted in the collection of successive interpretations of the meaning of the Scriptures, which had become articles of dogma. It was among doctors the subject of interminable discussions, most often on simple issues of words or forms, in the style of later theological disputes and subtleties of the scholasticism of the Middle Ages, from which came different sects and denominations

---

7 [Trans. note] Also known as Judas of Gamala or Judas of Galilee.

which claimed to have the monopoly of truth, and, as it happens almost always, cordially hated one another.

Among these sects was the most influential one of the Pharisees, led by Hillel, a Jewish physician born in Babylon, founder of a famous school where the teaching was that faith was due only to the Scriptures. Its origin dates back to the year 180 or 200 BC. The Pharisees were persecuted at various times, notably under Hyrcanus, sovereign pontiff and king of the Jews; Aristobulus and Alexander, king of Syria. However, the latter having given them their honors and possessions, they regained their power which they retained until the fall of Jerusalem, Around the year 70 AD their name disappeared as a result of the dispersion of the Jews.

The Pharisees had an active role in religious controversies. Servile observers of the external practices of worship and ceremonies, full of ardent zeal for proselytism, enemies of the innovators, they affected a great severity of principles. But under the appearance of a meticulous devotion, they hid dissolute morals, a great deal of pride and, above all, an excessive love of control and domination. Religion was for them a means to an end rather than the object of sincere faith. They had only the outside and the ostentation of virtue; but through this they exerted a strong influence on the people, in whose eyes they passed for holy individuals. That is why they were very powerful in Jerusalem.

They believed, or at least professed to believe, in Providence, the immortality of the soul, the eternity of punishment, and the resurrection of the dead (see Chapter **IV**, item **4** below). Jesus, who first of all took into account the simplicity and qualities of the heart, and who preferred in the law *the spirit that enlivens to the letter that kills*, endeavored, throughout his mission, to unmask their hypocrisy. As a result they became his fierce enemies, colluding with the high priests to stir up the people against him, and to ultimately destroy him.

SCRIBES – Name given in principle to the secretaries of the kings of Judah, and to certain stewards of the Jewish armies. Later this designation was applied especially to the teachers who taught Moses' law and interpreted it to the people. They made common cause with the Pharisees, whose principles and antipathy to innovators they shared, That is why Jesus includes them in the same reprobation.

SYNAGOGUE – (From Greek *sunagōgē* 'meeting,' 'congregation.') There was only one temple in Judea, that of Solomon at Jerusalem, where the great ceremonies of worship were celebrated. The Jews went there on pilgrimage for the main feasts every year, such as Passover, Dedication, and Tabernacles. It was on these occasions that Jesus made several journeys there. The other cities had no temples, but synagogues, buildings where the Jews were gathered on the Sabbath days to make sacrifices and public prayers, under the direction of Elders, scribes or doctors of the law. They also read from the sacred books that were explained and commented on; everyone could take part, That is why Jesus, without being a priest, taught in the synagogues on Sabbath days.

After the destruction of Jerusalem and the dispersion of the Jews, the synagogues in the cities they inhabited were used as temples for the celebration of worship.

SADDUCEES – Jewish sect which was formed around the year 248 BC, so named after Zadok (Hebrew *Sadoq*), its founder. The Sadducees did not believe in the immortality of the soul, nor in the resurrection, nor in good and bad angels. Nevertheless, they believed in God, yet not expecting anything after death. They served God only for temporal rewards, to which, according to them, God's providence limited itself. In their eyes, therefore, the satisfaction of the senses was the essential object of life. As for the Scriptures, they sticked to the text of the ancient law, admitting neither tradition nor any interpretation. They placed good deeds and the pure and simple execution of the law above the external practices of worship. They were, as we can see, the materialists, deists and sensualists of the time. This sect was small, but it had some important members; and as a political party, it constantly opposed the Pharisees.

ESSENES or ESSENIANS – Jewish sect founded around 450 BC in the time of the Maccabees, whose members led an ascetic life in places similar to monasteries, and formed a kind of moral and religious association among them. They distinguished themselves by their gentle manners and austere virtues; taught the love of God and neighbor, the immortality of the soul; and believed in the resurrection. They lived in celibacy, condemned servitude and war, held property in common, and engaged in agriculture. Opposed to the sensual Sadducees who denied immortality, and to rigid Pharisees for their outward practices, and in which virtue was only apparent, they took no part in the quarrels that divided those two sects. Their way of life was close to that of the early Christians, and the moral principles they professed led some people to think that Jesus was part of this sect before the beginning of his public mission. What is certain is that he must have known it, but there is nothing to prove that he was affiliated with it, and everything written about it is hypothetical.[8]

THERAPEUTAE – (From Greek *therapeutikos*, from *therapeuein* 'minister to, treat medically'; that is, servants of God or healers.) Contemporary Jewish sectarians contemporary with Christ, established mainly in Alexandria, Egypt. They had a great relationship with the Essenes, whose principles they professed. Like the latter they devoted themselves to the practice of all virtues. Their food was extremely frugal; devoted to celibacy, contemplation, and solitary life, they formed a true religious order. Philo, the Platonic Jewish philosopher of Alexandria, is the first to speak of Therapeutics; it has made it a sect of Judaism. Eusebius, St Jerome and other Church Fathers[9] thought they were Christians. Whether they were Jews or Christians, it is obvious that, like the Essenes, they form the link between Judaism and Christianity.

IV. SOCRATES AND PLATO, FORERUNNERS OF THE CHRISTIAN IDEA AND SPIRITISM

Based on the fact that Jesus must have known the sect of the Essenes, it would be wrong to conclude that he drew from it his tenets, and that, should he had lived in another milieu, he would have professed different principles. Great ideas never burst forth

---

8 Incidentally, *La Mort de Jésus* [*The Death of Jesus*] (4th ed. Paris: Dentu, 1864), supposedly written by an Essene monk, is a completely apocryphal book, written to serve an opinion, and which contains in itself the proof of its modern origin.

9 [Trans. note] The so-called Church Fathers are the most important authors of the early history of Christian literature, whose writings are regarded as especially authoritative.

suddenly; those based on truth always have forerunners that partly prepare the way for them. After that, when the time has come, God sends an individual with a mission to summarize, coordinate and complete these scattered elements, and to form a body of thought out of them. In this way the idea, not arriving abruptly, finds, at its appearance, minds ready to accept it. And so it was with the Christian idea, which was felt several centuries before Jesus and the Essenes, and of which Socrates and Plato were the main forerunners.

Socrates, like Christ, wrote nothing, or at least left no texts. Like him, he was executed as a criminal, victim of fanaticism, for having attacked received traditional beliefs, and put real virtue above hypocrisy and sham forms – in a word, for having fought religious prejudices. Like Jesus was accused by the Pharisees of corrupting the people by his teachings, he too was accused by his contemporary Pharisees – for types like these have existed in all ages – of corrupting the youth by proclaiming the dogma of the unicity of God, of the immortality of the soul, and future life. In the same way that we know of Jesus' tenets only by the writings of his disciples, we only know the teachings of Socrates by the writings left by his disciple Plato. I think it would be useful to summarize herein the highlights of his thought to show its agreement with the principles of Christianity,

To those who look at such a parallel as a profanation, and pretend that there can be no parity between the doctrine of a Gentile and that of Christ, I answer that the doctrine of Socrates was not pagan, since its object was to combat paganism; and that Jesus' doctrine, more complete and more refined than that of Socrates, has nothing to lose in comparison. The greatness of the divine mission of Christ cannot be diminished; and that besides it, there are historical facts that cannot be stifled. Humans have reached a point where light comes out of itself from under a bushel. We are ripe to look at it face to face; all the worse for those who dare not open their eyes. The time has come to consider things broadly and from higher above, and no longer from the petty point of view and narrow interests of sects and castes.

Furthermore, these citations will prove that, although Socrates and Plato had sensed in advance the Christian idea, the fundamental principles of Spiritism are also found in their philosophical tenets.

Summary of the doctrine of Socrates and Plato

I.   Every human being is an incarnated soul. Before its incarnation, it existed united to the primordial types, to the ideas of truth, good, and beauty. It separates itself by incarnating itself, and, remembering its past, it is more or less tormented by the desire to return to it.

The distinction and independence of the intelligent principle and the material principle could not be more clearly stated; it is, moreover, the doctrine of the preexistence of the soul; from the vague intuition the latter retains from another world to which it aspires; from its survival in the body, from its exit from the spiritual world to incarnate itself, and from its return to the same world after death. Finally, it is also the germ of the doctrine of fallen angels.

II.   The soul is lost and troubled when it uses the body to consider some object; it has vertigo as if it were drunk, because it is attached to things which are, by their nature, subject to change; whereas, when it contemplates its own essence, it moves towards what is pure, eternal, immortal, and, being of the same nature, it remains attached to it as long as it can. Then its mistakes cease, for it is united with that which is immutable, and this state of mind is what is called wisdom.

Thus to a human being who considers things from below, down to earth, from the material point of view, it becomes an illusion. In order to appreciate things with justice, one must see them from above, that is, from the spiritual point of view. The truly wise person must somehow isolate the soul from the body, to see with the eyes of the spirit. This is what Spiritism teaches (see Chapter **II**, item **5** below).

III.   As long as we have our body and the soul is immersed in this corruption, we will never possess the object of our desires: the truth. Indeed, the body arouses in us a thousand obstacles by the necessity that we have of taking care of it. Moreover, it fills us with desires, appetites, fears, a thousand chimeras, and a thousand follies, so that with it it is impossible to be wise even for one moment. But, if it is not possible to know anything purely while the soul is united to the body, two things should happen, namely, either the truth must never be known, unless it

is known after death, or once freed from the madness of the body, we will then converse – it is to be hoped – with equally freed souls; and we will know for ourselves the essence of things. That is why the true philosophers practice to die, and to them death does not seem to be something dreadful (see Allan KARDEC, *Heaven and Hell*, Part One, ch. II; and Part Two, ch. I).

This expresses the principle of the faculties of the soul obscured by the intermediate corporeal organs, and the expansion of these faculties after death. But this refers only to already purified elite souls, whereas the situation of impure souls is quite different.

IV. **In this state, an impure soul grows heavier and duller, and is dragged back to the visible world by its horror of what is invisible and immaterial. It then wanders, it is said, around monuments and tombs, near which we have sometimes seen dark ghosts, as must be the particular aspect of souls who have left the body without being entirely pure, and which retain something of the material form, so that the eye can see them. These are not the souls of the good but of the wicked, who are forced to wander in these places, where they bear the penalty of their former life, and where they continue to wander until the appetites inherent in the material form, to which they have given themselves, brings them back to a new body. Then they doubtlessly resume the same mores which, during their former life, were the object of their predilections.**

Not only is the principle of reincarnation clearly expressed here, but the state of those souls which are still under the influence of matter is described as Spiritism shows it in its evocations. There is more: it is said that reincarnation in a material body is a consequence of the impurity of the soul, while purified souls are freed from it. Spiritism does not say anything else, only adding that the soul that has taken good resolutions while they were in errant state (i.e., between incarnations), and that has acquired knowledge, brings back fewer defects, more virtues, and more intuitive ideas than it had in the past, during a previous existence. Thus each new existence marks for it an intellectual and moral progress (see Allan KARDEC, *Heaven and Hell*, Part Two, "Examples").

V. **After our death, the 'demon' (in Greek *daimōn* 'deity, genius') assigned to us during our life leads us to a place where all those who** are to be led to Hades will be judged. Souls, after staying in Hades for the necessary time, are brought back to this life for several long periods.

This is the doctrine of guardian angels or protector spirits, and successive reincarnations after longer or shorter intervals in the errant state (i.e. between incarnations).

VI. Demons fill the gap that separates heaven from Earth; they are the link that unites the Great All with itself. The divinity never comes into direct communication with humans; it is through demons that the gods trade and talk with humans, either during the waking state or during sleep.

The word *daimōn*, which originated the modern term demon,was not taken in a bad sense in ancient Greece as it is today. It did not refer exclusively to malevolent beings, but of all spirits in general, among which Greeks distinguished the higher spirits, which they called gods; and lower spirits, or so-called 'demons' properly speaking, which communicated directly with humans. Spiritism also says that spirits populate space; that God communicates Itself with humans only through the intermediary of pure spirits in charge of transmitting his will; that spirits communicate that spirits communicate during the day before and during sleep. If you replace the word demon by the word spirit, you will have the Spiritist doctrine; replace it instead by the word angel, and you will have the Christian doctrine.

VII. The constant concern of a philosopher (as understood by Socrates and Plato) should be to take the greatest care of the soul, less for this life, which lasts only an instant, than for eternity. If the soul is immortal, is it not wise to live for eternity?

Both Christianity and Spiritism teach this same principle.

VIII. If the soul is immaterial, it must pass, after this life, into a world as invisible and immaterial, just like the body, in decomposing itself, returns to matter. However it is important to distinguish clearly the pure soul, truly immaterial, which feeds, like God, on science and thoughts, from the soul more or less tainted with material impurities which prevent it from rising to the divine, and hold it in the places of its earthly stay.

As we can see, Socrates and Plato perfectly understood the different degrees of dematerialization of the soul. They insist on the difference of situation which results for the souls from their higher or lesser degree of purity. What they said by intuition, Spiritism proves by the many examples it places before our eyes (see Allan KARDEC, *Heaven and Hell*, Part Two).

IX. If death were the dissolution of the whole human being, it would be a great gain for the wicked, after their death, to be delivered at the same time from their bodies, their souls, and their vices. Only those who have adorned their souls, not with extraneous ornaments, but with that which is peculiar to oneself, can alone calmly wait for the hour of his/her departure to the other world.

In other words, materialism, which proclaims nothingness after death, would be the annulment of all subsequent moral responsibility, which would therefore incite the practice of evil. The wicked would thus have everything to gain from nothingness; yet only those individuals who have stripped themselves of their vices and have enriched themselves with virtues can wait quietly for their revival in the other life. Spiritism shows us, by the examples it places daily before our eyes, how painful it is for the wicked to pass from one life to another, and the entrance into the future life (see Allan KARDEC, *Heaven and Hell*, Part Two, ch. I).

X. The body preserves the well marked vestiges of the care taken of it or the accidents it has experienced. The same happens with the soul; when it is stripped of the body, it bears the obvious traces of its character, of its affections, and the imprints which each of the acts of its life have left in it. Thus the greatest misfortune that can happen to a human being is to go to the other world with a soul charged with crimes. You see, Callicles, neither you, nor Polus, nor Gorgias, can prove that we must lead another life that will be useful when we are there. Of so many different opinions, the only one which remains unshakable is that *it is better to receive than to commit an injustice*, and that before all things one must strive for, not to appear to be a good person, but to actually be one. (Socrates talking to his disciples in his prison.)

Here we find this other capital point, confirmed today by experience, that the unpurified soul retains the ideas, tendencies, character and passions it had on Earth. This maxim, *It is better to receive than to commit an injustice*, is not entirely Christian? It is the same thought that Jesus expresses by this saying: "To one who strikes you on the cheek, offer the other also (LUKE 6:29)." (See ch. **XII**, items **7**and **8** below.)

XI.   Of two things one is certain: either death is an absolute destruction, or it is the passage of a soul to another place. If everything is to be extinguished, death will be like one of those rare nights we spend without dreams and without any self-awareness. However, if death is only a change of residence, the passage to a place where the dead must meet, what happiness to meet those we have known! My greatest pleasure would be to examine closely the inhabitants of this place and to distinguish, as here, those who are wise from those who believe they are but are not. But it is time to leave, me to die, you to live. (Socrates addressing his judges.)

According to Socrates, human beings who have lived on Earth meet themselves again after death, and recognize one another. Spiritism shows them the relationships they have had, so that death is neither an interruption nor a cessation of life, but a seamless transformation, without any break of continuity.

Socrates and Plato would have known the teachings that Christ gave five hundred years later, and those now given by the spirits, that what they said was not in contradiction. In this there is nothing to be surprised, if one considers that great truths are eternal, and that the advanced spirits must have known them before coming to the Earth, where they introduced them. That Socrates, Plato, and the great philosophers of their time may have been, later on, among those who seconded Christ in his divine mission, and that they were chosen precisely because they were, more than others, able to understand his sublime teachings; and that they could at last become part of the galaxy of spirits charged with coming to teach humans the same truths.

XII.   *We must never render injustice for injustice, nor do any harm to anyone that has done harm to us.* Few, however, will admit this principle, and individuals who are divided on this matter do despise one another.

Is not this the principle of charitable love that teaches us not to render evil for evil, and to forgive our enemies?

XIII.   *A tree is recognized by its fruit.* **We must qualify each action according to what it produces: call it bad when it comes from evil, good when it is born from good.**

This maxim, "A tree is recognized by its fruit," is textually repeated several times in the Gospel.

XIV.   Wealth is a great danger. Every human being that loves riches does not love themselves or their own, but rather something that he/she does not like, and which is even more extraneous to them than what actually belongs to them (see Chapter **XVI** below).

XV.   The most beautiful prayers and the most beautiful sacrifices will please the Divinity less than a virtuous soul that strives to be like the latter. It would be a grave fault for the gods to have more regard for our offerings than for our souls, since by this means, the most culpable could make the gods propitious. Yet, no, there are truly just and wise human beings who, by their words and deeds, pay what they owe both to the gods and other humans (see Chapter **X**, items **7** and **8** below).

XVI.   I call a vicious person a vulgar lover who loves the body rather than the soul. Love is everywhere in Nature which invites us to exercise our intelligence; it is found even in the movement of the stars. It is love that adorns Nature with its rich carpets. It adorns itself and sets its home where it finds flowers and perfumes. It is still love that gives peace to humans, calm to the sea, silence to the winds and rest to pain.

Love, which must unite humans by a fraternal bond, is a consequence of Plato's theory of universal love as the law of Nature. Socrates having said that "Love is neither a god nor a mortal, but a great 'demon'," that is to say, a great spirit presides over universal love. This word was above all wrongly imputed to it as a crime.

XVII.   Virtue cannot be taught; it comes by a gift of God to those who possess it.

This is very close to the Christian doctrine about grace; but if virtue were a gift from God, it would be a favor, and one might ask why it is not granted to everyone. On the other hand, if it is a gift, it is without merit for the one who possesses it. Spiritism is more explicit: it says that one who possesses virtue has acquired it by one's own efforts and successive lives by gradually stripping oneself of one's imperfections. Grace is the strength of which God favors every human being of good will to abstain from evil and to do good.

XVIII. Each of us is naturally disposed to perceive in ourselves much less of our own defects than those we detect in others.

The Gospel says, "You see the speck that is in your brother's eye, but do not notice the log that is in your own eye." (See ch. **X**, items **9** and **10** below.)

XIX. If physicians fail in most diseases, it is because *they treat the body without the soul*, and that, if the whole being is not in good condition, it is impossible for a part of it to be truly well.

Spiritism gives the key to the relationship between the soul and the body, and proves that there is an incessant reaction of one to the other. It thus opens a new path to science. By showing to the latter the true cause of certain illnesses, it gives it the means to combat them. When it takes into account the action of the spiritual element in the process, it will fail less often.

XX. Every human being, starting from childhood, do much more harm than good.

This saying of Socrates touches on the serious issue of the predominance of evil on Earth, which would be insoluble without the knowledge of the plurality of worlds and the destiny of the Earth, where only a very small fraction of humanity lives. Spiritism alone provides the solution, which is further developed below in Chapters **II**, **III** and **V**.

XXI. There is wisdom in not pretending to know what you actually do not know.

This addresses people who criticize what they often do not know even the first word about. Plato completes this thought of Socrates by saying: "Let us first try to render them more honestly, if possible, in words; otherwise, do not worry about them, and seek only the truth. Let us try to instruct ourselves, but do not insult one another." Thus should spiritists act with regard to their good or bad faith adversaries. Should Plato be incarnated again today, he would find things almost the same as they were at his time, and could keep the same language. Socrates would also find people that would mock his belief in spirits, and treat him as a lunatic, and his disciple Plato as well.

It was for having professed these principles that Socrates was first ridiculed, then accused of impiety, and condemned to drink hemlock; which proves that great new truths, arousing against them the interests and prejudices they hurt, cannot be established without struggle and without making martyrs.

The Gospel

according to Spiritism

Chapter I
Do not think that I have come to abolish the Law

THE THREE REVELATIONS: MOSES; CHRIST; SPIRITISM · ALLIANCE OF SCIENCE AND
RELIGION · *INSTRUCTIONS FROM THE SPIRITS:* THE NEW ERA

1.   "Do not think that I have come to abolish the Law or the
Prophets; I have not come to abolish them but to fulfill them. For
truly, I say to you, until heaven and earth pass away, not an iota, not
a dot, will pass from the Law until all is accomplished (MATTHEW
5:12–18 ESV[10])."

MOSES

2.   There are two distinct parts in the Mosaic Law: the law of
God promulgated on Mount Sinai, and the civil or disciplinary law
established by Moses. One is invariable; the other is appropriate to
the customs and character of the people, and changes with time.

The law of God is formulated in the following ten commandments:
"And God spoke all these words, saying,

[i] 'I am the LORD your God, who brought you out of the land
of Egypt, out of the house of slavery. – 'You shall have no other
gods before me.' – 'You shall not make for yourself a carved image,
or any likeness of anything that is in heaven above, or that is in the
earth beneath, or that is in the water under the earth. You shall not
bow down to them or serve them...'

---

10 [Trans. note] With a few exceptions, all textual citations from the Bible
contained herein were excerpted from the *Holy Bible, English Standard Version* (ESV).

[II] 'You shall not take the name of the LORD your God in vain...'

[III] 'Remember the Sabbath day, to keep it holy....'

[IV] 'Honor your father and your mother, that your days may be long in the land that the LORD your God is giving you.'

[V] 'You shall not murder.'

[VI] 'You shall not commit adultery.'

[VII] 'You shall not steal.

[VIII] 'You shall not bear false witness against your neighbor.

[IX] 'You shall not covet your neighbor's wife...'

[X] 'You shall not covet your neighbor's house; or his male servant, or his female servant, or his ox, or his donkey, or anything that is your neighbor's' (*cf.* Exodus 20:1–17 ESV)."

This law is of all times and all places, and for that very reason has a divine character. All the others are laws established by Moses, obliged to subdue by fear a people naturally turbulent and undisciplined, in which he had to fight rooted abuses and prejudices drawn from their servitude in Egypt. To give authority to his own laws, he must have ascribed to them a divine origin, as all the legislators of primitive peoples have done. The authority of man was to rely on the authority of God; but only the idea of a terrifying God could impress ignorant people, in whom the moral sense and the sense of rightful justice were still little developed. It is quite evident that he who put in his commandments, "You shall not murder; [you shall not harm your neighbor]," could not contradict himself by turning extermination into a duty. The Mosaic laws, properly speaking, were therefore essentially transitory.

CHRIST

3. Jesus did not come to abolish the law, that is, the law of God; he came to fulfill it, that is, to develop it, to give it its true meaning, and to approximate it to the degree of advancement of human beings. That is why we find in this law the principle of duties toward God and towards our fellow beings, which form the foundation of his tenets. As for the laws of Moses, properly speaking, he has, on the contrary, profoundly modified them, either in substance or in form. He constantly fought the abuse of external practices and false interpretations, and he could not make them undergo a more radical transformation than by reducing them to these words, "To love God above all things, and your neighbor as yourself,"[11] and by saying, *This is the whole law and the prophets.*

With these words, "Until heaven and earth pass away, not an iota, not a dot, will pass from the Law until all is accomplished," Jesus meant that the law of God must be fulfilled, that is to say, practiced all over the Earth, in all its purity, with all its developments and all its consequences; for what would it be to have established this law if it were to remain the privilege of a few humans or even a single people? Since all humans are children of God, they are all without distinction, the object of the same solicitude.

4. Yet Jesus' role was not simply that of a moralist legislator, with no authority but his word: he came to fulfill the prophecies which had announced his coming; he held his authority through the exceptional nature of his spirit and his divine mission; he came to teach humans that the true life is not on Earth, but in the kingdom of heaven; to teach them the way that leads to it, the means to be reconciled to God, and to make them feel in advance the course of things in order to attain the fulfillment of human destinies. However, he has not said everything, and in many respects he has contented himself with depositing the germ of truths which he himself declares to be incapable of being understood at that time. He spoke of everything, but in more or less explicit terms. For one to grasp the hidden meaning of certain words, it was necessary that new ideas and new knowledge came to give the key, and these ideas could not come before a certain degree of maturity of the human spirit. Science was to contribute greatly to the hatching and development of these ideas; it was therefore necessary to give science time to evolve.

SPIRITISM

5. *Spiritism* is the new science which comes to reveal to human beings, by irrefutable proofs, the existence and the nature of the spiritual world, and its relations with the corporeal world. It shows it to us, no longer as something supernatural, but, on the contrary,

---

11 [Trans. note] "And you shall love the Lord your God with all your heart and with all your soul and with all your mind and with all your strength.' The second is this: 'You shall love your neighbor as yourself.' There is no other commandment greater than these (MARK 12:30–31 ESV)."

as one of the living and incessantly active forces of Nature, the source of a host of phenomena hitherto unappreciated and rejected, for this reason, in the domain of the fantastic and the marvelous. It is to these relationships that Christ refers in many circumstances, and that is why many things he said have remained unintelligible or have been misinterpreted. Spiritualism is the key by which everything is easily explained.

6. The Law of the Old Testament is personified in Moses; and that of the New Testament is in Christ. Spiritism is the third revelation of the law of God, but it is not personified in any individual, because it is the product of teachings given, not by a human being, but by the spirits, which are the voices of heaven, at every point of the Earth, and by a countless multitude of intermediaries. It is in a way a collective being comprising all the entities of the spiritual world, each of them bringing to humans the tribute of their lights, so as to make us better understand this world and the destiny that awaits us.

7. Just like Christ said, "I have not come to abolish the Law but to fulfill it," Spiritism also says, "II have not come to abolish the Christian law, but to fulfill it." It teaches nothing contrary to what Christ has taught, but it develops, completes, and explains, in clear terms to all, what was said only in allegorical form; It comes to fulfill, at the time predicted, what Christ has announced, by preparing the accomplishment of future things. It is therefore the work of Christ who presides over it, as he has similarly announced the regeneration which is taking place, and thus prepares the reign of God on Earth.

ALLIANCE OF SCIENCE AND RELIGION

8. Science and religion are the two levers of human intelligence: one reveals the laws of the material world and the other the laws of the moral world. However, *since the one and the other have the same principle, which is God,* they cannot contradict each other. If they were the negation of each other, one would be necessarily wrong and the other right and reason, because God cannot possibly wish to abolish Its own work. The incompatibility that we thought we detected between these two orders of ideas was due to a lack of observation and also because of too much exclusivism on both sides; hence a conflict from which unbelief and intolerance are born.

The times have come when the teachings of Christ must receive their complement; where the veil purposely thrown on some parts of this teaching must be lifted; where science, ceasing to be exclusively materialistic, must take into account the spiritual element; and where religion ceases to ignore the organic and unchanging laws of matter – these two forces, relying on one another, and walking together will lend mutual support to each other. Then religion, no longer receiving any denial from science, will acquire an unshakable power, because it will be in accord with reason, to which the irresistible logic of facts cannot be opposed.

Science and religion have not been able to understand each other to this day, because, since each considers things from its exclusive point of view, they repelled each other. It was necessary that something filled the void that separated them, a "hyphen" that would bring them together. This connecting hyphen is in the knowledge of the laws that govern the spiritual world and its relations with the corporeal world; laws as immutable as those which regulate the movement of the stars and the existence of beings. These reports, once ascertained by experience, shed a new light: faith has turned into reason, and reason has found nothing illogical in faith, and materialism has been vanquished. But in this as in all things, there are people who stay behind, until they are dragged by the general movement that crushes them if they want to resist it instead of surrendering to it. It is a whole moral revolution that is taking place at this moment and acting upon the spirits. After having been elaborated for over eighteen centuries, it now begins to reach its fulfillment, and will mark a new era for humanity. The consequences of this revolution are easy to predict; it must bring to social relations some inevitable modifications, to which it is not in anyone's power to oppose, because they are in the designs of God, and emerge from the law of progress, which is a law of God.

INSTRUCTIONS FROM THE SPIRITS

THE NEW ERA

9. God is unique, and Moses is the spirit whom God sent on a mission to make Itself known to humans, not only to the Hebrews, but also to the Gentiles. The Hebrew people were the instruments that God used to make Its revelation through Moses and the prophets, and the vicissitudes of this people were made to strike the eyes and bring down the veil that hid the divinity from human beings.

God's commandments as given by Moses bear the germ of the more extensive Christian morality. The commentaries of the Bible narrowed their meaning, because, should they have been implemented in all their purity, they would not have been understood at the time. Yet, the ten commandments of God remained nonetheless like the brilliant frontispiece, like the lighthouse which would illuminate humanity on the road it had to take.

The moral code taught by Moses was appropriate to the level of progress of the people he was called to regenerate; and such people, still half-savage in the development of their soul, would not have understood that they could worship God other than by burnt offerings, or that should render thanks to an enemy. Their intelligence, remarkable from the point of view of matter, and even in the arts and sciences, was far behind in moral principles, and would not have converted itself under the empire of an entirely spiritual religion. They needed a semi-material representation, as offered by the Hebrew religion at the time. Thus sacrificial offerings burnt on an altar spoke to their senses, while the idea of God spoke to their spirits.

Christ was the initiator of the purest, sublimest morality; that is, the Christian moral code contained in the Gospel, which ought to renew the world, bring human beings together and make them brothers and sisters. This in turn shall bring forth, in all human hearts, charity and love of neighbor, while creating among all humans a common solidarity; a moral conduct in the end, which must transform the Earth, and make it an abode for spirits superior to those that inhabit it today. This is the law of progress, to which Nature is subjected, and which is now being fulfilled – and today *Spiritism* is the lever which God has used to advance humanity.

The times have come when moral ideas must develop in order to fulfill the progress which is in the designs of God. They must follow the same road that the ideas of freedom have traveled, and which were their forerunner. But we must not believe that this development will be without struggles; no, in order to reach maturity, they need upheavals and debates, so that they attract the attention of the masses. Once the attention is fixed, the beauty and sanctity of morality will strike the spirits, and they will cling to a science which gives them the key of future life and opens to them the doors of eternal happiness. It was Moses who opened the way; Jesus continued the work; and Spiritism will finish it.

An Israelite Spirit (Mulhouse, France, 1861).

10. One day, God, in Its inexhaustible charity, allowed humans to see truth pierce darkness; that day was the coming of Christ. After the bright light, darkness came back; the world, after alternatives of truth and darkness, lost itself again. Then, like the prophets of the Old Testament, the spirits have begun to speak and warn you; the world will be shaken in its foundations; thunder will grow; stay firm!

Spiritism is of a divine order, since it rests on the very laws of Nature, and believe that all that is of divine order has a great and useful purpose. Your world was lost; science, developed at the expense of what is moral, while leading you to material well-being, turned to benefit the spirit of darkness. Christians, you know that heart and love must walk united to science. Alas! The reign of Christ after eighteen centuries, and despite the blood of so many martyrs, has not yet come. Christians, go back to the master who wants to save you. Everything becomes easy for anyone who believes and loves; let love fills you with an ineffable joy. Yes, my children, the world is shaken – as good spirits warn you often enough – bend under the gales foreshadowing the tempest to come, so as to not be overthrown by it. In other words, prepare yourself, and do not resemble the foolish virgins who were taken unawares by the arrival of the spouse.

The revolution being prepared is rather moral than material. Higher-order spirits, divine messengers, blow the faith, so that you all, enlightened and earnest workers, may make your humble voice heard; because, although you are but a grain of sand, without grains of sand there would be no mountains. Therefore these words, "We are small," have no meaning for you. To each his/her mission, to each his/her work. Does the ant not build the edifice of their republic, and tiny animalcules not raise continents? A new crusade has begun; apostles of universal peace and not of war; modern saints Bernard,[12] look and walk forward: the law of the world is the law of progress.

Fénelon[13] (Poitiers, France, 1861).

11. St. Augustine[14] is one of the greatest disseminators of Spiritism. His spirit has manifested itself almost everywhere; the reason why it has done so can be found in the life of this great Christian philosopher. He belongs to that vigorous phalanx of the Church Fathers, to whom Christendom owes its most solid foundation. Like many, he was torn from paganism or, to put it better, from the deepest impiety, by the brilliance of truth. When, in the midst of his excesses, he felt in his soul that strange vibration which reminded him of himself, and made him understand that happiness was elsewhere than in enervating and fleeting pleasures. When at last, on his way to Damascus, he too heard the holy voice call out to him, "Saul, Saul, why do you persecute me?" He cried, "My God! My God! forgive me, I am a believer, I am a Christian!" – and from then on he became one of the strongest supporters of the Gospel. In the remarkable Confessions that this eminent spirit has left us, we can read the words, at once characteristic and prophetic, which he wrote after having lost St. Monica: *"I am convinced that my mother will come back to visit me and give me advice by revealing what awaits us in the future life."* What a teaching in these words, and what a brilliant forecast of the future doctrine! It is for this reason that today, seeing the hour has arrived for the disclosure of the truth which he had previously sensed, that he has been its earnest disseminator, and has multiplied himself, so to speak, in order to answer to everyone that invokes him.

Erastus, disciple of the Apostle Paul (Paris, 1863).

---

12 [Trans. note] A symbolic reference to Bernard of Clairvaux (1090–1153). Another possible reference is to Bernard of Menthon (1020–1081).

13 [Trans. note] François Fénelon (1651–1715), French Roman Catholic archbishop, theologian, poet and writer.

14 [Trans. note] Augustine of Hippo (354–430 AD).

NOTE: Has Saint Augustine come to overthrow what he had taught before? Certainly not; but like so many others, he sees with the eyes of the spirit what he could not see as an incarnate human. His clear soul foresees new light; it understands what it did not understand before; new ideas have revealed to him the true sense of certain words. On Earth he judged things according to the knowledge he possessed, but when a new light was shed on him, he was able to judge them more healthily. Thus he had to reconsider his belief in incubus and succubus spirits, and the anathema he had launched against the antipodes theory. Now that Christianity appears to him in all its purity, he can, on certain points, think differently than during his lifetime, without ceasing to be the Christian apostle he always was. He can, without denying his faith, propagate Spiritism because he sees in it the fulfillment of the things predicted. In proclaiming it today, it only brings us back to a healthier and more logical interpretation of the texts. The same happens with other spirits that are in a similar position.

Chapter II
My kingdom is not of this world

1. "So Pilate entered his headquarters again and called Jesus and said to him, 'Are you the King of the Jews?' ... Jesus answered, '*My kingdom is not of this world.* If my kingdom were of this world, my servants would have been fighting, that I might not be delivered over to the Jews. But my kingdom is not from the world.'

Then Pilate said to him, 'So you are a king?' Jesus answered, 'You say that I am a king. For this purpose I was born and for this purpose I have come into the world – to bear witness to the truth. Everyone who is of the truth listens to my voice.' (JOHN 18:33,36-37 ESV)"

FUTURE LIFE

2. By these words, *future life* is clearly designated by Jesus, which he presents in all circumstances as the term toward which humankind is heading, and as the object of humans' main concerns on Earth. All these great maxims relate to this great principle. Without future life, most of his precepts of morality would indeed have no reason to be. That is why those who do not believe in future life, believing that he speaks only of current life, do not understand them, or find them puerile.

This dogma can therefore be considered as the pivot of Christ's teaching. That is why it is one of the first to be at the head of this work, because it must be the focus of all human beings. Only it can justify the anomalies of earthly life and agree with the justice of God.

3. The Jews only had quite uncertain ideas concerning future life. They believed in angels, whom they regarded as privileged beings of creation; but they did not know that humans could one day become angels and share their happiness. According to them, the observance of the laws of God was rewarded by the goods of the Earth, the supremacy of their nation, the victories over their enemies. Public calamities and defeats were punishment for their disobedience. Moses could say no more to an ignorant rustic people, who had to be touched first and foremost by the things of this world. Later, Jesus came to reveal to them that there is another world where the justice of God is going on: it is this world which he promises to those who keep God's commandments, and where the good will find their reward. Such a world is his kingdom, where he is in all his glory, and to where he would return after leaving Earth.

However, Jesus, conforming his teaching to the state of human beings of his time, did not think it his duty to offer them a complete light which would have dazzled without enlightening them, because they would not have understood it. He has confined himself to positing, as it were, future life in principle, as a law of Nature from which no one can escape. Therefore every Christian necessarily believes in a future life, but the idea that many make of it is vague, incomplete, and by that very fact false in several points. For many, it is only a belief which is not absolutely certain, beyond doubt or even unbelief.

Spiritism has come to complete in this point, as in many others, the teachings of Christ, when humans have become ripe to understand the truth. With Spiritism, future life is no longer a mere article of faith, a hypothesis; it is rather a concrete reality demonstrated by facts, for it is eyewitnesses who come to describe it in all its phases and vicissitudes, so that not only doubt is no longer possible, but even the most average intellect is able to represent it in its true aspect, like one imagines a country of which one has read a detailed description. Now, this description of future life is so detailed, the conditions of a happy or unhappy existence of those who are there are so rational, that one is convinced in spite of oneself that it cannot be otherwise, and that this is the true justice of God.

THE KINGSHIP OF JESUS

4. Jesus' kingdom is not of this world, that is what everyone understands; but on Earth does it not also have a kingship? The title of king does not always imply the exercise of temporal power; it is given by unanimous consent to those whose genius places them in the first rank in any order of ideas, which dominate their age, and influence the progress of humanity. It is in this sense that they say: The king or the prince of philosophers, artists, poets, writers, and so on. This kingship, born of personal merit and consecrated by posterity, does it not often have a preponderance far greater than that of those who actually bear a diadem? It is imperishable, while the other is the plaything of vicissitudes; it is always blessed for future generations, while the other is sometimes cursed. Earthly kingship ends in a lifetime, whereas moral royalty still reigns, especially after death. For this reason is Jesus not a king more powerful than many potentates? So he rightly said to Pilate: I am king, but my kingdom is not of this world.

THE POINT OF VIEW

5. A clear and precise idea of future life gives an unshakable faith in the future, and this faith has immense consequences for the moralization of human beings, in that it completely changes *the point of view under which they envisage earthly life.* For one who places himself/herself, through thought, in the spiritual life which is unlimited, bodily life is no more than a passage, a short stay in a an ungrateful country. Life's vicissitudes and tribulations are no more than incidents which he/she withstands with patience, because he/she knows that they are only of short duration and may be followed by a happier state. Death ceases to be alarming: it is no longer the door to nothingness, but a door of deliverance which opens to the exiled the entrance to a place of happiness and peace. Knowing that he/she is in a temporary and non-definitive place, these individuals tend to regard life's worries with more unconcern, which results for them in a calm of spirit which softens the bitterness.

By mere doubt about future life, humans carry all their thoughts back to earthly life. Uncertain of the future, they give everything to the present. Not perceiving more precious goods than those of the Earth, they are like children that see nothing beyond their toys. In order to get them, there is nothing they will not do; the loss of the least of their possessions is a burning sorrow; any disappointment, a frustrated hope; an unfulfilled ambition, an injustice of which he/she is a victim; hurt pride or vanity are all torments that make their life a perpetual anguish, *thus voluntarily inflicting a veritable torture against themselves at every moment.* Taking their point of view of terrestrial life as the center in which they are placed, everything takes vast proportions around them. The evil that afflicts them, like the good that belongs to others, everything acquires a great importance in their eyes. In the same way, to the one who is in the interior of a city, everything seems great, the individuals who are at the top of the ladder as well as the monuments – yet, should they go up a mountain, both individuals and things would seem very small to them.

Such is the view of those who consider earthly life from the point of view of future life: humanity, like the stars of the firmament, is lost in immensity. Then they realize that big and small are as mingled as ants on a clod of earth; that proletarians and potentates are of the same size; and they complain of the ephemera that cause them so much trouble to conquer a place which raises them so little, and which they must keep for a short time. Thus the importance attached to earthly goods is always in inverse ratio to faith in future life.

6. If everyone thought so, it will be said, nobody would care about the things of the Earth any longer, and everything would perish. No; humans instinctively seek their well-being, and even with the certainty of being only for a short time in a place, they still want to be in the best or the least well state possible. No one, once finding a thorn under his/her hand, will fail to extract it to avoid hurting themselves. Now, the search for well-being forces humans to improve all things, pushed by the instinct of progress and conservation, which is in the law of Nature. Human beings therefore works out of need, because it is their wish or their duty, and, in this, humans fulfill the designs of Providence which has placed them on Earth for this purpose. Only those who consider the future will attach merely relative importance to the present, and easily soothe themselves of their failures by thinking of the destiny that awaits them.

God, therefore, does not condemn earthly pleasures, but rather the abuse of these enjoyments to the detriment of the things of the soul. It is against this abuse that those who apply to themselves these words of Jesus are forbidden: *My kingdom is not of this world.*

Those who identify themselves with the idea of future life are like a rich person who loses a small sum without being moved by it; whereas those who concentrate their thoughts on earthly life are like a poor person who loses all possessions and despairs.

7.   Spiritism broadens one's thought, opening up new horizons for it. Instead of a narrow and petty vision which focus itself on current life – making the instant that one spends on the ground the unique and fragile pivot of the eternal future – it shows that this life is only a link, a ring in the harmonious and magnificent whole of the Creator's work. It shows the solidarity that connects all the existences of a same being, all the beings of a same world and the beings of all the worlds. Thus it gives a basis and a reason for being to universal fraternity, whereas the doctrine of the creation of the soul at the moment of birth of each body makes all beings extraneous to one another. This solidarity among the parts of the same whole explains what had remained inexplicable when we considered only one point. Such set of concepts could not be understood by people in the time of Christ. That is why he has reserved knowledge of it for other times.

INSTRUCTIONS FROM THE SPIRITS

AN EARTHLY KINGSHIP

8.   Who better than I can understand the truth of this word of Our Lord: "My kingdom is not of this world?" Pride caused me to lose myself on Earth. Who else then would understand the noth-ingness of the kingdoms of this world but me? What have I brought with me from my earthly kingdom? Nothing, absolutely nothing; and as if to make the lesson even more dreadful, it did not follow me to the grave. Queen I was among humans, queen I thought I also was entering the kingdom of heaven! What a disillusionment, what a humiliation, when, instead of being received as a sovereign, I saw above me, but far above, souls whom I had deemed very small and whom I despised, because they were not of noble blood! Ah! would that I understood back then how sterile are all the honors and magnificences which are so eagerly sought for on Earth!

However, to ready oneself for a place in this kingdom, self-denial, humility, charity in all its heavenly practice, benevolence toward everyone, are necessary. You are not asked what you have been, what rank you have occupied, but what good you have done and the tears you have shed.

O Jesus! You have said your kingdom is not here below, for one must suffer to reach heaven, and the steps of a throne do not bring you nearer; it is the most painful paths of life that lead to it; therefore seek the road through brambles and thorns, and not among the flowers.

Humans run after earthly goods as if they would always keep them; but here there is no more illusions; you soon perceive that you have seized only a shadow, and have neglected the only solid and durable goods, the only ones that give you some benefit for the celestial stay, the only ones which can grant you access to the latter.

Have mercy on those who have not earned the kingdom of heaven; help them with your prayers, for prayer brings humans closer to the Most High; it is the link between heaven and Earth: do not forget it.

A former queen of France (Le Havre, 1863).

Chapter III
In my Father's house are many rooms

DIFFERENT CONDITIONS OF THE SOUL IN THE ERRANT STATE · DIFFERENT
CATEGORIES OF INHABITED WORLDS · DESTINY OF THE EARTH — CAUSES OF
EARTHLY MISERIES · *INSTRUCTIONS FROM THE SPIRITS:* UPPER AND LOWER WORLDS ·
WORLDS OF TRIALS AND ATONEMENTS · REGENERATIVE WORLDS · PROGRESSION OF
WORLDS

1. "'Let not your hearts be troubled. Believe in God; believe also in me. *In my Father's house are many rooms.* If it were not so, would I have told you that I go to prepare a place for you? And if I go and prepare a place for you, I will come again and will take you to myself, that where I am you may be also' (JOHN 14:1–3 ESV)."

DIFFERENT CONDITIONS OF THE SOUL
IN THE ERRANT STATE[15]

2. The Father's house is the universe. The different dwellings are the worlds that circulate in infinite space, offering incarnate spirits adequate stays for their advancement.

Besides referring to the diversity of worlds, these words can also be understood as the happy or unhappy state of a spirit in the errant state. As it is more or less rid and free from material bonds, the environment in which it finds itself, the aspect of things, the sensations it experiences, the perceptions it possesses, will vary infinitely. While some cannot move away from the sphere where they lived, others rise and go through space and different worlds. Certain guilty spirits wander in darkness, whereas the happy ones enjoy resplendent brightness and the sublime spectacle of the infinite. Finally, as the wicked ones, filled with remorse and regret, often alone, without consolations, separated from the objects of their affection, groan

---

15 [Translation note] The term *errant state* (or *state of erraticity*, according to A. Blackwell's pioneering translation) does not denote a place, nor does it have any negative connotations. It basically means *itinerant state*, and refers to the period between one's incarnations.

under the embrace of moral sufferings, the righteous, reunited with those whom they love, experience the sweetness of indescribable bliss. Here too there are several dwellings, although they are neither circumscribed nor limited to a location.

DIFFERENT CATEGORIES OF INHABITED WORLDS

3. From the teaching given by the spirits, it follows that distinct worlds are in very different conditions from one another depending on the higher or lower evolutionary stage of their inhabitants. Among them, some are still lower in relation to Earth both physically and morally, while others are at the same degree, and others are more or less superior to it in all respects. In lower worlds existence is wholly material, passions reign supreme, moral life is almost null. As a world develops, the influence of matter diminishes, so that in the most advanced worlds life is, so to speak, wholly spiritual.

4. In intermediate worlds there is a mixture of good and evil, predominance of one or the other according to their degree of advancement. Although an absolute classification of the various worlds cannot be made, because of their state and their destiny, and based on their most marked nuances, a general classification is possible, dividing them into primitive worlds, assigned to the first incarnations of the human soul; worlds of trials and atonements, where evil still dominates; regenerative worlds, where souls that have yet to atone for their past, draw new strengths, while resting from the weariness of the struggle; happy worlds, where good outweighs evil; and celestial or divine worlds, the residence of purified spirits, where good reigns supreme. Earth belongs to the category of worlds of trials and atonements, which is why humans are still victim of so many miseries.

5. Spirits that are incarnated in a world are not attached to it indefinitely, and do not complete there all the progressive phases which they must traverse to reach perfection. When they have attained the degree of advancement necessary for it, they pass into another, more advanced world, and so on, until they have reached the state of pure spirits. These worlds are all stations at each of which they find elements of progress in proportion to their advancement. It is a reward for them to go to a higher-order world, as it is a punishment to prolong their stay in an unhappy world, or to be relegated to a world even more unhappy than the one they are forced to leave, if they stubbornly persist in evil.

Destiny of the Earth
Causes of earthly miseries

6. It is astonishing to find on planet Earth so much malice and bad passions, so many miseries and all sorts of infirmities, which leads to the conclusion that the human species is a sad affair. This judgment comes from the narrow point of view in which we place ourselves, and which gives a false idea of the whole. We must consider that on Earth we do not see all humanity, but a very small fraction of humankind. Indeed, the human species includes all sentient beings who populate the innumerable worlds of the universe. Now, what is the population of the Earth in relation to the total population of these worlds? Much less than that of a hamlet as compared to that of a great empire. The material and moral situation of Earth's humankind has nothing astonishing about it, if we take into account the destiny of the Earth and the nature of those who inhabit it.

7. One would make a false idea of the inhabitants of a big city if they were judged based on the population of tiny and squalid neighborhoods. In a hospital, we see only patients or disabled persons; in a galley we see all the turpitudes, all the vices united; in unhealthy places, most of the inhabitants are pale, frail and sickly. Well, imagine that the Earth is a suburb, a hospice, a penitentiary, an unhealthy place, for it is at once all off that, and it will be understood why afflictions prevail over enjoyments, for one does not send those who are well to a hospital, or those who have done no harm to houses of correction – and neither hospices nor houses of correction are blissful places.

Now, just like in a city not the whole population is in hospices or prisons, all humanity is not on Earth. Just like one leaves the hospital when one is cured, and leaves prison when one has done his/her time, a human soul leaves the Earth for happier worlds when he/she is cured of their moral infirmities.

INSTRUCTIONS FROM THE SPIRITS

UPPER AND LOWER WORLDS

8. The qualification of upper and lower worlds is rather relative than absolute. Such a world is inferior or superior to those above or below it in a progressive scale.

If Earth is taken as a point of comparison, one can form an idea of the state of an inferior world by supposing humans to be in the degree of savage races or in barbarous nations still found on its surface, and which are the remnants of our primitive state. In the most backward, the beings who inhabit them are somehow rudimentary; they have the human form, but without any beauty; and instincts are not tempered by any feeling of delicacy or benevolence, nor the notions of justice and injustice; brute force alone makes the law. Without industry, without inventions, people spend their lives seizing their food. However, God does not forsake any of Its created beings; in the depths of the darkness of their intelligence lie, latent and more or less developed, the vague intuition of a supreme Being. This instinct is enough to make them superior to one another and to prepare their blossoming for a fuller life; for they are not degraded beings, but rather children who are still growing up.

Between these lower and higher levels there are innumerable echelons, and among pure spirits, dematerialized and resplendent with glory, those which once animated these primitive beings can scarcely be recognized, just like in an adult person it is difficult to discern the embryo.

9. In worlds that have reached a higher level, the conditions of moral and material life are quite different from those found on Earth. The shape of the body is always, as everywhere, the human form, but embellished, perfected, and above all purified. The body has nothing of earthly materiality, and is consequently subject neither to the needs, nor to the diseases, or the deteriorations engendered by the predominance of matter. The senses, more refined, have perceptions which are stifled down here by the coarseness of our physical organs. The specific lightness of the bodies makes locomotion fast and easy; instead of crawling along the ground, one glides, so to speak, to the surface, or hovers in the atmosphere without any other effort than that of the will. In the same way we represent the angels, or the Ancients are pictured as manes in the Champs Elysées, humans preserve the features of their past migrations and appear to their nearest and dearest as they knew them, but illuminated by a divine light, always transfigured by their inner impressions. Instead of dullness in their faces, ravaged by sufferings and passions, intelligence and life radiate the brilliance that painters have translated by the nimbus or halo of the saints.

The little resistance offered by matter to spirits that are already very advanced, makes the development of their bodies rapid and childhood short or almost nonexistent. Life, free from worry and anxiety, is proportionally much longer than here on Earth. In principle, longevity is proportionate to the degree of advancement of the worlds. Death has none of the horrors of decomposition; far from being a subject of dread, it is considered a happy transformation, because there any doubt about the future does not exist. During life, the soul, not being concealed in compact matter, radiates and enjoys a lucidity that puts it in an almost permanent state of emancipation, which allows it free transmission of thought.

10. In such happy worlds, people-to-people relations, always friendly, are never troubled by any ambition to enslave one's neighbor, nor by wars which follow it. There are no masters, no slaves, no privileged at birth. Moral and intelligent superiority alone establishes difference in conditions and gives supremacy. Authority is always respected, because it is given only by merit, and it is always exercised with justice. *Humans do not seek to rise above other humans, but above themselves by perfecting themselves.* Their aim is to reach the rank of pure spirits, and this incessant desire is not a torment, but a noble ambition which makes them study with fervor in order to succeed in equating with them. All the tender and elevated sentiments of human nature are increased and purified; hatreds, petty jealousies, and low lusts of envy are unknown. A bond of love and fraternity unites all human beings; the strongest help the weak. They possess more or less according to what they have amassed through their intelligence, however no one suffers from lack of what is necessary for living, since no one is undergoing atonement – in a word, evil does not exist there anymore.

11.   In your world, you need evil to feel good, night to admire the light, illness to appreciate health, whereas in happy worlds, these contrasts are not necessary. Eternal light, eternal beauty, and eternal peace of the soul, procure an eternal joy which is not disturbed by the agonies of material life, or any contact with the wicked, who have no access to it. This is what the human spirit has the most trouble understanding; it has been ingenious in painting the torments of hell, but it has never been able to imagine the joys of heaven – and why is that so? Because, being lower-order spirits, they have endured only pains and miseries, and could not catch a glimpse of the celestial splendors. They can speak only of what they know; but as they rise and purify themselves, the horizon clears, and they understand the good that lies before them, as they have understood the evil that has remained behind.

12.   Yet these fortunate worlds are not privileged worlds, for God is not partial to any of Its children. God gives everyone the same rights and facilities to succeed; It makes them all depart from the same point, and endows them with nothing more than the others. The first ranks are accessible to all: it is up to them to conquer such ranks through their work; it is up to them to attain them as soon as possible, or else, to languish for centuries and centuries in the slums of humanity.

Higher-order Spirits (Summary of their teachings).

Worlds of trials and atonements

13.   What can I tell you of the worlds of atonement that you do not already know, since you only have to consider Earth where you live in? The superiority of intelligent life of many of its inhabitants indicates that it is not a primitive world destined for the incarnation of spirits that have just come out of the hands of the Creator. The innate qualities they bring with them are proof positive that they have already lived, and that they have made some progress; yet also the numerous vices to which they are inclined are indicators of a great moral imperfection. This is why God has placed them on an ungrateful land to atone for their faults through hard work and the miseries of life, until they have deserved to go to a happier world.

14. However, not all spirits incarnated on Earth are sent for atonement. Races you call savages are spirits barely out of infancy, which are on this planet for education and development in contact with more advanced spirits. Then come the semi-civilized races formed by these same spirits in progress. These are, as it were, the native races of the Earth, which have grown little by little as an outcome of many centuries. Some of these spirits have attained the intellectual perfection of the most enlightened peoples.

As for spirits undergoing atonement, they are, in a manner of speaking, exotic: they have already lived in other worlds from which they were excluded because of their obstinacy in evil, and because they became a cause of trouble for the good. They have been relegated, for a time, to live among the more backward spirits, whose advancement is their mission, for they have brought with them a more developed intelligence and the germ of acquired knowledge. That is why these punished spirits are among the most intelligent populations. They are also those for which the miseries of life carry the greatest bitterness, because in them there is more sensibility, and life's struggles are more testing for them than for the primitive peoples whose moral sense is more obtuse.

15. The Earth, then, represents one of the types of expiatory worlds, whose varieties are infinite, but which have the common characteristic of serving as a place of exile for spirits rebellious to God's law. There these spirits have to struggle at the same time against human perversity and against the inclemency of Nature – a double toil which, at the same time, helps develop the qualities of the heart and those of intelligence. It is in this way that God, in Its goodness, turns punishing into a benefit for the progress of the spirit.

St. Augustine (Paris, 1862).

REGENERATIVE WORLDS

16. Amongst those stars which glitter in the azure vault, so many worlds, like yours, are designated by the Lord for atonement and trial! Yet some are more miserable while others are better, as well as transitory ones that can be called regenerative worlds. Each planetary vortex, running around a common center in space, carries with it its primitive worlds of exile, trial, regeneration and bliss. You have been told of those worlds in which a nascent soul is placed, while still unaware of good and evil; it can walk toward God, as a master of itself, in possession of its free will. You have been told of what great faculties the soul has been endowed with to do good; but alas! there are some that succumb; and God, not wishing to annihilate them, allows them to go into those worlds where, from incarnation to incarnation, they are purified, regenerate themselves, and come back worthy of the glory which was meant to them.

17. Regenerative worlds serve as a transition between worlds of atonement and happy worlds. The soul that repents itself finds peace and repose in it by completing its purification. Undoubtedly, in these worlds humans are still subject to the laws that govern matter; humanity feels your sensations and desires, but it is freed from the disordered passions of which you are slaves. No longer pride that silences the heart, no more desire that tortures it, no more hatred that stifles it. The word love is written on all fronts; a perfect equity regulates social relations; everyone acknowledges God, and try to move toward It according to Its laws.

In such worlds, however, there is not yet perfect happiness, but the dawn of happiness. Humans are still made of flesh, and for that reason subject to vicissitudes of which only beings which have become completely dematerialized are exempt. Humans still have trials to undergo, but they do not suffer the poignant anguish of atonements. Compared to Earth, these worlds are very happy, and many of you would be contented to stop there, for it is like the calm after the storm, the recovery after a cruel illness. Yet those humans, less absorbed in material things, can see the future better than you do; they understand that there are other joys that the Lord promises to those who are worthy of them, when death has again reaped their bodies to give them real life. It is then that the emancipated soul will hover over all horizons. No material and gross senses any longer, but the senses of a pure and heavenly perispirit, aspiring to the emanations of God under the perfumes of love and charity that spread from Its bosom.

18. But alas! in these worlds, humans are still fallible, and the spirit of evil has not completely lost its empire. To not advance is to retreat, and if one is not firm on the path of good, one can fall back into the worlds of atonement, where new and more dreadful trials await him/her.

So contemplate this azure vault in the evening, at the hour of rest and prayer, and in those innumerable spheres that shine over your heads, ask those which lead to God, and pray that a regenerative world will open its womb to you after the atonement experienced on Earth.

St. Augustine (Paris, 1862).

PROGRESSION OF WORLDS

19. Progress is one of the laws of Nature; all beings of creation, both animate and inanimate, are subject to it by the goodness of God, which wants everything to grow and prosper. Even destruction, which seems the end of things to humans, is only a means of arriving through transformation to a more perfect state, for everything dies to be reborn, and nothing vanishes into nothingness.

At the same time that living beings evolve morally, the worlds they inhabit evolve materially. Whoever could follow a world in its various phases from the moment when the first atoms were used to form it, would see it traverse an incessantly progressive scale, but by imperceptive degrees for each generation, and offer to its inhabitants a more enjoyable stay as they themselves advance in the path of progress. Thus, at the same time that human progress advances, so does that of animals – their auxiliaries – plants and the environment, for nothing is stationary in Nature. How boundless is this idea, worthy of the majesty of the Creator, whereas, on the contrary, how narrow and unworthy of Its power to circumscribe Its solicitude and providence to this imperceptible grain of sand which is the Earth, thus restricting humanity to the few humans who inhabit it!

Earth, according to this law, had been materially and morally in a state inferior to what it is today, and will eventually attain under this double ratio a more advanced degree. It has now reached one of its periods of transformation, where from an expiatory world it will become a regenerative world. Then humans will be happy because the law of God will reign on this planet.

St. Augustine (Paris, 1862).

Chapter IV
Unless one is born again he cannot see the kingdom of God

RESURRECTION AND REINCARNATION · FAMILY TIES STRENGTHENED BY
REINCARNATION, BROKEN IF THERE WERE ONLY A SINGLE EXISTENCE ·
INSTRUCTIONS FROM THE SPIRITS: LIMITS OF INCARNATION · NECESSITY
FOR INCARNATION

1. "Now when Jesus came into the district of Caesarea Philippi, he asked his disciples, 'Who do people say that the Son of Man is?' And they said, 'Some say John the Baptist, others say Elijah, and others Jeremiah or one of the prophets.' He said to them, 'But who do you say that I am?' Simon Peter replied, 'You are the Christ, the Son of the living God.' And Jesus answered him, 'Blessed are you, Simon Bar-Jonah! For flesh and blood has not revealed this to you, but my Father who is in heaven. (MATTHEW 16:13–17; MARK 8:27–30 ESV)."

2. "King Herod heard of it, for Jesus' name had become known. Some said, 'John the Baptist has been raised from the dead. That is why these miraculous powers are at work in him.' But others said, 'He is Elijah.' And others said, 'He is a prophet, like one of the prophets of old.' — Now Herod the tetrarch heard about all that was happening, and he was perplexed, because it was said by some that John had been raised from the dead, by some that Elijah had appeared, and by others that one of the prophets of old had risen. Herod said, 'John I beheaded, but who is this about whom I hear such things?' And he sought to see him (MARK 6:14–15 ESV; LUKE 9:7–9 ESV).

3. (*After the transfiguration*) "And the disciples asked him, 'Then why do the scribes say that first Elijah must come?' He answered, 'Elijah does come, and he will restore all things. But I tell you that Elijah has already come, and they did not recognize him, but did to him whatever they pleased. So also the Son of Man will certainly suffer at their hands.' Then the disciples understood that he was speaking to them of John the Baptist (MATTHEW 17:10–13; *cf.* MARK 9:10–12 ESV)."

RESURRECTION AND REINCARNATION

4. *Reincarnation* was part of the dogmas that emerged under the name of resurrection; only the Sadducees, who thought that everything ended in death, did not believe in it. The ideas held by the Jews on this subject, as on many others, were not clearly defined, because they had only vague and incomplete notions about the soul and its connection with the body. They believed that a person who lived could revive, without realizing how exactly it could happen. They designated by the word *resurrection* what Spiritism more wisely calls *reincarnation*. Indeed, a resurrection supposes the return to life of the body that is dead, which science demonstrates to be physically impossible, especially when the elements of this body have long been dispersed and absorbed. *Reincarnation* is the return of the soul or spirit to bodily life, but in another newly formed body, which has nothing in common with the old. The word resurrection could thus apply to Lazarus, but not to Elijah or to other prophets. If then, according to their belief, John the Baptist was Elijah, John's body could not be that of Elijah, since we had seen John as a child, and we knew his father and his mother. John could therefore be Elijah *reincarnated* but not *resurrected*.

5. "Now there was a man of the Pharisees named Nicodemus, a ruler of the Jews. This man came to Jesus by night and said to him, 'Rabbi, we know that you are a teacher come from God, for no one can do these signs that you do unless God is with him.' Jesus answered him, 'Truly, truly, I say to you, *unless one is born again he cannot see the kingdom of God.*' Nicodemus said to him, 'How can a man be born when he is old? Can he enter a second time into his mother's womb and be born?' Jesus answered, 'Truly, truly, I say to you, unless one is born of water and the Spirit, he cannot enter the kingdom of God. That which is born of the flesh is flesh, and that which is born of the Spirit is spirit. Do not marvel that I said to you, 'You must be born again.' The wind blows where it wishes, and you hear its sound, but you do not know where it comes from or where it goes. So it is with everyone who is born of the Spirit.'

Nicodemus said to him, 'How can these things be?' Jesus answered him, 'Are you the teacher of Israel and yet you do not understand these things? Truly, truly, I say to you, we speak of what we know, and bear witness to what we have seen, but you do not receive our testimony. If I have told you earthly things and you do not believe, how can you believe if I tell you heavenly things?' (JOHN 3:1–12 ESV)."

6.   The thought that John the Baptist was Elijah, and that the prophets could live again on Earth, is found in many passages of the Gospels, especially in those quoted above (items **1**, **2** and **3**). If that belief had been an error, Jesus would not have failed to fight it, just as he had fought so many others; far from it, he corroborates it with all his authority, and posits it as a principle and as a necessary condition when he says: *Unless one is born again he cannot see the kingdom of God*; and he insists, by adding, *Do not marvel that I said to you, 'You must be born again.'*

7.   These words, *Unless one is born of water and the Spirit*, have been interpreted in the sense of regeneration by the water of baptism; but the primitive text simply bore: *Unless one is born of water and the Spirit*, while in some translations *the Spirit* has been substituted with *the Holy Ghost*; which would no longer correspond to the same thought. This crucial point emerges from the first comments made on the Gospel, until this will one day be unequivocally stated.[16]

8.   To understand the true meaning of these words, one must also refer to the meaning of the word *water*, which was not used in its proper sense.

The knowledge of the ancients about physical sciences was quite imperfect; they believed that the Earth had come out of the waters, which is why they regarded water as the absolute generative element. It is thus that in Genesis it is said, "The Spirit of God was hovering over the face of the waters. — 'Let the waters under the heavens be gathered together into one place, and let the dry land appear.' — 'Let the waters swarm with swarms of living creatures,

---

16 In French Bible translations, OSTERWALD's version conforms to the original text; it reads: "not reborn from water and the Spirit"; that of SACY says: "of the Holy Spirit"; and that of LAMENNAIS: "of the Holy Spirit."

and let birds fly above the earth across the expanse of the heavens' (GENESIS 1:2,9,20 ESV)."

According to this belief, water had become the symbol of material nature, just as the spirit was that of intelligent nature. These words, "Unless one is born of water and the Spirit," then actually mean, "If one is not reborn with one's body and soul." It is in this sense that they had been understood in principle.

Moreover, this interpretation is justified by these other words: *That which is born of the flesh is flesh, and that which is born of the Spirit is spirit.* Here Jesus makes a positive distinction between the spirit and the body. *That which is born of the flesh is flesh,* clearly indicates that the body *alone* proceeds from the body, and that the spirit is independent of the body.

9. *The wind blows where it wishes, and you hear its sound, but you do not know where it comes from or where it goes.* One can hear *the Spirit of God* which gives life to whom It wants, like the human soul in this last sense, *You do not know where it comes from or where it goes,* means that we do not know what has been, nor what will be the spirit. If the spirit, or soul, were created at the same time as the body, we would know where it came from, since we would know its beginning. In any case, this passage is the consecration of the principle of preexistence of the soul, and consequently of the plurality of existences.

10. "From the days of John the Baptist until now the kingdom of heaven has suffered violence, and the violent take it by force. For all the Prophets and the Law prophesied until John, and if you are willing to accept it, he is Elijah who is to come. He who has ears to hear, let him hear (MATTHEW 11:12–15 ESV)."

11. If the principle of reincarnation expressed in John the Evangelist could be interpreted , strictly speaking, in a purely mystical sense; it could not be the same in this passage of MATTHEW, which leaves no ambiguity: *He is Elijah who is to come* (MATTHEW 11:14 esv); there is neither figure nor allegory, it is a positive affirmation. - "From the days of John the Baptist until now the kingdom of heaven has suffered violence." What do these words mean, in view of the fact that John the Baptist was still living at that time? Jesus explains them by saying, "If you are willing to accept it, he is Elijah who is to come." Now, since John the Baptist is none other than Elijah, Jesus is referring to the time when John lived under the name of Elijah. "Until now the kingdom of heaven has suffered violence," is another allusion to the violence of the Mosaic Law which commanded the extermination of the infidels to win the Promised Land, the Hebrew Paradise, whereas, according to the new law, heaven is earned through charity and gentleness.

Then he adds: *He who has ears to hear, let him hear.* These words, so often repeated by Jesus, make it clear that not everyone was in a state of understanding certain truths.

12. "*Your dead shall live*; their bodies shall rise. You who dwell in the dust, awake and sing for joy! For your dew is a dew of light, and the earth will give birth to the dead (ISAIAH 26:19)."

13. This passage from Isaiah is just as explicit: "Your dead shall live; their bodies shall rise.... and the earth will give birth to the dead." If the prophet had heard of spiritual life, if he had meant to say that those who were killed did not die in the spirit, he would have said: they *still live*, and not *shall live*. In the spiritual sense, these words would be nonsense, since they would imply an interruption in the life of the soul. In the sense of *moral regeneration*, they would be the negation of eternal punishment, since they establish in principle that *all who are dead will live again.*

14. "But when a man is dead *once*, that his body, separated from his spirit, is consumed, what becomes of him? — A man being dead *once*, could he live again? In this war where I find myself every day of my life, I wait for my change to happen (Job 14:10,14 Sacy's Catholic French Bible)."

"But a man dies and is laid low; man breathes his last, and where is he? — If a man dies, shall he *live again*? All the days of my service I would wait, till my renewal should come (Job 14:10,14 ESV, similar to Ostervald's Protestant French bible)."

"When man is dead, he is still alive; when I finish the days of *my earthly existence*, I will wait, because *I will come back to it again* (Job 14:10,14 Greek Orthodox Bible)."

15. The principle of the plurality of existences is clearly expressed in these three versions. It cannot be supposed that Job wanted to speak of a regeneration by the water of baptism, which he certainly did not know. "A man being dead *once*, could he *live again?*" The idea of dying once and being reborn implies the idea of dying and living again many times. The version of the Greek Orthodox Church is even more explicit, if this is possible. "When I finish the days of my *earthly existence*, I will wait, because *I will come back to it again*"; that is to say, I will return to earthly existence. This is as clear as if someone said, I am leaving my house, but I will come back to it.

"In this war where I find myself every day of my life, I *wait for* my change to happen." Of course, Job wants to talk about his struggle, fighting against the miseries of life. He is *waiting for* his change, that is to say, he resigned himself to them. In the Greek version, I wait for my change to happen seem to apply to the new existence: "When I finish the days of my earthly existence, I *will wait*, because I will come back to it again"; Job seems to place himself, after his death, in the interval which separates one existence from the other, and to say that he will wait for his return.

16.   Therefore there can be no doubt that under the name of *resurrection* the principle of reincarnation was one of the fundamental beliefs of the Jews; that it was confirmed by Jesus and the prophets in a formal way; from which it follows that to deny reincarnation is to deny the words of Christ. His words will one day be authoritative on this subject, as on many others, when one analyze them without partiality.

17.   But to this authority, from the religious point of view, is added, from the philosophical point of view, that of the proofs which result from the observation of facts. When effects can be traced back to causes, reincarnation appears as an absolute necessity, as a condition inherent to humanity, in a word, as a law of Nature. It reveals itself by its results in a material manner, so to speak, as the hidden engine is revealed by its movement. This alone can tell human beings *where they come from, where they are going to, why they are on Earth,* and justify all the anomalies and all the apparent injustices offered by life.[17]

---

17 For developments of the dogma of reincarnation see A. KARDEC, *The Spirits' Book*, book two, ch. IV and V; A. KARDEC, *What is Spiritism?* ch. II; and PEZZANI, *La Pluralité des Existences de l'Âme* (Paris: Didier, 1865).

Without the principle of the preexistence of the soul and the plurality of existences, most of the maxims contained in the Gospel are unintelligible. That is why they gave rise to such contradictory interpretations; this principle is the key which should restore their true meaning.

FAMILY TIES STRENGTHENED BY REINCARNATION, BROKEN IF THERE WERE ONLY A SINGLE EXISTENCE

18. Family ties are not destroyed by reincarnation, as some people think; on the contrary, it strengthens and tightens them, it is the opposite principle that destroys them.

In the spiritual world, spirits form groups or families united by affection, affinity, and similarity of inclinations. Happy to be together, these spirits seek one another. Incarnation separates them only momentarily since, after their return to the errant state, they meet themselves again as friends coming back from a journey. Often they follow one another in an incarnation, being united in the same family, or in the same circle, working together for mutual advancement. True, some are incarnated and others are not, they are nonetheless united by thought; those who are free watch over those who are in captivity; the most advanced seek to advance the laggards. After each existence they have taken a step toward perfection. Less and less attached to matter, their affection is more lively by the very fact that it is more refined, that it is no longer troubled by selfishness or clouded by passions. They can thus traverse an unlimited number of bodily existences without any attack being made against their mutual affection.

It should be well understood that this is the real soul-to-soul affection, the only one that survives the destruction of the body, because beings who united here only by the senses have no reason to look for one another in the spiritual world. There are only lasting spiritual affections; carnal affections are extinguished with the cause which gave rise to them. Now, this cause no longer exists in the world of spirits, whereas the soul still exists. As for the persons united for reasons of interest alone, they are really nothing to one another: death separates them on Earth and in heaven.

19. The union and affection which exist between parents is a sign of previous affinity which has brought them together. It is also said when referring to a person whose character, tastes, and inclinations have no similarity whatsoever with those of the relatives, that he/she is not of the family. By saying this, one utters a greater truth than one may think. God allows, in families, these incarnations of antagonistic or extraneous spirits, with the double aim of serving as a test for some, and as a means of advancement for others. Then the bad ones improve little by little in contact with the good ones, and by the care they receive. Their character is softened, their habits and manners are purified, and aversions are effaced. It is thus that the fusion among different categories of spirits is established, like the one established on Earth among races and peoples.

20. The fear of an indefinite increase of kinship, as a result of reincarnation, is a selfish fear, which proves that one does not feel a love strong enough to share it with a large number of people. Does a father who has several children love them less than if he had only one? But – may the selfish stay reassured – this fear is unfounded. From the fact that a human being has had ten incarnations, it does not follow that he/she will find in the world of spirits ten fathers, ten mothers, ten spouses and a proportionate number of children and new relatives. Such person will always find there only the same objects of his/her affection which will have been attached to him on Earth, in various relationships, or maybe even the same ones.

21. Let us now see the consequences of the doctrine of nonreincarnation. This doctrine necessarily nullifies the preexistence of the soul. As souls are created at the same time as the body, there exists between them no previous link; they are completely foreign to each other; the parents are strangers to their children; the filiation of families is thus reduced to corporal filiation alone, without any spiritual connection. There is therefore no reason to boast of having illustrious personages as ancestors. With reincarnation, ancestors and descendants may have known one another, lived together, loved one another, and come together later to strengthen their sympathetic bonds.

22. So much for the past. As for the future, according to one of the fundamental dogmas that derive from nonreincarnation, the fate of souls is irrevocably fixed after a single existence. This definitive fixation of fate implies the cessation of all progress, for if there were any progress, there would no longer be a definitive fate. According to whether they have lived well or badly, they immediately go to the abode of the blessed or to eternal hell; *they are thus immediately separated forever, and without any hope of ever approaching one another again*, so that fathers, mothers and children, husbands and wives, brothers, sisters, friends, are never certain of seeing one another again: it is the most absolute break of family ties.

Conversely, with reincarnation, and the consequent progress, all who have loved one another meet again on Earth and in the spiritual world, and gravitate together to reach God. If there are some who fail on the way, they delay their advancement and their happiness, but all hope is not lost: helped, encouraged and supported by those who love them, they will one day come out of the quagmire in which they got stuck. Finally, with reincarnation, there is perpetual solidarity between the incarnate and the discarnate, hence the tightening of the bonds of affection.

23. In summary, four alternatives are presented to humans for their future beyond the grave: (1ST) Nothingness, according to the materialist doctrine; (2ND) Absorption in the universal whole, according to the pantheistic doctrine; (3RD) Individuality with definitive fixation of fate, according to the doctrine of the Church; (4TH) Individuality with indefinite progression, according to the Spiritist doctrine. According to the first two, family ties are broken after death, and there is no hope of meeting one another again; with the third, there is a chance to meet again, provided that one is in the same medium, and this environment can be either hell or paradise. With the plurality of existences, which is inseparable from the concept of gradual progression, there is certainty in the continuity of relationships among those who have loved one another, and this is what constitutes the true family.

INSTRUCTIONS FROM THE SPIRITS

LIMITS OF INCARNATION

24. *What are the limits of incarnation?*

Incarnation does not have clearly marked limits, strictly speaking, if we mean the envelope which constitutes the body of the spirit, since the materiality of this envelope decreases as the spirit purifies itself. In certain worlds more advanced than the Earth, it is already less compact, less heavy, and less coarse, and consequently subject to fewer vicissitudes. To an even greater degree, it becomes diaphanous and almost fluid; and thus from degree to degree, it becomes more and more dematerialized and ends up being confused with the perispirit. According to the world on which the spirit is called to live, this latter takes an envelope appropriate to the nature of this world.

The perispirit itself undergoes successive transformations. It becomes more and more ethereal until the complete purification which constitutes the state of pure spirit. If special worlds are designated, as stations, to very advanced spirits, these latter are not attached to them as in the lower worlds; their state of disengagement allows them to go wherever they are called by missions entrusted to them.

If we consider the incarnation from a material point of view, as it takes place on Earth, we can say that it is limited to lower worlds. Therefore, it depends on the spirit to emancipate itself more or less promptly by working on its purification.

It should also be taken into consideration that in the errant state, that is to say, in the interval between bodily existences, the situation of a spirit is in relation to the nature of the world of whose degree of advancement depends its own. Thus, in the errant state, a spirit may be more or less happy, more or less free and enlightened, according to its degree of dematerialization.

Saint Louis[18] (Paris, 1859).

NECESSITY FOR INCARNATION

25. *Is incarnation a punishment, and are only guilty spirits subject to it?*
The passage of spirits through bodily life is necessary for them to be able to accomplish, by means of material actions, the designs which God entrusts them with the execution. It is necessary for themselves, because the activity they are obliged to deploy helps the

---

18 [Trans. note] Saint Louis IX (1214–1270), a king of France and Catholic saint.

development of intelligence. God, being sovereignly just, must give an equal share to all Its children; that is why he gives everyone the same starting point, the same ability, *the same obligations to fulfill, and the same freedom to act.* Any privilege would be a preference, any preference an injustice. But, to all spirits, incarnation is only a transitory state; it is a task that God imposes on them at their beginning in life, as the first test of the use they will make of their free will. Those who fulfill this task with zeal move rapidly and less painfully through these first degrees of initiation, and enjoy the fruit of their labors earlier. On the contrary, those who make a bad use of the freedom that God grants to them retard their advancement. It is thus that, because of their obstinacy, they can prolong indefinitely the necessity of reincarnating, and it is then that incarnation becomes a punishment.

26. Note: A trivial comparison can make this difference be better understood. A pupil succeeds in getting good grades in science only after having traversed the series of lessons which lead to it. These lessons, whatever work they require, are a means to an end, not a punishment. A diligent schoolchild shortens the road and finds fewer thorns; otherwise, if negligent and lazy, they are compelled to repeat certain courses. It is not the work of the course lessons that is a punishment, but the obligation to undertake the same work again.

The same applies to all humans on Earth. For the spirit of a savage, who is almost at very beginning of his/her spiritual life, incarnation is a means of developing their intelligence. But for an enlightened individual in whom the moral sense is largely developed, and who is obliged to undertake again the stages of a bodily life full of anxieties, while he/she might already have arrived at a higher goal, it becomes a punishment due to the necessity to prolong his/her stay in lower and unhappy worlds. On the other hand, those who actively work on their moral progress, may not only shorten the duration of their material incarnation, but climb at once the intermediate degrees that separate them from higher worlds.

Could spirits incarnate only once on the same globe, and accomplish their different existences on different planets? This opinion would only be admissible if all humans on Earth were exactly at the same intellectual and moral level. However, the differences which exist among them, from the savage to the civilized person, show the degrees which they are called to go through. Moreover, incarnation must have a useful end; but what would be the usefulness of the ephemeral incarnations of children who die at an early age? They would have suffered without profit to themselves or to others: God, whose laws are supremely wise, does nothing useless. By reincarnation on the same globe, God wanted the same spirits to be in touch again, having occasion to repair their reciprocal wrongs. Due to the their previous relationships, God also wanted them to build family ties on a spiritual foundation, and to rest on a law of Nature the principles of solidarity, fraternity and equality.

Chapter V
Blessed are the afflicted

1. "'Blessed are the meek, for they shall inherit the earth.'

'Blessed are those who hunger and thirst for righteousness, for they shall be satisfied.'

'Blessed are those who are persecuted for righteousness' sake, for theirs is the kingdom of heaven' (MATTHEW 5:5–6,10 ESV)."

2. "And he lifted up his eyes on his disciples, and said:

'Blessed are you who are poor, for yours is the kingdom of God.'

'Blessed are you who are hungry now, for you shall be satisfied.'

'Blessed are you who weep now, for you shall laugh' (LUKE 6:20–21 ESV)."

"'But woe to you who are rich, for you have received your consolation.'

'Woe to you who are full now, for you shall be hungry.'

'Woe to you who laugh now, for you shall mourn and weep' (LUKE 6:24–25 ESV)."

JUSTICE OF AFFLICTIONS

3. The compensations that Jesus promises to the afflicted of the Earth can only take place in future life. Without the certainty of a future, these maxims would be nonsense – more than that, they would be a delusion. Even with such certainty it is difficult to understand the usefulness of suffering to be happy. It is, some say, to have more merit; but then one wonders why some suffer more than others; why some are born in misery while others in opulence, without having done anything to justify this condition; why nothing seems to succeed to some, while to others everything seems to smile? But what one understands even less is to see good and evil so unequally shared between vice and virtue; to see virtuous individuals suffer beside wicked ones that prosper. Faith in the future can comfort and make one have patience, but it does not explain these anomalies that seem to deny the justice of God.

However, since we admit the existence of God, we cannot conceive of It without Its infinite perfections. God must be all power, all justice, all goodness, otherwise It would not be God. If God is supremely good and just, It cannot act arbitrarily by caprice or partiality. Hence *the vicissitudes of life have a cause, and since God is always just, such cause must be just.* This is something of which everyone should become well aware. God has placed humans on the path of this cause by the teachings left by Jesus; and today, judging them to be ripe enough to understand it, God reveals it fully to them through *Spiritism*, that is to say, through *the voice of the spirits.*

CURRENT CAUSES OF AFFLICTIONS

4. The vicissitudes of life are of two kinds, or, if you will, have two very different sources, which it is important to distinguish. Some have their cause in current life, others outside of this life.

If one goes back to the source of earthly evils, it will be known that many are a natural consequence of the character and conduct of those who endure them.

How many people fall by their own fault! How many are victims of their own improvidence, their pride and their greed!

How many people ruined by a lack of order and perseverance, by misconduct, or for not being able to limit their desires!

What unhappy unions because they are the result of interest or vanity, in which the heart has no place!

How many dissensions and fatal quarrels could have been avoided by using more moderation and less susceptibility.

How many diseases and infirmities are the result of intemperance and excesses of all kinds.

How many parents are unhappy about their children, because they have not fought the bad tendencies of these latter since the start! Due to weakness or indifference, they have allowed seeds of pride, selfishness and stupid vanity to develop in them, drying out their heart. Then, later, when they harvest what they have sown, they are astonished and grieve for their children's ingratitude and lack of deference.

May all those who are struck in the heart by the vicissitudes and disappointments of life coldly examine their conscience; may they go back step by step to the source of the evils that afflict them, and they will see if, most often, they could not say: *If I had done, or had not done such and such a thing, I would not be in this situation.*

Who else should you blame for all these afflictions, if not yourself? Humans are thus, in a large number of cases, the architects of their own misfortunes; but, instead of recognizing it, they find it simpler and less humiliating for their vanity to blame fate, providence, unfavorable luck, their bad star, while their bad star actually lies in their own carelessness.

Evils of this nature certainly form a remarkable consignment of vicissitudes in one's life. Humans will avoid those when they work on their moral improvement as much as on their intellectual improvement.

5. Human laws can deal with certain faults and punish them. A condemned individual may say to himself/herself that he/she is suffering the consequence of what he/she has done; but human laws do not deal with and cannot reach all faults. Such laws strike more especially those which are harmful to society, and not those which harm only those people who commit them. But God wants the progress of all Its created beings; that is why It does not allow any deviation from the right path to go unpunished. There is not a single fault, slight as it may be, not a single infraction of God's law, which does not have strong and inevitable consequences which are more or less unfortunate. Whence it follows that in small as well as in great things human beings are always punished where they have sinned. The sufferings that ensue are a warning for them that they have done bad deeds. They give them experience, make them feel the difference between good and evil, and the need to improve themselves in order to avoid in future what has been a source of sorrows for them, otherwise they would have no motivation to amend themselves. Confident in impunity, they would delay their advancement, and consequently their future happiness.

But sometimes experience comes a little late, when life has been wasted and troubled, one's forces are worn out and evil is without remedy. Then the individual starts to say: If in the beginning of life I knew what I know now, how many missteps would I have avoided! *If I were to begin again,* I would do everything differently; but time is up! Like a lazy worker would say, "I lost my day," that person would think, "I lost my life." However, same as for the working person the Sun rises the next day, and a new day begins, allowing him/her to repair the time lost, for that individual also, after the night of the grave, the Sun of a new life shine, in which he/she will be able to use their experience of the past and their good resolutions for the future.

PRIOR CAUSES OF AFFLICTIONS

6.　But if there are evils of which humans are the first cause in this life, there are others to which they are, at least apparently, completely alien, and which seem to strike them as if by misfortune. Such are, for example, the loss of cherished beings, and the loss of breadwinners; such are also accidents which no foresight could have prevented; fortune's reversals that thwart any measures of prudence; natural plagues. Then there are infirmities of birth, especially those which deprive the unfortunate of means of gaining their living through work, such as deformities, lunacy, inanity, and so on.

Those who are born in such conditions have certainly done nothing in this life to deserve such a sad fate without compensation, that they could not avoid and that they are powerless to change for themselves, and puts them at the mercy of public compassion. Why, then, are there such distressed beings living side by side, under the same roof, in the same family, with others who are favored in every respect?

What can be said about these children who die at a young age and have only known suffering in life? Problems which no philosophy has yet been able to solve, anomalies which no religion could justify, and which would be the denial of god's goodness, justice and providence, on the assumption that one's soul is created at the same time as one's body, and that its fate is irrevocably fixed after a stay of a few moments on Earth. What have they done, those souls that would have just come out of the hands of the Creator, to endure so many miseries here below, and deserve a future or punishment of some kind, if they have not been able to do any good nor bad?

However, by virtue of the axiom that *every effect has a cause,* these miseries are effects which must have a cause; and since one admits the existence of a just God, this cause must be just. Now, since the cause always precedes the effect, and since it is not in current life, it must be prior to this life, that is, it belongs to a previous existence. On the other hand, God cannot punish us for the good we have done, nor for the evil we have not done. If we are punished, it is because we have done evil; if we have not done evil in this life, we have done it in another. It is an alternative from which it is impossible to escape, and whose logic on either side resides in the justice of God.

Human beings are not always punished, or completely atone for their errors in their current existence, but they never escape the consequences of their faults. The wicked's prosperity is only momentary; if they do not atone for it today, they will atone for it tomorrow, whereas those who suffer are atoning for their past. Misfortune, which at first seems unmerited, has its reason for being, and those who suffer may always say, "Forgive me Lord, for I have sinned."

7. Sufferings due to prior causes are often, like those of current faults, the natural consequence of a fault committed, that is to say, by a rigorous distributive justice, humans endure what they have done to others. If one was hard and inhuman, he/she can be treated in its turn harshly and inhumanly; if one has been proud, he/she may be born in humiliating conditions; if one has been stingy, selfish, or has misused his/her fortune, this person may be deprived of basic needs; if one has been a bad son or daughter, he/she may suffer from their own children, and so on.

Thus are explained, by the plurality of existences, and by Earth's role as a world of atonement, the anomalies which the distribution of happiness and misfortune presents between the good and the wicked here below. This anomaly exists in appearance only because one takes one's point of view only from current life. But if one rises, by thought, so as to encompass a series of existences, one will see that each and every one receives the share that he/she deserves, without detriment to the share they may be given in the world of the spirits; and that God's justice is never interrupted.

Humans must never lose sight of the fact that they are on an lower-order world where they are kept only by their imperfections. At each vicissitude, one must say to oneself that if he/she belonged to a more advanced world this would not happen; and that it depends on him/her not to come back here below, by working to improve oneself.

8. Tribulations of life can be imposed on hardened spirits, or too ignorant to make an informed choice, but they are freely chosen and accepted by repentant spirits who want to repair the evil they have done, and to try to do better. This is like the one who, having done his/her job badly, asks to do it again in order not to lose the benefit of his/her work. Such tribulations are therefore both atonements for the past which they punish, and trials for the future they are preparing. Let us give thanks to God which, in Its goodness, grants humans the possibility of reparation, and does not condemn it irrevocably on account of a first fault.

9. It should not be thought, however, that all suffering endured here below is necessarily indicative of a definite fault: they are often simple trials chosen by the spirit to complete its purification and hasten its advancement. Thus any atonement always serves as a test, but a test is not always an atonement. These are always signs of relative inferiority, because what is perfect no longer needs to be tested. A spirit may have acquired a certain degree of elevation, but, wishing to go further, it has solicited a mission, a task to be accomplished, of which it will be all the more rewarded, if it comes out victorious, the more painful the struggle will have been. Such are, more especially, those persons with naturally good instincts, with an elevated soul, with innate noble sentiments, who seem to have brought nothing bad from their former existence, and who endure with full Christian resignation the greatest pains, asking God strength to bear them without grumbling. On the contrary, we can consider as atonements the afflictions which incite grumbling and urge humans to revolt against God.

Suffering that does not incite grumbling may also be an atonement, but it is a sign that it was voluntarily chosen rather than imposed, and proof of a strong resolution, which is an indication of progress.

10. Spirits can aspire to perfect happiness only when they are pure: any impurity will prevent them from entering happy worlds. Like the passengers of a plague-infected ship, to whom the entrance into a city is forbidden until they have purified themselves, spirits are gradually stripped of their imperfections through various bodily existences. Life trials may contribute to our advancement when we bear them well. As expiations, they erase mistakes and purify; it is the remedy which cleans the wound and heals the patient; the more serious the harm, the more vigorous the remedy must be. Those who suffer too much ought to say that they had much to atone for, and rejoice at being healed soon. It depends on them, by their resignation, to render this suffering beneficial, and not to lose its fruit by grumbling, otherwise it would be necessary for them to start it all over again.

FORGETFULNESS OF THE PAST

11. In vain do some object to forgetfulness as an obstacle to their enjoyment of the experience of past lives. If God thought it appropriate to cast a veil over the past, it must have been for a good reason. Indeed, this memory would have very serious disadvantages. In some cases, it could conspicuously humiliate, or exalt our pride, and thereby hinder our free will. In any case, it would have brought an inevitable disturbance in social relations.

The spirit is often reborn again in the same environment where it has already lived, and is in touch with the same individuals, in order to repair the harm it has done to them. If the spirit recognized in them those it hated, its hatred might be revived; and in any case that spirit would be humiliated before those whom it had offended.

God has given us, in order to improve ourselves, just what is necessary and sufficient for us: the voice of conscience and our instinctive tendencies, while taking away anything that could harm us.

At birth, human beings bring what they had previously acquired; he is born what he has done; each new existence is for them a new starting point; it is not relevant to them to know what they were in previous lives: they are being punished because they have done evil; their current bad tendencies are indicative of what remains to be corrected in such spirits, and that is where they must focus their attention, because from what a spirit has been completely corrected no trace will be left. The good resolutions it has taken are the voice of conscience, warning it of what is good and what is evil, and giving it strength to resist temptation.

Moreover, such forgetfulness only takes place during corporeal life. Once a spirit returns to the spiritual world, it recovers the memory of the past. Therefore this forgetfulness is only a momentary interruption, like that which takes place in earthly life during sleep, which does not prevent anyone from remembering the next day what he or she have done the previous day and before.

Not only after physical death can a spirit recover the memory of its past. It can be said that it has never lost it, for experience proves that throughout incarnation, during the sleep of the body, when the spirit enjoys a certain freedom, it is aware of its previous actions. It knows why it suffers, and that this suffering is fair. The memory only disappears during the outer life of relation. But in the absence of a precise memory which could be painful to certain individuals and harmful to their social relations, they draw new strength in these moments of emancipation of the soul, provided they know how to put them to good use.

REASONS FOR RESIGNATION

12. With these words, *Blessed are the afflicted, for they shall be consoled,*[19] Jesus indicates both the compensation that awaits those who suffer, and the resignation that makes suffering be blessed as the prelude to healing.

These words can still be translated as follows: You must consider yourself happy to suffer, because your pains in this world are the

---

19 [Trans. note] Both French and English bibles vary in their translation of this passage from the Bible. The passage above, translated literally from A. KARDEC's citation appears in the *ESV* as follows: "Blessed are those who mourn, for they shall be comforted. (MATTHEW 5:4 ESV)."

debt of your past faults, and these pains, if endured patiently on Earth, will spare you centuries of suffering in future life. So you must be happy that God is reducing your debt by allowing you to pay off your debts now, which gives you peace of mind for the future.

Those who suffer are like a debtor who owes a large sum, and to whom the creditor says: "If you pay me today a hundredth part of your debt, I will leave you with all the rest, otherwise, should you fail to do it, I will pursue you until you pay the last penny." Would the debtor not be happy to endure all kinds of privations to free himself by paying only one hundredth of what he/she owes? Instead of complaining about the creditor, will the debtor not thank the latter?

This is the meaning of these words: "Blessed are the afflicted, for they shall be consoled." They are blessed, because they are paying off their debts, and after clearing the latter they will be free. But if, while clearing one side, you go into debt with another, you will never attain liberation. Now, every new fault increases the debt, because there is not a single one of them, whatever it may be, which does not bring with it its mandatory and inevitable punishment. If not today, it will be tomorrow; if not in this life, it will be in the other one. Among these faults, we must place in the first rank the lack of submission to the will of God. Therefore, if we grumble in afflictions we murmur, if we do not accept them with resignation and as something that we must have deserved; if we accuse God of injustice, we contract a new debt which makes us lose the benefit that we could draw from our suffering. That is why it will be necessary to start all over again, exactly as if, to a creditor who had previously tormented you, you had to start paying anew, each time you borrowed from him once more.

At its re-entry into the spiritual world, a spirit is still like the worker who presents himself/herself on payday. To some the master will say: "Here is the salary for your working days"; to others, to the happy-go-lucky of the Earth, to those who have lived in idleness, and those who have put their happiness in satisfying their self-esteem and worldly pleasures, he will say: "To you there is nothing, for you have already received your wages on Earth. Go back and repeat your task. "

13. Humans can soften or increase the bitterness of their trials by the way they regard earthly life. They will suffer all the more as they see the duration of the suffering to be lengthy. Now, whoever places oneself from the point of view of spiritual life encompasses at a glance corporeal life, sees it as a small point in the infinite, understands its brevity, and tells oneself that this painful moment will pass quickly, with the certainty of a happier near future providing moral support and encouragement. Then, instead of complaining, you thank heaven for the pains that make you go forward. Conversely, for those who can only see bodily life, it seems interminable to them, and pain weighs heavily on them with all its weight. The result of this way of looking at life is to lessen the importance of the things of this world, to make humans moderate their desires, and to be content with their position without envying the position of others, also softening the moral impression left by setbacks and disappointments they may experience. It draws calm and resignation which are as beneficial to the health of the body as to the health of the soul; whereas by envy, jealousy and ambition, one voluntarily exposes oneself to torture, thus adding to the miseries and anxieties of one's short life.

SUICIDE AND MADNESS

14. Calm and resignation in earthly life, and faith in the future, give the spirit a serenity which is the best antidote against *madness and suicide*. Indeed, it is certain that most cases of madness are due to the turmoil produced by vicissitudes that one does not have the strength to bear. Therefore, due to the manner by which Spiritism makes one think differently of the things of this world, he or she takes with indifference, even with joy, the setbacks and disappointments which would have been cause of despair in other circumstances. It is evident that this force, that places one above events, preserves one's reason from the jolts which otherwise would have shaken it.

15. It is the same with suicide. If we except those which are committed when someone is drunk or mad – which may be called unconscious – it is certain that, whatever their particular motives may be, they are always due to discontent. Now, anyone who is certain of being unhappy only one day and of feeling better the following days, will easily be patient. Such people will despair only if they see no end to their sufferings. What is human existence when compared to eternity, if not less than a single day? Yet for one who does not believe in eternity, and thinks that everything ends for him/her with life. If such people are overwhelmed by sorrow and misfortune, they can see an end to this state only in death. Devoid of any hope, they find it quite natural and logical to shorten their miseries by committing suicide.

16.   Unbelief, mere doubt about the future – in a word, materialistic ideas – are the major instigations of suicide: they cause *moral cowardice*. And when we see scientists and scholars rely on the authority of their knowledge to try to prove to their listeners or their readers that they have nothing to expect after death, are they not leading them to conclude that, if they are unhappy, they have nothing better to do than to kill themselves? What could they say to them in order to divert them from such a resolution? What compensation can they offer them? What hope can they give them? Nothing but nothingness. Hence it must be concluded that if nothingness is the only heroic remedy, the only prospect, it is better to surrender to it immediately than later, thus shortening one's sufferings.

The propagation of materialistic ideas is therefore the poison which inoculates thoughts of suicide in many individuals, and those who advocate such ideas assume a terrible responsibility for them. With Spiritism, since doubt is no longer possible, the aspect of life changes, the believer knows that life extends indefinitely beyond the grave, although under quite different conditions. Hence patience and resignation, which naturally divert one from thoughts of suicide, giving *moral courage* instead.

17.   In this respect, Spiritism also has another equally positive and perhaps more decisive result. It shows us the suicides themselves, accounting for their unfortunate situation, and proving that no one can violate God's law – which forbids humans to shorten their lives – with impunity. Among suicides, their suffering, albeit only temporary instead of eternal, is nonetheless dreadful, and of such a nature as to give food for thought to anyone who would be tempted to quit life down here before God's appointed time. Therefore Spiritists have several arguments as counterweights to the thought of suicide: the *certainty* of a future life in which they *know* they will be all the happier in proportion to how unhappy and resigned they were on Earth; the *certainty* that by abridging their lifetime they would arrive at a very different result from what they had hoped for; and that they would free themselves of an evil only to gain a much worse, longer and more dreadful one. They understand that it is a big mistake to believe that, by killing yourself, you go faster to heaven; that suicide is an obstacle to being reunited in the other world with the objects of their affections whom they hoped to find there – whence the consequence that by committing suicide, one will have only disappointments, as it is against one's own interests. So the number of suicides prevented by Spiritism is considerable, and it can be concluded that the day everyone becomes a Spiritist, there will be no more conscious suicides. Comparing the results of materialistic and Spiritist tenets from the sole point of view of suicide, we find that the logic of the former leads to it, while the logic of the latter diverts from it, which is confirmed by experience.

INSTRUCTIONS FROM THE SPIRITS

GOOD AND BAD SUFFERING

18.   When Christ said, "Blessed are the afflicted, for theirs is the kingdom of heaven,"[20] he was not referring to those who suffer in general, since all who are down here suffer, whether rich or poor; but alas! few suffer well, few understand that it is the enduring of trials what alone can lead them to the kingdom of God. Discouragement is a fault; God refuses to give you comfort when you lack courage. Prayer is a support for the soul, but it is not enough: it must be based on a strong faith in the goodness of God. It has often been said to you that God would not place a heavy burden on feeble shoulders, yet the burden is proportionate to one's forces, just like the reward will be proportionate to one's resignation and courage. A reward will be greater than an affliction is painful, but such reward must be deserved, and that is why life is full of tribulations.

---

20 [Trans. note] A. KARDEC seems to paraphrase the Gospel in this citation which is neither in SACY's or OSTERVALD's French bibles. *Cf.* MATTHEW 5:3 ESV: "Blessed are the poor in spirit, for theirs is the kingdom of heaven." See also J. DUPONT, *Les Béatitudes* (3 vols.; Paris: Gabalda, HI 1969, III 1973).

A soldier that is not sent to the line of fire is not happy, because staying back at the camp will not bring him/her any promotions. So then, be like the soldier and do not wish to rest back at the camp where your body would become weak and your soul numb. Be content when God sends you into combat. This struggle is not the fire of battle, but the bitterness of life, which is sometimes more discouraging than in a bloody fight, since even those who remain firm before the enemy, will bend down under the weight of a moral grief. Humans have no reward for this kind of courage, but God reserves victory laurels and a glorious place to them. When a reason for pain or annoyance comes to you, try to gain the upper hand; and when you have managed to control your impulses of impatience, anger or despair, say to yourself with just satisfaction: "I prevailed."

Therefore, *Blessed are the afflicted*, can be translated thus: Blessed are those who have the opportunity to prove their faith, their steadfastness, their perseverance and their submission to the will of God, because they shall receive a hundredfold the joy they lack on Earth – and after work comes rest.

Lacordaire[21] (Le Havre, 1863).

THE EVIL AND THE REMEDY

19.   Is Earth a place of joy, a paradise of delights? Does not the prophet's voice sound in your ears? Did he not cry that there would be weeping and gnashing of teeth for those born in this valley of sorrows? You who come to live in such a place, expect tears and bitter pains, and your pains will be sharp and deep; look up to heaven and bless the Lord, for wanting to test you! ... Human beings! Will you not acknowledge the power of your Master until he has healed the wounds of your body and crowned your days with bliss and joy? Will you acknowledge his love only when he has adorned your body with all glories, and restored it to its unblemished brightness? Try to imitate the one who was given to you as an example: after having arrived at the last degree of abjection and misery, and lying on a heap of dung, he says to God, "Lord, I have known all the joys of opulence, and you have reduced me to utter misery. Thank you,

---

21 [Trans. note] Jean-Baptiste Henri-Dominique LACORDAIRE (1802–1861), a French ecclesiastic, preacher, journalist, theologian and political activist.

thank you, O God, for having willed to test your servant!"How long will your eyes linger on horizons bounded by death? When will your soul finally want to go beyond the limits of the grave? Even if you were to cry and suffer for a lifetime, what is it beside the eternity of glory reserved for those who will have undergone the trials with faith, love and resignation? So seek consolation for your ills in the future that God has prepared for you, and the cause of your evils in your past. Those of you who suffer the most, consider yourselves the blessed of the Earth.

In the state of discarnate spirit, while you hovered in space, you chose your trials, because you thought you were strong enough to bear them – so why grumble now? If you are among those who asked for fortune and glory, it was to withstand the struggle against temptation and to overcome it. As for you who have asked to struggle in spirit and body against moral and physical evils, it is because you knew that the stronger the trial, the more the victory will be glorious, and that if you emerge triumphant, even if your body were thrown onto a dung heap, at death it would release a soul with unblemished brightness, made pure again by the baptism of atonement and suffering.

What remedy, then, is recommended to those who are suffering from cruel obsessions and harassed by stinging ills? There is one which is infallible: it is faith; it is look up to heaven. If, in the height of your most cruel sufferings, your voice would sing to the Lord, the angel by your bedside would show you the sign of salvation and the place you will occupy one day ... Faith is the sure remedy for suffering; it always shows the horizons of the infinite next to which the few dark days of the present fade away. Therefore do not ask us what remedy should be used to cure this ulcer or that wound, this temptation or that trial. Keep in mind that those who believe are strengthened by the remedy of faith, and those who doubt even for one second of its effectiveness are punished right away, because they experience at that very moment the poignant anguish of their affliction.

The Lord has marked with his seal all who believe in him. Christ has told you that through faith mountains can be moved, and I tell you that whoever suffers but is sustained by faith will be placed under his protection and will not suffer anymore; the moments of strongest pains will be for such a person the first notes of joy of eternity. This person's soul will disengage itself so much from the body that, while the latter is still writhing in convulsions, it will hover in the heavenly regions, singing with the angels hymns of gratitude and glory unto the Lord.

Happy are those who suffer and weep! May their souls be joyful, for they will be pervaded by God.

St. Augustine (Paris, 1863).

HAPPINESS IS NOT OF THIS WORLD

20. I am not happy! Happiness is not for me! – this is what one usually hears from people of all walks of life. My dear children, this proves better than all possible reasonings the truth of this maxim found in Ecclesiastes: "Happiness is not of this world." In fact, neither fortune, nor power, nor even a flourishing youth, are the essential conditions of happiness. I say more: not even these three coveted conditions together can bring happiness, since we constantly hear, even in the middle of the most privileged classes, people of all ages complaining bitterly about their situation.

Faced with such a result, it is inconceivable that the working and militant classes envy so much the position of those that fortune seems to have favored. Here below, regardless of social position, everyone has their share of toil and misery, their lot of suffering and disappointment. Hence it is easy to conclude that the Earth is a place of trials and atonements.

Therefore those who preach that the Earth is the only abode of humans; that it is only there, in a single existence, that one is allowed to attain the highest degree of happiness that its Nature entails, are fooling themselves and deceiving those who listen to them, since it is demonstrated by a centuries-old experience that this globe only exceptionally meets the conditions necessary for the complete happiness of an individual.

Generally speaking, it can be said that happiness is a utopia in the pursuit of which generations have sprung up successively without ever being able to reach it; for if wise persons are a rarity here below, an absolutely happy individual is even harder to find.

Happiness is so ephemeral on Earth that, for those who are not guided by wisdom, a year, a month, or a week of complete satisfaction, are followed by a series of grievances and disappointments – and note, my dear children, that I am speaking here of the joyous ones of the Earth, of those envied by the masses.

Consequently, if the stay on Earth is assigned to trials and atonements, it must be admitted that there are more favorable stays elsewhere, where the human spirit, still imprisoned in material flesh, enjoys in their fullest the enjoyments attached to human life. That is why God has sown in your vortex of stars those beautiful higher-order planets around which your efforts and your tendencies will make you gravitate one day, when you become sufficiently purified and perfected.

Nevertheless do not deduce from my words that the Earth is forever destined to be a penitentiary. No, certainly not! For, with the progress you have already made, you can easily predict further progress in future, and social improvements, new and more fruitful improvements. This is the immense task that the new philosophical and religious doctrine revealed by the spirits must fulfill.

So, my dear children, a holy emulation animates you, and each one of you should vigorously get rid of your old ways. You all owe to the popularization of Spiritism, which has already begun, your own regeneration. It is a duty to involve your brothers in the rays of sacred light. To work, my dear children! May all your hearts in this solemn meeting aspire to this grand goal to prepare future generations for a world where happiness will no longer be an empty word.

François-Nicholas-Madeleine, cardinal Morlot[22] (Paris, 1863.)

LOSS OF LOVED ONES
PREMATURE DEATHS

21. When death comes to mow into your families, randomly carrying away young people before the elders, you often say: God is not right, since It sacrifices who is strong and full of future, to preserve those who lived long years full of disappointments; since It removes those that are useful, while sparing those that are no longer useful for anything; and since It breaks a mother's heart by depriving her of the innocent creature who was all her joy.

---

22 [Trans. note] Francois-Nicholas-Madeleine Morlot (1795–1862), a French Catholic cardinal.

Humans, this is where you need to rise above mundane, down-to-earth issues of life so as to understand that good is often where you believe to see evil, wise foresight where you believe to see inexorable blind fate. Why measure divine justice using the same value of yours? Can you conceive of the master of the worlds willing, by mere whim, to inflict cruel punishment on you? Nothing is done without an intelligent goal, and whatever happens, everything has its reason for being. If you look harder at all the pains that strike you, you will always find a divine reason, a regenerative reason – and your petty interests would be a minor consideration that you would relegate to a secondary place.

Believe me, death is preferable, in the case of some incarnations of twenty years, to these shameful disturbances that desolate honorable families, break the heart of a mother, and make the parents' hair go gray before time. Premature death is often a great blessing that God gives to the individual who goes away, and who is thus preserved from the miseries of life, or from seductions that could have led to his/her death. Those who die in their prime of life are not victims of fate, but rather God has decided that it is beneficial for them not to remain longer on Earth.

It is a dreadful misfortune, you say, that a life so full of hopes was cut short so soon. What hopes are you talking about? Those of the Earth where the one who went away could have shone, making his/her way and fortune? Always it is this narrow view that prevents you from rising above matter. Do you know what would have been the outcome of such life so full of hopes for you? Who assures you that it would not be showered with bitterness? So you count for nothing the hopes of future life, instead preferring those of the ephemeral life that you lead on Earth? Do you think it is better to rank among human beings than among blessed spirits?

Rejoice instead of complaining when it pleases God to remove one of Its children from this valley of misery. Is it not selfish to wish that he/she remains on Earth to suffer with you? Ah! this pain is conceived by those who have no faith, and see in death an eternal separation. But you, Spiritists, know that the soul lives better free of its bodily envelope. Mothers, you know that your beloved children are close to you; yes, they are very near, their fluidic bodies surround you, their thoughts protect you, your memory suffuses them with joy;

yet also your unreasonable pains afflict them, because they denote a lack of faith, and they are a revolt against God's will.

You who understand spiritual life, listen to the words of your heart calling these dear loved ones; and if you pray to God to bless them, you will feel in you these powerful consolations that dry all tears, these prestigious aspirations which will show you the future promised by the sovereign Master.

Sanson, former member of the Parisian Society of Spiritist Studies (Paris, 1863).

IF THAT WERE A GOOD PERSON, HE/SHE WOULD HAVE BEEN KILLED

22.   You often say when talking of a bad person who has escaped some danger: *If that were a good person, he/she would have been killed.* Well, saying that you are right, because indeed it often happens that God gives a spirit, still young in the ways of progress, a longer trial than to a good spirit which will receive as a reward for its merit the favor that its test be as short as possible. So whenever you utter this axiom, you do not suspect that you are actually committing a blasphemy.

If a good person dies and beside his/her house lives a wicked person, you hasten to say: *It would be better if it were this one instead.* You are in great error, because the one who has left has finished his/her task, and the one who remains may not even have begun it. Why then would you want the wicked one to depart before having time to finish it, and the other, the good one, to remain attached to Earth? What about a prisoner who has finished serving his/her time, but that would be kept in prison while giving freedom to the one who is not entitled to it? Know then that true freedom is in being freed of the bonds of the body, and that as long as you are on Earth, you are in captivity.

Try not to blame what you cannot understand, and believe that God is righteous in all things. Often what seems to you to be evil is actually good; yet your faculties are so limited, that the great whole escapes your obtuse senses. Strive to get out of your narrow sphere through your thoughts; and, as you rise, the importance of material life will diminish in your eyes, because it will only appear to you as an incident in the infinite duration of your life, your spiritual existence, the only true existence.

Fénelon (Sens, 1861).

VOLUNTARY TORMENTS

23. Humans are incessantly pursuing a happiness which constantly eludes them, because unalloyed happiness does not exist on Earth yet. In spite of the vicissitudes that form the inevitable trail of life, people could at least enjoy of a relative happiness, but they seek it in perishable things and are subject to the same vicissitudes, that is to say, in material enjoyments, instead of seeking it in the enjoyments of the soul which are a foretaste of the imperishable heavenly enjoyments. Instead of seeking *peace of heart* – the only real happiness here below – they are eager for everything that can agitate and disturb them; and, singular thing, they seem to deliberately create torments for themselves which they alone could have avoided.

Are there any torments greater than those caused by envy and jealousy? For the envious and the jealous there is no rest, no letting go; they are perpetually feverish. What they do not have, and what others have, causes them insomnia; the success of their rivals make them dizzy; emulation is only exercised to overshadow their neighbors; all their joy consists in exciting in fools like them the rage of jealousy with which they are possessed. Poor fools, indeed, who do not think that tomorrow perhaps they will have to leave all these gewgaws they crave and which poison their lives! Since their woes and worries are not of the kind which will have their compensation in heaven, it is not to them that the following words apply: "Blessed are the afflicted, because they shall be comforted."[23]

Conversely, how many torments will spare those who know how to be contented with what they own, who look without envy at what they do not have, and who do not try to appear to be more than they are. Such people are always rich, because if they look below them, instead of looking above, they will always see people who have even less. They are calm because they do not create fanciful needs – and is the calm in the middle of the storms of life not a form of happiness?

---

23 [Trans. note] For terminological consistency, the biblical verse above was literally translated from A. KARDEC's French. See also footnote 19 above.

Fénelon (Lyon, 1860).

THE REAL MISFORTUNE

24. Everyone talks about misfortune, everyone has felt it and might think to know its multiple character. I now tell you that almost everyone is mistaken, and that real misfortune is not at all what human, that is to say unfortunate individuals, suppose it to be. They see it in deprivation; in a fireplace without fire; in a threatening creditor; in the empty cradle of a little angel who used to smile; in tears; in the coffin followed by a respectful retinue of mourners with uncovered heads and broken hearts; in the anguish of a betrayal; in the destitution of pride which should be clothed in purple but can barely conceal its nakedness under the rags of vanity. All these, and many other things, are called misfortune in human language. Yes, it is misfortune for those who see only the present; yet true misfortune lies in the consequences of something more than in the thing itself. Tell me if the happiest event for the moment, but which has fatal consequences, is not in reality more unfortunate than that which at first causes a great annoyance but ends up producing good. Tell me if the storm that breaks your trees, but cleans the air by dissipating unhealthy miasma that would have caused death, is not a fortunate event rather than a misfortune.

To judge something, it is necessary to see what comes after it; therefore to discern what is really fortunate or unfortunate for humans, it is necessary to go beyond one lifetime, because it is there that consequences are felt. Now, all that one calls misfortune according to one's narrow sight ceases with one's lifetime and finds its compensation in future life.

I will reveal misfortune to you in a new form, in the beautiful and flowery form that you welcome and desire it with all the strength of your deceived souls. Misfortune is joyfulness, it is pleasure, it is noise, it is vain agitation, it is the insane satisfaction of vanity which silences one's conscience, which squeezes the action of thought, which stuns the idea of future in humans. Misfortune is the opium of oblivion which you call for all your desires.

Keep hoping, you who cry! Tremble, you who laugh, because your body is satisfied! We cannot deceive God; we cannot evade destiny; or hardships, which are creditors more pitiless than the hordes unleashed by misery, watching for your moments of deceitful rest to plunge you suddenly into the agony of true misfortune, that which startles the soul softened by indifference and selfishness when it least expects.

So let Spiritism enlighten you, and place in their true light the truth and the error, so strangely disfigured by your blindness! Thus you will start acting like brave soldiers, who, far from fleeing danger, prefer the struggles of dangerous battles to a peace that cannot give them neither glory nor advancement. What does it matter to a soldier to lose in a fight all his/her weapons, luggage and clothes, provided that he/she comes out victorious and covered in glory! What does it matter to a soldier who has faith in the future to leave fortune and fleshly cloak on the battlefield of life, provided that his/her soul enters radiant into the heavenly kingdom?

Delphine de Girardin[24] (Paris, 1861).

MELANCHOLY

25. Do you know why a vague sadness sometimes seizes upon your hearts and makes you find life so bitter? It is your spirit that is aspiring to happiness and freedom, and which, riveted to the body which serves as a prison to it, has exhausted in vain all its efforts to get out of it. But realizing that its efforts are useless, the spirit falls into discouragement, and the body, undergoing its influence, falls into languor and dejection; and a kind of apathy seizes upon you, making you feel melancholic.

Believe me, you should resist with energy those impressions which weaken your willpower. Those aspirations for a better life are innate to the spirits of all human beings, but do not seek them here below. And now that God is sending you Its higher-order spirits to instruct you in the light that It has for you, wait patiently for the angel of deliverance that will help you break the bonds which hold your spirit captive. Bear in mind that you have to fulfill during your ordeal on Earth a mission which you cannot doubt, either by devoting yourself to your family, or by fulfilling the various duties that God has entrusted to you. And if, in the course of this ordeal, and while performing your task, you encounter worries, anxieties, and sorrows, be strong and courageous to bear them. Brave them

---

24 [Trans. note] Delphine de Girardin (1804–1855), French writer.

fearlessly, they are short-lived and should lead you to the friends you have mourned, who will rejoice at your arrival among them, and stretch out their arms to lead you to a place where Earth's sorrows have no access.

François de Genève (Bordeaux).

VOLUNTARY TRIALS
THE TRUE CILICE

26. You ask whether it is permissible to soften one's own trials. This question leads to the following: Is it permissible for those who are drowning to seek salvation? To those who have a thorn to try to remove it? To whoever is sick to call a doctor? Trials are intended to stimulate one's intelligence as well as patience and resignation. Some individuals may be born in a difficult and awkward position, precisely to compel them to seek the means of overcoming hardships. Merit consists in bearing without grumbling the consequences of evils that cannot be avoided, in persevering in the struggle, in not despairing if one does not succeed; but not in a slackness which would be laziness rather than virtue.

This question naturally leads to another: because Jesus said, "Blessed are the afflicted," is there any merit in seeking afflictions by aggravating one's trials through voluntary suffering? I will answer this question very clearly: Yes, there is great merit when such sufferings and privations are for the good of neighbor, for it is charity through sacrifice; but there is no merit, when they are aimed only at oneself, for it is selfishness through fanaticism.

Here there is a major distinction to be made: as for you personally, you should be contented with the trials that God sends you way, and not increase their burden, which sometimes is already so heavy; accept them without grumbling and with faith, that is all God asks of you. Do not weaken your body by inflicting unnecessary privations and aimless punishments on yourself, for you need all your strength to accomplish your mission of working on Earth. To intentionally torture and martyrize your body is to contravene God's law, which gives you the means to support and strengthen it; to unnecessarily weaken your body, is a veritable suicide. Use but do not abuse; such is the law. The abuse of the best things carries punishment by its inevitable consequences.

This is different from the suffering that is imposed for the relief of one's neighbor. If you endure cold and hunger to warm and nourish the one who needs it, and if your body suffers from it, this is a sacrifice that is blessed by God. You who leave your comfortable abode to go into a dismal hut to bring consolation; you who soil your delicate hands while tending somebody else's wounds; you who deprive yourself of sleep to watch over the bedside of a patient who is only your sibling in God's family; and finally, you who use your health in the practice of good deeds, this is your cilice, a truly blessed hair shirt, for the joys of the world have not dried up your heart. You have not fallen dormant in the enervating pleasures of fortune, but instead you have turned into consoling angels for the dispossessed, your poor fellow beings.

But you who withdraw from the world to avoid its seductions and live in isolation, of what use are you on Earth? Where is your courage in face of trials, if you are fleeing the struggle and deserting the fight? If you want a hair shirt, apply it to your soul and not to your body; mortify your spirit and not your flesh; repudiate your pride; take humiliations without complaining; punish your self-esteem; stiffen yourself against the pain of insults and calumny which are more poignant than physical pain. This is the true hair shirt whose wounds will be taken into account on your behalf, because they will bear witness of your courage and your submission to the will of God.

A guardian angel (Paris, 1863).

27. *Should we put an end to the trials of our fellow beings, when we can; or should we, out of respect for God's designs, let them follow their course?*

We have often and repeatedly told you that you are on this planet of atonement to complete your trials, and that all that happens to you is a consequence of your previous existences, the interest of the debt that you have to pay. But in some people this thought provokes notions that should be halted because they could have disastrous consequences.

Some think that as long as one is on Earth to atone, trials must take place. There are even some who go as far as to believe that not only nothing should be done to mitigate them, but that, on the contrary, one must be intensify the trials in order to make them more profitable. This is a big mistake. Indeed, your trials must follow the course that God has traced to them, but do you know this course? Do you know how far they have to go, and whether your merciful Parent has not said to the suffering of such and such of your brethren, "Do not go any further?" Do you know if Its providence has not chosen you, not as an instrument of torture to aggravate the sufferings of the guilty, but as a balm of consolation that must heal the wounds that God's justice had opened? Do not say, when you see one of your brothers and sisters hit, "It is the justice of God, it must have its course," but instead say, "Let me see what means the merciful God has put in my power to soften the suffering of my fellow being. Let me see if my moral consolations, my material support and my counsels cannot help my fellow being to overcome this trial with more strength, patience, and resignation; and let me see if God has not placed in my hands the means of putting an end to this suffering; if it was not given to me as a trial as well, perhaps as an atonement, to stop the iniquity and replace it with peace.

Therefore, always help one another in your respective trials and never regard yourselves as instruments of torment. Such a thought would be repugnant to any person of heart, especially to every Spiritist; for a Spiritist, better than any other, ought to understand the infinite extent of God's goodness. Spiritists should think that their whole lives must be an act of love and devotion; that whatever they do to thwart the designs of the Lord, Its justice will follow its course. One may therefore, without fear, make every effort to soften the bitterness of an atonement, but God alone can stop or prolong it as It sees fit.

Would there not be great pride on the part of humans in believing themselves to have, so to speak, the right to twist the knife in the wound? To increase the dosage of poison in the heart of someone who is suffering, under the pretext that it is his or her atonement? Ah! always regard yourselves as instruments chosen to make such suffering stop. Summing up: all of you are on Earth for atonement, yet all of you, without exception, must employ all your efforts to mitigate your neighbor's atonement according to the law of love and charity.

Bernardin, protector spirit (Bordeaux, 1863).

IS IT PERMISSIBLE TO SHORTEN THE LIFE OF A PATIENT WHO IS SUFFERING WITHOUT HOPE FOR A CURE?

28. *Someone is in agony, in the grip of extreme suffering – we know that his/her condition is hopeless. Is it permissible to take away a few moments of distress by hastening his/her end?*

Who, then, would give you the right to prejudge God's designs? Cannot God lead someone to the edge of the pit and then remove him or her from there, to make them come back to their senses and bring them to other thoughts? Whatever the state of a moribund person, no one can say with certainty that his/her last hour has arrived. Has science never been mistaken in its forecasts?

I know very well that there are cases which one can judge with reason as hopeless; but even if there is no grounded hope of a definite return to life and health, are there not innumerable examples where, at the moment of letting out the last breath, the patient revives and recovers consciousness for a few moments? Well then, this hour of grace granted to such a person may be of the greatest importance; for you are totally ignorant of the reflections which his/her spirit has been able to make while in the convulsions of agony, and what torments may sudden repentance save him/her.

Materialists, who see only the body and take no account of the soul, cannot understand these things. But Spiritists, who know what happens beyond the grave, know the value of one's last thought. Therefore soften the last sufferings as much as you can, but take care not to shorten anybody's life, even by a minute, for this minute may save many tears in the future.

Saint Louis[25] (Paris, 1860).

29. *Are persons that are disgusted with life but do not want to take it away, guilty for seeking death on a battlefield, with the intent of making their death useful?*

Whether one kills oneself, or have someone else do it, the aim is always to shorten one's own life, and consequently there is intention of committing suicide, if not the fact itself. The thought that

---

25 [Trans. note] View footnote 18 above.

one's death will serve some purpose is illusory; it is only a pretext for coloring one's action and excusing it in one's own eyes. If such individuals had a serious desire to serve their country, they would seek to live while defending it, and not to die, because once dead one has no use for it. True devotion consists in not fearing death when it comes to being useful, in braving danger, in making in advance and without regret the sacrifice of one's own life if it is necessary. Yet a *premeditated intention* of seeking death by exposing oneself to danger, even to render service, nullifies the merit of the action.

Saint Louis(Paris, 1860).

30. *When someone exposes himself/herself to imminent danger so as to save a fellow being, knowing in advance that they themselves will perish doing it, can this be regarded as suicide?*

If there is no intention to seek death, there is no suicide, but devotion and abnegation, even if one were certain of perishing. But who can have this certainty? Who can be sure that Providence had not reserved an unexpected means of salvation in the most critical moment? Could Providence have not saved even one standing in the mouth of a cannon? Often Providence may want to push the test of resignation to its last limit, when an unexpected circumstance would divert the fatal blow.

Saint Louis (Paris, 1860).

PROFIT FROM SUFFERING FOR OTHERS

31. *Do those who accept their suffering with resignation by submitting themselves to God's will and in view of their future happiness work only for themselves, or can they make their suffering profitable to others?*

Such suffering can be profitable to others both materially and morally. Materially, if through work, privations and the sacrifices thus imposed, they contribute to the material wellbeing of their fellow beings; morally, by the example they give of their submission to the will of God. This example of the power of the Spiritist faith can lead poor unfortunates to resign themselves, in order to save them from despair and its fatal consequences for the future.

Saint Louis (Paris, 1860).

Chapter VI
Christ the Consoler

THE EASY YOKE

1. "'Come to me, all who labor and are heavy laden, and I will give you rest. Take my yoke upon you, and learn from me, for I am gentle and lowly in heart, and you will find rest for your souls. For my yoke is easy, and my burden is light' (MATTHEW 11:28–30 ESV)."

2. All suffering: misery, disappointment, physical pain, loss of loved ones, find consolation in faith in the future and in trust in the justice of God, that Christ came to teach humankind. On the other hand, those who expect nothing after this life, or who simply doubts it, are scourged by heavy afflictions with no hope to soften their bitterness. This is what made Jesus say: *Come to me, all who labor and are heavy laden, and I will give you rest.*

However, Jesus sets a precondition on his aid, and on the happiness that he promises to the afflicted. This condition is in the law which he teaches, namely, that his yoke is the observation of this law. Yet this yoke is easy, and this law is light, since they impose love and charity as a duty.

THE PROMISED CONSOLER

3. "'If you love me, you will keep my commandments. And I will ask the Father, and he will give you another Helper, to be with you forever, even the Spirit of truth, whom the world cannot receive, because it neither sees him nor knows him. You know him, for he dwells with you and will be in you.' — 'But the Helper,[26] the Holy Spirit, whom the Father will send in my name, he will teach you all

---

26 [Trans. note] The Helper is also translated as the Consoler or the Comforter. the term *Consoler* is favored by Spiritists.

things and bring to your remembrance all that I have said to you'
(JOHN 14:15–17,26 ESV)."

4. Jesus promises another Consoler: it is *the Spirit of Truth*, which
the world does not yet know, because it is not ripe to understand it,
that the Father will send to teach all things, and to remember what
Christ said. If, then, the Spirit of Truth is to come later to teach all
things, Christ did not say all things; if he comes to remember what
Christ said, it is because it would be forgotten or misunderstood.

Spiritism comes at the appointed time to fulfill the promise of
Christ: the Spirit of Truth presides over its establishment; he reminds humans of the observance of the law; he teaches all things
by making you understand what Christ has said in parables. Christ
said, "He who has ears to hear, let him hear"; Spiritism comes to
open eyes and ears, for it speaks without figures and allegories; it
lifts the veil left intentionally on certain mysteries; finally, it comes
to bring supreme consolation to the disinherited of the Earth and
to all those who suffer, by giving a just cause and a useful goal to
all human pains.

Christ said, "Blessed are the afflicted, for they shall be comforted";
but how can one be happy to suffer if one does not know why one
suffers? Spiritism shows its cause in former existences and in the destination of the Earth where humans atone for their past wrongdoings;
he shows the purpose in those sorrows are like salutary crises that
bring about healing, and that they are the purification that ensures
happiness in future lives. Human beings can thus understand that
they have deserved to suffer, and they find their suffering fair. They
know that this suffering helps their advancement, and they accept
it without grumbling, like a working person accepts the work that
will earn him or her their salary. Spiritism gives them an unshakable
faith in the future, and excruciating doubt no longer has any hold
on their souls. By showing things from on high, the importance of
earthly vicissitudes is lost in the vast splendid horizons that they
embrace; and the prospect of the happiness that awaits them, gives
them patience, resignation and courage to endure until the end of
the road.

Thus Spiritism fulfills what Jesus said of the promised Consoler:
the knowledge of things that makes humans know where they come

from, where they are going, and why they are on Earth; a reminder of the true principles of God's law, and consolation by faith and hope.

INSTRUCTIONS FROM THE SPIRITS

ADVENT OF THE SPIRIT OF TRUTH

5.   As I once did among the lost children of Israel, I bring the truth and dispel the darkness. Listen to me. Spiritism, like my words formerly did, must remind unbelievers that above them reigns the immutable truth: the good God, the great God who makes the plants sprout and raises the waves. I revealed the divine doctrine; I, like a harvester, bounded in sheaves the good scattered in humanity, and said: Come to me, all who suffer!

Yet ungrateful humans have turned away from the straight and broad way that leads to the kingdom of my Parent, and have gone astray in the bitter paths of ungodliness. My Parent does not want to annihilate the human race; It wants you to help one another, dead and alive – that is to say, dead according to the flesh, because death does not exist. God wants you to help one another, and that, no longer through the voice of the prophets and apostles, but from the voice of those who no longer live on Earth: Pray and believe! For death is resurrection, and life is the chosen trial during which your cultivated virtues must grow and flourish like the cedar.

You frail humans who understand the darkness of your minds, do not take away the torch that divine clemency places in your hands to light your way and bring you, lost children, into the bosom of your divine Parent.

I am deeply touched with compassion for your miseries, for your immense weakness, and will never fail to extend a helping hand to the unfortunate misguided people who, despite seeing the sky, fall into the abyss of error. Believe, love, meditate on all things that are revealed to you; do not mix chaff with wheat, utopias with truths.

Spiritists! Love one another – that is the first lesson; educate yourselves – this is the second. All truths are found in Christianity; the errors that have taken root in it are all of human origin. And behold, beyond the grave, that you believed was nothingness, voices cry out to you: Brothers and sisters! Nothing perishes; Jesus Christ is the conqueror of evil, so you be the conquerors of ungodliness.

The Spirit of Truth (Paris, 1860).

6. I have come to teach and comfort the poor wretched ones; I have come to tell them that they are raising their resignation to the level of their trials. Let them cry, for pain was sacred in the Garden of Olives; but also let them have hope, for consoling angels will wipe away their tears.

Workers, trace your path; repeat on the next day the hard toil of the day before. The labor of your hands provides earthly bread for your bodies, but your souls should not be forgotten; and I, the divine gardener, cultivate them in the silence of your thoughts. When the hour of rest arrives, when the weft comes off of your hands, and your eyes are closed to the light, you will feel the sprout germinating in you my precious seed. Nothing is lost in the kingdom of our divine Parent, and your sweat, your miseries form the treasure that should make you rich in the higher spheres, where light replaces darkness, and where the most disinherited of all of you will perhaps be the most resplendent.

Truly I say to you, those who bear their burdens and assist their brothers and sisters are my beloved ones; be instructed in the precious doctrine which dispels the error of rebellion and teaches you the sublime purpose of human trials. Like the wind sweeps the dust, the breath of the spirits dissipates your jealousies against the rich of the Earth who are often very miserable, because their trials are more dangerous than yours. I am with you, and my apostle teaches you. Drink from the living source of love, and prepare yourself, a captive of life, to soar upwards one day, free and happy, into the bosom of the One which created you weak to make you perfectible, and which wants you yourselves to shape your soft clay, to be the artisans of your immortality.

The Spirit of Truth (Paris, 1861).

7. I am the great physician of souls, and I have come to bring you the remedy that must heal them. The weak, the distressed, and the infirm are my favorite children; I have come to save them. Come to me, all of you who are suffering and heavy laden, and you will be relieved and comforted. Do not look elsewhere for strength and consolation, for the world is powerless to give them. Through Spiritism, God makes a supreme call to your hearts; listen to it. Let ungodliness, falsehood, error and unbelief be extirpated from your sore souls; they are monsters that drink from your purest blood, and that almost always cause you deadly wounds. In future, humble and submissive to the Creator, you will practice Its divine law. Love and pray; be docile to the spirits of the Lord; invoke It from the bottom of your heart. Then It will send you Its beloved Son to instruct you and tell you these good words: Here I am; I come to you, because you called me.

The Spirit of Truth (Bordeaux, 1861).

8. God comforts the meek and give strength to the afflicted who ask for it. God's power covers the Earth, and everywhere beside each tear there is a balm that consoles. Devotion and self-denial are a continual prayer, and enclose a profound teaching; human wisdom lies in these two words. May all distressed spirits understand this truth, instead of crying out against their pains, the moral sufferings that are allotted to you here below. Take as a motto these two words, *devotion* and *self-denial*, and you will be strong because they summarize all the duties that charity and humility impose on you. The feeling of accomplished duty will give you peace of mind and resignation. The heart beats better, the soul calms down and the body no longer fails, because the body suffers all the more according to how deeply the spirit is struck.

The Spirit of Truth (Le Havre, 1863).

Chapter VII
Blessed are the poor in spirit

WHAT IS MEANT BY THE POOR IN SPIRIT?

1. "'Blessed are the poor in spirit, for theirs is the kingdom of heaven' (MATTHEW 5:3 ESV)."

2. Unbelief has been amused by this maxim, *Blessed are the poor in spirit*, as by many other passages, without understanding it. By the poor in spirit, Jesus does not mean humans without intelligence, but the meek: he says that the kingdom of heaven is for them, and not for the proud.

Individuals of science and of intellect according to the world, generally have such a high opinion of themselves and of their superiority, that they regard divine things as unworthy of their attention. They focus their gaze on their person and seem unable to rise it to God. This tendency to believe oneself to be above all things too often leads them to deny that which is above them and could belittle them, to negate even Divinity; or else, if they consent to admit It, they dispute one of its most beautiful attributes: Its providential action upon the things of this world, since they are convinced that they alone are enough to govern it well. Taking their intelligence for the measure of universal intelligence, and judging themselves capable of understanding everything, they cannot believe in the possibility of anything they do not understand. When they have passed judgment this is for them without appeal.

If they refuse to admit the invisible world and an extra-human power, it is not because that it is beyond their reach, but rather their pride revolts at the idea of a thing above which they cannot place themselves, which make them descend from their pedestal.

That is why they only have smiles of disdain for anything that is not visible and tangible; they attribute to themselves too much wit and knowledge to believe in things which, in their opinion, are good for *simple* people, thus regarding those who take them seriously as *poor in spirit*.

However, whatever they say about it, they will have to eventually enter, like the others, into this invisible world which they deride. It is there that their eyes will be opened and they will recognize their error. But God, which is righteous, cannot receive in the same way the one who has misjudged Its power and the one who has humbly submitted to Its laws, nor grant them an equal share.

In saying that the kingdom of heaven belongs to the simple, Jesus understands that no one is admitted without *the simplicity of the heart and the humility of the spirit*; that the ignorant person who possesses these qualities will be preferred to the scientist who believes more in himself/herself than in God. In all circumstances humility is placed in the rank of the virtues which draw one nearer to God, and pride as belonging the vices which depart from it; and that for a very natural reason humility is an act of submission to God, while pride is a revolt against It. Therefore it is better for the future happiness of humans to be *poor in spirit*, in the sense that the world understands it, but rich in moral qualities.

THOSE WHO EXALT THEMSELVES
WILL BE HUMBLED

3. "At that time the disciples came to Jesus, saying, 'Who is the greatest in the kingdom of heaven?' And calling to him a child, he put him in the midst of them and said, 'Truly, I say to you, unless you turn and become like children, you will never enter the kingdom of heaven. *Whoever humbles himself like this child is the greatest in the kingdom of heaven.* 'Whoever receives one such child in my name receives me, but whoever causes one of these little ones who believe in me to sin, it would be better for him to have a great millstone fastened around his neck and to be drowned in the depth of the sea (MATTHEW 18:1–5 ESV)."

4. "Then the mother of the sons of Zebedee came up to him with her sons, and kneeling before him she asked him for something. And he said to her, 'What do you want?' She said to him, 'Say that these two sons of mine are to sit, one at your right hand and one at your left, in your kingdom.' Jesus answered, 'You do not know what you are asking. Are you able to drink the cup that I am to drink?' They said to him, 'We are able.' He said to them, 'You will drink my cup, but to sit at my right hand and at my left is not mine to grant, but it is for those for whom it has been prepared by my Father.' And when the ten heard it, they were indignant at the two brothers. But Jesus called them to him and said, 'You know that the rulers of the Gentiles lord it over them, and their great ones exercise authority over them. It shall not be so among you. *But whoever would be great among you must be your servant, and whoever would be first among you must be your slave,* even as the Son of Man came not to be served but to serve, and to give his life as a ransom for many' (MATTHEW 20:20–28 ESV)."

5. "One Sabbath, when he went to dine at the house of a ruler of the Pharisees, they were watching him carefully. — Now he told a parable to those who were invited, when he noticed how they chose the places of honor, saying to them, 'When you are invited by someone to a wedding feast, do not sit down in a place of honor, lest someone more distinguished than you be invited by him, and he who invited you both will come and say to you, 'Give your place to this person,' and then you will begin with shame to take the lowest place. But when you are invited, go and sit in the lowest place, so that when your host comes he may say to you, 'Friend, move up higher.' Then you will be honored in the presence of all who sit at table with you. For everyone who exalts himself will be humbled, and he who humbles himself will be exalted (LUKE 14:1,7–11 ESV)."

6. Such maxims are consequence of the principle of humility which Jesus never ceases to lay down as an essential condition of the happiness promised to the elect of the Lord, and which he formulated with these words: "Blessed are the poor in spirit, for theirs is the kingdom of heaven." He takes a child as a type of the simplicity of the heart and says: "*Whoever humbles himself like this child* is the greatest in the kingdom of heaven"; that is to say, whoever has no claim to superiority or infallibility.

The same fundamental idea is found in this other maxim, *But whoever would be great among you must be your servant*, and also in this one, *For everyone who exalts himself will be humbled, and he who humbles himself will be exalted.*

Spiritism has come to corroborate theory by providing examples, showing us that those who are great in the spiritual world are those who were small on Earth; and that those who were the greatest and most powerful down here are very small indeed there. It is because at the time of death the former carry with them what alone can bring true greatness in heaven and is not lost, namely, one's virtues; whereas others have to leave behind what made their greatness on Earth, and cannot be carried away with them: fortune, titles, glory, noble birth. Having nothing else, they arrive in the other world deprived of everything, like castaways who have lost all their belongings, even their clothes, retaining only their pride which makes their new position even more humiliating, for they can see above them, resplendent with glory, those whom they had trampled underfoot on Earth.

Spiritism shows us another application of this principle in successive incarnations of those who have been at the highest position in one existence but lowered to the last rank in the following existence, if they were dominated by pride and ambition. So do not seek to be at the first place on Earth, nor to place yourself above the others, if you do not want to be forced to descend. Look, on the contrary, for the most humble and modest position, for God will be able to give you a higher one in heaven should you deserve it.

MYSTERIES HIDDEN FROM THE WISE
AND THE PRUDENT

7. "At that time Jesus declared, 'I thank you, Father, Lord of heaven and earth, that you have hidden these things from the wise and understanding and revealed them to little children' (MATTHEW 11:25 ESV)."

8. It may seem peculiar that Jesus gives thanks to God for having revealed these things to *the simple and the little ones*, who are the poor in spirit, and for having hidden them *from the wise and the prudent*, who would be apparently more apt to understand them. This is because we must understand by the first, *the meek* who humble themselves before God and do not believe themselves superior to everyone; and by the second, *the proud*, vain of their worldly science, who believe themselves to be prudent because they deny God, treating It as equals when they do not disown It; for, during antiquity, *sage* was synonymous with *scientist*. This is why God leaves to them the search for the secrets of the Earth, while revealing those of heaven to the simple and the meek who bow before the Creator.

9. It is the same today with the great truths revealed by Spiritism. Some unbelievers are astonished that the spirits do so little to convince them – this happens because the spirits take care of those who seek the light in good faith and with humility, in preference to those who believe they have all the light, and seem to think that God should be too happy to bring them back to Itself, by their proving that It exists.

God's power shines both in the smallest and in the largest things; it does not hide the light under a bushel, since it spreads it abundantly on all sides; therefore those who do not see it are blind. *God does not want to open their eyes forcibly, since they like to keep them closed.* Their turn will come, but not before they feel the anguish of darkness and *recognize God, not chance, in the hand that strikes their pride.* God uses the means that suit It according to each individual to overcome unbelief. It is not up to the incredulous to prescribe to God what It must do, and to say to It: If you want to convince me, you have to go about it in this or that way, at such and such time rather than at that or that other time, according to my convenience.

Therefore may unbelievers not be surprised if God, and the spirits that are the agents of Its will, do not submit to their demands. Let them wonder what they would think if the last of their servants wanted to impose themselves on them. God imposes Its conditions and does not submit to anyone; It listens kindly to those who speak to It with humility, and not to those who believe themselves to be superior to It.

10. Could God – it might be asked – not strike them personally by dazzling signs in the presence of which even the most hardened unbeliever would bow? No doubt God could do it, but then what would their merit be, and besides that what purpose would it serve? Do we not see it every day, certain people refusing the evidence and even saying, "If I saw it, I would not believe it, because I *know* that it is impossible"? If they refuse to admit the truth, it is because their spirit is not yet ripe to understand it, nor their heart to feel it. *Pride is the veil that obscures their sight*; what is the point of presenting light to a blind person? We must therefore first cure the cause of the evil; this is why, like a skillful doctor, God chastises pride first. Therefore God does not forsake Its lost children, for It knows that sooner or later their eyes will open. Yet God wants them to do it of their own free will; so when overcome by the torments of unbelief, they will throw themselves into Its arms and, like the prodigal son, ask for mercy!

INSTRUCTIONS FROM THE SPIRITS

PRIDE AND HUMILITY

11. May the Lord's peace be with you, dear friends! I come to encourage you to follow the right path.

To the poor spirits who once inhabited the Earth, God has given a mission to come and enlighten you. Blessed be God for the grace granted to us of being able to help you with your advancement. May the Holy Spirit enlighten me and help me make my words understandable, and grant me the grace to making them available to all! All of you incarnate beings, who are in pain and seek the light, may God's will help me make it shine in your eyes!

Humility is a virtue very much forgotten among you; the great examples which have been given to you are scarcely followed, and yet, without humility, can you be charitable towards your neighbor? Ah, definitely not, because this feeling levels all human beings; it tells them that they are brothers and sisters, that they must help each other, and it leads them toward good. Without humility, you adorn yourselves with virtues that you do not possess, as if you were wearing a coat to hide the deformities of your body. Remember the One who saved us; remember his humility which made him so great, and place him above all the prophets.

Pride is a terrible adversary of humility. If Christ promised the kingdom of heaven to the poorest, it is because the great of the Earth imagine that titles and riches are rewards given on account of their merit, and that their personal essence is purer than that of the poor. They believe that they are entitled to such distinctions. That is why, when God takes them away from them, they accuse It of injustice. Ah, what derision and blindness! Does God make a distinction among you based on your bodies? Is not the poor person's physical envelope the same as that of the rich person? Did the Creator make two species of humans? All that God does is great and wise; never attribute it to ideas that your proud brains gave birth to.

O you that are rich! While you sleep under your golden pavilion sheltered from the cold, do you ignore that thousands of your brothers and sisters who are worth the same as you are lying on the straw? Are not the unfortunate ones who suffer from hunger your equal? When hearing such words, I know your pride revolts; you may even feel like giving alms to them, but to fraternally shake their hands, never! "What?!" – You say – "Would I, born of noble blood, great on Earth, be the equal of this wretch who wears rags! Vain utopia of so-called philosophers! If we were equal, why would God have placed this person so low and me so high?" Indeed, it is true that your clothes hardly resemble one another; but if you were both stripped of them, what difference would there be between you? "The nobility of blood," you might say. However, chemistry has found no difference between the blood of a grand seigneur and that of a plebeian; between that of a master and that of a slave. Who can guarantee that once you too were not destitute and unhappy like this other person? Have you not begged for alms? Will you not beg for alms one day from the very one that you despise today? Are riches eternal? Do they not end with this body, which is the perishable envelope of your spirit? Ah! a return of humility on yourself. Finally direct your gaze on the reality of the things of this world, on what makes greatness and abasement in the other; remember that death will not spare you more than anyone else; that your titles and honors will not protect you from it; that it can hit you tomorrow, today, this very hour – and if you are buried full of pride, oh, then I pity you, because you will be worthy of pity!

And you, proud ones! What were you before you became powerful or members of the aristocracy? Perhaps you were lower than the last of your servants. So bow down your haughty foreheads which God can lower when you lift them higher. All humans are equal in the divine scale; virtues alone distinguish them in the eyes of God. All spirits are of the same essence, and all bodies are kneaded from the same dough. Your titles and names change nothing; they will remain in the grave, and it is not them that give the promised happiness to the elect, only charity and humility are titles of nobility.

Poor humans! You are parents, your children suffer; they are cold, they feel hunger; and you are going, bowed under the weight of your cross, to humble yourselves to get a piece of bread for them. Ah! I bow to you; how noble and holy you are in my eyes! Do hope and pray; happiness is not in this world. To the poor, the oppressed and those trusting in It, God gives the kingdom of heaven.

And you, young woman, poor child doomed to work, to deprivation, why these sad thoughts? Why cry? Devout and serene, may your gaze rise to God: even to little birds God gives laughter; so trust It, and It will not forsake you. The noise of the holidays, the pleasures of the world make your heart beat faster; you would also like to decorate your head with flowers and mingle with the happy ones of the Earth. You ask yourself, could you not, like these women you watch passing by, laughing wildly, be rich too. Oh, stop with these ideas, child! If you knew how many tears and nameless pains are hidden under these embroidered clothes, how many sobs are muffled under the noise of this joyful band, you would prefer your humble retreat and your poverty. Stay pure in the eyes of God, if you do not want your guardian angel to come up to God, with face hidden under its white wings, leaving you with remorse, without guide, without support in this world where you would be lost while waiting for your punishment in the other.

And all of you who suffer from the injustices of humans, be indulgent for the faults of your brothers and sisters, keeping in mind that you yourself are not without reproach. This is charity, but also humility. If you suffer from slander, bow your forehead under this ordeal. What do you care about the slanders of the world? If your conduct is pure, cannot God reward you for it? To courageously bear human humiliations is to be humble and to recognize that God alone is great and powerful.

Dear God, will it be necessary that Christ returns a second time to Earth in order to teach humans the laws that they have forgotten? Will he still have to drive out the temple vendors who sully God's house which should be exclusively a place of prayer? Who knows? O humans! if God granted you this grace, perhaps you would deny it as in the past; you would call him blasphemer, because he would lower the pride of the modern Pharisees; perhaps you would make him take the path of Golgotha all over again.

When Moses was on Mount Sinai to receive God's commandments, the people of Israel, left to their own devices, forsook the true God; men and women donated their gold and jewelry to make an idol they adored. Civilized humans, you do like them; Christ has left you his doctrine; he gave you the example of all virtues, but you have abandoned example and precepts. With each of you bringing his/her passions, you made yourself a God at your will: according to some, terrifying and bloodthirsty; to others, a God heedless of the interests of the world. The God you have made yourselves is still the golden calf that everyone appropriates for their tastes and ideas.

Come back to your senses, brothers and sisters, my friends. Let the voice of the spirits touch your hearts; be generous and charitable without ostentation; that is to say, do good humbly; let each and every one gradually demolish the altars which you have raised to pride; in a word, be true Christians, and you will have the reign of truth. No longer doubt the goodness of God, when It gives you so much proof. We have come to prepare the way for the fulfillment of the prophecies, when the Lord will give you a more dazzling manifestation of his mercy, and that the heavenly envoy will find in you only one large family. May your sweet and humble hearts be worthy of listening to the divine word that he will come to bring to you; may the chosen one finds on his path only palms deposited because of your return to good, to charity, and to fraternity – and thus your world will become paradise on Earth. But if you remain insensitive to the voice of the spirits sent to purify and renew your civilized society, so rich in science, and yet so poor in good feelings, alas, all that will be left for you to do is to cry and moan over your fate. But no, this will not be so; return to God the Parent, and thus, all of us, who will have been instrumental in the fulfillment of Its will, shall sing hymns of thanksgiving, to thank the Lord for his inexhaustible goodness, and to glorify him for ever and ever. So be it.

Lacordaire (Constantine, Algeria, 1863).

12. Humans, why do you complain about calamities that you yourselves have brought upon your heads? You have misunderstood the holy and divine morality of Christ, so do not be surprised that the cup of iniquity has overflowed over the brim on all sides.

Malaise has become widespread; who to blame, if not you who constantly seek to crush one another? You cannot be happy without mutual benevolence, but how can benevolence coexist with pride? Pride is the source of all your ills; endeavor therefore to destroy it, if you do not want to see perpetuate disastrous consequences. There is only one means available for you to achieve this, but this means is infallible: it is to take as an invariable rule of your conduct the law of Christ, that you have either rejected or distorted in its interpretation.

Why do you have so much esteem for what shines and charms your eyes, rather than for what touches the heart? Why is vice in opulence the object of your adulations, while you only have a look of disdain for the true merit that lies in obscurity? If a rich degenerate, lost both in body and soul, appears somewhere, all doors are open to him/her, all respects are paid to him/her, whereas one barely deigns to grant a salute to someone of good repute who earns a living with honesty. When the consideration given to individuals is measured by the weight of gold, whether because they own it or because the surname they bear, what interest can they have in correcting their faults?

It would be quite different if the vice of gold was castigated by public opinion the same as the vice in rags is; but pride is indulgent toward everything that flatters it. This is an era of greed and money, you may say. No doubt, but then why did you let material needs intrude on common sense and reason? Why does everyone want to rise above their fellow human beings? Today's society is suffering the consequences of such behavior.

Remember, such a state of affairs is always a sign of moral decay. When pride reaches the final stages, this indicates an impending fall, because God always strikes the haughty. If God sometimes lets them go up, it is to give them time to reflect and to improve themselves under the blows that, from time to time, It brings over their pride to warn them. But if instead of lowering themselves, they revolt, when the measure is full, it overturns them completely, and their fall is all the more terrible, the higher they were.

Poor humankind, whose selfishness has corrupted all routes, take courage, however, for in Its infinite mercy, God sends you a powerful remedy for your ills, an unexpected help in your distress. Open your eyes to the light: here are the souls of those who are no longer living on Earth, coming to remind you of your true duties. They will tell you, with the authority of experience, how paltry are the vanities and the grandeur of your fleeting existence in comparison to eternity. They will tell you that the greatest among you are those who have been the most humble of the little ones here below; that the ones who have loved their brothers and sisters the most are also the ones who will be the most loved in heaven; whereas the mighty of the Earth, if they have abused their authority, will be reduced to obeying their servants. Finally they will show you that charity and humility, these two siblings holding hands, are one's most effective means of obtaining grace before the Lord.

Adolphe, bishop of Algiers (Marmande, France, 1862).

MISSION OF INTELLIGENT HUMAN BEINGS ON EARTH

13. Be not proud of what you know, because this knowledge has very limited scope in the world you live in. But even supposing that you are one of the clever luminaries of this globe, you have no right to take pride in it. If God, in Its designs, has granted you to be born in an environment where you could develop your intelligence, it is because It wants you to use it for the good of everyone, for this is a mission which it has given to you, by putting in your hands the instrument with which to help backward intelligences to develop and be brought to God. Does not the nature of the instrument indicate the use to be made of it? Does not the spade that the gardener places in the hands of a workman show the latter that he must dig? And what would you say if this worker, instead of working, raised his spade to strike his master? You would say that it is nasty, and that the worker deserves to be driven out. Well, is it not the same with those who use their intelligence to destroy the idea of God and Providence among their fellow human beings? Are they not raising against their master the spade which was given to them so they could clear the soil? Are they entitled to the promised salary, or do they not deserve, on the contrary, to be driven out of the garden? They will certainly be, and then lead miserable lives full of humiliations until they have bowed down before the One to which they owe everything.

Human intelligence is rich in merits for the future, provided it is put to good use. If all individuals who are endowed with it used it according to the designs of God, the task of the spirits to advance humanity would be easier. Unfortunately many turn it into an instrument of pride and perdition for themselves. Humans abuse their intelligence like all their other faculties, and yet there is no shortage of lessons to warn them that a powerful hand can take away what was given to them.

Ferdinand, protector spirit (Bordeaux, 1862).

Chapter VIII
Blessed are the pure in heart

LET THE CHILDREN COME TO ME · SIN THROUGH THOUGHT − ADULTERY · TRUE
PURITY − UNWASHED HANDS · TEMPTATIONS TO SIN − IF YOUR HAND CAUSES YOU
TO SIN, CUT IT OFF · *INSTRUCTIONS FROM THE SPIRITS:* LET THE CHILDREN COME
TO ME · BLESSED ARE THOSE WHO HAVE THEIR EYES CLOSED

LET THE CHILDREN COME TO ME

1. "'Blessed are the pure in heart, for they shall see God' (MATTHEW 5:8 ESV)."

2. "And they were bringing children to him that he might touch them, and the disciples punished them. But when Jesus saw it, he was indignant and said to them, '*Let the children come to me;* do not hinder them, for to such belongs the kingdom of God. Truly, I say to you, whoever does not receive the kingdom of God like a child shall not enter it.' And he took them in his arms and blessed them, laying his hands on them (MARK 10:13–16 ESV)."

3. Purity of heart is inseparable from simplicity and humility; it excludes all thought of selfishness and pride. This is why Jesus takes childhood for the emblem of this purity, as he takes it for that of humility.

This comparison might not seem right, if we consider that the spirit of a child may be very old, and that it brings and revives imperfections in bodily life of which it has not been stripped in its previous lives – only a perfected spirit could give us the type of true purity. However it is exact from the point of view of current life; for the little child, not yet able to manifest any perverse tendency, offers us the image of innocence and candor; therefore Jesus does not say absolutely that the kingdom of God is *for them*, but *for those who are like them.*

4. Since the spirit of the child has already lived before, why does it not show itself, from birth, for what it is? Everything is wise in God's works. A child needs delicate care which only maternal tenderness can render, and such tenderness is increased by the child's weakness and ingenuousness. For a mother, her child is always an angel, and it has to be that way in order to win her solicitude. She would not have the same care toward her child, if she found, instead of naive grace and childish features, a developed character with the ideas of an adult – and even less if she was aware of her child's past.

Moreover, it was necessary that the activity of the intelligent principle should be proportional to the weakness of the child's body which could not have resisted too much activity from the spirit, as we see in too precocious individuals. That is why, with the approach of a new incarnation, the spirit enters a state of turmoil, gradually losing consciousness of itself. It is, for a certain time, in a sort of slumber during which all its acuity remains in a latent state. Such transient state is necessary to give the spirit a new starting point, and to make it forget, in its new earthly existence, the things that could have hindered it. The past, however, reacts to it; it is reborn into life larger and stronger both morally and intellectually, supported and seconded by the intuition which it retains from acquired experience.

From the birth onwards, such ideas recover their full vigor the person's limbs and organs are developed; whence it may be said that, during the first years, the spirit is truly a child, because the ideas which form the basis of its character are still dormant. During the time when its instincts are dormant, it is more flexible and for that very reason more accessible to impressions which can modify its nature and make it advance, thus making less difficult the task imposed on parents.

The spirit therefore puts on the robe of innocence for a while, and Jesus is right when, despite the anteriority of the soul, he takes the child as an emblem of purity and simplicity.

Sin through thought
Adultery

5. "'You have heard that it was said, 'You shall not commit adultery.' But I say to you that everyone who looks at a woman with lustful intent has already committed adultery with her in his heart' (MATTHEW 5:27–28 ESV)."

6. The word adultery should not be taken here in the exclusive sense of its proper meaning, but in a more general sense; Jesus often used it by extension to designate evil, sin, and any other bad thought, as, for example, in this passage:

"'For whoever is ashamed of me and of my words in this adulterous and sinful generation, of him will the Son of Man also be ashamed when he comes in the glory of his Father with the holy angels' (MARK 8:38 ESV)."

True purity is not only in acts; it is also in thought, for whoever has a pure heart does not even think of evil; that is what Jesus meant. He condemns sin, even in thought, because it is a sign of impurity.

7. This principle naturally leads to the following question: *Are we suffering consequences for bad thinking that has not actually materialized?*

There is an important distinction to make here. As the soul, taken down the wrong path, advances in spiritual life, it enlightens itself and gradually gets rid of its imperfections, according to the degree of good will it can bring to it by virtue of the soul's free will. Any bad thought is therefore the result of imperfections of the soul; but depending on the desire which the latter has conceived of purifying itself, this very same bad thought becomes an opportunity for the soul to advance itself, because the soul repels it with energy; it denotes a spot that it is trying to erase. The soul will not yield if the opportunity arises to satisfy a bad desire; and after it has resisted, it will feel stronger and happy in having prevailed over it.

Conversely, a soul which has not made good resolutions seeks an opportunity of carrying out a bad deed, and if it does not perform the wrongdoing, this is not the effect of the soul's will, but the result of a missed chance. The soul is therefore as guilty as if it had perpetrated it.

In short, in a person who does not even conceive of the thought of evil, his/her advancement has been accomplished; whereas, in the one to whom this thought comes, but who rejects it, advancement is still in process of being accomplished. Finally, those who still have this evil thought and takes pleasure in it, still possess such evil in all its force. In one the work is already done, in the other it remains to be done. God, which is just, takes all of these nuances into account in the accountability held by humans for their actions and thoughts.

True purity
Unwashed hands

8.   "Then Pharisees and scribes came to Jesus from Jerusalem and said, 'Why do your disciples break the tradition of the elders? For they do not wash their hands when they eat.'

He answered them, 'And why do you break the commandment of God for the sake of your tradition? For God commanded, 'Honor your father and your mother,' and, 'Whoever reviles father or mother must surely die.' But you say, 'If anyone tells his father or his mother, 'What you would have gained from me is given to God,' he need not honor his father.' So for the sake of your tradition you have made void the word of God.'

'You hypocrites! Well did Isaiah prophesy of you, when he said 'This people honors me with their lips, but their heart is far from me; in vain do they worship me, teaching as doctrines the commandments of men.'

And he called the people to him and said to them, 'Hear and understand: it is not what goes into the mouth that defiles a person, but what comes out of the mouth; this defiles a person.' Then the disciples came and said to him, 'Do you know that the Pharisees were offended when they heard this saying?' He answered, 'Every plant that my heavenly Father has not planted will be rooted up. Let them alone; they are blind guides. And if the blind lead the blind, both will fall into a pit.' But Peter said to him, 'Explain the parable to us.' And he said, 'Are you also still without understanding? Do you not see that whatever goes into the mouth passes into the stomach and is expelled? But what comes out of the mouth proceeds from the heart, and this defiles a person.'

For out of the heart come evil thoughts, murder, adultery, sexual immorality, theft, false witness, slander. These are what defile a

person. But to eat with unwashed hands does not defile anyone'
(Matthew 15:1–20 esv)."[27]

9. "While Jesus was speaking, a Pharisee asked him to dine
with him, so he went in and reclined at table. The Pharisee was
astonished to see that he did not first wash before dinner. And the
Lord said to him, 'Now you Pharisees cleanse the outside of the cup
and of the dish, but inside you are full of greed and wickedness.
You fools! Did not he who made the outside make the inside also?'
(Luke 11:37–40 esv)."

10. The Jews had neglected the true commandments of God,
to become attached to the practice of regulations established by
humans, whose rigid observers turned into matters of conscience.
The very simple background of God's commandments had eventually disappeared under the complication of the form. Since it was
easier to observe outward acts than to transform oneself morally, *by
washing their hands instead of cleansing their hearts*, humans deceived
themselves, and believed to be in good terms with God, as they
conformed to these practices, while remaining unchanged, for they
were taught that God asked nothing else from them. This is why
the prophet said: *In vain do they worship me, teaching as doctrines
the commandments of men.*

So it was with the moral tenets of Christ, which ended up being
relegated to a secondary rank, meaning that many Christians, like
the ancient Jews, believe their salvation is more assured by outward
practices than by those of a moral nature. It is to these additions
made by humans to God's law that Jesus alludes when he says: *Every
plant that my heavenly Father has not planted will be rooted up.*

The purpose of religion is to lead humans to God; or rather,
humans reach God only when they become perfect. Therefore any
religion that fails to make humans better does not reach the goal.
A religion on which we believe we can rely to do evil is either false
or distorted in principle. This is the result of all those in which
form prevails over substance. The belief in the effectiveness of
outward signs is null, if it does not prevent people from committing murders, from becoming adulterers and plunderers, or from

---

27 [Trans. note] Some verses of this biblical passage were cited in a different
order in the French original, now restored to their official sequence according both
to the esv and Sacy's French bible.

slandering and harming their fellow human beings. It can create superstitious, hypocritical or fanatical persons, but it does not make good individuals.

Therefore it is not enough for one to have the outward appearance of purity; above all it must exist inside one's heart.

TEMPTATIONS TO SIN[28]
IF YOUR HAND CAUSES YOU TO SIN, CUT IT OFF

11. "Woe unto the world because of offenses! for it must needs be that offenses come; but woe to that man by whom the offence cometh! Wherefore if thy hand or thy foot offend thee, cut them off, and cast them from thee: it is better for thee to enter into life halt or maimed, rather than having two hands or two feet to be cast into everlasting fire. — But whoso shall offend one of these little ones which believe in me, it were better for him that a millstone were hanged about his neck, and that he were drowned in the depth of the sea. — And if thine eye offend thee, pluck it out, and cast it from thee: it is better for thee to enter into life with one eye, rather than having two eyes to be cast into hell fire. Take heed that ye despise not one of these little ones; for I say unto you, That in heaven their angels do always behold the face of my Father which is in heaven. — And if thy right eye offend thee, pluck it out, and cast it from thee: for it is profitable for thee that one of thy members should perish, and not that thy whole body should be cast into hell. And if thy right hand offend thee, cut it off, and cast it from thee: for it is profitable for thee that one of thy members should perish, and not that thy whole body should be cast into hell. (MATTHEW 18:6–10 AKJV/PCE; MATTHEW 5:27–30 AKJV/PCE; also *cf.* the ESV)."[29]

12. In its common acceptation, *scandal* denotes any action which shocks morals or decorum in an overt manner. The scandal is not in the action itself, but in the impact it can have. The word scandal always implies the idea of some striking effect. Many people are content to avoid *scandal*, because their pride would suffer and

---

28 [Trans. note] *Scandal* (*scandale* in French) is the word used by A. KARDEC quoting the French Bible in the original, which is replaced by *temptation to sin* or by *offense* throughout the *English Standard Version* and the *Authorised King James Version*, as used herein.

29 [Trans. note] See footnote 27 above.

their standing in society would be diminished. As long as their turpitudes are ignored, that is enough for them, and their conscience is at rest. They are, according to the words of Jesus, "Like whitewashed tombs, which outwardly appear beautiful, but within are full of dead people's bones and all uncleanness. (MATTHEW 23:27 ESV)."

In the Gospel, the sense of the word scandal, so frequently used, is much broader, which is why we do not understand its meaning in some cases. It is no longer just what hurts the conscience of others, but rather all that is the result human vices and imperfections, any bad reaction from individual to individual with or without repercussions. The scandal, in this case, is *the effective result of a moral evil.*

13. *It it is necessary that scandals (temptations to sin, offenses) come,* said Jesus, because humans, being imperfect on Earth, are inclined to do evil, and bad trees give bad fruit. Therefore one should understand by these words that evil is a consequence of human imperfections, and not that humans have an obligation to do it.

14. *Scandals have to happen* because humans, who are in atonement on Earth, punish themselves by being brought into contact with their vices, of which they are the first victims, and whose disadvantages they eventually understand. When they get tired of suffering from evil, they will seek the remedy in good. Therefore their reaction to these vices serves both as punishment for some and trial for others. This is how God brings out good from evil, and humans themselves are able to benefit even from bad and objectionable things.

15. If this is so – some will say – then evil is necessary and will always exist; for should it disappear, God would be deprived of a powerful means of punishing the guilty; so there is no point in trying to improve humans. But if there were no more culprits, there would no longer be any need for punishment. Suppose the whole humanity transformed itself into people of good, then none would seek to harm neighbor, and all would be happy, because they would be good. Such is the state of the advanced worlds from which evil has been excluded; and such will be that of planet Earth when it has attained sufficient progress. However, as certain worlds advance, others are newly formed, populated by primitive spirits, but also serving as habitat, exile and atonement place for imperfect spirits, rebels, obstinate in evil, and those which have been rejected from worlds that have become happy.

16. *But woe to the one by whom the scandal (the temptation to sin) comes!* That is to say, evil being always evil, the one who has unwittingly served as an instrument for divine justice, and whose bad instincts have been used, has nonetheless done evil and must be punished. Thus, for example, an ungrateful child is a punishment or a trial for the parents who suffer from it, because such parents may have been bad children themselves who made their parents suffer, and are now suffering the pain of retaliation. Yet their children are no more excusable, and should in turn be punished in their own children or in another way.

17. *And if your hand … causes you to sin, cut it off and throw it away*; an energetic figure of speech which it would be absurd to take literally, and which simply means that one must destroy in oneself any cause of scandal, that is to say of evil; to tear from his/her heart all impure feelings and all vicious principles; that is to say, it would still be better for a someone to have had his/her hand cut, than if that hand had been for this person instrumental in committing a bad action; to be deprived of sight, only if your eyes had given you bad thoughts. Jesus said nothing absurd for anyone who understood the allegorical and profound meaning of his words; but many things cannot be understood without the key that Spiritism gives to it.

INSTRUCTIONS FROM THE SPIRITS

LET THE CHILDREN COME TO ME

18. Christ said, "Let the little children come to me." These words, so profound in their simplicity, did not refer to the simple appeal of children, but to that of souls that gravitate in the lower circles where misfortune ignores hope. Jesus called to him the intellectual infancy of fully grown individuals: the weak, the enslaved, the vicious. He could teach nothing to physical childhood, which is engaged in matter, subject to the yoke of instinct, and not yet belonging to the higher order of reason and willpower which are exercised around it and for it.

Jesus wanted people to approach him with the confidence of these little toddlers, and his calling won the hearts of women who are all mothers. Thus he subjected souls to his tender and mysterious authority. He was the torch that lights the darkness, the morning light that awakens the dawn. He was the initiator of Spiritism, which in turn must call to itself not small children, but fully-fledged individuals of good will. A vigorous process has begun; it is no longer a matter of instinctively believing and mechanically obeying; it is necessary for humans to follow the intelligent law which reveals to them their universality.

Dearly beloved, the time has come in which errors, once explained, will become truths. We will teach you the exact meaning of the parables, and we will show you the powerful correlation that links what has been and what is now taking place. Verily, verily I tell you the truth: the Spiritist manifestation is growing on the horizon; and here is its envoy which will shine like the Sun on the top of the mountains.

John the Evangelist (Paris, 1863).

19.   Let the little children come to me, for I have milk which strengthens the weak. Let those who are fearful and feeble, and in need of support and consolation, come to me. Let the ignorant come to me so that I enlighten them; let all those who suffer, the multitude of afflicted and poor individuals come to me, and I will teach them the great remedy that softens the evils of life, I will give them the secret to heal their wounds! What is it, my friends, this sovereign balm possessing virtue par excellence, this balm which is applied to all wounds of the heart, closing them? It is love, it is charity! If you have this divine fire, what is there to fear? You will say at all times in your life: God, may your will be done and not mine; please test me with pain and tribulation; be blessed, for it is for my own good; I know, that your hand is heavy on me. If it befits you, Lord, to have mercy on your weak created being, if you grant this heart its permitted joys, be blessed again; but make sure that divine love does not fall asleep in my soul, and that it constantly brings up the voice of my gratitude at your feet! ...

If you have love, you will have everything that is to be desired on Earth, you will possess the pearl par excellence that neither events, nor the wickedness of those who hate and persecute you will be able to take away. If you have love, you will have placed your treasures where worms and rust cannot reach them, and you will see imperceptibly effaced from your soul everything that can defile its purity. You will feel the weight of matter lighten day by day and, like the bird that hovers in the air and leaves the Earth behind, you will constantly climb, you will forever climb, until your exhilarated soul can drink from its element of life in the bosom of the Lord.

A protector spirit (Bordeaux, 1861).

BLESSED ARE THOSE WHO HAVE THEIR EYES CLOSED[30]

20.   Dear friends, you have called me – why? Is it to make me lay hands on the poor distressed person who is here, and heal her? Ah, what suffering, good God! She has lost her sight, and darkness has been made on her. Poor child! Let her pray and hope; I do not know how to work miracles, me, without the will of the good God. All the cures that I have been able to obtain, and which have been reported to you, attribute them only to God which is Parent to all. In your afflictions, therefore, always look up to heaven, and say from the bottom of your heart: "O God, heal me, but let my sick soul be healed before the infirmities of my body; may my flesh be chastised, if necessary, so that my soul may rise to you with the whiteness it had when you created it." After this prayer, my good friends, which the good Lord will always hear, strength and courage will be given to you, and perhaps also this healing which you will have asked only fearfully, as a reward for your selflessness.

But since I am here, in an assembly devoted above all to studying, I will tell you that those who are deprived of sight should consider themselves blessed in their atonement. Remember that Christ said that you needed to pluck your eye out if it was cause of evil; and that it was better that it be thrown into the fire than be the cause of your damnation. Alas! how many on Earth will one day curse in darkness for having seen the light! Oh, yes, how happy are those

30 This communication was given about a blind person, for whom the Spirit of J. B. Vianney, parish priest of Ars, had been evoked.

who in their atonement are struck in the eyesight! Their eyes will no longer be a subject of scandal and fall; they can live entirely in the life of souls; they can see more than you who can see clearly ... When God allows me to go and restore eyesight to some of these poor sufferers and give them back the light, I say to myself: Dear soul, why do you ignore all the delights of the spirit that lives in contemplation and love? You would not ask to see images that are less pure and less sweet than those that you have seen in your blindness.

Yes, indeed! Blessed is the blind person who wants to live with God; happier than you who are here, he/she can feel happiness, touch it, see other souls and soar with them in spiritual spheres that the predestined people of your very land cannot see. The open eye is always ready to make the soul tumble; the closed eye, on the contrary, is always ready to bring it up to God. Believe me, my dear good friends, blindness of the eyes is often the true light of the heart, while sight may often be the dark angel that leads to death.

And now a few words for you, my poor sufferer: take hope and courage! If I said to you: My child, your eyes will be opened, how happy you would be! But who knows if this joy would not make you completely lose yourself? Have confidence in the good God who made happiness and allowed sadness. I will do whatever I am allowed to do for you; but, in your turn, pray, and above all think of everything that I have just told you.

Before I leave, may all of you who are here receive my blessing.

Vianney, parish priest of Ars (Paris, 1863).

21. NOTE: When an affliction is not a consequence of the acts of current life, we must seek the cause of it in a previous life. The so-called whims of fate are nothing but the effects of God's justice. God does not impose arbitrary punishment; It wants that between fault and punishment, there is always a correlation. If, in Its kindness, God threw a veil over our past acts, It nevertheless puts us back on the path, saying, "Whoever lives by the sword shall perish by the sword"; words which can be translated thus: "We are always punished according to the nature of our sin." If therefore someone is afflicted by the loss of sight, it is because sight has been for this individual a cause of fall. Perhaps he/she was also the cause of loss of sight in another person; perhaps someone has become blind from the excessive work imposed on them, or as a result of ill-treatment, lack of care, etc.; and then the culprit suffers the pain of retaliation. The individuals themselves, in their repentance, were able to choose their atonement; which brings us to these words of Jesus: "If your eye causes you to sin, tear it out and throw it away."

Chapter IX
Blessed are the meek and the peacemakers

INSULTS AND VIOLENCE

1. "'Blessed are the meek, for they shall inherit the earth'
(MATTHEW 5:5 ESV)."

2. "'Blessed are the peacemakers, for they shall be called sons[31]
of God' (MATTHEW 5:9 ESV)."

3. "'You have heard that it was said to those of old, 'You shall
not murder; and whoever murders will be liable to judgment.' But
I say to you that everyone who is angry with his brother will be
liable to judgment; whoever insults his brother will be liable to the
council; and whoever says, 'You fool!' will be liable to the hell of
fire' (MATTHEW 5:21–22 ESV)."

4. Through these maxims, Jesus has made a law of meekness,
moderation, gentleness, affability and patience. He therefore condemns violence, anger and even all derogatory expressions toward
one's fellow human beings. *Raca[32]* was among the Hebrews a term
of contempt which meant *worthless person*, and was pronounced by
spitting and turning the head. He goes even further, since he threat-
ens with hellfire anyone who says to his brother or sister: *You fool!*

It is evident that here, as in all circumstances, the intention will
aggravate or mitigate the fault; but in what way can a simple word
have enough gravity to deserve such severe reprobation? This is so
because any offensive speech is the expression of a feeling contrary
to the law of love and charity which must regulate the relationships
of humans and keep harmony and union among them; furthermore
such feeling is an attack on mutual benevolence and fraternity, and

---

31 [Trans. note] Other English Bibles use the term *children* instead of *sons*.

32 [Trans. note] Following the French Bible, A. KARDEC mentions the word *raca*
("insane" in Aramaic) which was removed and replaced by the verb *insult* in the ESV.

it maintains hatred and animosity. Finally because, after humility toward God, charity toward neighbor should be the first law of every Christian.

5. But what does Jesus mean by these words, "Blessed are the meek, for they shall inherit the earth," in which he recommends renouncing the goods of this world and promises those of heaven?

While waiting for the goods of heaven, humans need those of the Earth to live. Jesus only recommends us not to attach more importance to the latter than to the former.

By these words, he means that, to this day, the goods of the Earth are monopolized by violent ones in detriment of those who are meek and peacemakers, and that often lack the necessary, while others have the superfluous. Jesus promises that justice will be done to them *on Earth as it is in heaven*, because they are called the children of God. When the law of love and charity shall become the law of Humanity, there will be no more selfishness; the weak and the peaceful will no longer be exploited or crushed by the strong and the violent. Such will be the state of the Earth when, according to the law of progress and the promise of Jesus, it becomes a happy world through the eviction of the wicked.

Instructions from the Spirits

Affability and meekness

6. Kindness toward others, fruit of love for neighbor, produces the affability and meekness which are its manifestation. However, do not always trust appearances; education and the use of the world can give one the veneer of these qualities. How many people are there whose feigned bonhomie is only an outward mask, a carefully tailored garment devised to conceal hidden deformities! The world is full of these people that have a smile on their lips but venom in their hearts; *that are meek provided that nothing contradict them, but will bite at the slightest provocation*; and whose golden tongue, when they talk face to face, is changed into a poisonous sting when they speak from behind.

Also to this class belong individuals, benign on the outside, who at home are domestic tyrants, making their families and their subordinates suffer the weight of their pride and their despotism. They seem to want to compensate themselves for the constraint they have imposed on themselves elsewhere. Not daring to exercise authority over strangers who would put them in their place, they thought fit to at least be feared by those who could not resist them; with their vanity enjoying being able to say: "Here I command and am obeyed"; without thinking that they could add with more reason: "And I am detested."

It is not enough that milk and honey flow from one's lips; if the heart has nothing to do with it, this is just hypocrisy. One whose affability and meekness are not feigned, never contradicts oneself; he/she is the same before the world and in privacy; and knows, moreover, that if one can deceive fellow human beings by appearances, one cannot deceive God.

Lazarus (Paris, 1861).

PATIENCE

7.   Pain is a blessing that God sends to Its elect; therefore do not grieve when you suffer, but on the contrary, bless the Almighty God who has marked you with pain here below for glory in heaven.

Be patient; it is an act of charity as well as an act of patience, and you must practice the law of charity taught by Christ, as sent from God. Charity which consists in the alms given to the poor is the easiest of charities; but there is one much more painful and consequently much more commendable: *it is to forgive those whom God has placed on our way to be the instruments of our sufferings and to put our patience to the test.*

Life is difficult, I know; it is made up of a thousand things which are like pinpricks and end up hurting; but we have to look at the duties that are imposed on us, the consolations and compensations that we have on the other hand, and then we will see that blessings are more numerous than pains. The burden seems lighter when you look up than when you bow your forehead toward the ground.

Courage, friends, Christ is your model; he suffered more than any of you, and he had nothing to reproach himself for, while you have to atone for your past and to strengthen yourselves for the future. So be patient; be Christians, this word encompasses everything.

A spirit friend (Le Havre, 1862).

OBEDIENCE AND RESIGNATION

8.   Jesus' doctrine teaches obedience and resignation everywhere, both quite vigorous companion virtues of meekness, although people mistakenly confuse them with the negation of feeling and will. *Obedience is the consent of reason; resignation is the consent of the heart.* Both are active forces, for they bear the burden of the trials which senseless revolt would let drop. The coward cannot be resigned, any more than the proud and selfish can be obedient. Jesus was the embodiment of these virtues despised by materialistic antiquity. He came at a time when Roman society was perishing through the moral failings of corruption; he came to shine, within a sagging humanity, the triumphs of self-sacrifice and carnal renunciation.

Each era is thus marked with the stamp of virtue or vice which ought to save or ruin it. The virtue of your generation is intellectual activity; its vice is moral indifference. I only say activity, because an individual of genius will suddenly emerge and discover alone horizons that the majority will be able to see only after him/her, while the intellectual activity is the meeting of the efforts of all to reach a less brilliant goal, but one which proves the intellectual elevation of an era. So submit yourselves to the impulsion we have just given to your spirits; obey the great law of progress which is the motto of your generation. Woe to lazy spirits, to those who obstruct their understanding! Woe indeed! For we which are the guides of humanity on the march of progress will strike them with the whip, and will compel their rebellious will under the double effort of the brake and the spur. Any proud resistance should subside sooner or later; but blessed are those who are meek, for they will lend a willing ear to our teachings.

Lazarus (Paris, 1863).

ANGER

9.   Pride leads you to believe that you are worth more than you actually are; unable to suffer any comparison that could demean you; and to see yourself, on the contrary, so much above your brothers and sisters, whether as a spirit, or because of your social position, or even on account of any personal advantage, that the slightest parallel will hurt and offend you – and then, as a result, you indulge in anger.

Look for the origin of these bouts of transient dementia that make you similar to brutes by causing you to lose your temper and mind. Search and you will almost always find hurt pride as their basis. Is it not your pride hurt by any contradiction that makes you reject right observations and angrily reject the wisest advice? The very impatience that often cause puerile annoyances is due to the importance attached to one's own personality, before which one might think that everyone and everything must yield.

In a frenzy, the angry person strikes everything, from raw nature to the inanimate objects he/she breaks, because these do not obey their will. Ah! if at such moments you could look at yourself with a cold-blooded regard, you would be afraid of yourself, or find yourself ridiculous! From this you can imagine the impression you are causing on others. If only out of self-respect, you should strive to overcome a propensity that makes you worthy of pity.

If they were aware that anger remedies nothing, that it affects their health and can even jeopardize their life, they would see that they themselves are its first victim. But yet another consideration should especially deter them: it is the thought that anger makes all those around them unhappy – if they have a heart, would it not make them remorseful to make suffer their nearest and dearest? And what thoughts of deep remorse would they harbor, if they had committed an act of anger which they would regret all their life!

In short, anger does not exclude certain qualities of the heart, but it prevents one from doing much good, and can cause one to do much harm. That should be enough to encourage one to make efforts to control it. Spiritists are also required to keep it in check for another reason, namely: anger is contrary to Christian charity and humility.

A protector spirit (Bordeaux, 1863).

10. According to the very false idea that one cannot transform one's own nature, one believes oneself exempt from making efforts to correct oneself for the faults which one has delighted in committing, or which would require too much perseverance. Thus, for example, a person inclined to anger will almost always give an excuse for his/her temper blaming his/her body for them, and therefore accusing God of their own misdeeds rather than admitting any guilt. This is another result of pride that we find mixed with all its other imperfections.

There is no question that some temperaments are more prone than others to violent actions, just like there are more flexible habits which lend themselves better than others to feats of force. Yet do not believe that this is the primary cause of anger, and instead rest assured that a peaceful spirit, even in a bilious body, will always be peaceful; and that a violent spirit in a lymphatic[33] body, will not be meek; only, the violence in this case will take on another character – not having an organization capable of seconding the spirit's violent nature, the anger will be condensed, and in the other case it will be unconstrained.

The body does not impart anger to anyone who does not have it, any more than it gives a person any other vices. All virtues and all vices are inherent in the spirit, otherwise where would the merit and responsibility be? A physically handicapped person cannot straighten his/her body because the spirit has nothing to do with it, but one can modify what concerns the spirit when one has a firm will. Has experience not proved to you, Spiritists, how far willpower can go, through the truly miraculous transformations that you see taking place? So be assured that humans only remain vicious because they want to remain vicious; but those who want to correct themselves can always do so, otherwise the law of progress would not exist for human beings.

Hahnemann (Paris, 1863).

---

33 [Trans. note] This mediumistic message bears the imprint of its author, the spirit of Samuel HAHNEMANN (1755–1843), founder of homeopathy, in its ancient use of the terms *bilious* and *lymphatic* as denoting an irascible temper.

Chapter X
Blessed are the merciful

FORGIVE SO THAT GOD CAN FORGIVE YOU

1. "Blessed are the merciful, for they shall receive mercy (MATTHEW 5:7 ESV)."

2. "For if you forgive others their trespasses, your heavenly Father will also forgive you, but if you do not forgive others their trespasses, neither will your Father forgive your trespasses (MATTHEW 6:14–15 ESV)."

3. "If your brother sins against you, go and tell him his fault, between you and him alone. If he listens to you, you have gained your brother. — Then Peter came up and said to him, 'Lord, how often will my brother sin against me, and I forgive him? As many as seven times?' Jesus said to him, 'I do not say to you seven times, but seventy times seven' (MATTHEW 18:15;21–22 ESV)."

4. Mercy is the complement of meekness; for those who are not merciful cannot be meek and peaceful. It consists in forgetting and forgiving injuries. Hatred and resentment denote a soul without elevation or greatness; forgetting injuries is a characteristic of a lofty soul that stands above the attacks that can be brought against it. One is always anxious, shady and full of gall; whereas the other is calm, full of leniency and charity.

Woe to those who say, "I will never forgive," for if he/she is not condemned by fellow human beings, he/she will certainly be condemned by God. By what right would someone claim forgiveness for one's own faults if one does not forgive those of others? Jesus teaches us that mercy must have no limits, when he says to forgive one's sibling, not seven times, but seventy times seven.

But there are two very different ways of forgiving: one great, noble, truly generous, without ulterior motive, delicately sparing the self-esteem and the susceptibility of the opponent, even if the latter is in the wrong; the second by which the injured, or whoever believes himself/herself to be, imposes on the other humiliating conditions, and makes feel the weight of a forgiveness which irritates instead of placating. If he/she reaches out, it is not with kindness, but with ostentation in order to be able to say to everyone: See how generous I am! In such circumstances, it is impossible for a reconciliation to be sincere from either side. No, this is not generosity, it is a way of satisfying one's pride. In any dispute, the one who shows himself/herself to be the most conciliatory, who demonstrates the most selflessness, charity and true greatness, will always win the sympathy of impartial people.

RECONCILE WITH YOUR ADVERSARIES

5. "Come to terms quickly with your accuser while you are going with him to court, lest your accuser hand you over to the judge, and the judge to the guard, and you be put in prison. Truly, I say to you, you will never get out until you have paid the last penny (MATTHEW 5:25–26 ESV)."

6. There is in the practice of forgiveness, and in that of good in general, more than a moral effect, there is also a material effect. Death, as we know, does not deliver us from our enemies; vindictive spirits often pursue with their hatred, beyond the grave, those against whom they bear a grudge. This is why the French proverb that says, "Dead the beast, dead the venom,"[34] is false when applied to humans. An evil spirit will wait for one it wants to harm, to be chained to a physical body and less free, in order to torment this individual more easily, to strike him/her in their interests or through their dearest affections. This fact should be regarded as the cause of most cases of obsession, especially those which present a certain severity,

---

34 [Trans. note] Known in English translations as the one above, it is akin to the old saying "Dead men tell no tales."

such as subjugation and possession. The obsessed and possessed are therefore almost always victims of a previous revenge, to which they have probably given rise by their own conduct. God allows it to punish them for the harm they themselves have done – or, if they have not done it, for having lacked indulgence and charity by not forgiving. It is therefore important, from the point of view of future peace, for such an individual to repair as soon as possible the wrongs that he/she had committed against his/her neighbor, to forgive their enemies, so as to extinguish, before dying, any reason of dissension, any founded cause of further animosity. Through this means, of a bitter enemy in this world, one can make a friend in the other; at least one puts good right on one's side, and God does not leave the one who has forgiven subject to revenge. When Jesus recommends to come to terms as soon as possible with one's adversary, it is not only with a view to appeasing a discord during the current existence, but to avoid that they are not perpetuated in future existences. You will not get out, he says, until you have paid the last penny, that is to say, until you have completely satisfied the justice of God.

THE MOST PLEASING SACRIFICE TO GOD

7. "So if you are offering your gift at the altar and there remember that your brother has something against you, leave your gift there before the altar and go. First be reconciled to your brother, and then come and offer your gift (MATTHEW 5:23–24 ESV)."

8. When Jesus said, "Leave your gift there before the altar and ... first be reconciled to your brother," he was teaching that the most pleasing sacrifice to the Lord is that of one's own resentment; that before presenting oneself to God to be forgiven, one oneself must have forgiven another fellow being, and that if one has done wrong to another of one's siblings, one must have repaired it first. Only then will the offering be accepted because it will come from a heart free from any evil thought. Jesus materializes this precept, because the Jews offered material sacrifices; he had to conform his words to their customs. Christians do not offer material gifts; they have spiritualized the sacrifice, but the precept has all the more force for that reason: Christians offer their soul to God, and their soul must be purified. *When entering the temple of the Lord, one* *must leave aside all feelings of hatred and animosity, all bad thoughts against one's fellow beings*; only then will one's prayer be carried by the angels to be deposited at the feet of the Lord. This is what Jesus teaches with these words: Leave your offering at the foot of the altar, and go first to be reconciled with your brother, if you want to be pleasing to the Lord.

THE SPECK AND THE LOG IN THE EYE

9. *"Why do you see the speck that is in your brother's eye, but do not notice the log that is in your own eye?* Or how can you say to your brother, 'Let me take the speck out of your eye,' when there is the log in your own eye? You hypocrite, first take the log out of your own eye, and then you will see clearly to take the speck out of your brother's eye (MATTHEW 7:3–5 ESV)."

10. One of humanity's faults is to see evil in others before seeing that which is in us. To judge yourself, you would have to be able to look in the mirror, somehow transport yourself outside, and consider yourself as another person, asking to yourself: What would I think if I saw someone else doing this that I am doing? Undoubtedly it is pride that leads humans to hide their own faults, both moral and physical. This flaw is essentially contrary to charity, because true charity is modest, simple and indulgent. Proud charity is nonsense, since these two feelings neutralize one another. How, indeed, a person vain enough to believe in the importance of his/her personality and the supremacy of his/her qualities, can they have at the same time enough self-denial to bring out, in others, the good which could eclipse it, instead of the evil that could enhance it? If pride is the parent of many vices, it is also the denial of many virtues – we find it at the bottom and as the motive of almost all actions. This is why Jesus set out to fight it as the main obstacle to progress.

JUDGE NOT, THAT YOU BE NOT JUDGED LET HIM WHO IS WITHOUT SIN CAST THE FIRST STONE

11. "Judge not, that you be not judged. For with the judgment you pronounce you will be judged, and with the measure you use it will be measured to you (MATTHEW 7:1–2 ESV)."

12.   "The scribes and the Pharisees brought a woman who had been caught in adultery, and placing her in the midst they said to him, 'Teacher, this woman has been caught in the act of adultery. Now in the Law Moses commanded us to stone such women. So what do you say?' This they said to test him, that they might have some charge to bring against him. Jesus bent down and wrote with his finger on the ground. And as they continued to ask him, he stood up and said to them, 'Let him who is without sin among you be the first to throw a stone at her.' And once more he bent down and wrote on the ground. But when they heard it, they went away one by one, beginning with the older ones, and Jesus was left alone with the woman standing before him.

Jesus stood up and said to her, 'Woman, where are they? Has no one condemned you?' She said, 'No one, Lord.' And Jesus said, 'Neither do I condemn you; go, and from now on sin no more' (JOHN 8:3–11 ESV)."

13.   "Let him who is without sin among you be the first to throw a stone at her," said Jesus. This maxim makes indulgence a duty for all of us, since there is no one who can do without it in relation to themselves. It teaches us that we must not judge others more harshly than we judge ourselves, nor condemn in others what we excuse in ourselves. Before blaming someone for a fault, let us see if the same blame cannot fall on us.

The blame cast on the conduct of others can have two motives: curbing evil, or discrediting the person whose actions are criticized. This last motive never has an excuse, because it comes from backbiting and wickedness. The former can be commendable, and even becomes a duty in some cases, since it must result in good, and without which evil would never be curbed in society. Moreover should humans not help the progress of their fellow beings? This principle should therefore not be taken in the absolute sense: "Judge not, that you be not judged," for the letter kills but the spirit gives life.[35]

Jesus could not possibly have forbidden us from accusing what is bad, since he himself gave us the example, and did it in vigorous terms; but he meant to say that authority to condemn lies in the moral authority of the one who pronounces it. To be guilty of what one condemns in others is to abdicate from this authority. It also

---

35 [Trans. note] 2Corinthians 3:6 ESV.

means taking away the right of curbing. Moreover, inner conscience refuses any respect and voluntary submission to those who, being invested with any power, violate the laws and principles that they are responsible for enforcing. *There is no legitimate authority in the eyes of God, if not founded on the example of goodness it provides.* This is also what transpires from the words of Jesus.

INSTRUCTIONS FROM THE SPIRITS

FORGIVENESS OF INJURIES

14. How many times should I forgive my fellow human being? You should forgive him/her not seven times, but seventy times seven. This is one of those words of Jesus that should strike your mind the most and speak the highest to your heart. Bring these words of mercy closer to the prayer so simple, so summarized and so great in its aspirations that Jesus has given to his disciples, and you will always encounter the same thought. Jesus, the just man par excellence, answers Peter: You will forgive, but without limits; you will forgive each offense as often as the offense is done to you; you will teach your brothers and sisters this self-forgetfulness which makes one immune to attack, bad practices and injuries. Once you become meek and humble of heart, never quantifying your indulgence, you will finally do what you want our Heavenly Parent to do for you. Often does God not have to forgive you, and does It count the number of times Its forgiveness comes down to erase your faults?

So listen carefully to this response from Jesus, and, like Peter, apply it to yourselves: forgive, be indulgent; be charitable, generous, even lavish with your love. Give, for the Lord will give you back; forgive, because the Lord will forgive you; lower yourself, for the Lord will elevate you; humble yourself, for the Lord will make you sit on Its right hand.

Dearly beloved, go study and comment on these words which I address to you on behalf of the One who, from the height of celestial splendors, always looks toward you, and continues with love the thankless task which he started eighteen centuries ago. So forgive your brothers and sisters as you yourselves need to be forgiven. If their actions were personally prejudicial to you, this is one more reason to be indulgent, because the merit of forgiveness is proportionate to the severity of the evil. There would be no need for forgiveness of the wrongs and injuries done by your brothers and sisters, if they had only caused you minor injuries. Spiritists, never forget that in words, as well as in actions, forgiveness of injuries must not be an empty saying. If you call yourselves Spiritists, then act as Spiritists: forget the harm that has been done to you, and think only of one thing, namely, the good that you can do. Whoever has taken this path must not depart from it even in thought, for you are responsible for your thoughts which are known by God. Therefore see that they are stripped of any feelings of resentment; for God knows what lies at the bottom of everyone's heart. *Blessed are those who can fall asleep each evening, saying: I hold nothing against my neighbor.*

Simeon[36] (Bordeaux, 1862).

15. To forgive your enemies is to ask forgiveness for yourself. To forgive one's friends is to give them proof of friendship; to forgive injuries is to show that we are getting better. Therefore do forgive, dear friends, so that God will forgive you; because if you are hard, demanding and inflexible, if you are rigorous even for a slight offense, how do you want God to forget that everyday you yourself have the greatest need of indulgence? Ah, woe to those who say, "I shall never forgive," for thus they are proclaiming their own condemnation. Moreover, who knows if, looking deep inside yourself, you were not the aggressor? Who knows if, in this fight that begins as a pinprick but escalates into a full-scale rupture, you have not started it by striking the first blow? If you did not let escape a hurtful remark? If you have failed to use the necessary moderation? No doubt your opponent is wrong for being too susceptible, but this is another reason for you to be indulgent and not deserve the reproach that you address to him/her. Suppose that you were really offended in a circumstance, who can say that you did not inflame it through reprisals, and that you did not degenerate it into a serious quarrel which could have easily been forgotten? If it was up to you to prevent it from happening, but you didn't, you are guilty. Finally, let us admit that you have absolutely no reproach to make yourself: you will have even more merit for being merciful

---

36 [Trans. note] There were four characters called Simeon in the Bible, three of them cited in Luke's Gospel and Acts.

However there are two very different ways of forgiving: there is forgiveness from the lips and forgiveness from the heart. Many people say of their adversary, "I forgive him/her," while internally deriving a secret pleasure from the misfortunes experienced by the latter, saying to themselves that he/she has only got what they deserve. How many say, "I forgive," and then add, "But I will never be reconciled; I will never see this person again in my life." Is this forgiveness according to the Gospel? No; true forgiveness, Christian forgiveness, is the one that casts a veil over the past; it is the only one which will be taken into account, because God is not satisfied with appearances: God searches the bottom of our hearts and the most secret thoughts; God cannot be fooled by words and vain simulations. A complete and absolute forgiveness of injuries is characteristic of great souls; bitterness being always a sign of debasement and inferiority. Remember that true forgiveness is found more in deeds than in words.

The Apostle Paul (Lyons, 1861).

INDULGENCE

16. Spiritists, we want to talk to you today about indulgence, a feeling so sweet and so fraternal that every human should have toward their brothers and sisters, but which only very few put into practice.

True indulgence does not see the faults in others; or if it sees them, it is careful not to speak about or to expose them. On the contrary, it hides them, so that they are known only to oneself; and if someone's malevolence discovers them, an indulgent person always has an excuse ready to remedy them, that is, a plausible, serious excuse, and never one that instead to mitigating a fault, actually highlights it with treacherous duplicity.

Indulgence never occupies itself with the wrongdoings of others, unless this is done to render a service. Yet it takes care to mitigate them as much as possible. It makes no shocking observations, utters no reproaches, only advice, which is most often veiled. When you throw criticism, what should be the consequences of your words? Would it be that you yourself, who blame, would not have done what you reproach; or could it be that you are better than the culprit. Humans, when will you judge your own hearts, your own thoughts, your own actions, instead of caring about what your brothers and sisters are doing? When will you direct your stern eyes only to yourselves?

Therefore be stern with yourself, but indulgent with others. Think of the One which judges in last instance, which can see the secret thoughts of each heart, and which often excuses the faults you blame in others, or condemns those you excuse, because God knows the motive behind all actions; and you yourself, who so loudly shout, "Anathema," would perhaps have made more serious mistakes.

Be indulgent, dear friends, because indulgence attracts, soothes and rectifies, whereas stern rigor discourages, drives away and inflames.

Joseph, protector spirit (Bordeaux, 1863).

17.   Be indulgent to the faults of others, whatever they may be; judge with severity only your own actions; and the Lord will be indulgent with you as you have been toward others.

Support the strong: encourage them to persevere; strengthen the weak by showing them the goodness of God which takes into account the slightest intention to repent; show everyone the angel of repentance spreading its white wings over the faults of humans, thus veiling them from the eyes of those who cannot yet see what is unclean. Understand the extent of your divine Parent's infinite mercy, and never forget to say to God through your thoughts and especially through your actions: "Forgive us our debts, as we also have forgiven our debtors." Understand the value of these sublime words, admirable not only textually, but also because of their teachings.

What do you ask of the Lord when asking for forgiveness? Is it only to forget your injuries? A forgetfulness that would leave you in nothingness, because if God were content to just forget your faults, *It would not punish, but neither would It reward you.* A reward cannot be the price of the good which one did not do, and even less of the evil which one did. Was such evil forgotten? By asking for forgiveness of your transgressions, you are asking God the favor of Its blessings so as not to fall again; the strength to enter a new path, a path of submission and love in which you can add reparation to repentance.

When forgiving your brothers and sisters, do not just spread the veil of oblivion over their faults; this veil is often quite transparent to one's eyes; bring love to them at the same time as forgiveness; do toward them what you will ask your Heavenly Parent to do toward you. Replace defiling anger with purifying love. Preach through example this active, tireless charity that Jesus taught you; preach it as he did himself throughout the time that he lived on the Earth visible to the eyes of the body, and as he still preaches incessantly since he became only visible to the eyes of the spirit. Follow this divine model; walk in his footsteps: they will lead you to the place of refuge where you will find rest after the combat. Like him, take up your cross, all of you, and climb painfully but courageously through your ordeal: at the top glorification is in store for you.

Jean, bishop of Bordeaux (Bordeaux, 1862).

18.   Dear friends, be severe with yourselves, forgiving of the weaknesses of others – still a practice of holy charity that very few people observe. All of you have bad inclinations to overcome, faults to correct, habits to modify; all of you have a more or less heavy burden to unload before you can climb to the summit of the mountain of advancement. Why then be so clairvoyant in relation to your fellow human beings, but so blind when it comes to yourselves? When will you cease to see in your siblings' eye the speck that hurts them, without looking at the log in yours that blinds you and makes you stumble from fall to fall? Believe your sibling spirits when they say: Those proud enough to believe to be superior in virtue and in merit to their incarnate brothers and sisters are foolish and guilty, and God will punish them in the day of Its justice. The true character of charity lies in the modesty and humility which consist in examining the faults of others only superficially and instead endeavor to assert what is good and virtuous in them. For, if the human heart is an abyss of corruption, in some of its most hidden folds there is always the rudiments of some good feelings, a living spark of spiritual essence.

Spiritism, this consoling and blessed doctrine, happy are those who get to know you and who take advantage of the salutary teachings of the Spirits of the Lord! For these people, the way is lighted, and all along the road they can read these words which show them the means to arrive at the goal: To practice charity; charity of the heart, charity for one's neighbor as for oneself; in a word, charity for all and love of God above all else, because the love of God sums up all our duties, and it is impossible to really love God without practicing the charity which It has made a mandatory law for all Its created beings.

Dufêtre, bishop of Nevers (Bordeaux).

19. *Since no one is perfect, does it follow that nobody has the right to scold their neighbor?*

Certainly not, since each of you must work for the progress of all, and especially of those whose guardianship has been entrusted to you. However this is a reason for doing it with restraint, for a useful purpose, and not, as one does most of the time, for the pleasure of bashing others. In the latter case, the blame lies in wickedness; in the first, it is a duty that charity commands you to accomplish with all possible care – and again the blame we throw on others, should at the same time be addressed to ourselves, and we should ask ourselves if we do not actually deserve it.

Saint Louis (Paris, 1860).

20. *Is it reprehensible to observe the imperfections of others, even if there cannot be any profit for them, and if one does not disclose them?*

It all depends on one's intention. Certainly it is not forbidden to see evil where evil exists; it would even be inconvenient to see only good everywhere, since such an illusion would hinder progress. What is wrong is to turn this observation for the detriment of others, by decrying it unnecessarily in public opinion. It would still be reprehensible to do it only to indulge ourselves with a feeling of malevolence and joy for finding others in fault. It is quite different when, by throwing a veil on someone's evil before the public, one contents oneself with observing it for personal gain; that is to say, studying oneself to avoid what one blames in others. Might this observation prove useful for the moralist? How would the latter be able to paint the flaws of humanity without studying examples?

Saint Louis (Paris, 1860).

21. *Are there cases in which it is useful to reveal the evil in others?*

This is a very delicate question which calls for a thorough understanding of charity. If a person's imperfections only harm oneself, there is never any point in making them known; but if they can harm others, the interest of the greatest number should be preferred over the interest of one. Depending on the circumstances, unmasking the practice of hypocrisy and lies may be a duty; for it is better for one person to fall than several others to become this person's dupes or victims. In such case, the sum of the pros and cons must be weighed up.

Saint Louis (Paris, 1860).

Chapter XI
Love your neighbor as yourself

THE GREATEST COMMANDMENT

1. "But when the Pharisees heard that he had silenced the Sadducees, they gathered together. And one of them, a lawyer, asked him a question to test him. 'Teacher, which is the great commandment in the Law?' And he said to him, 'You shall love the Lord your God with all your heart and with all your soul and with all your mind. This is the great and first commandment. And a second is like it: *You shall love your neighbor as yourself.* On these two commandments depend all the Law and the Prophets' (MATTHEW 22:34–40 ESV)."

2. "*'So whatever you wish that others would do to you, do also to them,* for this is the Law and the Prophets' (MATTHEW 7:12 ESV)."

"And as you wish that others would do to you, do so to them (LUKE 6:31 ESV)."

3. "'Therefore the kingdom of heaven may be compared to a king who wished to settle accounts with his servants. When he began to settle, one was brought to him who owed him ten thousand talents. And since he could not pay, his master ordered him to be sold, with his wife and children and all that he had, and payment to be made. So the servant fell on his knees, imploring him, 'Have patience with me, and I will pay you everything.' And out of pity for him, the master of that servant released him and forgave him the debt. But when that same servant went out, he found one of his fellow servants who owed him a hundred denarii,[37] and seizing him, he began to choke him, saying, 'Pay what you owe.' So his fellow

---

37 [Trans. note] *Denarius*, plural *denarii*, an ancient Roman coin.

servant fell down and pleaded with him, 'Have patience with me, and I will pay you.' He refused and went and put him in prison until he should pay the debt.

When his fellow servants saw what had taken place, they were greatly distressed, and they went and reported to their master all that had taken place. Then his master summoned him and said to him, 'You wicked servant! I forgave you all that debt because you pleaded with me. And should not you have had mercy on your fellow servant, as I had mercy on you?' And in anger his master delivered him to the jailers, until he should pay all his debt.

So also my heavenly Father will do to every one of you, if you do not forgive your brother from your heart (MATTHEW 18:23–35 ESV)."

4.   "Love your neighbor as yourself; do for others what you would like them to do for you" is the most complete expression of charity, because it sums up all the duties toward neighbor. There can be no safer guide in this regard than by taking into account what to do for others what you want for yourself. By what right would one demand from one's fellow beings more good practices, indulgence, benevolence and devotion than one oneself has toward them? The practice of these maxims leads to the destruction of selfishness; when humans take them as the rule for their conduct and the basis of their institutions, they will understand true fraternity, and will make peace and justice prevail among them. There will be no more hatred or dissension, but rather union, harmony and mutual benevolence.

GIVE TO CAESAR WHAT IS CAESAR'S

5.   "Then the Pharisees went and plotted how to entangle him in his words. And they sent their disciples to him, along with the Herodians, saying, 'Teacher, we know that you are true and teach the way of God truthfully, and you do not care about anyone's opinion, for you are not swayed by appearances. Tell us, then, what you think. Is it lawful to pay taxes to Caesar, or not?'

But Jesus, aware of their malice, said, 'Why put me to the test, you hypocrites? Show me the coin for the tax.' And they brought him a denarius. And Jesus said to them, 'Whose likeness and inscription is this?' They said, 'Caesar's.' Then he said to them, *Therefore render to Caesar the things that are Caesar's, and to God the things that are God's.'*

When they heard it, they marveled. And they left him and went away (MATTHEW 22:15–22; *cf.* MARK 12:13–17 ESV)."

6. The question put to Jesus was motivated by this circumstance, namely, that the Jews, who abhorred the tribute imposed on them by the Romans, had turned it into a religious issue. A large party had formed to refuse taxes; therefore to them the payment of the tribute was quite an irritating topic at the time, without which the question asked of Jesus – "Is it lawful to pay taxes to Caesar, or not?" – would have made no sense. This question was a trap because, depending on his reply, they hoped to stir up either Roman authorities or dissident Jews against him. "But Jesus, aware of their malice," sidesteps the difficulty by giving them a lesson in justice, and by saying to render to each one what is due to him. (See **INTRODUCTION**, III. Historical Data, entry "Publicans" above.)

7. This maxim, "Render to Caesar the things that are Caesar's," should not be understood in a restrictive and absolute manner. Like all the teachings of Jesus, it is a general principle condensed in a practical and usual form, and deduced from a particular circumstance. This principle is a consequence of the one that states, do unto others as you would have them do unto you. He condemns any material or moral prejudice inflicted on others, any violation of their interests. He prescribes respect for everyone else's rights, as everyone wants their own rights to be respected; it extends to the fulfillment of obligations contracted toward family, society, authority, as well as toward individuals.

INSTRUCTIONS FROM THE SPIRITS

THE LAW OF LOVE

8. Love sums up the whole doctrine of Jesus, because it is the sentiment par excellence, and sentiments are instincts raised to the height of progress accomplished. At their point of departure, humans have only instincts; once more advanced and corrupt, humans have only feelings; but as they become educated and purified, they have sentiments; and the exquisite point of sentiment is love. Not love in the common sense of the word, but this interior sun which condenses and gathers in its incandescent core all aspirations and all superhuman revelations. The law of love replaces personality with the fusion of beings; it destroys social miseries. Blessed are those who, going beyond their humanity, love with great love their distressed fellow beings! Happy are those who love, for they know neither the distress of the soul nor that of the body. Their feet are light, and they live as if transported out of themselves. When Jesus spoke this divine word, *love*, it thrilled human beings, and led the martyrs to descend, deeply imbued with hope, into the Roman circus arena.

Spiritism in turn has come to pronounce a second word in the divine alphabet – pay very close attention, because this word lifts the headstone from empty tombs – namely, *reincarnation*. And, by triumphing over death, reincarnation reveals to the amazement of humans, their intellectual heritage. It is no longer to torture that it leads them, but to the conquest of themselves, now elevated and transfigured. Blood redeemed the spirit, and today the spirit should redeem humans from matter.

Like I said, in the beginning humans had only instincts. Those in whom the instincts dominate are closer to the starting point than to the goal. To advance toward the goal, it is necessary to overcome instincts in favor of sentiment, that is to say, to perfect oneself by stifling the latent germs of matter. Instincts are the germination and the embryos of sentiment; they carry with them progress, as the acorn encloses the oak, and the least advanced beings are those which, by only stripping their chrysalis little by little, remain enslaved to their instincts. The spirit must be cultivated as a field crop; all future wealth depends on current plowing, and more than earthly goods, it will bring you glorious elevation. It is then that, by understanding the law of love which unites all beings, you will seek in it the sweet pleasures of the soul, which are the prelude to heavenly joys.

Lazarus (Paris, 1862).

9. Love is of divine essence, and from the first to the last of you, at the bottom of your heart you possess the spark of this sacred fire. Here is a fact often witnessed by everyone: even the most abject, the most vile, the most criminal individual has a lively and ardent affection for a being or for any object whatsoever, proof against everything that could attempt to diminish it, and frequently reaching the sublime.

I said "for a being or for any object whatsoever," because there are some among you who spend their love in abundance with their hearts overflowing toward animals, plants, and even material objects: they are like misanthropes complaining of humanity in general, hardening themselves against the natural inclination of their souls which would seek around them affection and affinity. They lower the law of love to the state of instinct. But whatever they do, they cannot stifle the perennial seed that God placed in their hearts when they were created. This seed develops and grows with morality and intelligence, and, although often curbed by selfishness, it is the source of the holy and sweet virtues that make sincere and lasting affections, and help you cross the steep, parched path of human existence.

There are some people to whom the reincarnation trial is repugnant in the sense that others participate in affectionate sympathies of which they are jealous. Poor brothers and sisters! It is your affection that makes you selfish; your love is restricted to an inner circle of relatives or friends, while remaining indifferent to everyone else. Well, then, in order to practice the law of love as God intends it, you must gradually love all your brothers and sisters indiscriminately. This task will be long and difficult, but it will be accomplished: God wills it, and the law of love is the first and most important precept of Spiritism, your new doctrine, because it is the one that should one day kill selfishness in whatever form it occurs; for, in addition to personal selfishness, there is also selfishness of family, social hierarchy and nationality. Jesus said, "Love your neighbor as yourself"; what does the idea of neighbor entail? Is it one's family, religion, and nation? No, it is the whole humanity. In higher worlds, what harmonizes and directs the advanced spirits that inhabit them is mutual love; and your planet, destined to imminent progress through social transformation, will see this sublime law practiced by its inhabitants, as a reflection of the Divinity.

The effects of the law of love are the moral improvement of humankind and happiness during earthly life. Even the most rebellious and most vicious individuals will have to transform themselves when they see the benefits produced by this practice: Do not do unto others what you do not wish others to do unto you, but on the contrary, do unto them all the good that you can.

Do not believe in the aridity and hardening of the human heart; it will eventually give in despite itself to true love, since it is a magnet which it cannot resist – and the contact of this love enlivens and fertilizes the seeds of this virtue which lies in your hearts in latent state. Earth, a planet of trial and exile, will then be purified by this sacred fire, and experience charity, humility, patience, devotion, self-denial, resignation, self-sacrifice – all virtues derived from love. Do not get tired of hearing the words of John the Evangelist; as you know, when infirmity and old age suspended the course of his preaching, he repeated only these sweet words: "Little children, love one another."

Dear beloved, take advantage of these lessons; their practice is difficult, but your souls can draw an immense good from it. Believe me, make this sublime effort that I ask of you: "Love one another," and you will soon see the Earth transforms itself and become an Elysium where the souls of the righteous will enjoy rest.

Fénelon (Bordeaux, 1861).

10.   Dear fellow disciples, the spirits here present say to you through my voice: Love well in order to be loved. This thought is so just, that you will find in it everything that comforts and calms our sorrows of everyday life; or rather, by practicing this wise maxim, you will rise so high above matter that you will spiritualize yourselves even before you discarnate. Spiritist studies have developed in you the understanding of the future, and now one thing is for sure: there really exists an advancement toward God, with all the promises that meet the aspirations of your soul. Therefore you must rise high enough to be able to pass judgment without the encumbrances of matter, and to avoid condemning your fellow human beings before taking your thoughts to God.

To love, in the deepest sense of the word, is to be loyal, honest, conscientious, and to do unto others as you would have them do unto you. It is to seek around oneself the inner meaning of all the pains which overwhelm your fellow human beings, in order to bring some soothing to them. It is to regard the great human family as your own, because you will meet this family again sometime in the future, in more advanced worlds – and, like you, the spirits that compose it are God's children, marked on the forehead to continue to rise to infinity. That is why you cannot refuse your brothers and sisters what God has given you liberally, since, for your part, you would be very glad that your fellow human beings gave you what you needed. Therefore, to all those who suffer, offer a word of hope and support, so that you may be entirely loving and just.

Believe that this wise saying, "Love well in order to be loved," will make its way: it is revolutionary, and follows a fixed, unchanging path. But you who have listened to me have already won; you are infinitely better than a hundred years ago; you have changed so much to your advantage that you accept without doubting a whole host of new ideas on freedom and fraternity that you would have rejected in the past. However, in a hundred years from now, you will accept with the same ease those which have not yet been able to enter your mind.

Now that the Spiritist movement has taken such a big step, see how quickly the ideas of justice and renewal contained in the Spiritist precepts are accepted by the average of intelligent people in the world. This happens because those ideas meet all that is divine in you; it is because you have been prepared by a fertile seed, namely, that of the last century, which has implanted in society great ideas of progress. And since everything is linked together under the command of the Most High, all the lessons received and accepted will be contained in this universal exchange of love for neighbor. Through it, you incarnate spirits, once able to better judge and feel, will stretch out your hands to the confines of your planet. Thus we will meet one another to get along with and love one another, and thus destroy all iniquities, all causes of misunderstanding among peoples.

The great thought of renewal through Spiritism, so well described in *The Spirits' Book*,[38] will produce the great miracle of the upcoming century, which will meet all material and spiritual interests of human beings, by the application of this maxim, now well understood: Love well in order to be loved.

Sanson, former member of the Parisian Society of Spiritist Studies (Paris, 1863)

---

38 [Trans. note] See bibliography: A. KARDEC, *The Spirits' Book.*

Selfishness

11. Selfishness, this plague of humanity, must disappear from Earth, whose moral progress it halts. The task of making it rise in the hierarchy of worlds is reserved for Spiritism. Selfishness is therefore the target toward which all true believers must direct their weapons, their forces, and their courage. I say "their courage," because it takes even more to defeat yourself than to defeat others. So let everyone put all their energy into fighting it within themselves, because this monster which devours all intelligent minds, this child of pride, is the source of all miseries here below. It is the negation of charity, and therefore the greatest obstacle to human happiness.

Jesus gave you the example of charity, as Pontius Pilate that of selfishness; for when the Just One was about to go through the holy stations of his martyrdom, Pilate washed his hands, saying: What does it matter to me! Then he said to the Jews, "This man is just, why do you want to crucify him?" – and yet he let him be led to his fatal torment.

It is due to this antagonism between charity and selfishness, to the invasion of this veritable leprosy of the human heart, that Christianity's mission has not yet been completely accomplished. It is on you, new apostles of the faith, enlightened by higher-order spirits, that the task and the duty fall of eradicating this evil in order to give to Christianity all its force, and to clear the way of the brambles that hinder its progress. Drive selfishness out from Earth so that it can rise in the scale of worlds, because it is time for humanity to put on its virile dress;[39] but first all of you must drive selfishness out of your hearts.

Emmanuel (Paris, 1861)

12. If human beings loved one another with mutual love, charity would be better practiced; but for that to happen, you should strive to get rid of this armor that blocks out your hearts, in order to become more sensitive to those who suffer. Inflexibility kills good sentiments. Christ was never put off: whoever addressed him,

---

39 [Trans. note] To symbolize the courage that comes with growing up, Emmanuel, once an ancient Roman citizen, uses the expression *toga virilis* (the toga of manhood), which was worn by Roman youths only after reaching a certain age, same as modern European society would have boys wear long trousers only after reaching puberty.

regardless of who they were, was not rejected. Both the adulterous woman and the criminal were rescued by him; he never feared that his own reputation would suffer from it. When will you take him as a model for all your actions? *If charity reigned on Earth, the wicked would no longer prevail, but rather flee ashamed and hide, because everywhere they would find themselves displaced.* Then, rest assured, evil would completely disappear.

Start by setting an example for yourselves: Be charitable to all without distinction; strive not to notice those who look down on you, and leave justice to God, for every day in Its kingdom God winnows the good wheat from the chaff.

Selfishness is the negation of charity. Now, without charity there can be no rest for society. I would say more: no safety for society either, given that with selfishness and pride – which join together – there will always be a race for the most dexterous, a struggle of interests where the most holy affections will be trampled underfoot, with even sacred family ties being thoroughly disrespected.

Pascal[40] (Sens, France, 1862).

FAITH AND CHARITY

13. I have told you recently, dear children, that charity without faith was not enough to keep among humans a social order capable of making them happy. I should also have added that charity is impossible without faith. You may indeed find generous impulses even in persons deprived of religion, but this self-denying charity which is exercised solely through self-renunciation, by constantly relinquishing self-interest, can only be inspired by faith, which helps us bear the cross of this life with love and perseverance.

Yes, dear children, it is in vain that those eager for enjoyment would want to deceive themselves about their destinies here on Earth, by maintaining that they are allowed to take care only of their own happiness. Indeed, God created us to be happy in eternity; however, earthly life should only serve for our moral perfecting, which is more easily acquired with the help of our organism and the material world. Besides the ordinary vicissitudes of life, the diversity of your tastes, inclinations, and needs is also a way to improve

---

40 [Trans. note] Blaise Pascal (1623–1662), French mathematician, physicist, religious philosopher, and writer.

yourselves by practicing charity. Because it is only through mutual concessions and sacrifices that you can maintain harmony among such diverse elements.

However, you will be right in affirming that happiness is intended for humans here below, if you seek it, not in material pleasures, but in the good. The history of Christianity tells of martyrs that went to martyrdom with joy. Today, to be a Christian in your society, you need neither the holocaust of martyrdom, nor the sacrifice of life, but only and simply the sacrifice of your own selfishness, your pride and your vanity. You will triumph, provided charity inspires you and faith supports you.

A protector spirit (Cracow, Poland, 1861).

CHARITY TOWARD CRIMINALS

14. True charity is one of the most sublime teachings that God has given to the world. A complete fraternity should be established among the true disciples of God's doctrine. You must love the wretched and the criminals like children of God, to whom forgiveness and mercy will be granted if they repent, as yourself, of the faults that they have committed against Its law. Remember that you are more reprehensible, more guilty than those to whom you refuse forgiveness and commiseration, because often they do not know God as you do, and it will be asked less of them than of you.

Do not judge, I say, do not judge anyone, dear friends, for the judgment which you pass will be applied to you still more severely, and you need indulgence for the sins which you incessantly commit! Do you not know that there are many actions which are crimes in the eyes of the God of purity, and which the world does not even consider to be slight faults?

True charity does not consist only in giving alms, nor even in the words of consolation which you may add to them. No, this is not just what God requires of you. The sublime charity taught by Jesus also consists in constant benevolence in all things given to neighbor. You can still exercise this sublime virtue upon many beings that need no alms, and those whom words of love, comfort and encouragement will bring to the Lord.

Times are near when, I say again, the great human fraternity will reign on this globe, and the law of Christ will govern human beings: it alone will be the restraint and hope that will lead souls to blissful realms. You should love one another as children of the same parent; do not differentiate between yourselves and those who are wretched, for it is God that wants us all to be equal. Do not despise anyone; God allows inveterate criminals to be among you, so that they may be a lesson to you. Soon, when humans are brought to the true laws of God, there will no longer be any need for such lessons, and *all unclean and rebellious spirits will be scattered in lower-order worlds that are attuned to their tendencies.*

You owe those who I mentioned the aid of your prayers: this is true charity. We must not say of a criminal: "He/she is a wretch; the Earth must be purged; death inflicted on them is too bland a punishment for beings of this kind." No, you should not speak like this. Look at your role model, Jesus; what would he say if he saw this wretched person near him? He would pity him; he would consider him/her as a very miserable patient; he would reach out to this person. Although you cannot do it in reality, at least you can pray for them, assist their spirits during the few moments that they still have to spend on Earth. Repentance can touch their hearts if you pray with faith. They are also your neighbors, as much as the best of your fellow beings. Their lost and rebellious souls have been created, just like yours, to perfect themselves; help them get out of the quagmire and pray for them.

Elizabeth of France[41] (Le Havre, 1863).

SHOULD ONE ENDANGER ONE'S LIFE FOR A CRIMINAL?

15. *Suppose someone is in danger of death; to save him/her, you will have to endanger your life; however you know that this person is a criminal, and that if he/she escapes, he/she will be able to commit new crimes. Should you, despite of this, endanger yourself to save this person?*

This is a very serious question which can naturally occur to anyone. I will answer according to my moral advancement, since we have already reached a point where we can know whether one should endanger one's own life even for a criminal. Devotion should be

---

41 [Trans. note] Elisabeth of France (1602–1644), also known as Isabel of Bourbon, was Queen Consort of Spain and Portugal.

blind: if you rescue an enemy, then you have to rescue an enemy of society as well, in a nutshell, a criminal. Do you believe that it is only at death that one should strive to rescue this wretched person? Maybe it should be throughout his/her whole past life. Because – think about it – during these fleeting moments in which the last minutes of this person's life flash before him/her, the lost soul looks back at its past lifetime, or rather, the latter stands before him/her. Death, perhaps, arrives too early for such a person; reincarnation can be terrible. So get started, humans! You that have been enlightened by Spiritist science; rush forward, rescue this person from his/her damnation, and then, perhaps, this individual who would have died while blaspheming, will throw himself/herself into your arms. However, you should not ask yourself if this person will or not do it; just go to this person's rescue regardless, because by saving him/her, you will follow this voice in your heart which tells you: "If you can save someone, save him/her!"

Lamennais[42] (Paris, 1862).

---

42 [Trans. note] Félicité Lamennais (1782–1854), French priest and philosophical and political writer.

Chapter XII
Love your enemies

RENDER GOOD FOR EVIL · DISCARNATE ENEMIES · IF ANYONE SLAPS YOU ON THE
RIGHT CHEEK, TURN TO HIM THE OTHER ALSO · *INSTRUCTIONS FROM THE SPIRITS:*
REVENGE · HATE · DUELS

RENDER GOOD FOR EVIL

1.   "You have heard that it was said, 'You shall love your neighbor and hate your enemy.' But I say to you, *Love your enemies and pray for those who persecute you*, so that you may be sons of your Father who is in heaven. For he makes his sun rise on the evil and on the good, and sends rain on the just and on the unjust. For if you love those who love you, what reward do you have? Do not even the tax collectors do the same? And if you greet only your brothers, what more are you doing than others? Do not even the Gentiles do the same? — For I tell you, unless your righteousness exceeds that of the scribes and Pharisees, you will never enter the kingdom of heaven (MATTHEW 5:20,43–47 ESV)."

2.   "'If you love those who love you, what benefit is that to you? For even sinners love those who love them. And if you do good to those who do good to you, what benefit is that to you? For even sinners do the same. And if you lend to those from whom you expect to receive, what credit is that to you? Even sinners lend to sinners, to get back the same amount. But *love your enemies, and do good, and lend, expecting nothing in return*, and your reward will be great, and you will be sons of the Most High, for he is kind to the ungrateful and the evil. Be merciful, even as your Father is merciful' (LUKE 6:32–36 ESV)."

3.   If love of neighbor is the principle of charity, loving one's enemies is its sublime application, for this virtue is one of the greatest victories won over selfishness and pride.

However, people generally misunderstand the meaning of *to love* in such circumstances; Jesus did not mean by this word that one must have toward one's enemy the tenderness that one feels for a sibling or friend. Tenderness presupposes confidence; now, we cannot possibly trust someone that we know for a fact wants to harm us; one cannot have outpourings of friendship for the latter, because one knows such a person is capable of abusing it. Between people who distrust each other, there cannot be the outbursts of affection and affinity that exist between those who are in communion of thoughts. Lastly, one cannot possibly have the same pleasure in being with an enemy as with a friend.

This very sentiment results from a physical law, namely, the one that governs the assimilation and repulsion of fluids. A malicious thought directs a fluid current whose impression is painful, whereas a benevolent thought envelops you in a pleasant fragrance – hence the difference in sensations one experiences when approaching a friend or an enemy. Therefore to love one's enemies cannot mean that one should not make any difference between those latter and one's friends. This precept may seem difficult, even impossible to practice, only to those who falsely believe that it prescribes to grant enemies the same place in one's heart. If the poverty of human language makes it necessary to use the same word to express various shades of feelings, reason must make up for such nuances depending on the case.

To love one's enemies is therefore not to have an affection for them, which is not in nature, for the contact of an enemy makes the heart beat in a very different way than that of a friend. It is rather to have neither hatred nor grudge, nor desire for revenge against them. It is to forgive them *without ulterior motive or precondition* the harm they may have done to us. It is to bring no obstacle to reconciliation, and to wish them good instead of wishing them evil. It is to rejoice instead of grieving in all the good that happens to them, and to extend a helping hand to them in case of need. It is to abstain *in words and actions* from anything that might harm them. Lastly, it is to render them good for evil, *without intention to humiliate them*. Whoever does this fulfills the conditions of God's command: Love your enemies.

4. To love your enemies is nonsense for unbelievers. Those for whom current life is all there is, see in one's enemy only a harmful being disturbing one's peace, and of whom death alone can rid oneself – hence the desire for revenge. The unbeliever has no interest in forgiving, except to satisfy his/her own pride in the eyes of the world. In certain cases, forgiveness even seems to be a weakness unworthy of oneself. If such a person does not take revenge, he/she will nevertheless retain a grudge and a secret desire for something evil to happen.

Conversely, for believers, but especially for Spiritists, the way of seeing it is quite different, because they look at the past and at the future, between which current life is only a point. They know that, by the very destination of the Earth, one must expect to find wicked and perverse persons there, and that the wickedness to which one is exposed is part of the trials one must undergo. Also that the higher point of view on which one may stand makes the vicissitudes of life less bitter, whether they come from humans or things, if one does not grumble against one's trials. *One should not grumble against those who are instruments of such trials.* If, instead of complaining, one thanks God for testing oneself, *one must thank the hand that gives oneself the opportunity to demonstrate one's patience and resignation.* This thought naturally gives a disposition to be forgiving. One also feels that the more generous one is, the more one grows in one's own eyes and finds oneself beyond the reach of the malicious traits of enemies.

Those who occupy a high rank in the world do not believe that they can be offended by insults of those whom they regard as their inferiors. So it is with those who rise in the moral world above material humankind: they understand that hatred and resentment would only demean and lower them. However, to be superior to one's adversary, one must have a greater, more noble, and more generous soul.

DISCARNATE ENEMIES

5.   Spiritists have still other reasons to exercise indulgence toward their enemies. First of all, they know that wickedness is not humans' permanent state; that it is due to a momentary imperfection, and that, just as children correct themselves for their faults, the wicked will one day admit their wrongs and become good.

Besides, they know that death only delivers them from the physical presence of their enemies, but that the latter can pursue them with their hatred, even after having left Earth. Thus any revenge misses its goal, which, on the contrary, has the effect of producing an even greater aggravation which can continue from one existence to another. It was up to Spiritism to prove, by experience and the law which governs the relations between the visible world and the invisible world, that the expression, *To quench hatred with blood*, is radically false; and that what is true, is that blood keeps hatred alive even beyond the grave. Consequently, this gives forgiveness an effective reason for being and a practical utility, in the sublime maxim of Christ: *Love your enemies*. There is no heart so perverse that it is not touched by good actions, even despite of itself. Through good actions, we at least remove any pretext for reprisals by an enemy, and we can make a friend before and after death. Through bad actions we irritate our enemies, *and it is then that they themselves serve as instruments of God's justice to punish the one who has not forgiven.*

6. We can therefore have enemies both among the incarnate and among the discarnate; the enemies of the invisible world manifest their malevolence through the spirit obsessions and subjugations to which so many people are exposed, and which are a modality of life trials. Such tests, like others, aid in our advancement and must be accepted with resignation, as a consequence of the inferior nature of the earthly globe. If there were no evil individuals on Earth, there would be no evil spirits roaming around the Earth. Therefore if one must have indulgence and kindness toward incarnate enemies, one must also have them toward those who are discarnate.

In the past, bloody victims were sacrificed to appease the infernal gods, who were none other than the evil spirits. The infernal gods have been succeeded by so-called demons, which are the same thing. Spiritism has come to prove that these demons are none other than the souls of perverse individuals who have not yet stripped off material instincts; that *one appeases them only by the sacrifice of one's hatred, that is to say, by charity* – and that charity has the effect not only of preventing them from doing evil, but of bringing them back onto the path of good, and of contributing to their own salvation. This is how the maxim, *Love your enemies*, is not limited to the narrow circle of the Earth and of current life, but fits into the great law of universal solidarity and fraternal love.

If anyone slaps you on the right cheek, turn to him the other also

7. "You have heard that it was said, 'An eye for an eye and a tooth for a tooth.' But I say to you, Do not resist the one who is evil. But *if anyone slaps you on the right cheek, turn to him the other also.* And if anyone would sue you and take your tunic, let him have your cloak as well. And if anyone forces you to go one mile, go with him two miles. Give to the one who begs from you, and do not refuse the one who would borrow from you. (Matthew 5:38–42 esv)."

8. The prejudices of the world, which we have agreed to call a point of honor, give them a shady susceptibility, born of pride and the exaltation of personality, which leads humans to render insult for insult, injury for injury, and that seems justice for one whose moral sense has not risen above earthly passions. This is why the Mosaic law said: an eye for an eye, a tooth for a tooth – a law which was in harmony with the time when Moses lived. Then Christ came, saying, *Render good for evil.* He also said: "Do not resist the one who is evil. *But if anyone slaps you on the right cheek, turn to him the other also.*" To the proud, this maxim sounds like cowardice, because they do not understand that there is more courage in bearing an insult than in taking revenge; and that always because one does not wish it to be carried beyond current time. Should we, however, take this maxim to the letter? No, no more than the one that says to pluck out your eye, if it is cause of scandal to you. Pushed to its ultimate consequences, it would condemn any repression, even when rightful and legal, thus leaving the field free to wicked individuals by taking away all fear from them. If their aggressions were not curbed, soon all good persons would be their victims. The very instinct for self-preservation, which is a law of Nature, says that an assassin's neck should not be stretched out on a voluntary basis. With those words Jesus therefore did not forbid defense, but rather condemned revenge. By saying to turn the other cheek to the aggressor when the right cheek has been struck, he meant to say, in another form, that no one should render evil for evil; that humans should humbly accept all that tends to lower their pride; that it is more glorious for one to be struck than to strike, and to patiently endure an injustice than to commit one oneself; and that it is better to be deceived than to be deceitful, to be ruined than to ruin others. It is at the same time the condemnation of the duel,[43] which is nothing other than a manifestation of pride. Faith in future life and in the justice of God, which never leaves evil unpunished, can alone give the strength to bear patiently any attacks on our interests and our self-esteem. This is why I keep saying: Look forward; the higher you rise in thought above material life, the less you will be offended by the things of the Earth.

INSTRUCTIONS FROM THE SPIRITS

REVENGE

9.   Revenge is one of the last remnants of barbaric customs which tend to disappear from the midst of humans. It is, like the duel, one of the surviving traces of savage customs under which humanity struggled in the beginning of the Christian era. This is why revenge is a sure indication of the backward stage of people who engage in it, and also of the spirits who can still inspire it. Therefore, my friends, this sentiment should never be harbored in the heart of anyone claiming to be a Spiritist. As you know, revenge is so contrary to Christ's precept, "Forgive your enemies," that whoever refuses to forgive is not only not a Spiritist, but not even a Christian. Revenge is all the more nefarious as an inspiration because it is frequently accompanied by falsehood and baseness. In fact, one who abandons oneself to such a nefarious and blind passion, almost never acts in the open when taking revenge. When he/she happens to be the strongest, he/she hardly ever falls on the one they call their enemy like a wild beast, at the sight of the former who ignites their passion, anger and hatred. Instead, they most often take on a hypocritical appearance, hiding in the deepest of their hearts the evil feelings that animate them. They employ devious subterfuges, following in the shadows their unsuspecting enemy, waiting for the right moment to strike the latter without any risk for themselves. They hide from their enemy while constantly spying on him/her. They set up heinous traps for their enemy, occasionally pouring some poison into the latter's cup.

---

43   [Trans. note] Despite being outlawed by then, when this book was written in the 19th century, and even later on, a duel was a prearranged fight with deadly weapons by two people in order to settle a quarrel over a point of honor.

When their hatred does not reach such extremes, they attack the enemy in his or her honor and affections. They do not shrink from calumny, and their treacherous innuendos, skillfully scattered to all winds, increase as they go along. Also, when the one they pursue presents himself/herself in circles where their venom has penetrated, such person is surprised to find cold countenances where he/she once met friendly and benevolent faces. He is amazed when the hands of those he/she seeks now refuse to shake his or hers. Finally this person is annihilated when his or her nearest and dearest turn and run away. Ah, the coward who takes revenge in this fashion is a hundred times guiltier than the one who goes straight to his/her enemy and openly insults the latter to their faces!

Away then with these savage customs! Let us abandon these customs from another era! Any Spiritist who today claims to still have the right to take revenge would no longer be worthy of joining the phalanx that took as its motto, *Without charity there is no salvation!* Yet no, I cannot accept the idea that a member of the great Spiritist family would ever give in to the impulse of revenge, instead of forgiving neighbor .

Jules Olivier[44] (Paris, 1862).

HATRED

10. Love one another, and you will be happy. Above all, take it upon yourself to love those who inspire you with indifference, hatred and contempt. Christ, whom you should take as your model, has given you the example of this revelation. As a missionary of love, he loved to the point of offering and giving his blood and his life. The self-sacrifice that forces you to love those who insult and persecute you is painful; but this is precisely what makes you superior to them. If you hate them as they hate you, you are no better than they are. It is a spotless offering that you should present to God on the altar of your heart, an offering of pleasant fragrance, the scents of which rise up to It. Although the law of love requires that we love all our brothers and sisters without distinction, it does not shield one's heart against bad actions; on the contrary, this is the most painful test of all – I should know, since during my last earthly existence, I

---

44 [Trans. note] The name Jules Olivier was relatively common in France, preventing this spirit's identity to be positively established today.

experienced this torture. But God is there, and It punishes in this life and in the next those who fail the law of love. Remember, my children, that love brings God closer, yet hatred draws It away.

Fénelon (Bordeaux, 1862).

DUELS

11. Truly great are only those who, considering life as a journey that must lead one to a goal, takes little notice of the roughness of the way. Such individuals never let themselves be diverted from the right path even for an instant; with their eyes constantly directed toward the final destination, it matters little to them that the brambles and thorns of the path threaten to scratch them – such obstacles only touch without reaching them, who continue their course regardless. To waste one's days taking revenge for an insult is to back away from the trials of life. This is always a crime in the eyes of God, and if you were not so misled by your prejudices, it would be ridiculous and a supreme folly in the eyes of fellow human beings.

There is crime in homicide by dueling – even your legislation recognizes it. No one has the right, whatever the case, to attempt against the life of fellow humans – a crime in the eyes of God which charted the right course of action for you. Here, more than anywhere else, you are judges in your own cause. Remember that you will be forgiven according to whether you yourselves have forgiven. Through forgiveness you approach Divinity, for mercy should be coupled with power. As long as a drop of human blood flows on Earth by the hand of humans, the true reign of God will not yet have arrived, this reign of conciliation and love which must forever banish animosity, discord and war from your globe. Then the word duel will no longer exist in your language except as a distant and vague souvenir of a past which is no more. Humans will experience no other antagonism among themselves than the noble rivalry of good.

Adolphe, bishop of Algiers (Marmande, France, 1861).

12. There is no doubt that a duel[45] can be, in certain cases, proof of physical courage, of disregard for life; but also undoubtedly, it bears proof of moral cowardice, as in suicide. A person who commits suicide lacks courage to face the vicissitudes of life, whereas

---

45 [Trans. note] See footnote 43 above.

the duelist does not have the courage to face offenses. Did Christ not tell you that there is more honor and courage in offering the left cheek to the one who has struck your right cheek, than to take revenge for an insult? Did not Christ say to Peter in the Garden of Olives, "Put your sword back into its place, for all who take the sword will perish by the sword"? With these words, has Jesus not condemned duels forever? Indeed, my children, what is this courage born of a violent, bloody and angry temper roaring at the first sign of offense? Where then is the greatness of soul of one who, at the slightest insult, wants to wash it in blood? Yet let such individuals tremble, because always, at the bottom of their conscience, a voice will cry to them: "Cain, Cain! what have you done of your brother?" To which they will answer, "I shed his blood to save my honor"; but the Lord will then answer to them: "You wanted to save your honor before humans for a few moments that you had left to live on Earth, but you did not think of saving it before God! You poor fool! How much blood would Christ ask of you for all the outrages he received! Not only did you hurt Jesus with the thorn and the spear, not only did you nail him to an infamous piece of wood, but also in the middle of his agony, one could hear the taunts that were lavished on him. What reparation, after so many outrages, did he ask of you? The last cry of the lamb was a prayer for its executioners. Ah, like him, do forgive and pray for those who have offended you!

Dear friends, remember this precept: "Love one another," and then to every blow of hatred you will respond with a smile, and to outrage with forgiveness. The world will no doubt rise up furiously and call you a coward; yet raise your head high, and then show that you are not afraid to also take thorns on your forehead, after the example of Christ, since your hand does not want to be an accomplice in a murder that is authorized, so to speak, by a false semblance of honor that is nothing but pride and self-esteem. In creating you, did God give you the right of life and death over one another? No, God only gave this right to Nature alone, to reform and rebuild; but to you, God does not even allow you to dispose of yourselves. Like the suicide, the duelist will be marked with blood when he/she arrives in God's presence – and to both, the Sovereign Judge has prepared harsh and long punishments. If the Lord has threatened with Its justice anyone who insults their fellow humans by calling them *raca*[46] ("insane"), how much more severe will the punishment be for those who appear before It with their hands reddened in their fellow humans' blood!

St. Augustine (Paris, 1862).

13. The duel is, as in the past what used to be called God's judgment, one of those barbaric institutions which still govern society. What would you say, however, if you saw the two antagonists plunge into boiling water or subjected to the contact of a hot iron to end their quarrel, and give reason to the one who would best undergo the test? You would regard these customs as totally insane. The duel is even worse than all this. For an emeritus duelist, it is an assassination committed in cold blood with intended premeditation, since the duelist is sure of the blow he/she would strike for the adversary almost certainly to succumb because of weakness or inability: a suicide committed with the coldest calculation. I know that we often try to avoid this equally criminal alternative by relying on chance; but then is it not another form of devolving judgment to God as conceived by the Middle Ages? And yet, at that epoch, we were infinitely less guilty. The very expression *God's judgment* indicates faith – naive, it is true, but still faith in the justice of God which could not allow an innocent to succumb, whereas in a duel we rely on brute force, so that it is often the offended party who succumbs.

O stupid self-esteem, you foolish vanity, you foolish pride, when will you be replaced by Christian charity, love of neighbor and humility of which Christ gave the example and left us the precept? Only then those monstrous prejudices which still govern humans – and which the laws are powerless to repress – will vanish; because it is not enough to prohibit evil and to prescribe good, it is necessary that the principle of good and a revulsion for evil become deeply embedded in human hearts.

A protector spirit (Bordeaux, 1861).

14. What opinion will people have of me – you often ask – if I refuse the reparation which is asked of me, or if I do not ask for one from the one who offended me? Mad people and backward individuals like you will certainly blame you; yet those who are

---

46 [Trans. note] See footnote 32 above.

enlightened by the torch of intellectual and moral progress will say that you are acting according to true wisdom. Just think a little: for a word often said on the part of one of your fellow human beings thoughtlessly or quite harmlessly, your pride gets hurt, and then you react to it in a sharp way, hence provoking animosity. Before reaching the decisive moment, ask yourself if you are acting as a Christian – what account will you owe to society if you deprive it of one of its members? Do you think of the remorse of having taken from a woman her companion, from a mother her child, from children their parent and support? Certainly whoever made the offense owes some reparation; but would it not be more honorable for one to give it spontaneously while acknowledging one's wrongs, than to expose the life of the one who has a right to complain? As for the offended, I agree that sometimes we can be seriously affected, either in our person, or in relation to our nearest and dearest. Then self-esteem is no longer just an issue, our heart is injured, it suffers. But apart from the fact that it is stupid to thwart one's life against a capable wretch, for an infamy, does the latter, once dead, the affront, whatever it is, cease to exist? Does not shed blood give more notoriety to a fact which, if it is false, would fade away by itself; and which, if it is true, should be kept in silence? Therefore, all that remains is the satisfaction of satisfied revenge; alas, a sad satisfaction which often leaves bitter regrets from this life. And if it is the offended that succumbs, where is the reparation?

When charity becomes the rule of conduct for humankind, they will conform their actions and their words to this maxim: "Do not do to others what you would not want done to you." Will all causes for dissension then disappear, and with them those of duels and wars, which are duels of nation against nation.

François-Xavier[47] (Bordeaux, 1861).

15. If a worldly person, a happy individual, who, because of a hurtful word, a slight motive, plays with their life which he/she owes to God, is also playing with the life of his/her fellow beings – which belongs only to God – this person is a hundred times guiltier than a wretch who, driven by greed, sometimes by need, enters a home to steal coveted goods, and kills those who oppose their purpose.

---

47 [Trans. note] Most probably Marie-François-Xavier Bichat (1771–1802), a French anatomist and physiologist.

The latter is almost always an uneducated person, having only imperfect notions of good and evil, while the duelist almost always belongs to the most enlightened social classes. One kills brutally, whereas the other does it methodically and politely, which makes society excuse him/her. I would even add that the duelist is infinitely more guilty than the wretch who, yielding to a feeling of revenge, kills in a moment of exasperation. A duelist has no excuse for being overthrown by passion, because between insult and reparation there is always time for one to think. A duelist therefore acts coldly and deliberately; everything is calculated and studied to more surely kill the opponent. It is true that the duelist also endangers his/her own life; and this is what rehabilitates the duel in the eyes of the world because we see in it an act of courage and no fear of losing one's own life. Yet is there real courage when you are so sure of yourself? The duel, a leftover from the times of barbarism when the right of the strongest was the law, will disappear with a healthier appreciation of what the true point of honor is, and as humans come to possess a more lively faith in future life.

St. Augustine (Bordeaux, 1861).

16. **Note:** Duels are becoming less and less frequent, and if we still witness some painful occurrences from time to time, their number is not comparable to what it used to be. Formerly one would not leave one's home without predicting a duel, so one always took precautions accordingly. A characteristic sign of the customs of a people and times, and of their habits is to be found in the use, whether visibly or hidden, of offensive and defensive weapons. The abolition of such use testifies to the softening of manners, and it is curious to follow its gradation from the time when the knights never rode without wearing armors and carrying a lance, until they started to sport of a simple sword, which has become more like an ornament and an accessory of a coat of arms than an aggressive weapon. Another trait of manners is that once person-to-person combats took place in the street, in front of the crowd which moved away to leave the field free, whereas today we hide. Nowadays the death of a person is regarded as an event, we are moved by it; whereas, in the past we would not pay attention to it. Spiritism will take away these last vestiges of barbarism, by instilling in humans a feeling of charity and fraternity.

Chapter XIII
Do not let your left hand know
what your right hand is doing

DOING GOOD WITHOUT OSTENTATION

1. "'Beware of practicing your righteousness before other people in order to be seen by them, for then you will have no reward from your Father who is in heaven. Thus, when you give to the needy, sound no trumpet before you, as the hypocrites do in the synagogues and in the streets, that they may be praised by others. Truly, I say to you, they have received their reward. But *when you give to the needy, do not let your left hand know what your right hand is doing*, so that your giving may be in secret. And your Father who sees in secret will reward you' (MATTHEW 6:1–4 ESV)."

2. "When he came down from the mountain, great crowds followed him. And behold, a leper came to him and knelt before him, saying, 'Lord, if you will, you can make me clean.' And Jesus stretched out his hand and touched him, saying, 'I will; be clean.' And immediately his leprosy was cleansed. And Jesus said to him, '*See that you say nothing to anyone*, but go, show yourself to the priest and offer the gift that Moses commanded, for a proof to them' (MATTHEW 8:1–4 ESV)."

3. Doing good without ostentation is a great merit. Hiding the hand that gives is even more meritorious; it is an indisputable sign of great moral superiority: because in order to see things higher than most people, it is necessary to disregard current life and to identify with future life. In short, it is necessary to place oneself above humanity to renounce any satisfaction obtained through the testimony of fellow humans and instead wait for God's approval. Whoever holds the judgment of humans above that of God, proves to has more faith in human beings than in God, and that current life means more to him/her than future life – or even that he/she does not believe in future life. Therefore, if preaching the opposite, such a person does not seem to believe in his/her own words.

How many there are who give to others only in hopes that the recipient will shout from the rooftops the benefit thus received; and who will give a large sum in broad daylight, but in the shadows would not give a single penny! This is why Jesus said that those who do good with ostentation have already received their reward. Indeed, whoever seek their own glorification on Earth by the good they do, have already rewarded themselves. God no longer owes them anything; there remains to them only to receive punishments for their pride.

Do not let your left hand know what your right hand is doing is a figure of speech which admirably characterizes acts of beneficence without ostentation. However, if on one side there is genuine lack of ostentation, on the other there can also be a feigned lack of ostentation, a simulated self-effacement. Such people hide the hand that gives, while taking care to let a bit out for being traced, then watch if someone sees it hiding there – what an unworthy parody of the maxims of Christ! If benefactors full of pride are despised by their own fellow beings, think how God will regard them! These too have already received their reward on Earth. We know them; they are self-satisfied for having been noticed: that is all they will get.

What will be the reward of benefactors who weigh heavily on the recipients of their benefits, in a way imposing testimonies of gratitude on the latter and making them feel their position in society by extolling the cost of the sacrifices that they had to impose on themselves in order to aid the needy? Ah, this sort of benefactor will not even have an earthly reward, for he/she will be deprived of the sweet satisfaction of hearing bless his/her name – and this is the first punishment for their pride. Instead of going up to heaven, the tears they dried up at the cost of their vanity will fall on the hearts of the afflicted, harming them. Any good they do will bring no profit to themselves, since they reproach it; because a benefit reproached is like adulterated and worthless currency.

To give without ostentation has a double merit: in addition to being material charity, there is moral charity. It spares the sensitivity of the recipient; it makes him/her accept the benefit without hurting their self-esteem. Also, by safeguarding their human dignity, people who would not receive alms, will accept a service. Now, to convert a service into alms – because of the way it is rendered – is to humiliate the one who receives it, and there is always pride and nastiness in humiliating someone. True charity, on the contrary, is delicate and ingenious in concealing a benefit so as to avoid to the least suspicion of giving alms, for any moral vexation would add to the suffering that arises from need. True charity knows how to find gentle and affable words which put the recipients at ease in front of the benefactor, whereas proud charity crushes them. The sublimity of true generosity is when the benefactor, by changing roles, finds a way of appearing to be the recipient to the one to whom he/she is rendering a service. This is what these words mean: Do not let your left hand know what your right hand is doing.

HIDDEN MISFORTUNES

4. In great calamities, charity is moved, and we see generous impulses to repair disasters; but, alongside these general disasters, there are thousands of private disasters that go unnoticed, people who lie on a pallet without complaining. It is these discreet and hidden misfortunes that true generosity knows how to find out without waiting for them to come and ask for assistance.

Who is that woman with a distinguished look, a simple yet neat appearance, followed by a girl dressed so modestly? She enters a sordid-looking house where she is probably known, because at the door she is greeted with respect. Where is she going? Up to the attic where lies a mother surrounded by small children. On her arrival joy shines on those emaciated faces, for she comes to calm all these pains. She brings them whatever is necessary seasoned with sweet and consoling words which make them accept the benefit without blushing, because these unfortunate people are not beggars by profession – the father is in hospital, and during this time the mother cannot meet the family's needs. Thanks to the benefactor, these poor children will not endure cold or hunger; they will go to school warmly dressed, and the mother's breast will not dry up for the little ones. If one of them is sick among them, no material care will cause repugnance on her part. From there, she goes to the hospital to bring the family's father some respite and to reassure him about the fate of his family. At the corner of the street, a carriage awaits her, a veritable store of everything she carries to her protégés, whom she visits successively. She does not inquire about their beliefs or opinions, since all human beings are brothers and sisters, and children of God. Once her errand is finished, she says to herself: I started my day very well. What is her name? Where does she live? Nobody knows. To the unfortunate her name would mean nothing; yet she is the angel of consolation; and, in the evening, a concert of blessings rises on her behalf toward the Creator: Catholics, Jews, Protestants, all bless her in unison.

Why is she dressed with such simplicity? Because she does not want to insult poverty with luxury. Why is she being accompanied by her young daughter? To teach her how one should practice charity. Her daughter also wants to practice charity, but her mother tells her; "What can you give, my child, since you have nothing of your own? If I give you something to pass it on to others, what merit will you have? It would still be me doing all the charity while you would take the merit – and that would not be fair. When we go visit the sick, you will help me care for them. Now, giving care is giving something. Doesn't that seem enough to you? Nothing could be simpler. Learn crafts such as sewing and knitting, and you will be able to make clothes for those small children; in this way you will give something coming from yourself." This is how this truly Christian mother trains her daughter to practice the virtues taught by Christ. Is she a Spiritist? Well, what does it matter!

In her private life, she is a lady, a society woman, because her position demands it. But we do not know what she owns, because she wants no other approval than that of God and her conscience. One day, however, an unforeseen circumstance brought one of her protégés to her home, selling some needlework. When the latter recognized her, she wanted to bless her benefactress: "Shush," she promptly said to the person, *"don't tell anyone."* Jesus also spoke in the same way.

THE WIDOW'S MITE

5. "And he sat down opposite the treasury and watched the people putting money into the offering box. Many rich people put in large sums. And a poor widow came and put in two small copper coins, which make a penny. And he called his disciples to him and said to them, 'Truly, I say to you, this poor widow has put in more than all those who are contributing to the offering box. For they all contributed out of their abundance, but she out of her poverty has put in everything she had, all she had to live on' (MARK 12:41–44; cf. LUKE 21:1–4 ESV)."

6. Many people regret not being able to do as much good as they would like, for want of sufficient resources; and if they desire wealth, it is, they say, to make good use of it. Their intention is laudable, no doubt; and may be very sincere in a few; but is it certain that they are completely disinterested when claiming it? Are there not some who, while wishing to do good to others, would actually be glad to begin by doing it to themselves, to give themselves a few more enjoyments, to procure a few of the inessentials they lack, except to give the rest to the poor? Such an ulterior motive, which they perhaps hide, but which they would find deep inside their hearts if they wanted to delve into it, cancels the merit of the good intention, because true charity thinks of others before thinking of itself. True sublimity of charity, in this case, would be in seeking to obtain through one's own work, and by the use of one's own strength, intelligence, and talents, the resources one may lack to accomplish one's generous intentions – this would be a more agreeable sacrifice to the Lord. Unfortunately most dream of easier ways to get rich all of a sudden and without difficulty, by running after chimeras, such as the discovery of buried treasures, a favorable random chance, the recovery of unexpected inheritances, etc. What can be said of those who hope to find auxiliaries among the spirits to aid them in researches of this nature? Surely they do not know or understand the sacred aim of Spiritism, and even less the mission of the spirits, which God allows to communicate with humans. Therefore they will be sorely disappointed (see Allan KARDEC, *The Mediums' Book*, items no. 294–295).

Those whose intention is pure, free of any personal interest, should comfort themselves for their powerlessness to do as much good as they would, by the thought that a poor person's small coin, who gives it by depriving himself/herself of essentials, weighs more in the scales of God than large amounts given by the rich who give without depriving themselves of anything. Our satisfaction would no doubt be great if we could largely help the needy; but if this is beyond your means, you must submit to reality and limit yourself to doing what you can. Besides, it is not only with gold that we can dry up tears, and we should not remain inactive because we do not possess it. Those who sincerely want to make themselves useful to their brothers and sisters will find a thousand opportunities to do so. Seek and you will find them; if not in one way, in another, for there is no one who, with the free enjoyment of one's faculties, cannot render any service, give comfort, alleviate physical or moral suffering, or make something useful to others. If one lacks money, does he/she not still have their labor, their time or their leisure to share with someone? There too lies the poor person's coin, the widow's mite.

INVITE THE POOR AND THE DISABLED

7. "He said also to the man who had invited him, 'When you give a dinner or a banquet, do not invite your friends or your brothers or your relatives or rich neighbors, lest they also invite you in return and you be repaid. But when you give a feast, invite the poor, the crippled, the lame, the blind, and you will be blessed, because they cannot repay you. For you will be repaid at the resurrection of the just.'

When one of those who reclined at table with him heard these things, he said to him, 'Blessed is everyone who will eat bread in the kingdom of God!' (Luke 14:12–15 esv)"

8. "When you give a feast," says Jesus, "do not invite your friends to it, but the poor and the crippled." These words, absurd if taken literally, are sublime in their inner meaning. Jesus could not have wanted to say that instead of one's friends, beggars on the street should be gathered at one's table – his language was almost always figurative, and for a people incapable of understanding the delicate nuances of thought, strong images were needed, producing the effect of sharp colors. The bottom of his thought is revealed in the following words: "You will be blessed, because they cannot repay you." This means that one should not do good expecting any return, but only for the pleasure of doing it. To make a striking comparison, he says: "Invite the poor, the crippled, the lame, the blind, and you will be blessed, because they cannot repay you." By *feast* he does not mean the meal itself, but sharing in the abundance that you enjoy.

However, that word can also be applied in a more literal sense. How many people invite to their table only those who can, as they say, do them honor, or who can invite them back in their turn! Others, on the contrary, find satisfaction in receiving those of their relatives or friends that are less fortunate – but who does not have at least one of these among his/her own? Sometimes this is doing them a great service without seeming to take notice of it. Those, without going as far as recruiting the blind and the disabled, are practicing Jesus' maxim, if they do it out of benevolence and without ostentation, knowing how to use sincere cordiality as they discreetly confer a benefit on someone.

INSTRUCTIONS FROM THE SPIRITS

MATERIAL AND MORAL CHARITY

9. "Love one another and do unto others as you would have them do unto you." All religion, all morality are contained in these two precepts. If they were followed here below, you all would be perfect: No more hatred, no more dissension and, I would say, even no more poverty, because from the surplus of each rich person's table, many poor people would be fed, and you would no longer see, in the gloomy districts in which I lived during my last incarnation, poor women dragging after them miserable children lacking everything.

You, rich ones, think about it! Help the poor as best you can. Give, so that God may give you back the good you have done, and so that you will find, after leaving your terrestrial envelope, a procession of grateful spirits that will receive you at the threshold of a happier world.

If you knew the joy I felt when I met up there with those I had been able to help during my last incarnation! ...

Therefore love your neighbor; love him/her as yourself, for you know them now, but this unfortunate person whom you reject was perhaps a sibling, a parent, a friend whom you turn away far from you; and then think what your despair will be upon recognizing this individual in the spirit world!

I hope that you understand well what *moral charity* can be, that which anyone can practice; that which *costs nothing* materially, and yet that which is most difficult to put into practice.

Moral charity is about supporting one another, which you scarcely do in this world where you are incarnated for a while. There is great merit, believe me, in knowing when to keep silent in order to let someone more foolish than yourself speak; and this again is a form of charity. Knowing how to play deaf when a mocking word escapes from a mouth used to make fun of others; and pretend not to notice the disdainful smile with which you are greeted by people who, often wrongly, believe themselves above you, but who in spirit life – which is *the only real one* – are sometimes quite beneath you. This has merit, not of humility, but of charity, because avoiding to take notice of other people's wrongs is moral charity.

However, this sort of charity should not prevent the other one. Above all, remember not to despise your fellow humans; remember all that I have already said to you: You must constantly remember that, in the poor rebel, you may be repelling a spirit that once was dear to you, and now is momentarily in a position inferior to yours. I met one of the poor in your land again, whom I had, luckily, been able to oblige sometimes, and from whom now it is my turn to implore.

Remember that Jesus said we are brothers and sisters, and always bear this in mind before pushing away the sick or the beggar. Farewell; think of those who suffer, and pray.

Sister Rosalie (Paris, 1860).

10.   Dear friends, I have heard many of you say to themselves: How can I do charity if often I lack the essentials of life myself!

Charity, dear friends, can be done in many ways. You can do charity in thoughts, words and actions. In thoughts, by praying for the poor outcasts who died without being able to see the light – a prayer from the heart relieves them. In words, by expressing some good views to your everyday companions in life – tell to those embittered by despair and hardship, and who blaspheme the name of the Most High: "I was like you – I suffered, I was unhappy – but I believed in Spiritism, and look at me: I am happy now." To old persons that may say to you: "This is useless; I am nearing the end of my life, and will die as I lived," tell them, "God's justice is equal for all; remember the workers of the tenth hour.[48] To very young people who, already tainted by their milieu, are going to be led astray, all too ready to succumb to bad temptations, tell them: "God can see you, dear young ones," and do not be afraid to often repeat these sweet words to them; they will end up taking root in their youthful minds – and instead of little rascals and layabouts, you will have made decent individuals of them. This is another form of charity.

Many of you will also say, "Bah! There are so many people on Earth, God cannot possibly see us all." Now, listen carefully, dear friends: When you are at the top of a mountain, does your gaze not encompass the billions of grains of sand that cover it? Well, then! This is how God sees you; It leaves you your free will, same as you let those grains of sand go with the wind that disperses them. Only, God, in Its infinite mercy, has placed deep inside your heart a vigilant sentinel called *conscience*. Listen to your conscience, it will only give you good advice. Sometimes you numb it by opposing the spirit of evil to it; then it is muted. But be sure that even the poor abandoned one will be heard as soon as you let it see a shade of remorse. Listen to it, query it, and often you will find comfort in the advice you receive from it.

Dear friends, to each new regiment the general presents a banner; as for me, I give you this maxim of Christ: "Love one another." Practice this maxim; rally all around this banner, and you will receive happiness and comfort.

A protector spirit (Lyon, 1860).

BENEFICENCE

11.   Beneficence, dear friends, will give you in this world the purest and sweetest pleasures, the joys of the heart which are disturbed neither by remorse nor by indifference. Ah, may you understand all that is great and sweet about the generosity of beautiful souls, this feeling that makes you look at others with the same eye that you look at yourself, that make you gladly take off your warm clothes to shelter your brother or sister. May you, dear friends, have no sweeter occupation than that of making other people happy! What feasts of the world can be compared to these joyous feasts of the

48 [Trans. note] *Cf.* Jesus' parable in MATTHEW 20:3–12.

heart, when, as representatives of the Divinity, you bring joy to these poor families who know only life's vicissitudes and bitterness; when you suddenly see these withered faces radiate with hope. For they had no bread, these unfortunates; and their little children, unaware that to live is to suffer, shouted, cried and repeated these words which sank like a sharp sword in the maternal heart: "I'm hungry!" ... Ah, understand how delicious are the impressions of one who sees joy be reborn where an instant before one could only find despair! Understand what your duties are toward your brothers and sisters! Go forward, ahead of misfortune; go especially to the aid of hidden miseries, because they are the most painful ones. Go forward, dearly beloved, and remember these words, as inferred by our Savior: "When you clothe one of these little ones, think that you are doing it to me!"

Charity! A sublime word which sums up all the virtues, it is you that will lead people to happiness. By practicing charity, they will create inner enjoyments for the future; and during their exile on Earth, it will be their comfort, the taste of the joys that they will experience later when they all unite together in the bosom of the God of love. It is you, Charity, divine virtue, that gave me the only moments of happiness that I tasted on Earth. May my incarnate brothers and sisters believe the voice of this friend who speaks to them, telling them: It is in charity that you must seek peace of heart, contentment of the soul, remedy for the afflictions of life. When you are about to accuse God, take a look beneath you and see that so many miseries remain to be relieved: poor children without families; a multitude old individuals lacking a friendly hand to help them and close their eyes when death approaches! So much good remains to be done! So do not complain but, on the contrary, thank God and lavish your sympathy, your love, your money with all your efforts, on those who, deprived of the goods of this world, languish in suffering and in isolation. Down here, you will thus gather very sweet joys, and later ... God only knows! ...

Adolphe, bishop of Algiers (Bordeaux, 1861).

12. Be good and charitable, it is the key to heaven which you hold in your hands; and all eternal happiness is contained in this maxim: Love one another. The soul can only rise to spiritual regions by devoting itself to neighbor; it finds happiness and comfort only in the impulses of charity. Therefore be good, support your brothers and sisters, leave aside the dreadful plague of selfishness. By fulfilling this duty you will certainly open the path to eternal happiness for yourselves. Besides, who among you has not felt the heart leap and inner joy expand on hearing the story of a beautiful devotion, of a truly charitable work? If you were only seeking for the pleasure that a good deed brings, you would always stay on the path of spiritual progress. You do not lack examples; only goodwill is scarce. See the crowd of good individuals whose devout memories are remembered by history.

Did Christ not tell you all that concerns the virtues of charity and love? Why do you leave aside these divine teachings? Why do you close your ears to his divine words and your hearts to his sweet maxims? I would like you to bring more interest, more faith, to the reading of the Gospel. We neglect this book, making hollow words of it, a closed letter. We allow this admirable moral code to get lost in oblivion: your ills come solely from the voluntary neglect of this summary of divine laws. So read these blazing pages of Jesus' devotion, and reflect upon them.

Strong individuals, gird yourselves up; but you, weak ones, arm yourselves with your gentleness and faith; have more persuasion, more constancy in the propagation of your new tenet. It is only an encouragement what we, spirits, have come to give you. It is only to stimulate your zeal and your virtues that God allows us to manifest ourselves to you. But if you really wanted to, you would only need the aid of God and your own will: Spiritist manifestations are only made for closed eyes and stubborn hearts.

Charity is the fundamental virtue which should support the whole edifice of earthly virtues; without it the others cannot exist. Without charity there is no hope for a better fate, no moral interest to guide us. Without charity there is no faith, for faith is only the pure ray which makes a charitable soul shine.

Charity is the eternal anchor of salvation on all worlds: it is the purest emanation of the Creator Itself; God's own virtue which It gives to all Its created beings. How would we wish to ignore this supreme goodness? What heart would be, with such thought, perverse enough to repress and drive away this divine feeling? What child would be evil enough to mutiny against this sweet caress called charity?

I dare not speak of what I have done in the past, for spirits should also keep modest and discrete about their deeds, but I believe that I have started one of those works which would contribute the most to the relief of our fellow human beings. I often see spirits asking for a mission to continue my task; I see them, sweet and dear daughters of charity, in their devout and divine ministry; I see them practicing the virtue that I recommend to you, with all the joy that comes from this existence of devotion and self-sacrifice; it gives me great pleasure to see how their character is honored, how much their mission is loved and gently protected. I ask all of you, right-minded people, of good and strong will, to unite in order to continue your great work of spreading charity. You will find the reward for this virtue through its very exercise; there is no spiritual joy that it cannot give since your current existence. Be united, love one another according to the Christ's precepts. So be it.

St. Vincent de Paul[49] (Paris, 1858).

13. I am called charity,[50] I am the main path that leads to God; follow me, for I am the goal that all of you should aim at achieving.

This morning I did my usual errands and, heartbroken, I have come to tell you: Ah, dear friends, how many miseries, how many tears I saw, and how much work you have to do to dry them all! I have vainly sought to comfort poor mothers; I whispered in their ears: Courage! There are good hearts watching over you that will not forsake you. Be patient for God is with you; you are loved, you are God's chosen ones. They seemed to hear me and turned their wide-open eyes to my side. I could read on their poor faces that their bodies, these tyrants of the spirit, were hungry, and that if my words comforted their hearts a little, they could not fill their stomachs. I kept repeating, Courage! Courage! Then a very young, poor mother nursing a small child, held the baby out in the empty space, as if to ask me to protect this poor little being who could only get insufficient nourishment from a sterile breast.

Elsewhere, dear friends, I have seen poor old men without work and soon without shelter, prey to all sufferings of hardship, and,

---

49 [Trans. note] Vincent de Paul (1581–1660), French Catholic priest at Ars who founded the Daughters of Charity of Saint Vincent de Paul, and devoted all his life to serving the poor.

50 [Translator note] This spirit calls itself Caritas, which means Charity.

ashamed of their misery, have never dared to beg, to go and implore pity from passers-by. With my heart moved with compassion, I who have nothing myself, have made myself a beggar for them, and will encourage charity everywhere, and inspire good thoughts in generous and compassionate hearts. This is why I have come to you, dear friends, telling you: There are unfortunate people out there whose huts are devoid of any food, their beds have no blankets, and there is no fire in their hearths. I would not pretend to tell you what to do – I leave the initiative to the kindness of your hearts. If I dictated to you the course of action to take, you would no longer have the merit of your good actions. I only say to you: I am charity, and I hold my hand out to you on behalf of your distressed brothers and sisters.

But if I ask, I also give, and give abundantly. I invite you to a big banquet, and I provide the tree where you all will be satiated. See how beautiful it is, how it is loaded with flowers and fruit! Go, pick all the fruits you can carry from this beautiful tree which is called charity. In place of the twigs you have taken, I will attach all the good deeds you will do, and then bring this tree back to God, so that It may load it with fruit again, because beneficence is inexhaustible. Follow me then, dear friends, so that I will count you among those enlisted under my banner. Fear not; I will lead you on the path of salvation, for I am *Charity*.

Caritas, martyrized in Rome (Lyon, 1860).

14. There are different ways to do charity that many of you mix up with alms; there is, however, a great difference. Alms, dear friends, are sometimes useful, because they relieve the poor; but it is almost always humiliating both for the one who gives and for those who receive them. Charity, on the contrary, binds the benefactor to the recipient, and can be disguised in so many ways! We can be charitable even toward our nearest and dearest, and our friends, by being indulgent to one another, and forgiving of our weaknesses; by taking care not to offend anyone's self-esteem. Also, when you Spiritists act in the way you do toward those who do not think like you; by bringing the less clear-sighted into believing, without attacking them, without cutting loose from their convictions, but rather by gradually and slowly bringing them to Spiritist meetings, where they will be able to hear us – the spirits – and where we will find an opening through which we can touch their hearts. This is another side of charity.

Now hear how you should do charity for the poor – underprivileged here on Earth; but rewarded by God, if they can accept their miseries without grumbling – which is dependent on you. To make myself better understood, I will give an example.

I see a ladies' meeting several times a week: there are people of all ages; for us, you know, they are all sisters. What are they doing? They work with great agility, their fingers are nimble. Also note how their faces are radiant, and how their hearts beat in unison! But what is their purpose? It is that they see winter approaching, which will be harsh for poor households. During summer, the "ants" were unable to gather enough grain for storage, and most of it has already been consumed. The poor mothers worry and cry as they think of the little children who will be cold and hungry this winter! But be patient, poor women! God has inspired some people who are more fortunate than you: they got together and are making you small clothes. Then one of these days, when the snow has covered the Earth and you grumble, saying, "God is not fair" – for it is a customary saying among you who suffer – you will see one of these young women who have made themselves workers for the poor. Yes, it was for you that they worked so diligently, and your grumbles will turn into blessings, because in the hearts of the unfortunate love soon succeeds hatred.

As all these workers need encouragement, I see communications from good spirits coming to them from all sides. Incarnate humans who are part of this society also contribute by doing one of these inspired readings which please so much; and we spirits, to reward the zeal of each and everyone in particular, promise these hardworking workers a good "clientele" who will pay them in blessings, which is the only currency in heaven, attending to them in greater numbers, and without fear to grow too much and fail them.

Caritas (Lyon, 1861).

15.   Dearest friends, every day I hear someone saying among you, "I am poor, I cannot do any charity;" and yet every day I see your lack of indulgence toward your fellow beings: you forgive them nothing, and often you set yourselves as harsh judges, without asking yourselves if you would like that the same was done with regard to you. Indulgence, is it not another form of charity? You who can only do charity through indulgence, at least do it, but do it a great deal. As for material charity, I want to tell you a story from the world beyond.

Two men had just died; then God said: "As long as these two men live, I will put in a bag each of their good deeds, and at their death I will weigh these bags." When the two men neared their last hour, God ordered that the two bags were brought to Its presence. One bag was big, tall, and well filled – so much so that it echoed the metal that filled it – whereas the other was very small and so thin, that one could see through it the few pennies it contained. Each of those men recognized his bag: "Here is mine," said the first, "I recognize it. I was rich and gave a lot." "And here is mine," said the other, "but alas! I have always been very poor and had almost nothing to share." However, what a surprise! When the two bags were placed on the scales, the larger one became light, and the small one got much heavier, so that it carried the other plate of the scales by far. Then God said to the rich man, "You have given much, it is true, but you have given with ostentation, and to see your name appear in all the temples of pride. Moreover, by giving you have not deprived yourself of anything; go to the left and be satisfied that alms still count for something small." Then he said to the poor one, "You have given very little, my friend; but each of the pennies which are on this scale represents a privation for you. If you have not given many alms, you still have done charity, and what is best, you have done charity naturally, without thinking that you would be taken into account. Moreover, you were indulgent; you have not judged your fellow beings; on the contrary, you have excused them all their actions. So pass to the right, an receive your reward."

A protector spirit (Lyon, 1861).

16. Can a rich, happy woman who does not need to use her time doing household chores devote a few hours to useful work for her fellow beings? May she with the surplus of her joys buy enough to clothe the unfortunate one who shivers with cold; let her make coarse but warm clothes with her delicate hands; may she help a mother cover her unborn child. If her own child ends up with a bit less lacework, the poor person's children will be warmer. To work for the poor is to work in the Lord's vineyard.

And you, poor home worker, who has no surplus, but still wishes, in your love for your brothers and sisters, to give whatever little you have, devote a few hours of your day, of your time – your only treasure – make these elegant handicrafts that entice the fortunate ones, sell them the work of your vigil, and you will also be able to give your brothers and sisters your share of relief. You may end up with fewer rags for yourself, but will provide shoes for those with bare feet.

As for you, religious women dedicated to God, also take part in God's work, but may your delicate and elaborate embroidered works be used not only to decorate your chapels, to draw attention to your dedication and even to your patience; but rather work, my daughters, and let the price of your works be devoted to the relief of your brothers and sisters in God. The poor are God's beloved children; to work for them is to glorify God. Be their Providence, which says: To the birds of the sky God provides food. May the gold and silver derived from the weaving of your fingers be changed into clothes and food for those in need. Do this, and your work will be blessed.

And each and every one of you who can produce something, please give. Give your genius, give your inspirations, give your heart that God will bless you. Poets, writers, who are only read by worldly people, do cater to their leisure, but let the product of some of your works be devoted to the relief of the unfortunate. Painters, sculptors, artists of all kinds, may your intelligence also help your brothers and sisters – you will have no less glory, and there will be some less suffering as a result.

Everyone can give; no matter what is your station in life, you all have something you can share. Whatever God has given you, you owe part of it to those who lack the essentials of life, because were you in their place you would be glad if another shared with you. Your earthly treasures will be somewhat diminished, but your heavenly treasures will be more abundant. You will reap a hundredfold the benefits you have sown for others here below.

Jean (Bordeaux, 1861).

COMPASSION

17. Compassion is the virtue that brings you closer to the angels; it is a sibling of charity which leads you to God. Ah, let your heart soften at the view of the miseries and sufferings of your fellow human beings; your tears are like balm poured over their wounds; and when, through sweet sympathy, you manage to give them hope and resignation, what delight this will bring you! True, such delight is mixed with a hint of bitterness, for it is born alongside unhappiness; but if it does not have the bitterness of worldly pleasures, it does not contain the poignant disappointments of the emptiness that the latter leave as an aftertaste. Instead, it possesses a penetrating sweetness that delights the soul. Compassion, when well-felt, is love. Love is devotion, and devotion is forgetting one's self – and this forgetfulness, this abnegation toward the unfortunate, is a moral virtue par excellence, the one that the divine Messiah practiced all his life, and which he taught in his utterly holy and sublime tenet. When this tenet is restored to its original purity, and when it is accepted by all peoples, it will bring happiness to the world by finally establishing a reign of harmony, peace and love.

The sentiments that most likely will make you progress by taming your selfishness and your pride, and that which can clothe your soul with humility, are beneficence and love of your neighbor, it is compassion! Such compassion that takes you down to your very soul, when witnessing the suffering of your brothers and sisters; which makes you reach out with a helping hand and move you to tears of deep sympathy. Therefore never stifle in your hearts this celestial emotion, do not act like these hardened selfish people who move away from the afflicted, because the sight of their misery would disturb their joyful existence for an instant. Dread staying indifferent when you can be of help. Tranquility bought at the price of guilty indifference is like the tranquility of the Dead Sea, which hides stinking mud and rotten matter at the bottom of its waters.

How far true compassion is from causing the trouble and the boredom dreaded by the selfish! Without a doubt one's soul experiences, in contact with the misfortune of others and by retreating into itself, a natural and deep seizure which makes vibrate all one's being and affecting it painfully; but this is greatly compensated, when you manage to give some courage and hope to an unhappy fellow being who is touched by the pressure of a friendly hand, and whose gaze, moist with both emotion and gratitude, turns gently toward you before settling on the sky to thank God for having sent a Consoler, a Helper. Compassion is the sad but celestial precursor of charity, this first of all virtues of which it is a sibling, and with which it prepares and ennobles all acts of beneficence.

Michel (Bordeaux, 1862).

ORPHANS

18. Dear brothers, love all the orphans; if you knew how sad it is to be alone and abandoned – specially at a young age! God allows orphans to exist so as to commit us to serve as parents to them. What a divine charity it is to help a poor little abandoned being, to prevent it from suffering of hunger and cold, to guide its soul so that it does not get lost in vice! Whoever reaches out to an abandoned child is pleasing to God because he/she understands and practices Its law. Also think that often the child you rescue was dear to you in a past incarnation; and if you could remember, it would no longer be charity, but a duty. So therefore, dear friends, every distressed being is your sibling and is entitled to your charity; but not a charity that hurts the heart, not alms that burns the hand in which it falls, because your handouts are often quite bitter! How often would such alms be rejected by the poor if, back at their miserable homes, illness and deprivation were not expecting them! So, give gently, add to your alms the most precious benefit of all: a kind word, a gentle touch, a friendly smile. Avoid using this patronizing tone that twists the iron into an already bleeding heart; and think that, by doing good, you are actually working for yourself and your nearest and dearest.

A familiar spirit[51] (Paris, 1860).

---

51 [Trans. note] In Spiritism, a *familiar spirit* is always a benevolent spirit usually related to some incarnate family (*cf.* A. KARDEC, *The Spirits' Book*, question no. 514).

BENEFITS REPAID WITH INGRATITUDE

19. *What should we think of people who, having been paid with ingratitude for all their benefits, no longer do good for fear of coming across ungrateful people?*

Such people have more selfishness than charity; for failing to do good only for fear of not receiving appreciation is not doing it disinterestedly – and only a selfless benefit is pleasing to God. It is also pride, because they indulge in the humility of recipients that show their appreciation by bowing at their feet. Those who seek on Earth the reward for the good they make will not receive it in heaven; however, God will take into account those who do not seek it on Earth.

One must always help the weak, even when knowing in advance that those to whom one does good will not be grateful. Know that if those to whom you are donating forget the benefit received, God will take it more into account than if you were already rewarded by the recipients' appreciation. *Sometimes God lets you to be paid back with ingratitude to test your resolve in doing good.*

Moreover, how do you know if this benefit, momentarily forgotten, will not later bear good fruit? On the contrary, rest assured that it is a seed that will eventually germinate. Unfortunately, over time you always see only the present; you work for yourself, not for others. Benefits given will eventually soften the most hardened hearts; they may be misunderstood here below, but when the spirit is rid of its carnal veil, it will remember it, and this memory will be its punishment. Then it will regret its ingratitude and wish to make up for its fault, to pay its debt in another existence, often even by accepting a life of devotion to its benefactor. Thus, without suspecting it, you will have contributed to this spirit's moral advancement, and later you will recognize all the truth contained in this maxim: "A good deed is never lost."[52] But in this way you will also have worked for yourself, for you will have the merit of having done good selflessly, and without being deterred by any disappointments.

Ah, dear friends, if you knew all the links which, in the current life, tie you to your previous existences; if you could encompass

---

52 [Trans. note] Maxim attributed to St. Basil (329–379 AD), bishop of Caesarea Mazaca in Cappadocia, Asia Minor.

the multitude of relationships that bring people together for their mutual progress, you would admire even better the wisdom and kindness of the Creator which allows you to be born again in order to reach It.

A spirit guide (Sens, 1862).

EXCLUSIVE BENEFICENCE

20. *Is beneficence better understood when it is exclusive to people of the same opinion, same belief or same party?*

No, it stands above any notion of sect or party which should all be abolished, because all humans are brothers and sisters. True Christians only see brothers and sisters in their fellow beings, and before rescuing the needy, they do not inquire from them what their belief is, or what opinion they hold on anything. Would you be following the precept of Jesus Christ, who says to love even one's enemies, if you reject a poor person, because he/she has a different faith from your own? Let everyone rescue him/her without asking for any account of his/her conscience, because if the latter is an enemy of religion, it is the means of making him/her love; whereas, by pushing such a person away, you would only make him/her be filled with hate.

St. Louis (Paris, 1860).

Chapter XIV
Honor your father and mother

1. "You know the commandments: 'Do not murder, Do not commit adultery, Do not steal, Do not bear false witness, Do not defraud, *Honor your father and mother.*' (MARK 10:19; *cf.* LUKE 18:20 and MATTHEW 19:19 ESV)."

2. "Honor your father and your mother, that your days may be long in the land that the LORD your God is giving you. (EXODUS 20:12 ESV)."

FILIAL PIETY

3. The commandment, "Honor your father and mother," is a consequence of the general law of charity and love of neighbor, for one cannot love one's neighbor without loving one's father and mother; but the verb *to honor* contains one additional duty toward them, namely, that of filial piety. God wanted to show by this that respect, consideration, submission and condescension should be added to love, which implies the obligation to accomplish toward them, even in a more rigorous way, all that charity commands toward neighbor. This duty naturally extends to people who take the role of father and mother, and who have all the more merit in that their dedication is less compulsory. Any violation of this commandment is to be always rigorously punished by God.

To honor your father and mother is not only to respect them, it is also to help them when in need; it is to guarantee them repose in old age; it is to surround them with care as they did for us in our childhood.

It is especially toward parents destitute of resources that one must show real filial piety. Are those, who believe they are making a great effort by giving their parents just enough not to starve, following this commandment, when they themselves do not deprive themselves of anything? By relegating their parents to the smallest rooms in the house, so as not to leave them on the street, while reserving the best, the most comfortable ones for themselves? Such parents should count themselves happy that their children do not do it grudgingly and do not make them pay for the time they have left in this life by being burdened with the fatigues of housework! So, should old and ailing parents be the servants of young and strong children? Did their mother bargain for her milk when they were still in the cradle? Did she count her vigils when they were ill, her steps to get them what they needed? No, it is not only the bare necessities that children owe to their poor parents: it is also, as much as they can, superfluous little treats, the attentions and delicate cares, which should be regarded as the rightful interest on what they received, the payment of a sacred debt. Only thus there is filial piety accepted by God.

Woe to those who forget what they owe to those who supported them in their childhood frailty; who, with material life, gave them moral life; who often imposed hardship on themselves in order to ensure their children's well-being. Woe to the ingrate, for they will be punished by ingratitude and neglect; they will be struck in their dearest affections, *sometimes starting in their current life*, but certainly in another existence, where they will endure what they have made others endure.

It is true that certain parents disregard their duties, and do not behave toward their children the way they should; but it is up to God and not to their children to punish them. It is not up to the latter to blame them, because perhaps they themselves deserved it to be so. If charity makes a law of rendering good for evil, of being indulgent to imperfections of others, of not vilifying one's neighbor, of forgetting and forgiving wrongs, of loving even one's enemies, how much greater this obligation should be toward one's parents! Children should therefore take as a rule of conduct toward them, all the precepts of Jesus concerning neighbor, and be convinced that any blameworthy process vis-à-vis strangers is even more so vis-à-vis those nearest to them; and that, what might be only a fault in the first case, can become a crime in the second, because then to a lack of charity one must add filial ingratitude.

4. God said, "Honor your father and your mother, that your days may be long in the land that the LORD your God is giving you." Why then does God promise life on Earth and not heavenly life as a reward? The explanation is in these words: "That the Lord will give you,"[53] deleted in the modern formula of the Decalogue, which distorts its meaning. To understand this word, it is necessary to consider the context and Hebrew ideas when it was said. They did not yet understand future life; their sight did not extend beyond bodily life; therefore they must have been more affected by what they could see than by what they did not see at all. This is why God speaks to them a language within their reach, and, as with children, gives them in perspective what can satisfy their minds. They were then in the desert; the land which God *will give* them was the Promised Land, the goal of their aspiration. They wanted nothing else, and God tells them that they will live there a long time, that is to say, that they will possess it for a long time if they observe God's commandments.

But later on, when Jesus came, their ideas were more developed. When the moment had come to give them less coarse food for thought, he initiated them into spiritual life by saying: "My kingdom is not of this world; it is there, and not on Earth, that you will receive the reward for your good deeds." With these words, the material Promised Land is transformed into a celestial homeland. Also, when he reminds them to observe the commandment, "Honor your father and your mother," it is no longer the Earth that he promises them, but heaven (see Chapters **II** & **III** above).

WHO IS MY MOTHER AND WHO ARE MY BROTHERS?

5. Then he went home, and the crowd gathered again, so that they could not even eat. And when his family heard it, they went out to seize him, for they were saying, *'He is out of his mind.'* — And his mother and his brothers came, and standing outside they sent to him and called him. And a crowd was sitting around him, and they said to him, 'Your mother and your brothers are outside, seeking you.' And he answered them, *'Who are my mother and my brothers?'*

---

53 [Trans. note] A. KARDEC uses the future tense, "will give," whereas both French and English Bibles use either the simple present or the present continuous, "is giving," in this passage (*cf.* EXODUS 20:12).

And looking about at those who sat around him, he said, 'Here are my mother and my brothers! For whoever does the will of God, he is my brother and sister and mother' (MARK 3:20–21,31–35; *cf.* MATTHEW 12:46–50 ESV)."

6.   Certain words seem strange coming from Jesus' mouth, in contrast with his kindness and his unalterable benevolence toward all. Unbelievers did not fail to weaponize them by saying that he contradicted himself. An indisputable fact is that his doctrine has as its essential basis, as its cornerstone, the law of love and charity. Therefore he could not destroy on one side what he established on the other; from which it is necessary to draw a rigorous consequence, namely that, if certain maxims are in contradiction with the principle, it is that some words attributed to him were either badly rendered, badly understood, or not uttered by him at all.

7.   One is astonished, with reason, to see in this circumstance, Jesus showing so much indifference for his close relatives, and somehow negating his own mother.

As for his brothers, we know that they never had any sympathy for him. Little advanced spirits, they had not understood his mission; his conduct, in their eyes, was strange, and his teachings had not touched them in any way, since he had no disciple among them. It would even seem that they shared to some extent the prejudices of his enemies. Moreover, it is certain that they welcomed him more as a stranger than as a brother when he appeared in the family, and John the Evangelist positively said, "*Not even his brothers believed in him* (JOHN 7:5 ESV)."

As for his mother, no one could dispute her tenderness for her son; but it must also be admitted that she does not seem to have had a very fair idea of his mission, because we have never seen her follow his teachings, nor bear witness to him, as did John the Baptist. Maternal concern must have been the dominant feeling in her. With regard to Jesus, to suppose him to have negated his mother would be to disregard his character; such a thought could not animate the one who said, *Honor your father and your mother.* We must therefore seek a different meaning for his words, almost always veiled in allegorical form.

Jesus would not overlook any opportunity to teach; he therefore seized the one offered to him by the arrival of his family to establish the difference which exists between bodily kinship and spiritual kinship.

BODILY KINSHIP AND SPIRITUAL KINSHIP

8.   Blood ties do not necessarily create connections among spirits. The body originates from the body, but the spirit does not originate from the spirit, because the spirit already existed before the body was formed. Parents do not create the spirit of their children, they only provide them with a bodily envelope, albeit still expected to help them in their moral and intellectual development in order to make them progress.

The spirits that incarnate in one same family, especially among close relatives, are most often sympathetic spirits, united by previous relationships which are expressed by their affection during earthly life. But it may also happen that these spirits are completely foreign to one another, divided by equally earlier antipathies, which are likewise expressed by their antagonism on Earth, which serves as a test for them. True family ties are therefore not those of consanguinity, but those of affinity and communion of thoughts which unite spirits *before, during* and *after* their incarnation. Whence it follows that two beings born of different parents can be more brothers and sisters in spirit than if they had blood ties. They can feel attracted by one another, seek one another out, please one another out, whereas two consanguineous siblings can repel each other, as we see every day – a moral problem which Spiritism alone could solve by revealing the plurality of existences (see Chapter **IV**, no. **13** above).

There are therefore two kinds of families: *families by spiritual ties, and families by bodily ties.* The first, which are lasting, are strengthened through purification and perpetuated in the spiritual world, through the various migrations of the soul. The seconds, fragile as matter, die out over time and often cease to exist morally in one's current life. This is what Jesus wanted to make clear by saying of his disciples: "Here are my mother and my brothers" – that is to say my family by the bonds of the spirit – "for whoever does the will of God, he is my brother and sister and mother."

The hostility of his brothers is clearly expressed in Mark's story, since, as he says, they set out to seize him, under the pretext that he was *out of his mind*. At the announcement of their arrival, knowing their feelings about him, it was natural that he would say in speaking of his disciples, that from the spiritual point of view, "These are my true brothers." His mother was with them, he generalized the teaching, which does not imply in any way that he claimed that his bodily mother was nothing to him as a spirit, and that he felt completely indifferent toward her. In other circumstances, his conduct has sufficiently proved otherwise.

INSTRUCTIONS FROM THE SPIRITS

CHILDREN'S INGRATITUDE
AND FAMILY TIES

9.   Ingratitude is one of the most immediate fruits of selfishness. It always causes revulsion to honest hearts; however, children's ingratitude toward parents has an even more odious dimension. It is more specifically from this viewpoint that I will analyze its causes and effects. Here, as everywhere, Spiritism sheds light on one of the problems of the human heart.

When a spirit leaves Earth, it takes with it the passions or virtues inherent in its nature, and returns to the spiritual world either to perfect itself or remaining stationary until it wishes to see the light. Therefore some have left still carrying with them powerful hatreds and unfulfilled desires for revenge; yet to some of them, more advanced than the others, it is allowed to glimpse a corner of the truth; they acknowledge the fateful effects of their passions, and it is then that they make good resolutions. They understand that in order for them to go to God, there is only one password: *charity*. However, there can be no charity without forgetting insults and outrages; no charity with hatred in the heart and without forgiveness.

Then, with an incredible effort, they look back at those they hated on Earth. But at this sight their animosity is reawakened; they revolt at the idea of forgiving – even more than that of renouncing themselves – especially a the idea of loving those who have perhaps destroyed their fortune, their honor, their family. However, the hearts of these unfortunates are shaken; they hesitate, they stray, agitated by contrary feelings. If the right resolution wins, they pray to God and beseech the good spirits to give them strength at the most decisive moment of their trial.

Finally, after a few years of meditations and prayers, the spirit takes advantage of a physical body which is being prepared in the family of the one the spirit hated, and asks the spirits charged with transmitting the supreme orders, to go and fill on Earth the destinies of this fleshly envelope which has just been formed. What will be this spirit's conduct in this family? It will depend on the more or less persistence of its good resolutions. The constant contact with the beings it hated is a terrible ordeal under which it sometimes succumbs, if its will is not strong enough. Thus, depending on whether a good or bad resolution wins, this spirit will be the friend or the enemy of those in whose midst it is called to live. This explains these hatreds, these instinctive repulsions which one notices in certain children and which no previous occurrence seems to justify. Nothing, indeed, in the current existence, could have provoked such an aversion; to realize its cause, one would have to look at the distant past.

Spiritists, understand today the great role of humanity! Understand that when you produce a body, the soul which incarnates in it comes from the spiritual world to evolve. Know your duties, and put all your love into bringing this soul closer to God: this is the mission which is entrusted to you, and whose reward you will receive if you accomplish it faithfully. Your care, the education you will give this child will help his/her development and future well-being. Bear in mind that, from each father and each mother, God will ask: What have you done with the child in your care? If such child is backward because of your fault, your punishment will be to see this spirit among the distressed spirits, while it was up to you that it would be happy. Then you yourselves, full of remorse, will ask to make up for your fault; you will seek a new incarnation for you and for that spirit, in which you will surround it with a more enlightened care, and it, full of gratitude, will surround you with its love.

Therefore do not reject the child who repels his/her mother in the cradle, nor the one who repays you with ingratitude. It was not chance that did it and brought it onto you. An imperfect intuition of the past may be revealed, and from there judge that one or the other has already hated or has been deeply offended by one another; that now has come either to forgive or to atone. Mothers! Kiss the child who is causing you grief, and say to yourself: One of us has been guilty. Earn the divine joys that God attaches to motherhood, by teaching this child that he/she is on Earth in order to perfect himself/herself, to love, and to bless. However, alas, many of you, instead of driving out through education any bad innate tendencies of previous existences, keep and develop these same tendencies by a guilty weakness or by carelessness; and, later, your heart, ulcerated by the ingratitude of your children, will become for you, already in current life, the beginning of your atonement.

This task is not as difficult as you might think; it does not require a worldly knowledge: the ignorant as well as the scientist can fulfill it. Besides, Spiritism has come to facilitate it by making known the cause of the imperfections of the human heart.

From the cradle a child manifests the good or bad instincts it has brought from its previous existence; we should apply our efforts in studying them. All evils have their beginnings in selfishness and pride; therefore watch for the slightest signs which reveal the germ of these vices, and endeavor to fight them without waiting for them to create deep roots. Do like the good gardener, who pulls out the bad weeds as soon as he sees them appear on the tree. If you let selfishness and pride grow, do not be surprised if you are later repaid with ingratitude. When parents have done all they could for the moral advancement of their children, if they do not succeed, they cannot be blamed for the failure, and their conscience may be at rest. However to the very natural sorrow which they feel at the failure of their efforts, God has reserved a great, an immense consolation, in the *certainty* that it is only a postponement of their task, and that they will have the opportunity to complete another existence the work started in this one; and that one day the ungrateful child will reward them with his/her love (see Chapter **XIII**, no. **19** above).

God does not give anyone a test above the strength of those who request it; God only allows tests that one can accomplish. Therefore, if one does not succeed, it is not for lack of possibility, but for a lack of willpower. How many are there who, instead of resisting bad inclinations, let themselves be dragged by them! It is to these that weeping and wailing are reserved in their later existence. But admire the goodness of God, who never closes the door of repentance. A day comes when culprits get tired of suffering, where their pride is finally tamed. It is then that God opens Its kind and protective arms to Its prodigal children who throws themselves at Its feet.

Understand when I say that *the hardest trials are almost always an indication of the end of suffering and of perfecting of the spirit, when they are accepted with a view to God.* It is a supreme moment, when it is especially important not to fail by grumbling, if one does not want to lose the fruit of it and thus have to start all over again. Instead of complaining, thank God, which gives you the opportunity to win the combat so as to give you the prize of victory. So when, leaving the whirlwind of the earthly world, you reenter the world of spirits, you will be acclaimed like the soldier who comes out victorious from the middle of the fray.

Of all life's trials, the most painful ones are those that affect one's heart. People who courageously endure misery and material privations will nevertheless succumb under the weight of domestic sorrows, bruised by the ingratitude of their nearest and dearest. Indeed, this is such a poignant anguish! But what can better raise one's moral courage in such circumstances than the knowledge of the causes of the evil, and the certainty that, even when heartbreaks are too long, there is no eternal despair, since God cannot possibly wish that Its created beings suffer forever? What could be more consoling, more encouraging, than this thought that one depends on oneself, on one's own efforts, to shorten suffering by destroying in oneself the causes of evil? Yet, if only for that, you should stop looking to the ground and seeing only one existence. You all must rise and hover in the infinity of the past and the future. Then God's immense justice is revealed to your eyes, and you learn to wait patiently, because you find out the explanation of what you thought were life's enormities on Earth. The wounds you receive here now seem to you only scratches. This glance cast on the whole now shows family ties in their true light, more like fragile bonds of matter which unite its members, whereas the lasting bonds of the spirit are perpetuated and consolidated by being purified, instead of being broken, by reincarnation.

Spirits whose similarity of taste, identity of moral progress and affection bring together, form families. These same spirits, in their earthly migrations, seek to group themselves as they do in space; this is how united and homogeneous families are born. And if, in their wanderings, they are momentarily separated, they meet again later, happy with their newly acquired progress. But as they must not work only for themselves, God allows that less advanced spirits come to incarnate among them to draw from their advice and good examples in the interest of their advancement. They sometimes cause trouble on Earth, but there lies the trial, there lies the task. So welcome them as brothers and sisters; help them, and later on, in the spiritual world, the family will congratulate themselves for having saved forsaken individuals who, in turn, will be able to save others.

St. Augustine (Paris, 1862).

Chapter XV
Without charity there is no salvation

WHAT IT TAKES TO BE SAVED

1. "When the Son of Man comes in his glory, and all the angels with him, then he will sit on his glorious throne. Before him will be gathered all the nations, and he will separate people one from another as a shepherd separates the sheep from the goats. And he will place the sheep on his right, but the goats on the left. Then the King will say to those on his right, 'Come, you who are blessed by my Father, inherit the kingdom prepared for you from the foundation of the world. For I was hungry and you gave me food, I was thirsty and you gave me drink, I was a stranger and you welcomed me, I was naked and you clothed me, I was sick and you visited me, I was in prison and you came to me.' Then the righteous will answer him, saying, 'Lord, when did we see you hungry and feed you, or thirsty and give you drink? And when did we see you a stranger and welcome you, or naked and clothe you? And when did we see you sick or in prison and visit you?' And the King will answer them, 'Truly, I say to you, as you did it to one of the least of these my brothers, you did it to me.'

"Then he will say to those on his left, 'Depart from me, you cursed, into the eternal fire prepared for the devil and his angels. For I was hungry and you gave me no food, I was thirsty and you gave me no drink, I was a stranger and you did not welcome me, naked and you did not clothe me, sick and in prison and you did not visit me.' Then they also will answer, saying, 'Lord, when did we see you hungry or thirsty or a stranger or naked or sick or in prison, and did not minister to you?' Then he will answer them, saying, 'Truly, I say to you, as you did not do it to one of the least of these, you did not do it to me.' And these will go away into eternal punishment, but the righteous into eternal life (MATTHEW 25:31–46 ESV)."

2.   "And behold, a lawyer stood up to put him to the test, saying, 'Teacher, what shall I do to inherit eternal life?' He said to him, 'What is written in the Law? How do you read it?' And he answered, 'You shall love the Lord your God with all your heart and with all your soul and with all your strength and with all your mind, and your neighbor as yourself.' And he said to him, 'You have answered correctly; do this, and you will live.'

But he, desiring to justify himself, said to Jesus, 'And who is my neighbor?' Jesus replied, 'A man was going down from Jerusalem to Jericho, and he fell among robbers, who stripped him and beat him and departed, leaving him half dead. Now by chance a priest was going down that road, and when he saw him he passed by on the other side. So likewise a Levite, when he came to the place and saw him, passed by on the other side. But a Samaritan, as he journeyed, came to where he was, and when he saw him, he had compassion. He went to him and bound up his wounds, pouring on oil and wine. Then he set him on his own animal and brought him to an inn and took care of him. And the next day he took out two denarii and gave them to the innkeeper, saying, 'Take care of him, and whatever more you spend, I will repay you when I come back.' Which of these three, do you think, proved to be a neighbor to the man who fell among the robbers?' He said, 'The one who showed him mercy.' And Jesus said to him, 'You go, and do likewise' (LUKE 10:25–37 ESV)."

3.   The whole moral of Jesus can be summed up as charity and humility, that is to say, in the two virtues contrary to selfishness and pride. In all his teachings, he shows these virtues as being the path to eternal bliss. Blessed, he says, are the poor in spirit – that is to say the humble – for theirs is the kingdom of heaven; blessed are the pure in heart; blessed are the meek and the peacemakers; blessed are the merciful; love your neighbor as yourself; do unto others as you would have them do unto you; love your enemies; forgive offenses, if you want to be forgiven; do good without ostentation; judge yourself before judging others. Humility and charity, this

is what he never ceases to recommend, and of which he himself set an example. As for pride and selfishness, he has never ceased to fight against them; yet he does more than recommend charity: he places it clearly and explicitly as the absolute condition for future happiness.

As in many other passages, in the scenario of the last judgment as presented by Jesus, it is necessary to make some allowance for figures of speech and allegories. To people like those to whom he spoke, still incapable of understanding purely spiritual things, he had to present material images, both striking and capable of impressing their minds. To be better accepted, he could not afford to stray too far from received ideas as to form, always reserving for the future the true interpretation of his words and points about which he could not explain himself clearly. But next to the accessory and figurative part of the scenario he painted out, there is a dominant idea, namely, of happiness and bliss awaiting the just, and misfortune reserved for the wicked.

In that supreme judgment, what are the articles taken into account when passing the sentence? On what grounds is the indictment based? Does the judge ask whether this or that formality has been fulfilled, or whether some exterior practice has been more or less observed? No; he only inquires about one thing: the practice of charity, saying: You who have assisted your brothers and sisters, pass to the right; and you who have been hard on your fellow beings, pass to the left. Does he inquire about the orthodoxy of faith? Does he make any distinction between one who believes in one way and one who believes in another way? No; for Jesus places the Samaritan – then regarded as a heretic, but who has love of neighbor – above the orthodox who lacks charity. Jesus therefore does not make charity only one of the conditions of salvation, but the sole condition. If there were other virtues to fulfill, he would have named them. If he places charity in the forefront of virtues, it is because it implicitly contains all the others: humility, meekness, benevolence, indulgence, justice, etc. – and also because it is the utter and complete negation of pride and selfishness.

THE GREATEST COMMANDMENT

4. But when the Pharisees heard that he had silenced the Sadducees, they gathered together. And one of them, a lawyer, asked him a question to test him. 'Teacher, which is the great commandment in the Law?' And he said to him, 'You shall love the Lord your God with all your heart and with all your soul and with all your mind. This is the great and first commandment. And a second is like it: You shall love your neighbor as yourself. On these two commandments depend all the Law and the Prophets' (MATTHEW 22:34–40 ESV)."

5. Charity and humility are therefore the only path to salvation, whereas selfishness and pride pave the path to perdition. This principle is formulated in precise terms in the following words: "You shall love the Lord your God with all your heart and with all your soul and with all your mind.... You shall love your neighbor as yourself. *On these two commandments depend all the Law and the Prophets.*" And so that there is no ambiguity in the interpretation of the love of God and of neighbor, he adds: "And a second is like it"; that is, one can neither truly love God without loving one's neighbor, nor love one's neighbor without loving God; therefore anything you do against neighbor is done against God. Unable to love God without practicing charity toward one's neighbor, all human duties are summed up in this maxim: *Without charity there is no salvation.*

THE NEED FOR CHARITY ACCORDING TO THE APOSTLE PAUL

6. "Though I speak with the tongues of men and of angels, and have not charity, I am become as sounding brass, or a tinkling cymbal. And though I have the gift of prophecy, and understand all mysteries, and all knowledge; and though I have all faith, so that I could remove mountains, *and have not charity, I am nothing.* And though I bestow all my goods to feed the poor, and though I give my body to be burned, and have not charity, it profiteth me nothing.

Charity suffereth long, and is kind; charity envieth not; charity vaunteth not itself, is not puffed up, Doth not behave itself unseemly, seeketh not her own, is not easily provoked, thinketh no evil; Rejoiceth not in iniquity, but rejoiceth in the truth; Beareth all things, believeth all things, hopeth all things, endureth all things. And now abideth faith, hope, charity, these three; but the greatest of these is *charity* (PAUL, 1CORINTHIANS 13:1–7,13 AKJV/PCE)."[54]

7. The Apostle Paul understood this major truth so much, that he said: "*Though I speak with the tongue ... of angels, ... and though I have the gift of prophecy, and understand all mysteries, and all knowledge; and though I have all faith, so that I could remove mountains, and have not charity, I am nothing. And though I bestow all my goods to feed the poor, and though I give my body to be burned, and have not charity, it profiteth me nothing.... And now abideth faith, hope, charity, these three; but the greatest of these is charity.*" Thus he places charity unequivocally above even faith, since charity is within the reach of everyone, of both the ignorant and the learned, the rich and the poor; also because it is independent of any particular belief.

More than this, he defines true charity, showing it to be not only beneficence, but also the gathering of all the qualities of the heart, and kindness and benevolence toward neighbor.

WITHOUT THE CHURCH THERE IS NO SALVATION
WITHOUT TRUTH THERE IS NO SALVATION

8. Whereas the maxim, *Without charity there is no salvation*, is based on a universal principle, opening to all God's children access to supreme happiness, the dogma, *Without the Church*[55] *there is no*

---

54 [Trans. note] The passage above was extracted from the ancient AUTHORISED KING JAMES VERSION/ PURE CAMBRIDGE EDITION where the word *charity* is used. However, in more recent English Bibles, such as the ENGLISH STANDARD VERSION, the word *love* is used instead: "If I speak in the tongues of men and of angels, but have not love, I am a noisy gong or a clanging cymbal. And if I have prophetic powers, and understand all mysteries and all knowledge, and if I have all faith, so as to remove mountains, but have not love, I am nothing. If I give away all I have, and if I deliver up my body to be burned, but have not love, I gain nothing.

Love is patient and kind; love does not envy or boast; it is not arrogant or rude. It does not insist on its own way; it is not irritable or resentful; it does not rejoice at wrongdoing, but rejoices with the truth. Love bears all things, believes all things, hopes all things, endures all things.

So now faith, hope, and love abide, these three; but the greatest of these is love (PAUL, 1CORINTHIANS 13:1–7,13 ESV)."

55 [Trans. note] See footnote 1 above.

salvation, is based, not so much on a fundamental faith in God, the immortality of the soul, and a faith common to all religions, but rather on *a special faith in specific dogmas*. It is exclusive and absolute: instead of uniting God's children, it divides them; instead of arousing them for the love of others, it maintains and sanctions the sectarian nuisance among different beliefs and religions, which reciprocally consider one another as being cursed in eternity, even parents or friends in this world. By ignoring the great law of equality in the tomb, this dogma separates them even after death. Conversely the maxim, *Without charity there is no salvation*, is the confirmation of the principle of equality before God and freedom of conscience. With this maxim as a rule, all humans are brothers and sisters, and whatever their manner of worshiping the Creator, they reach out and pray for one another. But with the dogma, *Without the Church there is no salvation*, people launch anathema against one another, and persecute one another, living as enemies: parents do not pray for their children, neither do children pray for their parents, nor a friend for another friend, if they all believe one another to be irredeemably damned. Such a dogma is therefore essentially contrary to the teachings of Christ and to the Gospel's law.

9. *Without truth there is no salvation* would be the equivalent of *Without the Church there is no salvation*, and just as exclusive, because there is not a single creed or religion which does not claim to have the privilege of the truth. Who is the person who can pride himself/herself on knowing it all, when the horizon of knowledge is constantly expanding, and ideas are being rectified every day? Absolute truth is only known to spirits of the highest order, and earthly humanity cannot claim it, because it is not given to humans to know everything. Human beings can only aspire to a relative truth proportional to their advancement. If God had made possession of absolute truth the express condition for future happiness, it would be like a general proscription edict; whereas charity, even in its broadest sense, can be practiced by each and every one. Spiritism, in agreement with the Gospel, by admitting that anyone can be saved regardless of one's belief, provided that one observes God's law, does not say, *Without Spiritism there is no salvation*. And since it does not pretend to teach the whole truth; yet, it does not say either that,

Without truth there is no salvation – a maxim which would divide instead of uniting, and thus perpetuate antagonism.

INSTRUCTIONS FROM THE SPIRITS

WITHOUT CHARITY THERE IS NO SALVATION

10. Dear children, the maxim, *Without charity there is no salvation*, contains the destinies of all human beings on Earth as well as in heaven. On Earth, because under the shadow of this banner they will live in peace. In heaven, because those who have practiced charity will find favor before the Lord. This motto is the celestial torch, the luminous column which guides humans in the desert of life, leading them to the Promised Land. It shines in heaven like a holy halo on the forehead of the elect, and on Earth it is engraved in the hearts of those to whom Jesus will say: Pass to the right, you blessed by my Father. You can recognize them by the scent of charity that they spread around them. Nothing expresses Jesus' thought better, nothing sums up human duties better than this divine maxim. Spiritism could not prove its divine origin better than by giving it as a rule, because it is the reflection of the purest Christianity. With such a guide, human beings will never go astray. Try therefore, dear friends, to understand its deep meaning and consequences; to seek for yourself all its applications. Submit all your actions to the control of charity, and your conscience will respond to you. Not only will it prevent you from doing evil, but it will make you do good: for nothing comes from an inactive virtue, there must be an active virtue. In order to do good, one always needs the action of one's will; while simply avoiding to do harm often does not require more than inertia and a lack of concern.

Therefore, dear friends, thank God for having allowed you to be able to enjoy the light of Spiritism. Not that only those who possess it can be saved, but because by helping you to better understand the teachings of Christ, it makes you better Christians. So make it so that those who see you can say that a true Spiritist and true Christian are one and the same thing, because all those who practice charity are disciples of Jesus, regardless of their creed or religion.

The Apostle Paul (Paris, 1860).

Chapter XVI
One cannot serve God and mammon

THE SALVATION OF THE WEALTHY

1. "No servant can serve two masters: for either he will hate the one, and love the other; or else he will hold to the one, and despise the other. *Ye cannot serve God and mammon* (LUKE 16:13 AKJV/PCE)."[56]

2. "And behold, a man came up to him, saying, 'Teacher, what good deed must I do to have eternal life?' And he said to him, 'Why do you ask me about what is good? There is only one who is good. If you would enter life, keep the commandments.' He said to him, 'Which ones?' And Jesus said, 'You shall not murder, You shall not commit adultery, You shall not steal, You shall not bear false witness, Honor your father and mother, and, You shall love your neighbor as yourself.' The young man said to him, 'All these I have kept. What do I still lack?' Jesus said to him, 'If you would be perfect, go, sell what you possess and give to the poor, and you will have treasure in heaven; and come, follow me.' When the young man heard this he went away sorrowful, for he had great possessions.

And Jesus said to his disciples, 'Truly, I say to you, only with difficulty will a rich person enter the kingdom of heaven. *Again I tell you, it is easier for a camel to go through the eye of a needle than for a*

---

56 [Trans. note] Ancient English versions of the Bible use *mammon* (from Aramaic "riches" or "wealth") as A. KARDEC did, instead of *money* as used by the ENGLISH STANDARD VERSION: "No servant can serve two masters, for either he will hate the one and love the other, or he will be devoted to the one and despise the other. You cannot serve God and money (LUKE 16:13)."

rich person to enter the kingdom of God' [57] (MATTHEW 19:16–24. See also LUKE 18:18–25 and MARK 10:17–25 ESV)."

BEWARE OF AVARICE

3. "Someone in the crowd said to him, 'Teacher, tell my brother to divide the inheritance with me.' But he said to him, 'Man, who made me a judge or arbitrator over you?' And he said to them, 'Take care, and be on your guard against all covetousness, for one's life does not consist in the abundance of his possessions.' And he told them a parable, saying, 'The land of a rich man produced plentifully, and he thought to himself, 'What shall I do, for I have nowhere to store my crops?' And he said, 'I will do this: I will tear down my barns and build larger ones, and there I will store all my grain and my goods. And I will say to my soul, Soul, you have ample goods laid up for many years; relax, eat, drink, be merry.' But God said to him, 'Fool! This night your soul is required of you, and the things you have prepared, whose will they be?' So is the one who lays up treasure for himself and is not rich toward God' (LUKE 12:13–21 ESV)."

JESUS AT ZACCHAEUS' HOUSE

4. "He entered Jericho and was passing through. And there was a man named Zacchaeus. He was a chief tax collector and was rich. And he was seeking to see who Jesus was, but on account of the crowd he could not, because he was small of stature. So he ran on ahead and climbed up into a sycamore tree to see him, for he was about to pass that way. And when Jesus came to the place, he looked up and said to him, 'Zacchaeus, hurry and come down, for I must stay at your house today.' So he hurried and came down and received him joyfully. And when they saw it, they all grumbled, 'He has gone in to be the guest of a man who is a sinner.'" (See **Introduction**, III. Historical Data, entry "Publicans" above.)

"And Zacchaeus stood and said to the Lord, 'Behold, Lord, the half of my goods I give to the poor. And if I have defrauded anyone of

---

57 This bold metaphor may seem a bit forced, since one cannot see any relation between a camel and a needle. This happened because in Hebrew the same word was used to mean both a *cable* and a *camel*. In translations it was given the latter meaning. However it is probable that Jesus was referring to the first meaning, as it is at least more natural.

anything, I restore it fourfold.' And Jesus said to him, 'Today salvation has come to this house, since he also is a son of Abraham. For the Son of Man came to seek and to save the lost' (LUKE 19:1–10 ESV)."

PARABLE OF THE EVIL RICH MAN

5. "There was a rich man who was clothed in purple and fine linen and who feasted sumptuously every day. And at his gate was laid a poor man named Lazarus, covered with sores, who desired to be fed with what fell from the rich man's table. Moreover, even the dogs came and licked his sores. The poor man died and was carried by the angels to Abraham's side. The rich man also died and was buried, and in Hades, being in torment, he lifted up his eyes and saw Abraham far off and Lazarus at his side. And he called out, 'Father Abraham, have mercy on me, and send Lazarus to dip the end of his finger in water and cool my tongue, for I am in anguish in this flame.'

But Abraham said, 'Child, remember that you in your lifetime received your good things, and Lazarus in like manner bad things; but now he is comforted here, and you are in anguish. And besides all this, between us and you a great chasm has been fixed, in order that those who would pass from here to you may not be able, and none may cross from there to us.'

And he said, 'Then I beg you, father, to send him to my father's house for I have five brothers so that he may warn them, lest they also come into this place of torment.' But Abraham said, 'They have Moses and the Prophets; let them hear them.' And he said, 'No, father Abraham, but if someone goes to them from the dead, they will repent.' He said to him, 'If they do not hear Moses and the Prophets, neither will they be convinced if someone should rise from the dead' (Luke 16:19–31 esv)."

PARABLE OF THE TALENTS

6. "For it will be like a man going on a journey, who called his servants and entrusted to them his property. To one he gave five talents,[58] to another two, to another one, to each according to his

---

58 [Trans. note] A *talent* was an ancient unit of weight of approximately 75 pounds, also used as currency worth that weight in silver (or even gold).

ability. Then he went away. He who had received the five talents went at once and traded with them, and he made five talents more. So also he who had the two talents made two talents more. But he who had received the one talent went and dug in the ground and hid his master's money. Now after a long time the master of those servants came and settled accounts with them. And he who had received the five talents came forward, bringing five talents more, saying, 'Master, you delivered to me five talents; here I have made five talents more.' His master said to him, 'Well done, good and faithful servant. You have been faithful over a little; I will set you over much. Enter into the joy of your master.' And he also who had the two talents came forward, saying, 'Master, you delivered to me two talents; here I have made two talents more.' His master said to him, 'Well done, good and faithful servant. You have been faithful over a little; I will set you over much. Enter into the joy of your master.' He also who had received the one talent came forward, saying, 'Master, I knew you to be a hard man, reaping where you did not sow, and gathering where you scattered no seed, so I was afraid, and I went and hid your talent in the ground. Here you have what is yours.' But his master answered him, 'You wicked and slothful servant! You knew that I reap where I have not sown and gather where I scattered no seed? Then you ought to have invested my money with the bankers, and at my coming I should have received what was my own with interest. So take the talent from him and give it to him who has the ten talents. For to everyone who has will more be given, and he will have an abundance. But from the one who has not, even what he has will be taken away. And cast the worthless servant into the outer darkness. In that place there will be weeping and gnashing of teeth' (MATTHEW 25:14–30 ESV)."

PROVIDENTIAL USEFULNESS OF WEALTH

7. If wealth were an absolute obstacle to the salvation of those who possess it – as one could infer from certain words of Jesus, if considered only according to their letter and not to their spirit – then God, which dispenses it, would have put in the hands of certain individuals an instrument of destruction without remission, the mere idea of which is repugnant to reason. Wealth is undoubtedly a very slippery trial, more dangerous than poverty because of its

enticements, the temptations it draws forth, and the fascination it exerts. It is the supreme instigator of pride, selfishness and sensual life. It is the most powerful bond that keeps a human being attached to Earth and turns his/her thoughts away from heaven. Wealth produces such vertigo that we often see those who go from poverty to wealth quickly forget their former position, those who shared it and those who helped it, thus becoming insensitive, selfish and vain. But from the fact that it makes one's path harder, it does not follow that it makes it impossible, and that it cannot become a means of salvation in the hands of those who know how to use it, like certain poisons can restore health if used wisely and appropriately.

When Jesus said to the rich young man who questioned him about the means of earning eternal life, "Sell all your possessions and follow me," he did not mean to establish as an absolute principle that everyone should give up all that he or she has, and that salvation can only be obtained at this price, but rather that *attachment to earthly goods* is an obstacle to salvation. That young man actually thought himself quits with God because he had observed certain commandments, and yet he shrank from the idea of renouncing his possessions, since his desire for eternal life did not go as far as making this sacrifice.

The proposal made to him by Jesus was a decisive test for bringing to light the substance of his thought. Of course he could have been a perfectly good and righteous person in the eyes of the world, doing no harm to anyone, nor slandering neighbor, being neither vain nor proud, and honoring his father and mother. But he did not possess true charity, for his virtue did not go as far as self-denial. This is what Jesus wanted to demonstrate; it was an application of the principle, *Without charity there is no salvation.*

The consequence of that proposal, if taken in its strict sense, would be to abolish wealth as it was harmful to future happiness and a source of all sorts of evils on Earth. Moreover, this would be the condemnation of work which can generate wealth, an absurd assumption that would make people revert to a primitive nature, which, for this very reason, would be in contradiction with the law of progress, a law of God.

If wealth is the source of many evils, if it excites so many bad passions, even if it causes so many crimes, it is necessary to attack not wealth itself, but the those who abuse it, like those who abuse any of God's gifts of God. Abuse renders pernicious what could be most useful to us; it is the consequence of the state of inferiority in which the earthly world finds itself. If wealth were to produce only evil, God would not have allowed it on Earth; it is up to humans to bring out the good in it. Although it is not a direct element of moral progress, it is undoubtedly a powerful element of intellectual progress.

Indeed, humans' mission is to work for the material improvement of the globe: we must clear it, clean it up, and dispose of it to receive one day all the population which its area can comprise. To feed this constantly growing population, it is necessary to increase production; if the production of a given region is insufficient, it must be sought somewhere else. For this very reason, people-to-people relations become a necessity; to make them easier, all material obstacles which separate them must be vanquished, making communications faster. For work endeavors that took centuries, humans had to draw materials from the entrails of the Earth. People sought in science means of carrying them out more efficiently and more quickly; but to accomplish it we need resources: necessity has made us create wealth, as it has made us discover science. The activity required by such endeavor made human intelligence grow and develop. Such intelligence which we first concentrated on satisfying our material needs, would later help us understand the great moral truths. Since wealth is the first and foremost means of execution, without it there would not be major work, greater activity, more motivation, more research. It is therefore rightly regarded as an element of progress.

INEQUALITY OF WEALTH

8.   One problem that we seek in vain to solve is inequality of wealth, if we consider only current life. The first question that arises is the following: Why are not all people equally wealthy? They are not for a very simple reason, namely, *because they are not equally intelligent, active and industrious to acquire, level-headed and far-sighted to conserve it.* It is, moreover, a mathematically demonstrated point, that equally distributed wealth would give each individual a minimal and insufficient share; and that, supposing that this distribution was made, balance would soon be broken by the diversity of characters and skills. Even supposing it possible and lasting, with each person having barely enough to live, it would mean the end of all major works which contribute to the progress and well-being of humanity. Also, if supposing that it would give each one the essentials of life, there would no longer be the motivation that drives great discoveries and useful enterprises. Therefore, if God concentrates it here or there, this happens so that it will spread in sufficient quantity, according to general needs.

Even with this being admitted, one wonders why God gives wealth to people incapable of making it bear fruit for the good of all. Here again is another proof of God's wisdom and goodness. By giving humans free will, God wanted them to succeed, through their own experience, in telling the difference between good and evil, and that the practice of good was the result of their efforts and their own will. One is not inexorably led neither to good nor to evil; without free will we would only be passive and irresponsible instruments, like animals. Wealth is a means of testing us morally; but since, at the same time, it is a powerful means of action for progress, God does not want it to remain unproductive for a long time, which is why *it constantly changes hands.* Everyone must have it, to try and use it, and prove the use they can make of it. However it is materially impossible for all to have it at the same time. Besides, if everyone possessed it, nobody would work, and improvement of the globe would suffer from it. Hence *each and every one will possess it in their turn:* someone who did not have it today already had it once or will have it in another existence; and whoever has it now may no longer have it tomorrow. There are rich and poor, because God, being just and fair, determines that everyone has to work in turn. For some people poverty is a test of patience and resignation, while for others wealth is a test of charity and self-denial.

One grumbles with reason when seeing the pitiful use that certain people make of their wealth, the vile passions that provoke lust, and then wonders if God is really just and fair by giving wealth to such people? It is certain that if a person had only one lifetime, nothing could justify such a distribution of earthly goods; but if, instead of limiting our view to current life, we consider all successive existences, we are able to see that everything is balanced with justice. The poor therefore no longer have any reason to accuse Providence, nor envy the rich; and the rich no longer have to boast about their possessions. If the latter abuse them, it is neither with decrees, nor with sumptuary laws,[59] that such evil will be remedied. Laws can temporarily change the outside, but they cannot change one's heart; this is why they have only a temporary effectiveness, and are always followed by a more frantic relapse. The source of evil lies in selfishness and pride; abuses of all kinds will cease of their own accord when humans settle themselves on the law of charity.

INSTRUCTIONS FROM THE SPIRITS

TRUE OWNERSHIP

9.   Humans own only what they can take from this world. What they find when they arrive and what they leave behind when they depart, they enjoy during their stay. However, since they are all forced to abandon it, they can only enjoy it temporarily, and not actually possess anything. What do they have then? Nothing that is for the use of the body, everything that is for the use of the soul: intelligence, knowledge, moral qualities; this is what people bring and what they take with themselves, something that is no one's power to take away from them, and which will serve them even better in the world beyond than in this one. Everyone depends on being richer on their departure than on their arrival, because on what he/she will have acquired in good deeds depends their future position. When people travel to a distant country, they fill their luggage with belongings that have some currency in the new country, but care nothing about those that would be useless to them. So do the same for your future life, and stock up only on what can be useful for you in the next destination.

A traveler who arrives at an inn is given fine accommodation if he/she can afford it; to those who have little, a less pleasant one is provided. As for the one who has nothing, such a person will have to sleep on straw. So it is with souls on their arrival in the spiritual world: their place there will depend on what they actually possess; but one cannot pay for it with gold. No one will ask you: How much did you have on Earth? What position did you hold there? Were

---

59 [Trans. note] Common in the 13th to 15th centuries, *sumptuary laws* were designed to restrict luxury or extravagance.

you a prince or a humble craftsman? Instead, you will be asked: What do you bring in? It is not the value of your earthly goods or titles that will be taken into account, but the sum of your virtues. Now, in this respect, the craftsman can be richer than the prince. In vain will the latter allege that before his departure he had paid for his entry with gold; to this he will be replied: Places cannot be bought here, they are earned by the good that one has done; with the earthly money, you were able to buy fields, houses and palaces; however, here everything is paid for with the qualities of the heart. Are you rich in such qualities? Then welcome, and go to the first place where plenty of congratulations await you; but if you are poor go to the last one where you shall be treated according to your merit.

Pascal (Geneva, 1860).

10. All the goods of the Earth belong to God which dispenses them at will, with humans being merely usufructuaries, their more or less honest and clever administrators. So barely are they the individual property of humans, that God often frustrates all predictions, when wealth escapes those who firmly believe they are entitled to it.

You may say that this is understandable when it comes to hereditary wealth, but that it is not the same with the wealth that one acquires through work. Undoubtedly, if there is legitimate wealth, this is the one, when it is acquired honestly, for *private property is only legitimately acquired when, in order to own it, no one has been harmed in the process.* You will be accountable for ill-gotten money to the detriment of others. But if some individuals owe their wealth to themselves, does it give them any advantage when dying? Aren't the precautions they take to transmit it to their offspring often futile? For, if God does not want it to fall to them, nothing can prevail against Its will. Can one use it and abuse it with impunity during one's life without being held accountable? No; by allowing one to acquire it, God may have wanted to reward this person, during this life, for their efforts, courage and perseverance. But if this person only uses it to satisfy his/her senses or pride; if it becomes a cause of fall in his/her hands, it would have been better for such a person not to have owned it. On the one hand this person loses what he/she has earned and, on the other, by canceling the merit of his/her work, and after leaving the Earth, they will hear from God: You have already received your reward.

M., a protector spirit (Bruxelles, 1861).

THE USE MADE OF WEALTH

11. You cannot serve God and mammon;[60] remember this well, you that are governed by the love of gold, you who would sell your soul to possess treasures, because these can raise you above other people and give you all the pleasures of flesh, that you cannot possibly serve God and mammon! If therefore you feel your soul is governed by the lusts of the flesh, you must hasten to shake off the yoke which weighs you down, for God, being just and severe, will tell you: What have you done, unfaithful treasurer, with the goods that I had entrusted to you? Such powerful means for good works, you have only used for your own personal satisfaction.

So what is the best use of wealth? Find it in these words, "Love one another," the solution to this problem. Therein lies the secret of making good use of one's wealth. Those who are animated by the love of neighbor thoroughly adopt this course of action. The use that pleases God is charity; not this cold and selfish charity which consists in spreading around a few superfluous crumbs of a wealthy existence, but rather true charity full of love which seeks out misfortune and relieves it without humiliating it. You rich, that give of your superfluous goods, do better than that: give something of your necessary possessions, because even your necessary possessions are still superfluous. However, give with wisdom, do not reject a plea for fear of being deceived, but go to the source of the evil, first relieve, then educate yourself, and see if the effort, the advice, the affection itself will not be more effective than your alms. Spread around you, with ease, the love of God, the love of work and love of neighbor. Put your wealth in a fund that you will never lose and that will bring you big interests, namely, good deeds. The wealth of intelligence must be useful to you like that of gold. Spread around you the treasures of education; pour out on your brothers and sisters the treasures of your love, and they will bear fruit.

Cheverus[61] (Bordeaux, 1861).

---

60 [Trans. note] See footnote 56 above.
61 [Trans. note] Cardinal Cheverus (1768–1836), former archbishop of Bordeaux.

12. When I consider the brevity of life, I am painfully affected by your incessant concern for material well-being, while attaching so little importance, and devoting so little or no time at all, to your moral improvement, which is what matters for all eternity. One would think, seeing the activity that you are doing, that it is a matter of the highest interest for humanity, while it almost always is a matter of merely putting yourselves in a position to satisfy exaggerated needs, vanities, or to indulge in excesses. What pains, worries and torments one gives oneself, how many sleepless nights, only to increase one's fortune which is often more than enough! Adding insult to injury, it is not uncommon to see those who an immoderate love of wealth and the pleasures it procures, subject themselves to hard toils, take advantage of a so-called existence of sacrifice and merit, as if working for others and not for themselves. That is simply insane! So you really think that you will be taken into account for care and efforts of which selfishness, greed or pride have been the motive, while neglecting the care of your future, as well as the duties that fraternal solidarity imposes on all who enjoy the benefits of social life? You have thought only of your physical body; its well-being, its enjoyments were the sole object of your selfish solicitude. When it dies, you will have neglected your spirit which will live forever. Thus the pampered and caressed master you chose, has become your tyrant; it commands your spirit which has turned into its slave. Is that the purpose of existence given to you by God?

A protector spirit (Cracow, Poland, 1861).

13. A person being the depositary, the manager of the goods that God places into his/her hands, they will be asked to give a strict account of the use they will have made of this wealth by virtue of their free will. Bad use consists in making it serve only for their personal satisfaction. Conversely, good use is found whenever there is good deeds to others. Merit is commensurate with the self-sacrifice that is required. Beneficence is only a method of using wealth; it relieves current poverty, it appeases hunger, it preserves from the cold and gives shelter to the one who lacks it. But an equally imperative, equally meritorious duty, consists in preventing poverty; it is above all the mission of great fortunes by works of all kinds which are made possible by wealth. And if someone would derive a legitimate profit from it, good would still be done, because opportunities for work develop intelligence and enhance the dignity of people who are always proud to be able to say that they have earned the bread they eat, whereas alms often humiliate and degrade. Wealth concentrated in one hand should be a source of living water that spreads fertility and well-being around it. You rich people, that use it according to the Lord's direction, will be the first to have your hearts quench your thirst at this beneficent fountain. Already in this life you will experience the ineffable enjoyments of the soul instead of the material enjoyments of selfishness which leave a void in the heart. Your name will be blessed on Earth, and when you leave it, the sovereign master will address to you these words from the parable of the talents: "Well done, good and faithful servant, enter into the joy of your master." In this parable, is it not the servant that has buried in the ground the money entrusted to him, an image of the miser in whose hands fortune is unproductive? If, however, Jesus speaks mainly of alms, it is because at that time and in the country where he lived, they did not yet know the works that the arts and industry have created since, and how wealth could be beneficially used for the general good. To all those who can give whether a little or a lot, I therefore say: Give alms when necessary, but as much as possible convert it into wages, so that whoever receives them does not feel embarrassed or ashamed.

Fénelon (Algeria, 1860).

Detachment from earthly goods

14. I come, dear brothers and sisters, my friends, to bring a small contribution to help you walk boldly on the path of improvement which you have taken. We owe each other; it is only through a sincere and fraternal alliance between spirits and incarnate humans that regeneration is possible.

Your love for earthly goods is one of the strongest obstacles to your moral and spiritual advancement. By such an attachment to possessions, you ruin your loving faculties by transferring them entirely to material things. Be frank; does wealth give you unalloyed happiness? When your coffers are full, is there not always a void left in your hearts? At the bottom of this basket of flowers, isn't there always a hidden viper? I understand that a person who, by diligent and honorable work, has won a fortune, may experience some satisfaction, which is quite just and natural. Yet between such a satisfaction, very natural and approved by God, and an attachment which absorbs all other sentiments and paralyzes the tenderness of the heart, there is a great distance, as far as the one between sordid greed and exaggerated extravagance, two vices between which God has interposed charity, this holy and salutary virtue that teaches the rich to give without ostentation, so that the poor can receive without being debased.

Whether wealth comes to you inherited from your family, or whether you earned it through your own work, there is one thing you should never forget: everything comes from God and everything goes back to God. Nothing belongs to you or anyone on Earth, not even your poor body: death strips you of it as of all material goods. Make no mistake, you are depositaries and not owners. God has lent you everything, you must give it back; and God will lend you on condition that at least what is superfluous to you is distributed to those who lack the essentials of life.

Suppose that one of your friends lends you a sum; as long as you are honest, you make a point of paying it back, and you remain grateful for it. Well, that is the situation of every rich person: God is the heavenly friend who lent them wealth. God only asks for love and recognition, but demands that in turn the rich give to the poor who are as much God's children as they are.

The goods which God has entrusted to you excites in your hearts an intense mad lust for money. When you get too attached to wealth, as perishable and passing like you, have you ever thought a day will come when you will have to give an account to the Lord, owner of everything which is in your possession? Do you forget that, with wealth, you have been invested with the sacred position of ministers of charity on Earth, as intelligent dispensers? Then what should you be considered, given the fact that you have used what has been entrusted to you only for your own profit, if not as unfaithful depositaries? What were the results from this voluntary neglect of your duties? Death will inflexibly and inexorably tear the veil beneath which you hide, and force you to give your account to the very friend that had obliged you, and which at that moment will be wearing the judge's toga for you.

In vain you seek to deceive yourselves on Earth, by disguising as virtue what is often only selfishness; and what you call prudent economy and foresight actually being nothing but greed and avarice; or calling generosity what is nothing but lavishness for your sole benefit. A parent, for example, will refrain from doing charity, while saving and piling up gold on gold, which, he/she claims, is for the purpose of leaving their children as much money as possible, thus preventing them from falling into poverty. This is a very righteous and proper resolution on their part, I agree, and one could not find fault with it; but is this still really only reason guiding such parent? Is it not often an excuse of their conscience to justify in their own eyes and in the eyes of the world their personal attachment to earthly goods? However, even admitting that parental love is their only motive; would it be a reason to forget one's fellow beings before God? If one already possess the superfluous, will he/she leave their children in poverty, for having a little less of this superfluous in future? Instead, is it not giving them a lesson on how being selfish and hardening their hearts? Is it not stifling love for neighbor? Fathers and mothers, you are in great error, if you think that this is a way of increasing the affection of your children for you, while teaching them to be selfish for others. On the contrary, you are teaching them to be selfish toward yourselves.

When a person has worked hard and well, and by the sweat of the brow has amassed goods, you will often hear this person say that when money is earned you learn to value it better. Nothing could be truer. Now, if this person, who admits to knowing the true value of money, does charity within his/her means, he/she will have more merit than the one who, born in abundance, ignores the rough fatigues of work. Conversely, if this same person that remembers his/her tribulations and labors, is selfish and hard on the poor, he/she will be much more guilty compared to those people mentioned above; for the more one knows for oneself the hidden pains of poverty, the more one should be inclined to relieve such suffering in others.

Unfortunately pride is a sentiment always present in those who have a strong attachment to wealth. It is not uncommon to see a parvenu stun an unfortunate individual who begs assistance on account of his/her work and know-how. Instead of coming to the unfortunate person's aid, he/she tells him: "Do what I have done." According to the parvenu, the goodness of God has nothing to do with his/her wealth; the merit is all his/her own. Pride has put a blindfold over their eyes and plugged their ears tight. They do not realize that, despite all their intelligence and skills, God can sink them with a single blow.

Squandering one's fortune means not detachment from earthly goods, but carelessness and indifference. A person, as a mere custodian of these goods, has no more right to squander them than to confiscate them for his/her own profit. Prodigality is not generosity, it is often a form of selfishness. Someone who throws handfuls of gold to satisfy a whim would not give a single coin for service. True detachment from earthly goods consists in giving money its just value, namely, in using it for others and not for oneself; in not sacrificing the interests of future life; in losing it without grumbling if it pleases God to take it away from you. If, by unforeseen setbacks, you become another biblical Job, say like him: "The LORD gave, and the LORD has taken away; blessed be the name of the LORD."[62] This is real detachment. Be submissive first; have faith in the One who gave and took away from you, and can give you back. Courageously resist dejection and despair that paralyze your strength. When God strikes you, never forget that next to the greatest trial, It always provides a consolation. But think above all that there are goods infinitely more precious than those of the Earth, and this thought will help you detach from them. The low value we attach to something makes us less sensitive to losing it. Those who attach themselves to the goods of the Earth are like children who care only about the present moment; whereas those who do not hold to earthly goods are like grown-ups who care about more important things, for they understand these prophetic words of our Savior: "My kingdom is not of this world."

The Lord does not order anyone to divest oneself of one's possessions and to be reduced to voluntary begging, because then one would become a burden to society. To act like that would be to misunderstand detachment from earthly goods; it would be another type of selfishness, because it would mean to rid oneself of the responsibilities that wealth imposes upon those who possess it.

---

62 [Trans. note] JOB 1:21 ESV.

God gives it to whomsoever It pleases so that they manage it for the benefit of all. The rich therefore have a mission; a mission that he can make beautiful and profitable. To reject wealth when God gives it to you is to renounce the benefit of the good that can be done by managing it wisely. By knowing to do without it when you do not have it, and knowing how to use it usefully when you do, and how to sacrifice it when necessary, will be acting in accordance with the Lord's will. Let the one who happens to be granted what the world calls good fortune exclaim: "God, you have sent me a new task, give me the strength to fulfill it according to your holy will."

This, dear friends, is what I intended to teach you as detachment from earthly goods. I will sum up by saying: Know how to be content with little. If you are poor, do not envy the rich, because wealth is not necessary for happiness. If you are wealthy, do not forget that these goods are entrusted to you, and that you will have to justify their use as you would in a guardianship account. Do not be unfaithful trustees, by making the goods serve for the satisfaction of your pride and your sensuality. Do not think you are entitled to use only for yourself what is actually a loan, and not a donation. If you cannot give back, you no longer have the right to ask, and remember that those who give to the poor pay off the debt they contracted with God.

Lacordaire (Constantine, Algeria, 1863).

15. *Does the principle by which a person is only the depositary of the wealth which God allows him/her to enjoy during life, deprive them of the right to transmit it to their descendants?*

Anyone can perfectly transmit after death what he/she enjoyed during life, because the effect of this right is always subject to the will of God which can, when It wants, prevent descendants from enjoying it. This is how we see the crumbling of fortunes which seemed to be most solidly established. A person's will to keep his/her fortune in his/her lineage is therefore powerless, which does not deprive such a person of the right to transmit the loan received, since God will withdraw it when It sees fit.

Saint Louis (Paris, 1860).

Chapter XVII
Be perfect

CHARACTERISTICS OF PERFECTION

1. "Love your enemies and pray for those who persecute you, so that you may be sons of your Father who is in heaven. For he makes his sun rise on the evil and on the good, and sends rain on the just and on the unjust. For if you love those who love you, what reward do you have? Do not even the tax collectors do the same? And if you greet only your brothers, what more are you doing than others? Do not even the Gentiles do the same? *You therefore must be perfect, as your heavenly Father is perfect* (MATTHEW 5:44–48 ESV)."

2. Since God is infinitely perfect in all things, taken literally, this maxim, "You therefore must be perfect, as your heavenly Father is perfect," would presuppose the possibility of achieving absolute perfection. However, if created beings could be as perfect as their Creator, they would become equal to It, which is inconceivable. But the people to whom Jesus talked would not understand such nuance; so he simply presented them with a model and told them to strive to achieve it.

These words must therefore be understood as meaning relative perfection, of which humanity is susceptible and which brings us closer to the Divinity. But what sort of perfection is this? Jesus said: "Love your enemies, do good to those who hate you, pray for those who persecute you." By this he shows that the essence of perfection is charity in its broadest sense, because it involves the practice of all other virtues.

Indeed if we observe the consequences of all vices, and even simple faults, we will recognize that none of them can in the least alter the sentiment of charity, for they are all rooted in the principle of selfishness and pride, which are its negation; for everything that excites one's feeling of personality destroys, or at least weakens, the elements of true charity, namely, benevolence, indulgence, self-denial and commitment. Love of neighbor, extended to the love of one's enemies, unable to ally itself with any defect contrary to charity, is by this very fact always an indication of greater or lesser moral superiority. Whence it follows that one's degree of perfection is relative to the extent of this love; which is why Jesus, after giving his disciples the rules of the sublimest charity, said to them: "You therefore must be perfect, as your heavenly Father is perfect."

Good persons

3.   A truly good human being is one who practices the law of justice, love and charity in its greatest purity. If people would inquire their conscience about their own acts, they would find out whether they have violated this law and done any harm. Whether they did *all the good they could* or voluntarily neglected an opportunity to be useful; or if no one has anything to complain against them. And, lastly, whether they have done unto others as they would have others do unto them.

Good persons have faith in God, in God's kindness, in God's justice and wisdom. They know that nothing happens without Its permission, and submit themselves in all things to God's will.

They have faith in the future – this is why they place spiritual goods above temporal goods.

They know that all the vicissitudes, all the pains, and all the disappointments of life are trials or atonements, which they accept without grumbling.

Persons imbued with the feeling of charity and love of neighbor do good for the sake of good, without expecting any return. They render good for evil, defend the weak against the strong, and always sacrifice their own interest to the requirements of justice.

They find satisfaction in the benefits they spread, in the services they render, in the happiness they bring, in the tears they dry up, in the comfort they give to the afflicted. Their first impulse is to think of others before thinking of themselves, to seek the interest of others before their own. The selfish person, on the contrary, calculates the profits and losses of any generous action.

Such individuals are good, humane and benevolent toward everyone, *without distinction of race or creed*, because they regard all human beings as brothers and sisters.

They respect in others any sincerely held convictions, and do not condemn those who think differently from them.

In all circumstances, they are guided by charity. It is said that anyone who harms others with malicious words, who offends the susceptibility of others by pride and disdain, who does not shy away from the idea of causing pain – even slight annoyances, when they could be avoided – fails in the duty of love of neighbor, and thus does not deserve the Lord's mercy.

Good persons harbor no hatred, no grudge, no desire for revenge. Following the example of Jesus, they forgive and forget all offenses, and remember only acts of kindness; for they know that those who forgive will themselves be forgiven.

They are indulgent to weaknesses in others, because they know they need to have indulgence toward themselves, and remember these words of Christ: "Let him who is without sin cast the first stone."

They do not take pleasure in finding or pointing out the faults of others. If necessity obliges them to give their opinion, they always seek good points that can mitigate the evil.

They examine their own imperfections, and constantly work to combat them. All their efforts aim at being able to say the next day that there is something better in them than the day before.

They do not seek to assert neither their wit nor their own talents at the expense of others. On the contrary, the seize every opportunity to highlight what is to the advantage of others.

They have no vanity either in their wealth or personal advantages, because they know that whatever was given to them can be taken away from them.

They use, but do not abuse, the goods which are granted to them, because they know that it is a deposit which they will be required to give an account to God; and that the most harmful use that they could make of it for themselves, would be to make it serve the satisfaction of their passions.

When social order places humans under its protection, it treats them with kindness and benevolence, because they are equal before God. It uses its authority to raise their morale, not to crush them under its pride. It avoids anything that could make their subordinate position more painful.

Subordinates, for their part, will thus understand the duties of their position, and be scrupulous in fulfilling them conscientiously (see Ch. **XVII**, n° **9** above).

Lastly, all good persons do respect in their fellow beings all the rights which the laws of Nature have give them, as they would like such laws to be respected with regard to themselves.

There is not a list of all the qualities which distinguish a good person, but whoever strives to have these is on the way of possessing all the others.

GOOD SPIRITISTS

4. Spiritism, when well understood but above all deeply felt, leads to the above results, which characterize a true Spiritist as a true Christian, with one mirroring exactly the other. Spiritism creates no new moral code; it rather facilitates humans to understand and practice Christ's moral code, by imparting a strong and enlightened faith to those who doubt or waver.

But many of those who believe in the facts of spirit phenomena do not understand their consequences or moral significance. Or, if they do understand them, they do not apply them to themselves. Why is that so? Is this due to some lack of precision in the Spiritist tenets? No, since Spiritism does not contain allegories or figures of speech which could give rise to false interpretations. Its very essence is clarity, and that is what makes it powerful, because it goes straight to the intellect. There is nothing mysterious about it, and its initiates are not in possession of any secret hidden from anyone else.

In order to understand Spiritism, does one must have extraordinary intelligence? No, because we see individuals with marked intellectual capacity who do not understand it, while regular, common people – even young people barely out of adolescence – seize with admirable accuracy its most delicate nuances. This comes from the fact that the somewhat *material* part of science requires only eyes to be seen, while the *essential* part needs a certain degree of sensitivity which could be called *a developed moral sense*. Such developed sense is independent of age or degree of education, because it is inherent in the development, in a special sense, of an incarnate spirit.

In some people, the bonds of matter are still too tenacious to allow the spirit to free itself from the things of the Earth. The thick fog that surrounds them hides from them the sight of the infinite; which is why they do not easily break with their habits and preferences, incapable of conceiving of anything better than what they already have. The belief in spirits is for them a mere fact, which modifies little or nothing of their instinctive tendencies. In a word, they see only a sliver of light, insufficient to move them and give them a powerful aspiration, capable of overcoming their addictions. They attach themselves more to spirit phenomena than to moral effects, which seem banal and monotonous to them. They insistently ask the spirits to initiate them in new mysteries, without wondering if they have made themselves worthy of being informed about the Creator's secrets. So these are imperfect spiritists, some of whom stay on the way while others move away from their brothers and sisters in faith, because they recoil before the necessity of transforming themselves, or else they reserve their sympathies only for those who share their same weaknesses or prejudices. However, the acceptance of the basic principle of Spiritism is a first step which will make the second one easier for them in another existence.

Those who can rightly be called true and sincere Spiritists are at a higher level of moral advancement. When there is predominance of spirit over matter, it gives one a clearer perception of the future; the principles of Spiritist tenets stir up every fiber of one's being, which remain silent among the former. In a word, the latter are *touched deep in their hearts*, therefore their faith is unshakable. One is like a musician who is moved by certain chords, while the other can hear only sounds. *True Spiritists are recognized by their moral transformation, and by the efforts they make to subdue their bad inclinations.* While the former delight in their limited horizon, the latter, who discern something better, strive to detach themselves from it, and always succeed when they have a firm will.

PARABLE OF THE SOWER AND THE SEED

5. "That same day Jesus went out of the house and sat beside the sea. And great crowds gathered about him, so that he got into a boat and sat down. And the whole crowd stood on the beach. And he told them many things in parables, saying: 'A sower went out to sow. And as he sowed, some seeds fell along the path, and the birds came and devoured them. Other seeds fell on rocky ground, where they did not have much soil, and immediately they sprang up, since they had no depth of soil, but when the sun rose they were scorched. And since they had no root, they withered away. Other seeds fell among thorns, and the thorns grew up and choked them. Other seeds fell on good soil and produced grain, some a hundredfold, some sixty, some thirty. He who has ears, let him hear' (MATTHEW 13:1–9 ESV)."

"Hear then the parable of the sower: When anyone hears the word of the kingdom and does not understand it, the evil one comes and snatches away what has been sown in his heart. This is what was sown along the path.

As for what was sown on rocky ground, this is the one who hears the word and immediately receives it with joy, yet he has no root in himself, but endures for a while, and when tribulation or persecution arises on account of the word, immediately he falls away.

As for what was sown among thorns, this is the one who hears the word, but the cares of the world and the deceitfulness of riches choke the word, and it proves unfruitful.

As for what was sown on good soil, this is the one who hears the word and understands it. He indeed bears fruit and yields, in one case a hundredfold, in another sixty, and in another thirty (MATTHEW 13:18–23 ESV)."

6. The parable of the sower and the seed perfectly represents the nuances that exist in the manner of using the teachings of the Gospel. Indeed, how many people are there for whom it is nothing but dead letter, which, like the seed sown on rocky ground, yield no fruit!

This parable finds an equally just application in the different categories of Spiritists. Is it not the emblem of those fixated only on material spirit phenomena, and draw no consequence from them, because they see in them a mere object of curiosity? Or of those who seek only dazzling spirit communications, and are only interested in them as long as they satisfy their imagination, but who, after having heard them, remain as cold and indifferent as before? Also of those who find the advice very good and admire it, but apply it to others but not to themselves? Finally, of those for whom these instructions are like seeds sown in good soil, which yield plenty of fruit?

INSTRUCTIONS FROM THE SPIRITS

DUTY

7.   Duty is this sentiment of obligation with regard to oneself first and to others afterwards. Duty is the law of life; it is found in the smallest details, as well as in the highest acts. Here I am referring only to moral duty, not to that imposed by one's profession or occupation.

In the order of sentiments, duty is very difficult to fulfill, because it finds itself in antagonism to the seductions of interest and of the heart. Its victories have no witnesses, its defeats no suppression. A person's inner duty is abandoned at the mercy of his/her own free will. Although the sting of conscience – this guardian of inner uprightness – will warn and support the individual, he/she often remains powerless before the fallacies of passion. Duty of the heart, when faithfully observed, elevates you. Yet, how to specify this duty? Where does it start? Where does it stop? *Duty starts precisely at the point you threaten the happiness or peace of others, and stops at the boundaries you would not want others to violate with respect to yourself.*

God created all people equal as regards pain. Both young and old, ignorant or enlightened, suffer from the same causes, so that each and every one can conscientiously consider the harm that they can do. The same criterion does not exist in relation to good, which is infinitely more varied in its expressions. *The equality in pain is a sublime foresight of God, which wants Its children, educated by common experience, to stop committing evil, once unable to claim ignorance of its effects.*

Duty is the practical summary of all moral speculations; it is an act of bravery of the soul which confronts the anguish of the struggle; it is both austere and flexible: quick to bow to various difficulties, it remains adamant before temptations. *Anyone who fulfills their duty loves God more than their fellow humans, and fellow humans more than themselves.* They are both judge and witness, lord and serf, in their own cause.

Duty is the most beautiful jewel of reason; it reports back to it, as the child reports to its mother. Humans should love duty, not because it preserves them from the evils of life, from which humanity cannot escape, but because it gives one's soul the stamina necessary for its development.

Duty grows and radiates in a higher form at each of the higher stages of humanity. Moral obligation never ceases from the created being to God; it must reflect the virtues of the Eternal One which does not accept an imperfect sketch, for It wants the beauty of Its work to shine before Its presence.

Lazarus (Paris, 1863).

VIRTUE

8.   Virtue, in its highest degree, comprises the whole of all the essential qualities which constitute a good person. Being good, charitable, hardworking, sober, modest, are all qualities of virtuous persons. Unfortunately they are often accompanied by slight moral infirmities which mismatch and decrease them. Those who display their virtue are not virtuous, since they lack its main quality: modesty; and instead possess its most contrary vice: pride. Virtue truly worthy of its name does not seek to put itself on display; you can guess it, but it prefers to remain unnoticed and flees flattery and compliments of others. Saint Vincent de Paul, the worthy parish priest of Ars, was virtuous like many others little known to the world, but known to God. All these good persons themselves did not know that they were virtuous; they let themselves be aware of their holy inspirations, and practiced good with complete disinterestedness, and completely oblivious to themselves.

It is to this sort of virtue thus understood and practiced that I invite you, dear children. It is to this truly Christian and Spiritist virtue that I urge you to devote yourselves – yet be sure to remove from your hearts any thought of pride, vanity or self-esteem which always mismatches the most beautiful qualities. Do not imitate a person who poses as a model and advocates his/her own qualities to all complacent ears. This virtue of ostentation often hides a series of small turpitudes and odious cowardice.

In principle, those who exalt themselves, who raise a statue to their own virtue, destroy by this very fact all the effective merit they can have. But what can I say of those whose entire value resides in seeming to be what they are not? I am willing to admit that someone who does good feels some inner satisfaction at the bottom of his/ her heart, but as soon as such satisfaction is expressed outward to receive praise, it degenerates into self-esteem.

All of you who have been warmed up by the Spiritist faith, and who know how far humans are from perfection, never give in such folly. Virtue is a grace that I wish to all sincere Spiritists, but I would also like to add: Better have less virtue with modesty than much with pride. It is through pride that successive civilizations have lost their way; it is through humility that they must one day redeem themselves.

François Nicolas Madeleine[63] (Paris, 1863).

SUPERIORS AND SUBORDINATES

9.   Authority, like wealth, is a delegated power of which those who are invested with it will be held accountable. Do not think that it is given to someone to procure him or her the vain pleasure of commanding; nor, as most of the powerful of the Earth falsely believe, as a right, a property. Meanwhile God has sufficiently proved to them that it is neither, since It takes it away when It wills. If authority were a privilege attached to one person, it would be irremovable. Therefore no one can say that something belongs to them, when it can be taken from them without their consent. Authority is given as a *mission* or test when God wills; and likewise it is withdrawn.

Whoever is the depositary of authority, whatever its extent, from a master over his/her subordinates to a sovereign over his/her people, must not forget the fact that he/she is in charge of souls. Such persons will be held accountable for the good or bad command they exerted over their subordinates; and for the faults which these latter will be able to commit, or the vices to which they will be drawn, as a result of his/her authority or *bad example*, which will fall back on the depositary of authority. Conversely, such a person will collect the fruits of his/her solicitude in bringing their subordinates to good. Every human being has a small or big mission to perform on Earth; whatever it may be, it is always given for the cause of good.

---

63 [Trans. note] François Nicolas Madeleine Morlot (1795–1862), French Catholic cardinal and archbishop of Paris.

Therefore anyone who adulterates and distorts its principle, will have failed it.

God will ask the rich: What have you done with the wealth that was intended to become in your hands a copious stream spreading fertility all around? And God will ask those who have any sort of authority: What use have you made of this authority? What evil did you stop? What progress have you brought about? If I gave you subordinates, it was neither to make them slaves of your will, nor docile instruments of your whims or greed: I made you strong and entrusted you with the weak for you to support them and help them come up to me.

Superiors who are permeated by the words of the Christ do not despise any of those who are under them, because they know that social distinctions do not rank them before God. Spiritism teaches you that if others obey you today, they may have previously commanded you, or will one day command you – and then they will treat you as you would have treated them yourselves.

If superiors have duties to fulfill, subordinates also have their own which are no less sacred. If the latter are Spiritist, their conscience will tell them even better that they are not exempt from duties, even when their superiors do not fill theirs, because they know that one must not return evil for evil, and that the faults of some do not authorize the faults of others. If subordinates suffer for their station and rank, they should bear in mind that they undoubtedly deserved it, since they themselves may have once abused their authority, and now they must feel in turn the disadvantages of what they made others suffer. If subordinates are forced to undergo this position, failing to find a better one, Spiritism teaches them to resign themselves to it as a test of humility, necessary for their advancement. Their belief guides them in such conduct; they behave as they would want their subordinates to do unto them if instead they were their superiors. For this very reason they are more scrupulous in the fulfillment of their obligations, because they understand that any negligence in the work entrusted to them would cause loss to the person who pays them and to whom they owe their hired time and care. In a word, they are bound by a feeling of duty as entrusted and assigned by their superiors, and by the certainty that any deviation from the right path is a debt that will have to be paid sooner or later.

François Nicolas Madeleine (Paris, 1863).

THE INDIVIDUAL IN THE WORLD

10.   A sentiment of piety must always animate the hearts of those who gather before the eyes of the Lord imploring the assistance of good spirits. So purify your hearts, do not let any worldly or futile thoughts linger in them, raise your spirit toward those that you invoke, so that, finding in you the necessary disposition, they can profusely throw the seed which must germinate in your hearts to bear the fruit of charity and justice.

Do not think, however, that by constantly exhorting you to prayer and mental evocation, we are committing you to lead a mystical life that keeps you away from the laws of society, in which you are sentenced to live. On the contrary, you ought to live with the fellow humans of your time, as all people should live; and sacrifice for the needs, even for the frivolities of the day, but do it with a feeling of purity that can sanctify them.

You are called to put yourself in contact with spirits of different natures and contrasting characters: be sure not to offend any of those with which you happen to be around you. Be cheerful and happy, but with the gaiety that a good conscience gives, and the happiness of an heir to heaven counting the days that bring you closer to your allotted heritage.

Virtue does not consist neither in putting on a severe and gloomy countenance, nor in repelling the pleasures that your human condition allow. It suffices to relate all the actions of one's life to the Creator which gave you this life. It is enough, when one begins or completes a work, to raise his/her thoughts toward the Creator, asking from God, in an impetus of the soul, either Its protection for one to succeed, or Its blessing for the finished work. Whatever you do, go back to the source of all things; never do anything without the remembrance of God coming to purify and sanctify your actions.

Perfection lies entirely, as the Christ said, in the practice of absolute charity; yet the duties of charity extend to social positions, from the humblest to the highest. The individual who would rather live alone would have no charity to exercise; it is only in contact with fellow beings, in the most painful struggles, that one finds the opportunity to practice it. Those who isolate themselves voluntarily deprive themselves of the most powerful means to achieve perfection. If you think of no other but yourself, your life becomes that of an egoist (see chapter **V**, no. **26** above).

Therefore do not assume that, to live in constant communication with us and under the eye of the Lord, it is necessary to put on a haircloth and cover yourselves with ashes.[64] Absolutely not. Be happy in accordance with the needs of humanity, but do not let your happiness be tainted by any thought or action that might offend or cloud the face of those who love you and direct you. God is love and blesses those whose love is saintly.

A protector spirit (Bordeaux, 1863).

Caring for body and soul

11. Does moral perfection consist in mortification of the body? To resolve this question, I will rely on some elementary principles, and begin by demonstrating the necessity of caring for the body, which, in view of the alternatives of health and disease, has a very important influence on the soul, which, by its turn, must be considered as held captive to the flesh. In order for this prisoner to live, move about and even conceive of the illusion of freedom, the body must be healthy, willing and physically staunch. Let us make a comparison: Suppose that one's body and soul are both in perfect condition, what should be done in order to keep the balance between their very different abilities and needs?

Here two systems are present: that of the ascetics, who want to mortify the body; and that of the materialists, who want to diminish the soul. Two types of violence, one being almost as insane as the other. Beside these groups of people swarms the large tribe of the indifferent, who, without any conviction or passion, love lukewarmly and enjoy parsimoniously. Where then is wisdom? Where is the science of living? It is nowhere to be found; and this great problem would remain entirely unsolved if Spiritism had not come to the aid of researchers, showing them the relation which exists between body and soul, and saying that, since they are necessary for each other, you have to look after both of them. Therefore love your soul, but also look after your body, the instrument of the soul. To

---

64 [Trans. note] A symbolic figure of penitence in biblical times.

ignore the needs which are indicated by Nature itself is to ignore the God's law. Do not chastise it for the faults that your free will made it commit, and for which it is as blameless as a misguided horse would be for the accidents which it caused. Will you thus be more perfect if, while mortifying the body, you remain nonetheless selfish, proud and ungodly toward neighbor? No, perfection is not there; it is entirely in the transformation to which you will subject your spirit by bending it, subduing it, humiliating it, and mortifying it. This is the way to make it docile to the will of God, and the only one that leads to perfection.

Georges, a protector spirit (Paris, 1863)

Chapter XVIII
Many are called but few are chosen

PARABLE OF THE WEDDING FEAST

1. "And again Jesus spoke to them in parables, saying, 'The kingdom of heaven may be compared to a king who gave a wedding feast for his son, and sent his servants to call those who were invited to the wedding feast, but they would not come. Again he sent other servants, saying, 'Tell those who are invited, See, I have prepared my dinner, my oxen and my fat calves have been slaughtered, and everything is ready. Come to the wedding feast.' But they paid no attention and went off, one to his farm, another to his business, while the rest seized his servants, treated them shamefully, and killed them. The king was angry, and he sent his troops and destroyed those murderers and burned their city. Then he said to his servants, 'The wedding feast is ready, but those invited were not worthy. Go therefore to the main roads and invite to the wedding feast as many as you find.' And those servants went out into the roads and gathered all whom they found, both bad and good. So the wedding hall was filled with guests.

'But when the king came in to look at the guests, he saw there a man who had no wedding garment. And he said to him, 'Friend, how did you get in here without a wedding garment?' And he was speechless. Then the king said to the attendants, 'Bind him hand and foot and cast him into the outer darkness. In that place there will be weeping and gnashing of teeth.' *For many are called, but few are chosen'* (MATTHEW 22:1–14 ESV)."

2. Unbelievers smile at this parable which seems childishly naive to them, because they do not understand how someone could possibly go through so many difficulties to attend a feast, and even less that guests could show resistance to the point of slaying the envoys of the master of the house. "Parables," they say, "are undoubtedly symbolical, but still they must not push the limits of plausibility."

The same can be said of all allegories, the most ingenious fables, if we do not strip them from their envelopes to seek their hidden meaning. Jesus drew his own from the most ordinary customs of life, and adapted them to the customs and character of the people to whom he spoke. Most of them were intended to introduce the idea of spiritual life to the masses; the meaning of the parables often seems unintelligible only because one does not start from this point of view.

In this particular parable, Jesus compares the kingdom of heaven – where everything is joy and happiness – to a feast. As first guests, he alludes to the Hebrews[65] whom God had called first to the knowledge of Its law. The king's envoys are the prophets who came to exhort them to follow the path of true bliss; yet their words were seldom heard, their warnings were despised, and several of them were even slain like the servants of the parable. The guests who excuse their absence by claiming that they had to tend their fields and to their business, are the emblem of the worldly people who, absorbed by earthly things, are indifferent to heavenly things.

It was a common belief, among the Jews of the day, that their nation should gain supremacy over all others. In fact, did not God promise Abraham that his seed would cover the whole Earth? But still, taking form for content, they believed in an effectively material domination.

Before the coming of Christ, with the exception of the Hebrews, all peoples were idolaters and polytheists. If certain individuals, superior to the average, could conceive the idea of divine unicity, this idea remained in the state of a personal system, nowhere accepted as a fundamental truth, except by some initiates who hid their knowledge under a mysterious veil impenetrable to the masses. The Hebrews were the first to publicly practice monotheism. It is

---

65 [Trans. note] Jews of ancient Israel and Palestine, descendants of the patriarch Jacob, grandson of Abraham.

to them that God transmitted Its law, first through Moses, then through Jesus. It is from this tiny source that light was to spread over the whole world, defeating paganism, and giving to Abraham a spiritual posterity "as numerous as the stars of the firmament." But the Jews, while rejecting idolatry, had neglected the moral law to attach themselves to the externalities of form. Evil was at its height; that enslaved nation was torn apart by factions, divided by sects; even unbelief had penetrated into the inner sanctum. It was then that Jesus appeared, sent to remind them to observe the law, and to open to them the new horizons of future life. However, as the first invited to the banquet of universal faith, they rejected the word of the heavenly Messiah, and destroyed him. Thus they lost the fruit which they would have gathered from their earlier initiative.

It would be unfair, however, to accuse the whole people of this state of affairs; the responsibility rests primarily with the Pharisees and Sadducees who led to the nation's loss through the pride and fanaticism of some, and through the unbelief of others. It is they above all that Jesus equates to the guests who refuse to go to the wedding dinner. Then he adds: "Go therefore to the main roads and invite to the wedding feast as many as you find." By this he meant that the word would be preached to all other peoples, pagans and idolaters, and that those accepting it would be admitted to the feast instead of the first guests.

But it is not enough to be invited; it is not enough to wear the label of Christian or to sit at the table to take part in the celestial feast. It is necessary, first and foremost and as an express condition, to be clothed in the nuptial robe, that is to say, to have purity of heart, and to practice the law according to its spirit. Now, this law is entirely contained in the following words: *Without charity there is no salvation.* Yet, among all those who hear the divine words, how few are there who keep them and use them! How few are there who are worthy to enter the kingdom of heaven! This is why Jesus said: *Many are called, but few are chosen.*

THE NARROW GATE

3. "'Enter by the narrow gate. For the gate is wide and the way is easy that leads to destruction, and those who enter by it are many.

For the gate is narrow and the way is hard that leads to life, and those who find it are few' (MATTHEW 7:13–14 ESV)."

4. "And someone said to him, 'Lord, will those who are saved be few?' And he said to them, 'Strive to enter through the narrow door. For many, I tell you, will seek to enter and will not be able. When once the master of the house has risen and shut the door, and you begin to stand outside and to knock at the door, saying, 'Lord, open to us,' then he will answer you, 'I do not know where you come from.' Then you will begin to say, 'We ate and drank in your presence, and you taught in our streets.' But he will say, 'I tell you, I do not know where you come from. Depart from me, all you workers of evil!'

In that place there will be weeping and gnashing of teeth, when you see Abraham and Isaac and Jacob and all the prophets in the kingdom of God but you yourselves cast out. And people will come from east and west, and from north and south, and recline at table in the kingdom of God. And behold, some are last who will be first, and some are first who will be last' (LUKE 13:23–30 ESV)."

5. The gate to perdition is wide, because bad passions are numerous, and the road to evil is frequented by the greatest number of people. Conversely, the gate to salvation is narrow, because those who want to cross it must make great efforts on themselves in order to overcome their bad tendencies, and only a few are resigned to it. This is the complement of the maxim: *Many are called, but few are chosen.*

Such is the current state of earthly humanity because, as the Earth is a world of atonement, evil still predominates on it. When it is transformed, the path to good will be the busiest. These words must therefore be understood in a relative sense and not in an absolute sense. If that were to be the normal state of humanity, God would have willingly destroyed the vast majority of Its created beings; an inadmissible supposition, as soon as one acknowledges that God is all justice and kindness.

But what misdeeds could humanity have done to deserve such a sad fate in its present and in its future, if it were all relegated to Earth, and if the soul had not had other existences? Why would there be so many obstacles sown on its way? Why is this gate so narrow that it is given to the smallest number of people to cross, if the fate of one's soul is fixed forever after death? In this way, with the idea of experiencing only a single existence, one is incessantly at odds with oneself and with the justice of God. Conversely, with the concept of anteriority of the soul and the plurality of worlds, the horizon widens, light is shed on the most obscure points of faith, the present and the future are united with the past. Only then can we understand all the depth, all the truth and all the wisdom of the maxims of Christ.

NOT EVERYONE WHO SAYS, "LORD, LORD," WILL ENTER THE KINGDOM OF HEAVEN

6. "'Not everyone who says to me, 'Lord, Lord,' will enter the kingdom of heaven, but the one who does the will of my Father who is in heaven. On that day many will say to me, 'Lord, Lord, did we not prophesy in your name, and cast out demons in your name, and do many mighty works in your name?' And then will I declare to them, 'I never knew you; depart from me, you workers of lawlessness' (MATTHEW 7:21–23 ESV)."

7. "'Everyone then who hears these words of mine and does them will be like a wise man who built his house on the rock. And the rain fell, and the floods came, and the winds blew and beat on that house, but it did not fall, because it had been founded on the rock. And everyone who hears these words of mine and does not do them will be like a foolish man who built his house on the sand. And the rain fell, and the floods came, and the winds blew and beat against that house, and it fell, and great was the fall of it' (MATTHEW 7:24–27; cf. LUKE 6:46–49 ESV)."

8. "'Therefore whoever relaxes one of the least of these commandments and teaches others to do the same will be called least in the kingdom of heaven, but whoever does them and teaches them will be called great in the kingdom of heaven' (MATTHEW 5:19 ESV)."

9. All those who confess faith in Jesus' mission say, "Lord! Lord!" But what is the use of calling him Master or Lord if one does not follow his precepts? Can be called Christians those who honor him by external acts of devotion while at the same time never renouncing

their pride, selfishness, greed and all their passions? Are his real disciples those who spend days in prayer and become neither better, nor more charitable, nor more indulgent toward their fellow beings? No, because, like the Pharisees, they have prayer on their lips and not in their hearts. With the apparent form, they can impose it on humans, but not on God. In vain they will say to Jesus, "Lord, we have prophesied, that is to say, taught in your name; we have cast demons out on your behalf; we drank and ate with you." To this he will reply: "I do not know you; withdraw from me, all you who commit iniquities, you who belie your words by your actions, who slander your neighbor, who plunder widows and commit adultery; away from me, you whose hearts distill hatred and gall, you who shed the blood of your brothers and sisters in my name, who incite tears instead of drying them. Your reward shall be weeping and gnashing of teeth, for the kingdom of God is reserved for those who are gentle, humble and charitable. Do not hope to soften the justice of the Lord by the multiplicity of your words and your genuflections; the only way open to you to find grace before God, is the sincere practice of the law of love and charity."

Jesus' words are eternal, because they are the truth. They are not only the safeguard of celestial life, but the pledge for peace, tranquility and stability in the things of earthly life. This is why all human, political, social and religious institutions which are based on these words will be stable like the house built on stone; humans will keep them because they will find their happiness there. However, those who violate them will be like a house built on sand, which the wind of revolutions and the river of progress will carry away.

MUCH WILL BE ASKED OF THOSE WHO HAVE BEEN GIVEN MUCH

10. "And that servant who knew his master's will but did not get ready or act according to his will, will receive a severe beating. But the one who did not know, and did what deserved a beating, will receive a light beating. Everyone to whom much was given, of him much will be required, and from him to whom they entrusted much, they will demand the more (LUKE 12:47–48 ESV)."

11. "Jesus said, 'For judgment I came into this world, that those who do not see may see, and those who see may become blind.' Some of the Pharisees near him heard these things, and said to him, 'Are we also blind?' Jesus said to them, 'If you were blind, you would have no guilt; but now that you say, 'We see,' your guilt remains (JOHN 9:39–41 ESV)."

12. These maxims find their application above all in the teachings of the spirits. Anyone who knows the precepts of Christ is surely guilty of not practicing them; but besides that, the Gospel, which contains them, is spread only in the Christian religions. But among these, how many are there who do not read it; and among those who read it, how many of them who do not understand it! As a result, the very words of Jesus are lost to the greatest number of people.

The teachings of the spirits, which reproduce these maxims in different forms, develop and comment on them, thus making them available to all, have the particularity of not being circumscribed. So everyone, both literate and illiterate, believers or unbelievers, Christian or not, can receive these teachings, since spirits communicate everywhere. None of those who receive them, directly or through intermediaries, can pretend ignorance; neither can they claim lack of education, nor difficulties and obscurity of the allegorical meanings. Those who do not avail themselves of them for the purposes of their own improvement, who admires them as interesting and curious things without being touched in the heart; and who are no less vain, no less proud, no less selfish, no less attached to material goods, and no better for their neighbor, are all the more blameworthy because they have more means of knowing the truth.

Mediums who obtain good communications are even more reprehensible for persisting in evil, because often they write their own condemnation, and if they were not blinded by pride, they would recognize that it is to them that the spirits address themselves. But, instead of taking the lessons that they write, or that they see being written for them, their only thought is to apply them to others, thus fulfilling these words of Jesus: "You see the speck that is in your brother's eye, but do not notice the log that is in your own eye"(see Chapter **X**, n ° **9** above).

By these other words, "If you were blind, you would have no guilt," Jesus implied that guilt is due to the lights one may have.

Now, the Pharisees, who pretended to be, and who were in fact, the most enlightened part of the nation, were more reprehensible in the eyes of God than the ignorant people. The same occurs today.

Therefore much will be asked of Spiritists because they have received much; but also to those who have benefited from it, much will be given.

The first thought of every sincere Spiritist should be to seek, in the advice given by the spirits, whether there is something that can concern him or her directly and personally.

Spiritism comes to multiply the number of those who are *called*. By the faith it gives, it will also multiply the number of those who are *chosen*.

INSTRUCTIONS FROM THE SPIRITS

TO EVERYONE WHO HAS WILL MORE BE GIVEN

13. "Then the disciples came and said to him, 'Why do you speak to them in parables?' And he answered them, 'To you it has been given to know the secrets of the kingdom of heaven, but to them it has not been given. For to the one who has, more will be given, and he will have an abundance, but from the one who has not, even what he has will be taken away. This is why I speak to them in parables, because seeing they do not see, and hearing they do not hear, nor do they understand. Indeed, in their case the prophecy of Isaiah is fulfilled that says:

'You will indeed hear but never understand, and you will indeed see but never perceive' (MATTHEW 13:10–14 ESV)."

14. "'Pay attention to what you hear: with the measure you use, it will be measured to you, and still more will be added to you. For to the one who has, more will be given, and from the one who has not, even what he has will be taken away' (MARK 4:24–25 ESV)."

15. "To the one who has, more will be given, ... but from the one who has not, even what he has will be taken away." Ponder these great teachings that have often seemed paradoxical to you. Those who received are the ones who have the sense of the divine word; they received only because they tried to make themselves worthy of it, and because the Lord, in his merciful love, encourages efforts toward good. When sustained and persevering, such efforts attract the blessings of the Lord; it is a magnet which attracts to them what is progressively better, abundant blessings which make you stronger, so as to climb the holy mountain, at the top of which one finds rest after labor.

"From the one who has not, even what he has will be taken away." Take this as a figurative opposition. God does not take away from Its created beings the good which It has granted them. Blind and deaf humans! Open your minds and your hearts, see through your spirit, hear through your soul, and do not interpret in such a grossly unjust manner the words of him who made the righteousness of the Lord shine in your eyes. It is not God who withdraws from those who had received little, it is one's spirit itself who lives lavishly and carefree, does not know how to keep what it has, and how to increase, by cultivating it, the little coin fallen into its heart.

Whoever fails to cultivate the field that their father's work has earned them, and which they inherited, will see this field covered with parasitic herbs. Is it their father who takes away the crops that they did not deign to prepare? If they have left the seeds, intended to produce in this field, to rot for lack of care, should they accuse their father if the seeds do not produce anything? Absolutely not. Instead of accusing the one who had prepared everything for them and criticize the gifts they have received, let them resume their labor and accuse the true causes of their distresses and misery, and then, repentant and diligent, let them set to work with courage, breaking and clearing the ungrateful soil by the effort of their will. Let them plow it to the heart with the help of repentance and hope, throw with confidence the seed with which they will have chosen good over evil. May they sprinkle those seeds with love and charity, and God – which is the God of love and charity – will give more to them who have already received. Then they will see their efforts crowned with success, and one grain will produce a hundred, and these a thousand-fold more. Courage, plowmen; take your harrows and your plows; plow your hearts; tear out the tares; sow the good seed which the Lord entrusts to you, and the dew of love will make it bear the fruit of charity.

A spirit friend (Bordeaux, 1862).

TRUE CHRISTIANS ARE RECOGNIZED
BY THEIR DEEDS

16. "Not everyone who says to me, 'Lord, Lord,' will enter the kingdom of heaven, but the one who does the will of my Father who is in heaven."

Hear these words from the Master, all of you who reject Spiritism as a work of the devil. Open your ears, the moment to hear has arrived.

Is it enough to wear the Lord's livery to be a faithful servant? Is it enough to say, "I am a Christian," to follow the Christ? Seek true Christians and you will recognize them by their deeds. "No good tree bears bad fruit, nor again does a bad tree bear good fruit" – "Every tree that does not bear good fruit is cut down and thrown into the fire."[66] These are the words of the Master; disciples of Christ, understand them well. What are the fruits that the tree of Christianity must bear, a mighty tree whose bushy branches cover part of the world with their shade, but have not yet sheltered all those who would line up around it? The fruits of the tree of life are fruits of life, hope and faith. Christianity, as it has been done for many centuries, still preaches these divine virtues; it tries to spread these fruits, but how few actually pick them! The tree is still good, but the gardeners are not. They wanted to shape it to their concept; they wanted to shape it according to their needs. So they cut it, shrunk it and mutilated it – its sterile branches do not bear bad fruit, but they no longer bear any fruit. The weathered travelers who stop under its shadow, looking for the fruit of hope which should restore their strength and courage, finds only arid branches foreshadowing the storm. In vain they ask for the fruit of life from the tree of life: the leaves fall down completely dry; their seeking hands injured so much that they got burned out.

So open your ears and your hearts, dearly beloved! Cultivate this tree of life whose fruit gives eternal life. The one who planted it urges you to tend to it with love, and you will see it still bearing abundantly its divine fruit. Leave it as Christ gave it to you: do not mutilate it; its immense shadow wishes to extend over the universe, so do not shorten its branches. Its beneficial fruits fall in abundance to nourish the thirsty traveler who wants to reach the goal. Do not

---

66 [Trans. note] LUKE 6:43; MATTHEW 7:19 ESV.

pick them up, these fruits, to lock them up and let them rot, thus making them useless. "Many are called but few are chosen;" for there are some monopolists of the bread of life, as there often are those of material bread. Do not rank with their number; the tree which bears good fruits must spread them for all. Therefore go find those who are thirsty; bring them under the branches of the tree and share with them the shelter it offers you."Grapes are not picked from a bramble bush."[67] Therefore, brothers and sisters, keep away from those who call you to present you the brambles of the path, and follow instead those who lead you to the shade of the tree of life.

The divine Savior, who is just par excellence, said so, and his words will never pass: "Not everyone who says to me, 'Lord, Lord,' will enter the kingdom of heaven, but the one who does the will of my Father who is in heaven."

May the Lord of blessing bless all of you; may the God of light enlighten you; may the tree of life spread its fruit over you in abundance! Believe and pray.

Simeon (Bordeaux, 1863).

---

67 [Trans. note] *Cf.* LUKE 6:44 ESV.

Chapter XIX
Faith can move mountains

THE POWER OF FAITH

1. "And when they came to the crowd, a man came up to him and, kneeling before him, said, 'Lord, have mercy on my son, for he is an epileptic and he suffers terribly. For often he falls into the fire, and often into the water. And I brought him to your disciples, and they could not heal him.' And Jesus answered, 'O faithless and twisted generation, how long am I to be with you? How long am I to bear with you? Bring him here to me.' And Jesus punished the demon, and it came out of him, and the boy was healed instantly. Then the disciples came to Jesus privately and said, 'Why could we not cast it out?' He said to them, 'Because of your little faith. For truly, I say to you, *if you have faith like a grain of mustard seed, you will say to this mountain, 'Move from here to there,' and it will move,* and nothing will be impossible for you' (MATTHEW 17:14–20 ESV)."

2. In its literal sense, it is certain that confidence in one's own strength makes one capable of performing material things that one cannot do when one doubts oneself; but here it is only in the moral sense that we must understand these words. The mountains which faith moves are the difficulties, the resistances, the bad will, in short, which one usually meets among human beings, even when it is a matter of everyone's best interests. The prejudices of routine, material interest and selfishness; the blindness of fanaticism; prideful passions, are those numerous mountains that block the path of anyone who works for the progress of humankind. Robust faith gives perseverance, energy and resources to overcome obstacles, both in small things as well as great ones; whereas a wavering faith gives uncertainty and hesitation which reinforce the very obstacles one wants to fight: it does not seek the means to win, because it does not believe that it can win.

3. In another sense, faith is the confidence that one has in the accomplishment of something, the certainty of reaching a goal. It gives a kind of lucidity which shows, through thought, the term towards which one is tending, and the means of getting there, so that whoever possesses it moves on, so to speak, without fail. In either case it can make great things happen.

Sincere and true faith is always calm; it gives patience which knows how to wait, because since it is based on intelligence and understanding of things, it is certain to arrive. Doubtful faith feels its own weakness; when it is stimulated by interest, it becomes furious, and thinks that it can compensate with violence the power it lacks. Calmness in the struggle is always a sign of strength and confidence, whereas violence is evidence of weakness and self-doubt.

4. We must be careful not to confuse faith with presumption. True faith is blended with humility; those who possess it place their trust in God more than in themselves, because they know that, as mere instruments of the will of God, they can do nothing without the Creator; that is why good spirits help them. Presumption is less the product of faith than of pride – and pride is always chastised sooner or later by disappointment and failure inflicted upon it.

5. The power of faith receives direct and special application in magnetic action; through it humans are able to act on the universal cosmic fluid, modifying its qualities, and giving it an almost irresistible impulsion. This is why those already possessing great normal fluidic power, when impelled by an ardent faith, can by directing their will toward good alone, operate these strange phenomena of cures and others which formerly passed for miracles, but actually are only the consequences of a natural law. This is the reason why Jesus said to his apostles, you could not heal "Because of your little faith."

Religious faith
The state of unshakable faith

6. From a religious point of view, faith is belief in particular dogmas which constitute the different religions. All religions have their articles of faith. In this respect, faith can be a reasoned faith or be blind. By examining nothing, blind faith accepts without control the false as the true, and collides at each step against evidence and reason. Pushed to excess, it produces *fanaticism*. When faith rests on terror, it collapses sooner or later; when based on truth it is the only one assured of lasting into the future, for it has nothing to fear from the progress of enlightenment, since *whatever is true in the shadow, is also so in broad daylight*. Each religion claims to be in exclusive possession of the truth. *To advocate blind faith on a point of belief is to admit your powerlessness to demonstrate that you are right.*

7.   It is commonly said that *faith cannot be commanded*; hence many people say that it is not their fault if they do not have faith. While faith, no doubt, cannot be commanded, the following is even more just: *faith cannot be imposed.* No, it cannot be controlled, but it can be acquired, and there is no one who is denied the right to possess it, even among the most unyielding individuals. I am referring to fundamental spiritual truths, and not to any particular belief. It is not up to faith to look for people, but to people to look for faith – and if they seek it with sincerity, they will most certainly find it. So take it for granted that those who say, "We would not ask more than being able to believe, but we cannot believe," say it from the lips and not from the heart, because by saying that, they are actually covering their ears. Evidence, however, is plentiful around them; then why do they refuse to see it? With some it is because of carelessness; with others for fear of being forced to change their habits; with most, it is their pride that refuses to recognize a higher power, because they would have to bow to it.

In some people, faith somehow seems innate, a single spark is enough to develop it. This ease of assimilation of spiritual truths is an obvious sign of previous evolvement. Conversely, in others, they penetrate only with difficulty, which is no less evident a sign of a backwards nature. The former have already believed and understood; they bring back to life the intuition of what they already knew: their education is done. As for the latter, they still have everything to learn: their education still needs to be done. It will be done, and if it is not finished in this existence, it will be concluded in another.

The unbelievers' resistance, it must be admitted, often comes less from themselves than from the way in which things are presented to them. There must be a foundation to faith, and this basis should be a perfect understanding of what one must believe. To believe, it is not enough to see, but above all it is necessary to *understand*. Blind faith is no longer fitting for the current century. Nowadays, it is precisely the dogma of blind faith that today creates the greatest number of current non-believers, because it wants to impose itself, and because it requires the abdication of one of the most cherished prerogatives of humankind: reasoning and free will. It is this sort of faith against which, above all, the unbeliever stiffens up, and of which it is true to say that it cannot be commanded. Refusing to admit evidence, it leaves in the mind a wave from which doubt arises. Reasoned faith – that which is based on facts and logic – leaves no obscurity as to its beliefs. One believes when one is certain; and one is only certain when one has understood – that is why it does not falter, because *unshakable faith is only that which can meet reason face to face in every human epoch.*

It is to this result that Spiritism leads, thus triumphing over unbelief whenever it does not encounter systematic and interested opposition.

PARABLE OF THE BARREN FIG TREE

8. "On the following day, when they came from Bethany, he was hungry. And seeing in the distance a fig tree in leaf, he went to see if he could find anything on it. When he came to it, he found nothing but leaves, for it was not the season for figs. And he said to it, 'May no one ever eat fruit from you again.' And his disciples heard it.

As they passed by in the morning, they saw the fig tree withered away to its roots. And Peter remembered and said to him, 'Rabbi, look! The fig tree that you cursed has withered.' And Jesus answered them, 'Have faith in God. Truly, I say to you, whoever says to this mountain, 'Be taken up and thrown into the sea,' and does not doubt in his heart, but believes that what he says will come to pass, it will be done for him' (MARK 11:12–14;20–23 ESV)."

9. The barren fig tree is the symbol of people that have only the appearance of good, but actually produce nothing good. For instance, speakers that have more brilliance than substance, present an outward veneer in their words. They please the ears, but when you examine them, you find nothing substantial for the heart. After hearing them, one wonders what benefit they have derived from them.

The barren fig tree is also the emblem of all people that have the means to be useful but are not; of all utopias, of all empty systems, of all doctrines without a solid foundation. Most of the time, what is lacking is true faith, fruitful faith, a faith that can stir the fibers of the heart – in a word, the faith that can move mountains. These are the trees that have leaves, but bear no fruit. This is why Jesus condemns them to sterility, for the day will come when they will be dried up to the root; that is to say, all the systems, all the doctrines that will have produced no good for humanity, will fall into nothingness; and all people that are voluntarily useless, for want of having used the resources which were in them, will be treated like the dried fig tree.

10. Mediums are the interpreters of spirits; they supply the physical organs which the latter lack to transmit their instructions to us – that is why they are endowed with faculties for this purpose. In these times of social renewal, they have a particular mission: these are trees which must give spiritual nourishment to their brothers and sisters. They are multiplied, so that food is aplenty and found everywhere, in all countries, in all walks of society, among the rich and the poor, among the great and the small, so that no one is deprived, and to prove to human beings that *each and every one is called*. However, if they divert the precious faculty granted to them for this providential purpose, if they make it serve futile or harmful objectives, if they put it at the service of worldly interests, if instead of salutary fruits they give unhealthy ones, if they refuse to improving themselves by making it beneficial for others, they become like the barren fig tree. God will take away a gift that has become useless in their hands – the seed that they do not know how to make bear fruit – and will let them fall prey to evil spirits.

INSTRUCTIONS FROM THE SPIRITS

FAITH, THE PARENT OF HOPE AND CHARITY

11. Faith, to be fruitful, must be active; it should never go numb. Parent of all virtues that lead to God, it should closely monitor the development of the offspring it gives birth to.

Hope and charity are a consequence of faith – these three virtues form an inseparable trinity. Is it not faith that gives you hope of seeing our Lord's promises fulfilled, for if you have no faith, what will you expect? Is it not faith that gives love, for if you have no faith, what recognition will you have, and therefore what love?

Faith, divine inspiration of God, awakens all the noble instincts which lead a person to good; it is the foundation of personal regeneration. Therefore its foundation must be strong and durable, because if the slightest doubt can shake it, what will become of the edifice that you build on it? So build up this edifice on an unshakable foundation; may your faith be stronger than the sophistry and taunts of unbelievers; since a faith that does not stand up to the ridicule of humans is not true faith.

Sincere faith is catchy and contagious; it is communicated to those who did not have it, or even would not want to have it. It finds persuasive words which go to the soul, whereas an apparent faith has only sonorous words which leave one cold and indifferent. Instead, preach by example of your faith to give it to fellow humans; lead by example of your deeds, to make them see the merit of faith; preach with your unshakable hope to make them see the confidence that strengthens and can face all the vicissitudes of life.

Therefore have faith in all that is beautiful and good, in its purity, in its reasoning. Do not admit faith without verification, a blind child born of blindness. Love God, but understand why you love It; believe in God's promises, but know why you believe; follow our advice, but be aware of the objective we show you and the means we provide for you to achieve it. Believe and hope without ever faltering, for miracles are operated by faith.

Joseph, a protector spirit (Bordeaux, 1862).

DIVINE FAITH AND HUMAN FAITH

12. Faith is the innate feeling that exists in every human being of their future destiny; it is the awareness that they have immense faculties whose germ has been deposited in them, in latent state at first, and which must hatch and grow through each person's active will.

Hitherto faith has been understood only from the religious standpoint, because Christ recommended it as a powerful lever, and because one saw in him only the head of a religion. But Christ, who performed material miracles, showed by these very miracles, what humans can do when they have faith, that is, *the will to want*, and the certainty that this will can achieve its fulfillment. Did not the apostles also work miracles? Now, what were such miracles, if not natural effects whose cause was unknown to humans then, but which is largely explained today, and which will be completely understood through the study of Spiritism and magnetism?

Faith can be human or divine, depending on whether a person applies their faculties to their earthly needs or to heavenly and future aspirations. Persons of genius, who pursue the realization of some great enterprise, will succeed if they have faith, because they feel in themselves that it can and must happen – and this certainty gives them immense strength. Good individuals who, believing in their heavenly future, want to fill their current life with noble and beautiful deeds, draw on their faith, in the certainty of the happiness that awaits them, the necessary strength – and thus again miracles of charity, of dedication and self-denial are accomplished. Finally, with faith, there is not a single bad inclination that one cannot overcome.

Magnetism is one of the greatest proofs of the power of faith put into action. It is by faith that one heals and produces these strange phenomena formerly called miracles.

I repeat, faith can be *human or divine*; if all the incarnates were well persuaded of the power which they have in them, and if they wanted to put their will at the service of this force, they would be able to accomplish what until now, we called prodigies, and which are simply a development of human faculties.

A protector spirit (Paris, 1863).

Chapter XX
Last-hour workers

INSTRUCTIONS FROM THE SPIRITS: THE LAST WILL BE FIRST · SPIRITISTS' MISSION · THE LORD'S WORKERS

1. "'For the kingdom of heaven is like a master of a house who went out early in the morning to hire laborers for his vineyard. After agreeing with the laborers for a denarius a day, he sent them into his vineyard. And going out about the third hour he saw others standing idle in the marketplace, and to them he said, 'You go into the vineyard too, and whatever is right I will give you.' So they went. Going out again about the sixth hour and the ninth hour, he did the same. And about the eleventh hour he went out and found others standing. And he said to them, 'Why do you stand here idle all day?' They said to him, 'Because no one has hired us.' He said to them, 'You go into the vineyard too.'

And when evening came, the owner of the vineyard said to his foreman, 'Call the laborers and pay them their wages, beginning with the last, up to the first.' And when those hired about the eleventh hour came, each of them received a denarius. Now when those hired first came, they thought they would receive more, but each of them also received a denarius. And on receiving it they grumbled at the master of the house, saying, 'These last worked only one hour, and you have made them equal to us who have borne the burden of the day and the scorching heat.'

But he replied to one of them, 'Friend, I am doing you no wrong. Did you not agree with me for a denarius? Take what belongs to you and go. I choose to give to this last worker as I give to you. Am I not allowed to do what I choose with what belongs to me? Or do you begrudge my generosity?' *So the last will be first, and the first last'* (MATTHEW 20:1–16. See also The Parable of the Wedding Feast, MATTHEW 22:1–14 ESV)."

INSTRUCTIONS FROM THE SPIRITS

THE LAST WILL BE FIRST

2. Last-hour workers are also entitled to their wages, provided their good will have kept them at the disposal of the master who has employed them – and such tardiness in being hired should not be due to laziness or bad will on their part. They are entitled to wages because, since dawn, they have been impatiently waiting for the one who would finally call them to work – they are hard-working and, before that, only lacked work to do.

But if they had refused work at every hour of the day saying: "Let us be patient, rest is sweet to me. When the last hour strikes, it will be time to think of the day's wages. Why do I need to bother myself with a master whom I do not know and not even like! The later the better." Well, this sort of people, dear friends, would not have earned the wages of working laborers, but those of laziness.

What then will become of those who, instead of simply remaining inactive, have used the hours intended for the labor of the day to commit guilty acts; who have blasphemed God, shed the blood of their fellow beings, thrown trouble into families, ruined trusting persons, abused innocence; and who, all things considered, have wallowed in the many infamies of humanity? What will become of them? Will it be enough for them to say at the last hour: "O Lord, I have wasted my time; hire me until the end of the day, that I do a little, very little of my task, and pay me the wages of the worker of good will"? No, absolutely not. The master will tell them, "As of now, I have no work for you. You wasted your time, you forgot what you had learned, you no longer know how to work in my vineyard. So start learning again, and when you are better prepared, you will come to me, and I will open up my vast field to you, and then you will be able to work on it at any time of the day."

Good Spiritists, dearly beloved, know that you are all last-hour workers. Very proud would be the one who could say: I started work at dawn and will not finish until sunset. All of you came when you were called, some a little earlier, others a little later, by the incarnation of which you wear the chain – but for how many centuries have piled up with the master calling you to his vineyard without you ever deigning to enter it! You are nearing the moment of receiving your wages; make good use of this last hour that you have left, and never forget that your existence, however long it may seem to you, is only a fleeting moment in the immensity of time that forms eternity for you.

Constantine, a protector spirit (Bordeaux, 1863).

3. Jesus was fond of the simplicity of symbols, so, in his virile language, the workers who arrived at the earliest hours are the prophets, Moses, and all the initiators who marked the stages of progress, which was continued through the centuries by the apostles, the martyrs, the Church Fathers, the scholars, the philosophers, and finally the Spiritists. These latter, who came last, were announced and foreseen at the dawn of the Messiah, and they will receive the same reward as their forerunners – what do I say, indeed a higher reward. As newcomers, Spiritists profit from the intellectual labors of their predecessors, because humans must inherit from humans, and their works and results should be collective: God blesses solidarity. Many of them are living again today, or will live tomorrow, to complete the work they started long ago. More than one patriarch, more than one prophet, more than one disciple of Christ, more than one disseminator of the Christian faith, can be found among them, but more enlightened, more advanced, and working, no longer at the foundations, but on the crowning of the building. Their wages will therefore be proportional to the merit of the work.

Reincarnation, this most beautiful dogma, perpetuates and clarifies spiritual filiation. The spirit, called to account for its earthly deeds, understands the continuity of the task interrupted but always resumed. It sees, it feels that it has caught on the fly the thought of its predecessors, and it reenters the jousting lists, matured by experience, to advance still further. Thus everyone, whether workers of the first or the last hour, with their eyes drawn to the deep justice of God, no longer grumble but instead worship the Creator.

This is one of the true meanings of this parable which contains, like all those which Jesus addressed to the populace, the germ of the future, and also, in all forms and images, the revelation of this magnificent unity which harmonizes all things in the universe, this solidarity which links all the beings in the present to those in the past and those in the future.

Heinrich Heine[68] (Paris, 1863).

SPIRITISTS' MISSION

4. Can't you already hear the storm which must sweep away the old world and engulf in nothingness the sum of earthly iniquities? Ah, bless the Lord, all of you that put your faith in Its sovereign justice, and who, like new apostles of the belief revealed by the higher prophetic voices, will preach the new dogma of reincarnation and gradual elevation of the spirits, according to how well or badly they have accomplished their missions and endured their earthly trials.

Tremble no more! Tongues of fire[69] are coming down on your heads. True followers of Spiritism, you are the elect of God! Go and preach the divine word. The time has come when you must sacrifice your habits, your jobs, your futile occupations for its dissemination. Go and preach: the spirits from on high are with you. You will certainly speak to people who will not want to listen to the voice of God, because that voice constantly reminds them of self-denial. You will preach disinterestedness to the miser, abstinence from debauchery, indulgence toward domestic tyrants as well as to despots – lost words, I know it. But whatever! It is necessary to sprinkle with your own sweat the ground that you must sow, because otherwise it will not bear fruit, and will produce only under the repeated efforts of the Gospel spade and plow. Go onward and preach!

Yes, all of you, persons of good faith, who are aware of your inferiority when gazing at the worlds scattered in the infinite, launch a crusade against injustice and iniquity. Go and overthrow this cult of the golden calf, which becomes more and more invasive every day. Go, God leads you! Simple and ignorant people, your tongues will be untied, and you will speak like no other speaker can. Go and preach, and the attentive people will gladly receive your words of comfort, fraternity, hope and peace.

---

68 [Trans. note] Heinrich Heine (1797–1856), German poet and writer.

69 {Trans. note] A figure taken from the Gospel, at Pentecost: "And divided tongues as of fire appeared to them and rested on each one of them." Acts 2:3 esv.

What will the pitfalls strewn in your pathway matter? Only wolves will be caught in wolf traps, since shepherds will be able to defend their sheep against sacrificial butchers.

Go, great individuals before God, who, happier than the biblical Thomas, believe without asking to see, and accept the facts of mediumship even when they have never succeeded in obtaining them themselves. Go, the Spirit of God leads you.

So, onward, march imposing phalanx moved by your faith, and the large battalions of unbelievers will vanish before you like the mists of the morning at the first rays of the rising sun.

Faith is the virtue that can move mountains, Jesus told you; but heavier than the heaviest mountains are impurity and all the vices of impurity that lie in the hearts of humans. So leave with courage to overthrow this mountain of iniquities that future generations must know only as a vague legend, as you yourselves only very imperfectly retain the memory of times before pagan civilization.

Indeed, moral and philosophical upheavals will certainly erupt on all points of the globe; for the hour approaches when the divine light will appear on the two worlds.

THE LORD'S WORKERS

5.   You are nearing the time when the fulfillment of things announced for the transformation of humanity will take place. Happy will be those who will have worked in the Lord's field with selflessness and having no other motive than charity! Their working days will be paid a hundredfold of what they would have hoped for. Happy will be those who will have said to their fellow beings: "Brothers and sisters, let us work together, and let us unite our efforts so that the master will find the work finished on his arrival," because the master will say to them: "Come to me, you who have been good servants, you who have laid down your jealousies and disagreements so as not to leave the work unfinished! But woe to those who, by their dissensions, have delayed the hour of the harvest, for a storm will come and they will be swept away by the whirlwind! They will cry out, "Have mercy on us!" But the Lord will say to them, "Why do you ask for mercy, you who did not have mercy on your brothers and sisters, and who refused to reach out to them; you who crushed the weak instead of supporting them? Why do you ask for mercy, you who have sought your reward in Earth's joys and in the satisfaction of your pride? You have already received your reward as you wanted it, ask no further: heavenly rewards are for those who have not asked for the rewards of the Earth."

God is counting his faithful servants right now, and has marked with Its finger those who only have the appearance of revelation, so that they do not usurp the wages of courageous servants, for only those who will not shrink from their task will be entrusted with the most difficult part of the great work of regeneration through Spiritism, thus fulfilling these words: "The last will be first, and the first last" in the kingdom of heaven!

The Spirit of Truth (Paris, 1862).

Chapter XXI
False christs and false prophets will arise

A TREE IS RECOGNIZED BY ITS FRUIT

1. "'For no good tree bears bad fruit, nor again does a bad tree bear good fruit, for each tree is known by its own fruit. For figs are not gathered from thorn bushes, nor are grapes picked from a bramble bush. The good person out of the good treasure of his heart produces good, and the evil person out of his evil treasure produces evil, for out of the abundance of the heart his mouth speaks' (LUKE 6:43–45 ESV)."

2. "'*Beware of false prophets,* who come to you in sheep's clothing but inwardly are ravenous wolves. You will recognize them by their fruits. *Are grapes gathered from thorn bushes, or figs from thistles?* So, every healthy tree bears good fruit, but the diseased tree bears bad fruit. *A healthy tree cannot bear bad fruit, nor can a diseased tree bear good fruit.* Every tree that does not bear good fruit is cut down and thrown into the fire. Thus you will recognize them by their fruits' (MATTHEW 7:15–20 ESV)."

3. "'See that no one leads you astray. For many will come in my name, saying, 'I am the Christ,' and they will lead many astray.'

'And many false prophets will arise and lead many astray. And because lawlessness will be increased, the love of many will grow cold. But the one who endures to the end will be saved.'

'Then if anyone says to you, 'Look, here is the Christ!' or 'There he is!' do not believe it. For false christs and false prophets will arise and perform great signs and wonders, so as to lead astray, if possible, even the elect' (MATTHEW 24:4–5,11–13,23–24. *Cf.* MARK 13:5–6,21–22 ESV)."

THE PROPHETS' MISSION

4. The gift of revealing the future is usually attributed to prophets, hence the words *prophecies* and *predictions* have become synonymous. In the Gospel sense, the word *prophet* has a more extensive meaning; it relates to all persons sent from God with the mission of instructing their fellow human beings and revealing to them the hidden things and the mysteries of spiritual life. A man can therefore be a prophet without making predictions. That was the idea that the Jews had of the term in Jesus' time – which is why, when he was brought before the high priest Caiaphas, the scribes and the elders being assembled, spat in his face, punched him and slapped him, saying: "Prophesy to us, you Christ! Who is it that struck you?"[70] However, it did indeed happen that prophets had foreknowledge of the future, either by intuition or by providential revelation, in order to send warnings to humankind. As these events were accomplished, the gift of predicting the future was regarded as one of the attributes of being a prophet.

GREAT SIGNS AND WONDERS OF FALSE PROPHETS

5. "For false christs and false prophets will arise and perform great signs and wonders, so as to lead astray, if possible, even the elect." These words give the true meaning of the word wonder (prodigy). In theological acceptation, wonders and miracles are exceptional phenomena, outside the laws of Nature. Since the laws of Nature are the work of God alone, It can undoubtedly derogate from them if It so pleases, but simple common sense shows that God cannot have given to inferior and perverse beings a power equal to Its own, and much less the right to undo what It has done. Jesus could not possibly have sanctioned such a principle. Therefore if, according to the meaning attached to these words, the evil spirit has the power to perform such wonders that can deceive the even elect themselves, it would follow, that being able to do what God does, wonders and miracles are not the exclusive privilege of God's envoys, and would prove nothing, since nothing distinguishes the miracles of the saints from the miracles of the devil. We must therefore seek a more rational meaning to such words.

---

70 [Trans. note] MATTHEW 26:68 ESV.

In the eyes of little enlightened people, any phenomenon whose cause is unknown passes for supernatural, amazing and miraculous; but once the cause is known, we recognize that the phenomenon, as extraordinary as it may seem, is nothing other than the application of a law of Nature. Thus the circle of supernatural facts narrows as the circle of science broadens. Humans have always exploited – for satisfying their ambition, their personal interests and their domination – any particular knowledge they possessed, in order to give themselves the prestige of a so-called superhuman power or of an alleged divine mission. These are false christs and false prophets; the dissemination of scientific enlightenment kills their credit, which is why the number of such individuals decreases as human beings become more enlightened. The fact of their operating what, in the eyes of certain people, passes for prodigies, is therefore not a sign of divine mission, since it can result from mere knowledge which anyone can acquire; or from special organic faculties that the most unworthy as well as the most worthy people can possess. True prophets are recognized for possessing a more serious and exclusively moral character.

Do not believe every spirit

6. "Beloved, *do not believe every spirit*, but test the spirits to see whether they are from God, for many false prophets have gone out into the world (1 John 4:1 esv)."

7. Spiritist phenomena, far from endorsing false christs and false prophets, as some claim it does, on the contrary, has come to strike one final blow to them. Do not ask Spiritism for miracles or wonders, for it formally declares that it does not produce such. Like physics, chemistry, astronomy, geology came to reveal the laws of the material world, Spiritism comes to reveal other unknown laws, those which govern the rapports between the corporeal world and the incorporeal world, and which, like their elders of science, are not less laws of Nature. By providing the explanation of a certain set of phenomena misunderstood until today, it destroys what is still ascribed to the domain of the marvelous. Consequently, those who would feel tempted to exploit such phenomena for their own personal profit, by posing as messiahs of God, would not be able to abuse credulity for long, and would soon be unmasked. Besides, as already said, these phenomena alone prove absolutely nothing: a divine mission proves itself by moral effects which are not given to the first comer to produce. This is one of the results of the development of Spiritist science: by scrutinizing the cause of certain phenomena, it lifts the veil on several mysteries. As for those who prefer darkness to light, they are only interested in fighting it. However truth is like the Sun: it dissipates even the thickest fog.

Spiritism came to reveal another, much more dangerous, category of false christs and false prophets, who are found, not among the incarnate, but among discarnate spirits, namely, that of deceptive, hypocritical, proud and falsely sage individuals, who, have passed into error from their days on material Earth, and now adorn themselves with revered names in order to seek to accredit, behind the mask with which they conceal themselves, the most bizarre and absurd ideas. Before mediumistic communications were known, they usually exerted their action in a less conspicuous manner, by means of inspiration, or through hearing and speaking unconscious mediumship. A considerable number of those which, at various times, but especially in recent times, have presented themselves as being some of the ancient prophets, as Christ himself, as Mary, mother of Christ, and even as God. John the Evangelist warns against them when he says: "Beloved, do not believe every spirit, but test the spirits to see whether they are from God, for many false prophets have gone out into the world." Spiritism gives the means to test them by indicating the characters through which one recognizes good spirits – such characteristics are *always moral and never material.*[71] The following words of Jesus can be applied above all to the discernment of good and bad spirits: "A tree is recognized by its fruit. A healthy tree cannot bear bad fruit, nor can a diseased tree bear good fruit." We judge spirits by the quality of their deeds, like a tree by the quality of its fruit.

---

71 About how to distinguish among spirits, see A. Kardec, *The Mediums' Book,* ch. XXIV *et seq.*

INSTRUCTIONS FROM THE SPIRITS

FALSE PROPHETS

8. If you are told, "Here is the Christ," do not go, but instead beware, for there will be many false prophets. Yet do you not see the fig tree's leaves starting to turn white; do you not see its numerous sprouts in vain awaiting the flowering season, and did not Christ tell you that a tree is recognized by its fruit? Therefore if the fruit is bitter, you ought to conclude that the tree is bad; but if it is sweet and beneficial, you should say: Nothing pure can come out of a bad stock.

It is thus, dear brothers and sisters, that you must judge; it is the deeds that you should examine. If those who claim to be clothed with divine power bear all signs of such a mission; in other words, if they possess to the highest degree the eternal Christian virtues of charity, love, indulgence, and kindness which reconciles all hearts; and if, in support of their words, they add their actions; only then you will be able to say: These are truly, definitely, envoys of God.

But beware of honeyed words, beware of scribes and Pharisees who pray in public places, dressed in long robes. Beware of those who claim to have an exclusive monopoly on truth!

No, Christ is definitely not there, since those whom he sends to disseminate his holy doctrine, and to regenerate his people, like the Master, will be meek and humble of heart above all things. Those who must, by their examples and their advice, save humanity from plunging itself into ruination and from wandering in tortuous paths, will be above all modest and humble. Anything revealing even an atom of pride should be avoided like a contagious plague which corrupts everything it touches. Remember that *each and every created being bears on its forehead, but above all in its deeds, the stamp of its greatness or decadence.*

Therefore go, dearly beloved children, advance without delay and without any ulterior motives, on the blessed path which you have taken. Go, keep going without fear; courageously keep away everything that could hinder your progress toward the eternal goal. Travelers, you will only remain in darkness and the pain of trials for a very short time, if you let your hearts go to this sweet doctrine which came to reveal the eternal laws to all of you, and to satisfy all your soul's aspirations toward the unknown beyond. From now on, you can give substance to these ethereal sylphs that you saw passing in your dreams, and which, ephemeral, could only charm your spirit, but said nothing to your heart. Now, dearly beloved, death has disappeared to make way for the radiant angel you know, the angel of both farewell and reunion! Now, you who have successfully accomplished the task imposed by the Creator, have nothing more to fear from God's justice, because God is parent and always forgives Its lost children who cry out for mercy. So keep going, keep moving onward, may your motto be that of progress, of continuous progress in all things, until you finally reach the happy destination where all those who have preceded you are waiting for you.

Louis (Bordeaux, 1861).

CHARACTERISTICS OF TRUE PROPHETS

9. *Beware of false prophets.* This recommendation is useful in all times, but especially in moments of transition when, like the current one, a transformation of humanity is being prepared, because then a multitude of ambitious and scheming people will pose as reformers and messiahs. It is against these impostors that we must be on our guard; and it is the duty of every honest person to unmask them. You will no doubt ask how we can recognize them; here is a description of such individuals:

The command of an army can only be entrusted to a skillful general, capable of directing it. So, do you believe that God would be less cautious than humans? Rest assured that God entrusts important missions only to those whom It knows to be capable of fulfilling them, since great missions are heavy burdens which would crush anyone too weak to carry them. As in all things, a master must know more than the schoolchild. Hence, in order to morally and intellectually advance humanity, we need people of superior intelligence and morality! This is why it is always spirits already very advanced – having proven themselves in previous existences – who incarnate for this purpose; because if they are not superior to the environment in which they must function, their action will be null.

Having said this, one can conclude that true missionaries of God must justify their mission through their superiority, through their virtues, through greatness, and by the result and the moralizing influence of their deeds. Again, the same conclusion can be drawn that, if anyone stands, by their character, by their virtues, and by their intelligence, beneath the mission they have assigned themselves – or beneath the characters of those under whose revered names they shelter – they are nothing but mediocre impersonators of examples they cannot even imitate.

Another consideration is that most of the true missionaries of God are not aware of themselves; they accomplish what they are called to do by the force of their genius seconded by the hidden power that inspires and directs them without their knowledge and without premeditated design. In a word, *true prophets are revealed by their deeds – we can guess their nature – whereas false prophets just pose as messengers of God;* the first are humble and modest, the latter are proud and full of themselves, speaking haughtily and, like all liars, always seem to fear that they would not be believed.

We have seen these impostors pass themselves off as the apostles of Christ, others still as Christ himself, and what stands to the shame of humankind is that they find people gullible enough to lend faith to such turpitudes. However, a quite simple consideration should suffice to open the eyes of the most blind, namely, that if Christ was reincarnated on Earth, he would return with all his power and all his virtues, unless he admitted – which would be absurd – that he would somehow have degraded. Now, just as if you take away from God only a single one of his attributes you would no longer have God, should you take away only one of the virtues of Christ, you would no longer have Christ. Do those who pass themselves off as Christ have all his virtues? That is the question; examine, scrutinize their thoughts and deeds, and you will recognize that they lack above all the distinctive qualities of Christ – humility and charity – while possessing what he certainly did not have, namely, greed and pride. Moreover note that there are now, and in different countries, several so-called Christs, as there are several so-called Elijahs, Saint Johns or Saint Peters, which obviously cannot be altogether credible. Keep in mind that these are people who exploit gullibility and find it convenient to live at the expense of those who listen to them.

So beware of false prophets, especially in a time of renewal, because many impostors will claim to be envoys of God; they get vain satisfaction on Earth, however, you can rest assured that a terrible justice awaits them.

Erastus (Paris, 1862)

FALSE PROPHETS IN THE ERRANT STATE[72]

10. False prophets are not found only among the incarnate; there are also, and in much greater numbers, lots of them among proud spirits that, under false pretenses of love and charity, sow disunity and delay the work of humankind's emancipation, by surreptitiously introducing systems after winning over their mediums' acceptance. Then, in order to better fascinate those they want to abuse, and to impart more weight and authority to their theories, they unscrupulously adorn themselves with names that humans would only pronounce with reverence.

They are the ones who sow seeds of antagonism among groups, causing them to isolate themselves from one another, and to see one another with a bad light. That alone would suffice to unmask them, since, by doing so, they themselves provide the most blatant denial of what they profess to be. Therefore, blind are those who let themselves fall in such a crude trap.

But there are many other ways to recognize false prophets. Spirits of the order to which they claim to belong must not only be very kind, but also eminently rational. Well, sift their systems through reason and common sense, and see what will remain of it. You will therefore agree with me that, whenever a spirit indicates as a remedy for the evils of humanity, or as a means of accomplishing self-transformation, clearly utopian and impracticable things, or puerile and ridiculous measures; when it formulates a system that contradicts even the most elementary notions of science, it can only be an ignorant, lying spirit.

On the other hand, rest assured that if truth is not always appreciated by individuals, it is always appreciated by the common sense of the masses – and this is another criterion. If two principles contradict each other, you will have the measure of their intrinsic value

---

72 [Trans. note] *In the errant state* simply means *as discarnate souls in the spiritual world.* The term *errant* (i.e., itinerant), once favored by Allan Kardec, only refers to the intervening period between one's incarnations (see footnote 15 above).

by seeking the one that finds the most sympathetic reverberation. Actually, *it would be illogical to admit that a doctrine which would see the number of its adherents diminish would be truer than that which sees its own increase.* God, wanting truth to happen to all, does not confine it in a small circle: God makes it emerge in different points, so that everywhere light can be found next to darkness.

Vigorously reject all those spirits which purport to offer exclusive advice, while preaching division and isolation. They are almost always conceited and mediocre spirits that tend to impose themselves on weak and gullible people by lavishing exaggerated praise on them, in order to allure them and keep them under their domination. Such spirits are generally hungry for power, that were public or household despots during their incarnate lifetime, and now, after death, want to have more victims to tyrannize. *Generally speaking, beware of spirit communications that bear a mystical or strange character, or that prescribe ceremonies and bizarre acts*, since these usually give a legitimate reason for suspicion.

On the other hand, please be aware that when a truth is to be revealed to humankind, it is instantly communicated, so to speak, to all serious mediumistic groups who possess serious mediums, and not to such and such at exclusion of others. No one can be a perfect medium if he/she is obsessed by a spirit, and there is manifest obsession when a medium is only able to receive communications from a special spirit, no matter how lofty a rank such spirit may claim to possess. Consequently, any medium, any mediumistic group, that believe to be favored by spirit communications which only they can receive, and which, moreover, are prone to practices that border on superstition, are undoubtedly under the grip of an evident obsession, especially when the dominating spirit prides itself on a name that virtually everyone, both incarnate and discarnate, are expected to honor and respect, and not debase in any way.

It is indisputable that after submitting all the data and all spirit communications to the severe test of reason and logic, it will be easy to reject any absurdity or error. A medium can be fascinated, a whole group can be exploited; but the strict control adopted by other groups, the scientific advancement acquired, and the high moral authority of group leaders, besides communications received by the main mediums, which bear the stamp of logic and authenticity of our best communicating spirits, will quickly debunk these cunning and untruthful dictations emanating from a few deceitful or wicked spirits.

Erastus, disciple of the Apostle Paul (Paris, 1862).

(See above, **Introduction**, "II. The authority of Spiritism: Universal control of spirits' teachings." See also Allan KARDEC, *The Mediums' Book*, Chapter XXIII, "Obsession.")

JEREMIAH AND THE FALSE PROPHETS

11. "Thus says the LORD of hosts: 'Do not listen to the words of the prophets who prophesy to you, filling you with vain hopes. They speak visions of their own minds, not from the mouth of the LORD. They say continually to those who despise the word of the LORD, 'It shall be well with you'; and to everyone who stubbornly follows his own heart, they say, 'No disaster shall come upon you.'

For who among them has stood in the council of the LORD to see and to hear his word, or who has paid attention to his word and listened? — I did not send the prophets, yet they ran; I did not speak to them, yet they prophesied. — I have heard what the prophets have said who prophesy lies in my name, saying, 'I have dreamed, I have dreamed!' How long shall there be lies in the heart of the prophets who prophesy lies, and who prophesy the deceit of their own heart —

'When one of this people, or a prophet or a priest asks you, 'What is the burden of the LORD?' you shall say to them, 'You are the burden, and I will cast you off, declares the LORD' (JEREMIAH 23:16–18, 21, 25–26 and 33 ESV)."

It is of this passage from the prophet Jeremiah that I will now speak to you, dear friends. God speaking through his mouth said, "They speak visions of their own minds." These words clearly indicate that already, at that time, charlatans and disturbed people were abusing and exploiting the gift of prophecy. They therefore exploited the simple and almost blind faith of the populace by predicting good and pleasant things *in exchange for money*. This kind of deception was fairly general among the Jewish nation, and it is easy to understand that poor people, in their ignorance, were unable to distinguish the good from the bad, so they were always more or less fooled by so-called prophets who were nothing but impostors or fanatics. Is there anything more significant than the following words, "I did not send the prophets, yet they ran; I did not speak to them, yet they prophesied"? Later he said: "I have heard what the prophets have said who prophesy lies in my name, saying, 'I have dreamed, I have dreamed!'." Jeremiah thus indicated one of the means employed to exploit the confidence that one deposited in them. The crowds, always credulous, did not think of challenging the veracity of those dreams or visions; they found it all natural and always invited these prophets to speak.

After the words of the prophet, listen to the wise counsel given by John the Evangelist, when he said, "Do not believe every spirit, but test the spirits to see whether they are from God." Because, among the invisible ones, there are also some that like to make dupes when they find the opportunity. These dupes are, of course, mediums who do not take enough precautions. This is undoubtedly one of the greatest pitfalls which beset many people, especially when they are new to Spiritism. It is a trial for them in which they can only succeed by exercising great caution. Therefore you should learn, before anything else, to distinguish between good and bad spirits, so as not to become false prophets yourselves.

Luoz, a protector spirit (Karlsruhe, Germany, 1861).

Chapter XXII
Let no one separate what God has joined together

THE INDISSOLUBILITY OF MARRIAGE · DIVORCE

THE INDISSOLUBILITY OF MARRIAGE

1. "And Pharisees came up to him and tested him by asking, 'Is it lawful to divorce one's wife for any cause?' He answered, 'Have you not read that he who created them from the beginning made them male and female, and said, 'Therefore a man shall leave his father and his mother and hold fast to his wife, and the two shall become one flesh'? So they are no longer two but one flesh. *What therefore God has joined together, let not man separate.*'

They said to him, 'Why then did Moses command one to give a certificate of divorce and to send her away?' He said to them, 'Because of your hardness of heart Moses allowed you to divorce your wives, but from the beginning it was not so. And I say to you: whoever divorces his wife, except for sexual immorality, and marries another, commits adultery' (MATTHEW 19:3–9 ESV)."[73]

2. Only that which comes from God is immutable; everything that is the work of humans is subject to change. The laws of Nature are the same in all times and in all places, whereas human laws change according to time, place and intellectual progress. In marriage, what is divine is the union of the sexes from which springs the renewal of the population; and yet the conditions that regulate this union are so much confined to human conventions, that there are not in the whole world – not even in Christendom – two countries where they are absolutely alike; and there is no country – not a single one – where they have not changed over time. Hence, in the eyes

---
73 [Trans. note] In the French Bible used by A. KARDEC (based on the Latin Vulgate) there is an additional sentence at the end of verse 9 above, absent from the ESV but found in the ancient AKJV/PCE, which reads: "... *and whoso marrieth her which is put away doth commit adultery.*"

of civil law, what is perfectly acceptable in one country in a certain time, is considered adultery in another country in a different time. This occurs because civil law aims to regulate the interests of families, and such interests vary according to local customs and needs. It is thus that, for example, in certain countries, religious marriage is the only legitimate one, whereas in others it is required in addition to civil marriage, while in others still, civil marriage alone is sufficient.

3. But in the union of the sexes, alongside the physical aspect of divine law, common to all living beings, there is another divine law, which is unchanging like all the laws of God, which is exclusively moral, namely, the law of love. God wanted all beings to be united, not only by the bonds of the flesh, but also by those of the soul, so that the mutual affection of spouses would be transferred to their children, and that they might be two, instead of one, to love them, to care for them and to make them progress. In the ordinary conditions of marriage, it is this law of love taken into account? Not at all; what we seek to ascertain is not the affection of two beings that a mutual feeling draws toward each other – an affection which is oftentimes broken off; what we seek is not the satisfaction of one's heart, but that of pride, vanity, greed – in short, of all material interests. When everything suits these interests best, we say that the marriage is adequate; and when financial means are well matched, we say that the spouses are also – and ought to be – very happy.

However, neither the civil law, nor the marriage engagements which it causes to be contracted can replace the law of love if this law does not preside over the union. From which follows that often, *what one has united by force separates by itself;* and that the vow which is pronounced at the foot of the altar becomes perjury if it is said as a banal formula. Hence the unhappy unions, which end up becoming criminal; a double misfortune which one would avoid if, in the conditions for marriage, one did not disregard the only one which sanctions it in God's eyes: the law of love. When God said, "The two shall become one flesh";[74] and when Jesus said, "What God has joined together, let not man separate," it should be understood as a union according to the unchanging law of God, and not according to the changing law of humans.

74 [Trans. note] EPHESIANS 5:31 ESV.

4. Does that mean that civil law is superfluous, and that we should all return to marriages according to Nature? Certainly not. The aim of civil law is to regulate social relationships and family interests, according to the requirements of civilization; that is why it is useful, necessary, but variable. It should be far-sighted, because civilized people cannot live like savages; but nothing, absolutely nothing prevents it from being the corollary of the law of God. Obstacles to the fulfillment of divine law come from prejudice and not from civil law. Such prejudices, although still persisting, have already lost their influence among enlightened nations. Prejudices will disappear with the advancement of moral progress, which will finally open our eyes to countless evils, faults, even crimes that result from marital unions contracted for the sole purpose of material interests – and one will wonder one day if it is more human, more charitable, more moral to bring one person to another who cannot live together, than to give them freedom; and if the prospect of an indissoluble chain does not increase the number of irregular unions.

Divorce

5. Divorce is a human law which aims at legally separating what is actually separated. It is not contrary to the law of God, since it only reforms what humans have done, and should only be applicable in cases where the divine law has not been taken into account. If it were contrary to this law, the Church[75] itself would be forced to regard as prevaricators some of its leaders who, on their own authority and in the name of religion, have imposed divorce in more than one occasion – a double prevarication then, since it was for temporal interests alone, and not to satisfy the law of love.

However, Jesus himself has never consecrated the absolute indissolubility of marriage. Did he not say, "Because of your hardness of heart Moses allowed you to divorce your wives"? This means that, from the time of Moses, since mutual affection was not the sole aim of marriage, separation might become necessary. "But," he adds, "from the beginning it was not so." That is to say, that at the origin of humanity, when humans were not yet perverted by

75 [Trans. note] See footnote 1 above.

selfishness and pride, they lived according to the law of God, when unions, based on affinity and not on vanity or ambition, did not give rise to repudiation.

He goes further: he specifies adultery as the case in which divorce can take place. Now, adultery does not exist where there is genuine mutual affection. It is true that he forbids anyone from marrying a divorced woman, but then again the manners and habits of the men of his time must be taken into consideration. Mosaic law, in this case, prescribed stoning; however, wanting to abolish this barbaric practice, a penalty was still required. He finds it in the dishonor represented by the prohibition of a second marriage.[76] It was somehow a civil law substituted for another civil law, but which, like all laws of this nature, had to stand the test of time.

76 [Trans. note] See footnote 73 above.

Chapter XXIII
Strange morals

IF ANY COME TO ME AND DO NOT HATE THEIR OWN FATHER AND MOTHER

1. "Now great crowds accompanied him, and he turned and said to them, 'If anyone comes to me and does not hate his own father and mother and wife and children and brothers and sisters, yes, and even his own life, he cannot be my disciple. Whoever does not bear his own cross and come after me cannot be my disciple.

So therefore, any one of you who does not renounce all that he has cannot be my disciple' (LUKE 14:25–27, 33 ESV)."

2. "Whoever loves father or mother more than me is not worthy of me, and whoever loves son or daughter more than me is not worthy of me (MATTHEW 10:37 ESV)."

3. Certain words, albeit very rare, make such a strange contrast in the mouth of Christ, that one instinctively rejects their literal meaning, and the sublimity of his doctrine has not been affected by them. Having been written after his death – since no Gospel was written during his lifetime – it is possible to believe that, in this case, the gist of his thought was not properly conveyed, or – which is no less probable – the original meaning of the words may have undergone some alteration in passing from one language to another. It is often enough for a mistake to be made once, for it to be repeated by scribes, as is often the case when dealing with historical facts.

The word *hate*, in this sentence from Luke, "If anyone comes to me and does not hate his own father and mother," is one such instance – and no one would have thought of attributing it to Jesus. It would therefore be redundant to discuss it, let alone seek to justify it here. First we should ascertain if he did pronounce those words, and, if so, whether in the language in which he spoke, the word hate had the same meaning as in ours. In this passage from John, "Whoever *hates* his life in this world will keep it for eternal life,"[77] it is certain that he does not express the idea that we usually attach to that word.

The Hebrew language was not as rich as other languages, and had many words with several different meanings. Such is for example the word that, in Genesis, designates the phases of creation, and used both to express any period of time and a diurnal revolution – hence, later on, its translation as the word day, and the belief that the world was created in six times twenty-four hours. This is also what happened to the word that meant both camel and cable – because cables were made of camel hair – which was translated as camel in the allegory of the eye of a needle (see chapter **XVI**, no. **2** above).[78]

It is also necessary to take into account the mores and the character of the peoples, which influence the particular genius of the language they speak. Without this knowledge the true meaning of certain words is elusive: from one language to another, the same word may have a more or less forceful meaning; it may be an insult or blasphemy in one but quite insignificant in the other, depending on the idea attached to it. In one same language certain words may lose their significance a few centuries apart; this is why a rigorously literal translation does not always convey the thought perfectly, and that for it to be exact, it is sometimes necessary to use, not the corresponding words, but equivalent ones or periphrases.

---

77 [Trans. note] JOHN 12:25 ESV.

78 Note by André PEZZANI as added by Allan KARDEC: "*Non odit* in Latin, *kai* or *mise* in Greek, does not mean *to hate*, but *to love less*. What the Greek verb *misein* means, the Hebrew verb which Jesus must have used, express even better, for it does not only mean *to hate*, but *to love less*, that is, *not to love as much as or the same as another*. In the Syriac dialect (derived from Aramaic, the native language of Jesus), which it is said that Jesus used most often, this latter meaning is even more accentuated. It is in this sense that it appears in GENESIS 29:30–31 ESV: "So Jacob went in to Rachel also, and he loved Rachel more than Leah ... When the LORD saw that Leah was *hated* ..." It is obvious that here the true meaning is *less loved*, which is how it should have been translated. In several other Hebrew passages, and especially in Syriac, the same verb is used in the sense of *not loving as much as or the same as another* – and it would be a mistake to translate it as *hating*, which has another well defined meaning. Moreover, MATTHEW's text leaves no doubt on the subject."

Such considerations are especially useful when interpreting biblical texts, and the Gospels in particular. If one does not take into account the environment in which Jesus lived, one runs the risk of making mistakes about the meaning and significance of certain expressions and facts, as a result of the habit of assimilating others to oneself. In any event, it is necessary to exclude from the word hate its modern meaning as being contrary to the spirit of Jesus' teachings (see also Chapter **XIV**, no. 5 *et seq.* above).

FORSAKING ONE'S OWN FATHER, MOTHER AND CHILDREN

4. "And everyone who has left houses or brothers or sisters or father or mother or children or lands, for my name's sake, will receive a hundredfold and will inherit eternal life (MATTHEW 19:29 ESV)."

5. "And Peter said, 'See, we have left our homes and followed you.' And he said to them, 'Truly, I say to you, there is no one who has left house or wife or brothers or parents or children, for the sake of the kingdom of God, who will not receive many times more in this time, and in the age to come eternal life' (LUKE 18:28–30 ESV)."

6. "Yet another said, 'I will follow you, Lord, but let me first say farewell to those at my home.' Jesus said to him, 'No one who puts his hand to the plow and looks back is fit for the kingdom of God' (LUKE 9:61–62 ESV)."

Without discussing the words, here we must seek the thought they express, which is obviously this: "The interests of future life prevail over all human interests and considerations" – because it agrees with the essence of Jesus' doctrine, whereas the idea of forsaking one's family would be its negation.

Moreover, have we not already before us the application of those maxims in the sacrifice of family interests and affections for one's homeland? Do we blame a soldier for leaving his father, mother, siblings, wife, children to march in defense of country? Quite on the contrary, for do we not consider to be a soldier's merit to tear themself away from the sweet warmth of the domestic hearth, and from the embraces of friendship, in order to accomplish a duty? There are therefore some duties which do prevail over other duties. Are those newly married not legally bound to leave their parents to follow their spouses? The world is teeming with cases where the most painful separations need to take place; but affections are not severed by that; parting does not diminish the respect or the care owed to one's parents or the tenderness owed to one's children. Therefore it is clearly evident that, even taken to the letter, except for the word *hate*, those words would not be a negation of the commandment which prescribes honoring one's father and mother, or of the feeling of parental tenderness, all the more so if one takes the spirit into consideration. Their purpose was to show by hyperbole how imperious was the duty to care for future life. Besides, such words must have been less shocking for a people and in a time when, as a result of customs and manners, family ties had less force than in more advanced moral civilizations. These bonds, weaker among primitive peoples, are strengthened with the development of sensitivity and the moral sense. Separation itself is necessary for progress; there are families as well as races that would degrade if there were no miscegenation, if people did not graft on each other. It is a law of Nature as much in the interest of moral progress as of physical progress.

Things are considered here only from the earthly standpoint; Spiritism makes us see them from a higher perspective, by showing us that the real bonds of affection are those of the spirit and not those of the body. These bonds are not broken off by separation, or even by the death of the body. Let them be strengthened in the spiritual life by the purification of the spirit, a consoling truth which gives one great strength in enduring life's many vicissitudes (see Chapter **IV**, no. **18** and Chapter **XIV**, no. **8** above).

LEAVE THE DEAD TO BURY THEIR OWN DEAD

7.   "To another he said, 'Follow me.' But he said, 'Lord, let me first go and bury my father.' And Jesus said to him, 'Leave the dead to bury their own dead. But as for you, go and proclaim the kingdom of God'(LUKE 9:59–60 ESV)."

8.   What can these words mean: "Leave the dead to bury their own dead"? The foregoing considerations show first of all that, in the circumstances in which they were pronounced, they could not express a reprimand against one who regarded it as a duty of filial piety to go and bury one's parents; but they contain a deep meaning that only a more complete knowledge of spiritual life could make comprehensible.

Spiritual life is in fact the real life. It is the normal life of the spirit, since its earthly existence is only transitory and fleeting; a kind of death if we compare it to the splendor and activity of spiritual life. The body is merely a coarse garment which the spirit momentarily puts on, a veritable chain which binds it to the soil of the Earth, and from which it is happy to be delivered. The respect that we have for the dead does not relate to matter, but – through memory – to the absent spirit. It is analogous to that which one has for the objects which belonged to oneself, which one used to touch, and which those who love the departed keep as relics. This is what that man was not able to understand by himself; hence Jesus taught him by saying: Do not worry about the body, but rather think of the spirit; go and proclaim the kingdom of God; go and tell your fellow beings that their homeland is not on Earth but in heaven, the sole place where real life exists.

I HAVE NOT COME TO BRING PEACE BUT DIVISION

9. "'Do not think that I have come to bring peace to the earth. I have not come to bring peace, but a sword. For I have come to set a man against his father, and a daughter against her mother, and a daughter-in-law against her mother-in-law. And a person's enemies will be those of his own household' (MATTHEW 10:34–36 ESV)."

10. "'I came to cast fire on the earth, and would that it were already kindled! I have a baptism to be baptized with, and how great is my distress until it is accomplished! Do you think that I have come to give peace on earth? No, I tell you, but rather division. For from now on in one house there will be five divided, three against two and two against three. They will be divided, father against son and son against father, mother against daughter and daughter against mother, mother-in-law against her daughter-in-law and daughter-in-law against mother-in-law' (LUKE 12:49–53 ESV)."

11. Is it really Jesus, the personification of meekness and good-ness – he who never stopped preaching the love of neighbor – that said: I have not come to bring peace, but a sword; I have come to separate son from father, husband from wife; I came to cast fire on the earth, and would that it were already kindled. Are these words not in flagrant contradiction to his teaching? Is it not blasphemy to attribute to him the language of a bloodthirsty and devastating conqueror? No, there is neither blasphemy nor contradiction in those words, for it is indeed he who spoke them, and they testify to his high wisdom; only the slightly ambiguous form fails to accurately convey his thought, causing us to misapprehend their true meaning. If taken literally, they might transform his entirely peaceful mission into a mission of unrest and discord, an absurd consequence which common sense makes one dismiss it, because Jesus could not have contradicted himself (see Chapter **XIV**, no. **6** above).

12. Every new idea inevitably meets opposition, and there is not a single one that has been established without struggles. However, in such a case, the resistance is always due to the impor-tance of the expected results, because the greater it is, the more it injures certain interests. If an idea is notoriously false and judged to be of no consequence, nobody acknowledges it, instead letting it pass away, for they know that it has no endurance. But, con-versely, if it is true, if it rests on a solid foundation, if they foresee a future for it, a secret foreboding warns its antagonists that it is a danger for them and for the order of things which they have a vested interest in maintaining. That is why they attack the idea and its supporters.

The measure of the importance and the results of a new idea is thus found in the emotion which it causes at its advent, in the violence of the opposition it raises, and in the degree and persistence of the anger of its opponents.

13. Jesus came to proclaim a doctrine which undermined the abuses of which the Pharisees, the scribes and the priests of his time lived off. For that reason, they killed him, believing they were killing the idea by killing the person; but the idea survived, because it was true; it grew up, because it was in the plans of God; and, leaving an obscure village of Judea, it would plant its flag in the very capital of the pagan world, in front of its most bitter enemies, those who had the most interest in fighting it, because it overturned secular beliefs in which many were much more interested than in their religious convictions. The most terrible struggles awaited his apostles; the victims were innumerable, yet the idea always grew and came out triumphant, because it prevailed as truth over its predecessors.

14. It should be noted that Christianity arrived when Paganism was in decline and struggling against the lights of reason. It was still practiced in form, but the belief had disappeared and self-interest alone supported it. Interest is tenacious; it never gives in to the obvious, it becomes all the more irritated as the reasoned thoughts which are opposed to it become more authoritative and better demonstrate its error; and it knows very well that it is in error, but that is not what touches it, for true faith is not in its core. What it dreads the most is the light that opens the eyes of the blind, for the error benefits it. That is why it clings to it and fiercely defends it.

Had not Socrates also issued a doctrine to a certain point analogous to that of the Christ? Then why it did not prevail at that time among one of the most intelligent civilizations on Earth? The time had not yet come; his crops were planted in untilled soil; paganism had not yet *worn out*. As for Christ, he received his providential mission at an auspicious time. Not all people of his time were advanced enough to live up to Christian ideas, but there was a more general aptitude for assimilating them, because they had begun to feel the void that pagan beliefs left in their souls. Socrates and Plato had opened the way by predisposing minds. (See **Introduction**, section **IV**, *"Socrates and Plato, forerunners of the Christian idea and Spiritism"* above).

15. Unfortunately the followers of the new doctrine did not agree on the interpretation of the words of the Master, most of them veiled under allegories and figures of speech, which caused from the beginning the appearance of numerous sects that claimed to possess the exclusive truth, and which even after eighteen centuries have been unable to reach an agreement. Forgetting the most important of the divine precepts, the one which Jesus had made the cornerstone of his edifice as the express condition of salvation – namely charity, fraternity and love of neighbor – these sects dismissed one another, and wrecked them one on top of the other, with the strongest crushing the weakest, stifling them in the blood, the tortures and the flame of the pyres. Christians, the victors of Paganism, from persecuted became persecutors. It was with iron and fire that they planted the cross of the spotless lamb of God in both worlds. It is a notorious fact that the wars of religion have been the cruelest of all, and have claimed more victims than political wars, by committing the most heinous acts of atrocity and barbarism.

Is Christ's doctrine to blame for it? Certainly not, because it formally condemns all sorts of violence. Did it say to its adherents somewhere, to go, kill, massacre and burn all those who will not believe like them? No, on the contrary, it said to them: All humans are brothers and sisters, and God is supremely merciful; love your neighbor; love your enemies; do good to those who persecute you. Moreover, it said to them: "All who take the sword will perish by the sword."[79] Therefore the blame is not on Jesus' teachings, but on those who misinterpreted it, making it an instrument to serve their passions; on those who have misunderstood this saying: "My kingdom is not of this world."

Jesus, in his deep wisdom, foresaw what was to happen; but these things were inevitable, because they were due to the inferiority of human nature which could not suddenly be transformed. Christianity had to go through this long and cruel test of eighteen centuries[80] to show all its power; for, despite all the evil committed in its name, it came out pure; it has never been called into question; blame has always fallen on those who have abused it; in view of every act of intolerance, one would always say: If Christianity was better understood and better practiced, this would never happen.

16. When Jesus said, "'Do not think that I have come to bring peace, but a sword,'" what he meant is as follows:

"Do not think that my doctrine will be established peacefully; it will bring bloody struggles, for which my name will be the pretext, because humans will not have understood me, or will not have wanted to understand me. Brothers and sisters, separated by their beliefs, will draw the sword against each other, and division will

---

79 [Trans. note] MATTHEW 26:52 ESV.

80 [Trans. note] Here as throughout this book, "eighteen centuries" is roughly the time elapsed since Jesus' crucifixion for those reading it in the 19th century.

reign among members of the same family who will not have the same faith. I have come to set fire to Earth so as to clean it of errors and prejudices, like one sets fire to a field to destroy the weeds, and I cannot wait for it to light up so that purification comes sooner, because from this conflict truth will come out triumphant. Peace will succeed war; universal fraternity will succeed the hatred of factions; and the radiance of enlightened faith will succeed the darkness of fanaticism. So when the field is prepared, I will send you *the Consoler*,[81] *the Spirit of Truth, who will come to restore all things;* that is to say, by making known the true meaning of my words that, at last, more enlightened people will be able to understand. This will put an end to the fratricidal struggle which divides the children of the same God. Tired finally of a dead-end fight, which only drags after itself nothing but desolation, and brings trouble even into the bosom of families, humans will recognize where their real interests lie regarding this world and the next. They will see on which side the friends and the enemies of their peace stand. Everyone will then come to shelter under one same flag, which is that of charity; and things will be restored on Earth according to the truth and the principles that I have taught you."

17. Spiritism has come to fulfill the promises of Christ in due time; however, it cannot do so without destroying abuses. Like Jesus, it encounters in its path pride, selfishness, ambition, greed, blind fanaticism, which, for being hunted down in their last entrenchments, try to block its way and raise obstacles and persecutions. This is why it must also fight; yet the time of bloody struggles and persecutions has passed; those which it will have to undergo are all of a moral nature, and their end is coming nearer. The former struggles and persecutions have lasted for centuries, whereas the latter will last barely a few years, because light, instead of emanating from a single point source, now springs up on all points of the globe, and will sooner open the eyes of the blind.

18. These words of Jesus must therefore be understood by the antagonisms that he foresaw that would be raised by his doctrine. Momentary conflicts that were going to be the consequence of the struggles that it was going to withstand before becoming established,

---

81 [Trans. note] In English also referred to as the Helper or the Comforter.

as it was with the Hebrews before reaching the Promised Land. It was not a premeditated plan on Jesus' part to sow disorder and confusion. Evil had to come from humans, not from the Christ. He was like the doctor who comes to heal, but whose remedies trigger a salutary crisis by stirring the unhealthy humors of the patient's body.

Chapter XXIV
Do not hide your lamp under a bushel

LAMP UNDER A BUSHEL
WHY JESUS SPEAKS IN PARABLES

1. "'Nor do people light a lamp and put it under a basket,[82] but on a stand, and it gives light to all in the house' (MATTHEW 5:15 ESV)."

2. "'No one after lighting a lamp covers it with a jar or puts it under a bed, but puts it on a stand, so that those who enter may see the light. For nothing is hidden that will not be made manifest, nor is anything secret that will not be known and come to light' (LUKE 8:16–17 ESV)."

3. "Then the disciples came and said to him, 'Why do you speak to them in parables?' And he answered them, 'To you it has been given to know the secrets of the kingdom of heaven, but to them it has not been given.... This is why I speak to them in parables, because seeing they do not see, and hearing they do not hear, nor do they understand. Indeed, in their case the prophecy of Isaiah is fulfilled that says: 'You will indeed hear but never understand, and you will indeed see but never perceive. For this people's heart has grown dull, and with their ears they can barely hear, and their eyes they have closed, lest they should see with their eyes and hear with their ears and understand with their heart and turn, and I would heal them' (MATTHEW 13:10–11,13–15 ESV)."

4. It is astonishing to hear Jesus say that we should not hide the light under a bushel, when he himself constantly hides the meaning

---

82 [Trans. note] *Basket* in the *ESV* is the same as *bushel* in older English Bibles.

of his words under the veil of allegory which cannot be understood by everyone. He explains himself by saying to his apostles: I speak to them in parables, because they are not in a condition to understand certain things; seeing they do not see, and hearing they do not hear, nor do they understand; telling them everything would therefore be useless for the moment. But to you I tell it, because it is given to you to understand these mysteries. He therefore acted with the populace as we do with children whose ideas are not yet developed. Thus he indicates the true meaning of the maxim: You should not put a lamp under a bushel, but on the candlestick, so that those who enter may see the light. This does not mean that all things must be thoughtlessly revealed; all teaching must be proportional to the intelligence of the person one is addressing, for there are people who would be stunned and dazzled instead of being enlightened by too bright a light.

This happens with people in general as well as individuals in particular; each generation has its childhood, its youth and its mature age; everything must come in due time, and the seed sown out of season will not bear fruit. But what requires to be silenced momentarily by prudence should sooner or later be discovered, because, once a certain degree of development is reached, people themselves will seek a brighter light, for darkness will start to weigh on them. Since God gave humans intelligence to understand and to guide themselves in both earthly and heavenly things, they eventually wish to reason their faith. It is then that one should not hide the lamp under a bushel, because *without the light of reason, faith dwindles* (see Chapter **XIX**, no. 7 above).

5.   If therefore, in its foreseeing wisdom, Providence reveals truths only gradually, it always unveils them as time goes by, as humanity becomes ripe to receive them. It keeps them in reserve but not under wraps; yet individuals who are in possession of them, most of the time will hide them from their fellow beings only in order to dominate them. Such individuals are the ones who really keep the light under wraps. It is thus that all religions have had their mysteries and questioning was forbidden. But while these religions lagged behind, science and intelligence marched forward and tore open the mysterious veil. Ordinary people, having matured, wished to penetrate the bottom of things, and rejected in their faith everything that was contrary to observation.

There can be no absolute mysteries, and Jesus is right when he says that there is nothing secret that should not be revealed. All that is hidden will one day be unveiled, and what humans cannot yet understand on Earth will be successively revealed to them in more advanced worlds, when they become purified. Down here, we are still in a haze.

6. One wonders what benefit the populace could get from this multitude of parables whose meaning remained hidden for them? It should be noted that Jesus expressed himself in parables only regarding the somewhat abstract parts of his doctrine; but having made both charity toward neighbor, and humility, the express condition of salvation, everything he said in this regard is perfectly clear, explicit and unambiguous. It had to be so, because it was the rule of conduct, a rule that everyone had to understand in order to observe it. It was essential for the ignorant crowd to which he limited himself to saying: This is what must be done to gain the kingdom of heaven. On the other parts of his doctrine he elaborated on his thought only to his closer disciples. Since they were more advanced morally and intellectually, Jesus had been able to initiate them into more abstract truths; therefore he says: *To everyone who has, more will be given*[83] (see Chapter **XVIII**, no. **15** above).

However, even with his apostles, he remained vague on many points whose full comprehension was reserved for later times. It was these points that gave rise to such diverse interpretations, until science, on the one hand, and Spiritism, on the other, came to reveal the new laws of Nature that made their true meaning plain.

7. Today Spiritism has come to shed light on a host of obscure points; however it does not do it rashly. The spirits give their instructions with admirable caution; only successively and gradually they approached the various known parts of the doctrine, and this is how the other parts will be revealed when time is right to bring them out of the shadow. If they had presented everything complete from the start, it would have been accessible only to a small number of

---

83 [Trans. note] Luke 19:26; cf. MATTHEW 13:12 ESV.

individuals. Furthermore, it would have frightened those who were not prepared for it, a fact that would have hindered its dissemination. Therefore if the spirits do not yet overtly reveal everything, it is not because of any mysteries reserved for the privileged, or because they hide the lamp under a bushel, but rather because everything has to come at the appropriate time. The spirits give an idea time to mature and be disseminated before presenting another one, and *allow events time in which to prepare its acceptance.*

GO NOWHERE AMONG THE GENTILES

8. "These twelve Jesus sent out, instructing them, 'Go nowhere among the Gentiles and enter no town of the Samaritans, but go rather to the lost sheep of the house of Israel. And proclaim as you go, saying, 'The kingdom of heaven is at hand' (MATTHEW 10:5–7 ESV)."

9. Jesus proves in many circumstances that his views are not confined to the Jewish people, but rather embrace all humankind. If therefore he told his apostles not to go among the Gentiles, it was not out of disdain for the conversion of the latter, which would have been unhelpful, but because the Jews, who believed in the unity of God and waited for a Messiah, were prepared, by the law of Moses and the prophets, to receive his word. Among the pagans, since the very base was lacking, everything was still to be done, and the apostles were not yet sufficiently enlightened for such a heavy task. Hence he said to them, Go to the lost sheep of Israel, that is to say, go and sow on land already plowed, as he knew full well that the conversion of the Gentiles would come in due time. Later, in fact, it was at the very center of paganism that the apostles went to plant the cross.

10. These words can also be applied to the followers and disseminators of Spiritism. Systematic unbelievers, obstinate mockers, interested adversaries, are to Spiritists what the Gentiles were to the apostles. Following the example left by the latter, let first seek proselytes among people of goodwill, that is, those who desire the light and in whom we find a fertile seed – and there are quite a lot of such people – without wasting time on those who refuse to see and hear, and instead stiffen all the more, out of pride, when someone seems to attach more value to their conversion. It is better to open the eyes of a hundred blind persons who do wish to see clearly, than of one who delights in remaining in the dark, because in this way you increase the number of supporters of the cause in a greater proportion. Leaving others alone is not indifference, but good policy; their turn will come when they are somehow swayed by general opinion, and when they hear the same thing constantly repeated around them. In this way they will believe to accept the idea voluntarily and of their own volition, and not under the pressure of some individual. Moreover, ideas are like seeds: they cannot germinate before the right season, and only in a prepared soil; this is why it is better to wait for the favorable time, and to cultivate first those which do germinate, for fear of thwarting others by having pushed them too hard.

In the time of Jesus, and as a result of the restricted and materialistic ideas of that time, everything was circumscribed and localized. The house of Israel was a small nation, and the Gentiles were small surrounding nations. Nowadays ideas are universalized and more spiritualized. The new light is not the privilege of any nation and have no more barriers. It has its home everywhere and all humans are regarded as brothers and sisters. But also the Gentiles are no longer a people, it is rather an opinion that one meets everywhere, and whose truth gradually gains dominance as Christianity once triumphed over paganism. It is no longer with the weapons of war that we fight them, but with the power of an idea.

THOSE WHO ARE WELL HAVE NO NEED
OF A PHYSICIAN

11. "And as Jesus reclined at table in the house, behold, many tax collectors and sinners came and were reclining with Jesus and his disciples. And when the Pharisees saw this, they said to his disciples, 'Why does your teacher eat with tax collectors and sinners?' But when he heard it, he said, 'Those who are well have no need of a physician, but those who are sick' (MATTHEW 9:10–12 ESV)."

12. Jesus addressed himself especially to the poor and the underprivileged, because they are the ones who most need comfort; to the blind who are willing to learn and have good faith, because they ask to see, and not to the proud ones who think they possess all the light and need nothing. (See **Introduction**, III. Historical Data, entries "Publicans" and "Toll collectors" above.)

These words, like so many others, find their application in Spiritism. It is sometimes surprising that mediumship is given to people who are unworthy and capable of misusing it. It would seem that such a precious faculty should be the exclusive attribute of the most deserving human beings.

First and foremost, it should be pointed out that mediumship comes from a purely organic faculty that any person can possess, just like the ordinary senses of seeing, hearing and speaking. There is not a single one that humans, by virtue of their free will, cannot abuse; and if God had given the ability of speaking, for example, only to those who are incapable of saying bad things, there would be more mutes than speaking people in the world. So God has given humans many faculties, also giving them the freedom to use them as they wish. However, God always punishes those who abuse their faculties.

If the power to communicate with the spirits was given only to the most worthy, who would dare to claim it? Moreover, where would be the boundaries between worthiness and unworthiness? Mediumship is given without distinction, so that spirits can carry light into all ranks, in all walks of society; among the poor as well as the rich; among the wise to strengthen them in the good; among the vicious and wicked in order to correct them. Aren't these the patients who need a physician? Why should God, who does not want the sinners' demise, deprive them of the help that can get them out of the quagmire? Good spirits therefore come to their aid, and give them advice, which they receive directly – which is likely to impress them more vividly than if they received it through indirect means. God, in Its goodness, to spare them the trouble of seeking the light far away, puts it in their hands – is one not much more culpable for not looking at it? Will he or she be able to apologize for their ignorance, when they have written themselves, seen with their eyes, heard with their ears, and pronounced their own condemnation with their mouths? If one does not benefit from it, only then he/she is punished by the loss or by the perversion of their faculty, which evil spirits will seize to obsess and deceive them, without prejudice to the real afflictions with which God strikes all unworthy servants, and any hearts hardened by pride and selfishness.

Mediumship does not necessarily imply recurring communication with higher-order spirits; it is simply the *aptitude* for serving as a more or less flexible instrument used by spirits in general. A good medium is therefore not one who receives spiritual communications with ease, but the one who is sympathetic to good spirits and only assisted by them. It is only in this sense that the excellence of moral qualities is of almighty importance in mediumship.

THE COURAGE OF FAITH

13. "'So everyone who acknowledges me before men, I also will acknowledge before my Father who is in heaven, but whoever denies me before men, I also will deny before my Father who is in heaven' (MATTHEW 10:32–33 ESV)."

14. "'For whoever is ashamed of me and of my words, of him will the Son of Man be ashamed when he comes in his glory and the glory of the Father and of the holy angels.' (LUKE 9:26 ESV)."

15. The courage of showing one's opinion in public has always been held in esteem among humans, because there is merit in braving the dangers, the persecutions, the contradictions, and even the simple sarcasm, to which those who are not afraid to admit lofty ideas that are not those of everyone else, are almost always exposed. Here, as in everything, merit depends on the circumstances and the importance of the result. There is always weakness in backing away from the consequences of one's opinion, and to deny it, but there are some cases where it is as great a cowardice as fleeing during combat.

Jesus decries such cowardice, specially with regard of his doctrine, saying that if anyone is ashamed of his words, he will also be ashamed of them; that he will deny those who denied him, whereas those who will confess him before fellow beings, will be recognized by him before his Parent in heaven. In other words: *Those who are afraid to confess themselves disciples of the truth, are not worthy of being admitted into the kingdom of the truth.* They will lose the benefit of their faith, because it is a selfish faith, which they keep for themselves, but otherwise hide it lest it harm them in this world, whereas those who, putting truth above their material interests, overtly proclaim it, work simultaneously for their future and that of others.

16. So it will be with the followers of Spiritism, since its doctrine is none other than the development and application of the Gospel's tenets. Also, it is to them that those words of Christ are addressed. They sow on Earth what they will reap in spiritual life. It is there that they will reap the fruits of their courage or their weakness.

Take up one's cross
Whoever would save one's life, will lose it

17. "'Blessed are you when people hate you and when they exclude you and revile you and spurn your name as evil, on account of the Son of Man! Rejoice in that day, and leap for joy, for behold, your reward is great in heaven; for so their fathers did to the prophets' (Luke 6:22–23 esv)."

18. "And calling the crowd to him with his disciples, he said to them, 'If anyone would come after me, let him deny himself and take up his cross and follow me. For what does it profit a man to gain the whole world and forfeit his soul?'

For whoever would save his life will lose it, but whoever loses his life for my sake will save it. For what does it profit a man if he gains the whole world and loses or forfeits himself?' (Mark 8:34–36; Luke 10:23–25. *Cf.* Matthew 10:39 and John 12:24–25 esv)."

19. Rejoice, said Jesus, when people hate you and persecute you because of me, because you will be rewarded in heaven. These words can be translated as follows: Be joyful when people, on account of their ill will toward you, provide you with an opportunity to prove the sincerity of your faith, because the harm they do to you will turn to your benefit. Therefore feel sorry for their blindness but do not curse them.

Then he adds: "If anyone would come after me, let him deny himself and take up his cross," that is to say, all those who courageously endure the tribulations that their faith will cause them; for whoever wishes to save their lives and their possessions by renouncing Jesus, will lose the advantages of the kingdom of heaven, whereas those who will have lost everything down here, even their own lives, for the triumph of truth, will receive, in future life, a reward for their courage, perseverance and selflessness. However, to those who sacrifice heavenly goods for earthly enjoyments, God will say: You have already received your reward.

Chapter XXV
Seek and you will find

HELP YOURSELF AND HEAVEN WILL HELP YOU

1. "'Ask, and it will be given to you; *seek, and you will find*; knock, and it will be opened to you. For everyone who asks receives, and the one who seeks finds, and to the one who knocks it will be opened. Or which one of you, if his son asks him for bread, will give him a stone? Or if he asks for a fish, will give him a serpent? If you then, who are evil, know how to give good gifts to your children, how much more will your Father who is in heaven give good things to those who ask him!' (MATHEW 7:7–11 ESV)."

2. From the earthly standpoint, the maxim, *Seek and you will find*, is analogous to, *Help yourself and heaven will help you*.[84] It expresses the principle of the *law of work*, and consequently of the *law of progress*, because progress is the offspring of work, due to the fact that work activates the forces of intelligence.

During the infancy of humankind, people applied their intelligence only in the search for food, means to protect themselves from bad weather, and to defend themselves against their enemies. But God gave them, beyond that which was also given to animals, *a constant drive for the best*. It is this desire for the best that drives humans to seek ways to improve their condition, which leads them to make discoveries and inventions, and to increasingly develop science, for it is science which gives humans what they lack. Through study and research, their intelligence grows, morals are purified. Besides physical needs, there are also spiritual needs; after material food, spiritual food is needed – this is how human beings go from being primitive to being civilized.

---

84 [Trans. note] *Aide-toi, le ciel t'aidera* is a French proverb attributed to the poet LA FONTAINE (1621–1695).

But the progress that each person achieves individually during a lifetime is very little, even imperceptible in many cases. So how could humanity progress without a preexistence and a *re-existence* of the soul? Should souls leave each day to never return, humanity would constantly renew itself only with primitive individuals, still having everything to do, everything to learn. Therefore there would be no reason why man should be more advanced today than in the first ages of the planet, since at each birth all intellectual work would have to be started all over again. Conversely, the soul returning with its already accomplished progress, and each time adding something more to it, thus gradually passes from a primitive state to *material civilization,* and from this latter to *moral civilization* (see Chapter **IV**, no. **17** above).

3.   If God had freed humans from the work of the body, the limbs would be atrophied. If God had freed humans from the work of intelligence, their spirits would have remained in infancy, in the state of animal instinct. That is why the Creator made work a necessity, telling humans, *Seek and you will find, work and you will produce;* in this way you will become the outcome of your deeds, you will have the merit and be rewarded according to what you have done.

4.   By applying this principle, the spirits do not come to spare humans the work of study and research, by bringing them ready-made discoveries and inventions, so humans only have to take what would be put in their hands, without having the trouble to bend down and pick it up, not even the effort of thinking. If this were so, the laziest could get rich, and the most ignorant become savants, and both take credit for what they would not have done. No, *the spirits do not come to free human beings from the law of work, but rather to show them the goal which they must reach and the road which leads to it, by saying to them: Walk onward and you will get there.* You will find stones under your feet; look out and take them away yourself; we will give you the necessary strength if you are willing to use it (see Allan KARDEC, *The Mediums' Book*, Chapter XXVI, items no. 291 *et seq.*).

5.   From a moral point of view, these words of Jesus mean: Ask for the light that should illuminate your way, and it will be given to you; ask for strength to resist evil, and you will have it; ask for the assistance of good spirits, and they will come to accompany you, and like Tobit's[85] angel, they will serve you as guides; ask for good advice, and it will never be denied; knock on our door, and it will be opened to you. Yet ask sincerely, with faith, earnestness and confidence; make your case with humility and not with arrogance. Without that you will be left to your own strength, and the very tumbles you take will be a punishment for your pride.

Such is the meaning contained in these words: Seek, and you will find; knock, and it will be opened to you

LOOK AT THE BIRDS OF THE AIR

6. "'Therefore I tell you, do not be anxious about your life, what you will eat or what you will drink, nor about your body, what you will put on. Is not life more than food, and the body more than clothing?

Look at the birds of the air: they neither sow nor reap nor gather into barns, and yet your heavenly Father feeds them. Are you not of more value than they? And which of you by being anxious can add a single hour to his span of life?

And why are you anxious about clothing? Consider the lilies of the field, how they grow: they neither toil nor spin, yet I tell you, even Solomon in all his glory was not arrayed like one of these. But if God so clothes the grass of the field, which today is alive and tomorrow is thrown into the oven, will he not much more clothe you, O you of little faith?

Therefore do not be anxious, saying, 'What shall we eat?' or 'What shall we drink?' or 'What shall we wear?' For the Gentiles seek after all these things, and your heavenly Father knows that you need them all. But seek first the kingdom of God and his righteousness, and all these things will be added to you.

Therefore do not be anxious about tomorrow, for tomorrow will be anxious for itself. *Sufficient for the day is its own trouble*' (MATHEW 6:25–34 ESV)."

---

85 [Trans. note] Tobit, Tobiah or Tobias, also called *The Book of Tobias*, is an apocryphal work not recognized by Jews and Protestants, but included in the Roman Catholic canon.

7. Taken literally, these words would be the negation of all foresight, of all work, and therefore of all progress. With such a principle, people would be reduced to an expectant passivity; their physical and intellectual strengths would be left without activity. If such were their normal condition on Earth, they would never have left the primitive state; and if they had made it their current law, they would only have to live without having to do anything. This cannot have been what Jesus meant to say, for it would be in contradiction with what he said elsewhere and with the very laws of Nature. God created humans without clothing or shelter, but granted them intelligence to make and build what they needed (see Chapter **XIV** no. **6**; Chapter **XXV** no. **2** above).

Therefore we should see in these words only a poetic allegory of Providence, which never forsakes those who put their trust in It, but wants them to work and do their part. If it does not always come to the aid through material help, it inspires the ideas with which we find the means to help ourselves out of predicaments (see Chapter **XXVII**, no. **8** below).

God knows our needs, and provides for them as necessary; but humans, insatiable in their desires, do not always know how to content themselves with what they may have. For them, having the essential is not enough, they need the superfluous. It is then that Providence leaves them to themselves. Often they are unhappy by their own fault and for having misunderstood the voice which warned them through their conscience. Then God lets them suffer the consequences, so that these will serve as a lesson to them in future (see Chapter **V**, no. **4** above).

8. Earth produces enough to feed all its inhabitants, when humans can properly manage the goods it produces, in accordance with the laws of justice, charity and love of neighbor. The day fraternity reigns among diverse nations, as well as among provinces of the same empire, the momentary surplus of one will make up for the momentary shortage of the other, and thus each will have the essentials. The wealthy will then regard themselves as individuals with a large quantity of seeds; if he or she spreads them, they will produce a hundredfold for them and for others; however, if they eat these seeds on by themselves, and if they waste and lose the surplus of what they eat, they will produce nothing, and there will be enough for everybody. Also, if they stockpile the seeds in their silos, they end up being eaten by worms. This is why Jesus said: Do not lay up for yourselves treasures on Earth, which are perishable, but lay up for yourselves treasures in heaven, where they are eternal.[86] In other words, do not attach more importance to material goods than to spiritual goods, and know how to sacrifice the former for the sake of the latter (see Chapter **XVI**, no. **7** *et seq.* above).

Charity and fraternity cannot be established by legal decree. If they are not found in one's heart, selfishness will always stifle them. Making them enter the heart is the task of Spiritism.

ACQUIRE NO GOLD NOR SILVER NOR COPPER

9. "'Acquire no gold nor silver nor copper for your belts, no bag for your journey, nor two tunics nor sandals nor a staff, for the laborer deserves his food' (MATTHEW 10:9–10 ESV)."

10. "'And whatever town or village you enter, find out who is worthy in it and stay there until you depart. As you enter the house, greet it. And if the house is worthy, let your peace come upon it, but if it is not worthy, let your peace return to you.

And if anyone will not receive you or listen to your words, shake off the dust from your feet when you leave that house or town. Truly, I say to you, it will be more bearable on the day of judgment for the land of Sodom and Gomorrah than for that town' (MATTHEW 10:11–15 ESV)."

11. These words addressed by Jesus to his apostles, when he first sent them to announce the Good News, were nothing strange at the time: they were according to the patriarchal customs of the East, where a traveler was always received under the tent. But back then travelers were rare, whereas among modern nations the increase in people's flow would create new habits and customs. We find those of ancient times only in remote regions where a great movement of persons has not yet built up. Therefore if Jesus returned today, he would no longer be able to say to his apostles, "Go without provisions."

Besides their literal sense, these words have a very profound moral sense. Jesus thus taught his disciples to trust in Providence. Also,

---

86 [Trans. note] *Cf.* MATTHEW 6:19–20 ESV.

by having no possessions, they would not entice the greed of those who received them – it was a means of distinguishing the charitable from the selfish – which is why he said to them: "Find out who is worthy in it and stay there until you depart" – in other words, find out who is humane enough to lodge a traveler who does not have enough to pay, because these are worthy to hear your words; it is through their charity that you will recognize them.

As for those who will neither receive them nor listen to them, did he tell his apostles to curse them, to impose themselves on them, to use violence and coercion to convert them? No, but rather to go purely and simply elsewhere, and to seek people of good will.

Thus Spiritism says today to its adherents: Neither violate any conscience, nor force anyone to leave their belief in order to adopt your own. Do not cast anathema on those who do not think like you; welcome those who come to you but leave those who reject you at peace. Remember the words of the Christ: Once heaven was taken by force, today it is taken by gentleness (see Chapter **IV**, no. **10** and **11** above).

Chapter XXVI
Freely you have received, freely give

THE GIFT OF HEALING

1. "Heal the sick, raise the dead, cleanse lepers, cast out demons. *You received without paying; give without pay* (MATTHEW 10:8 ESV)."

2. "You received without paying; give without pay," said Jesus to his disciples. By this precept he prescribed them to give freely as they themselves had freely received. Now, what they had received for free was the ability to heal the sick and cast out demons, that is to say, evil spirits. This gift had been given to them free of charge by God for the relief of all those who suffered, and for helping the propagation of the faith – and Jesus told them not to traffic in it, nor to turn it into an object of financial speculation or a means of living.

PAID PRAYERS

3. "And in the hearing of all the people he said to his disciples, 'Beware of the scribes, who like to walk around in long robes, and love greetings in the marketplaces and the best seats in the synagogues and the places of honor at feasts, *who devour widows' houses and for a pretense make long prayers.* They will receive the greater condemnation' (LUKE 20:45–47; *cf.* MARK 12:38–40 and MATTHEW 23:14 ESV)."

4. Jesus also said: Do not charge for your prayers; do not act like the scribes who, *"devour widows' houses and for a pretense make long prayers"* – that is to say, grab people's money. Prayer is an act of charity, an outburst of the heart; to charge for prayers that one addresses to God on behalf of others, is to transform oneself into a salaried intermediary. Then a prayer becomes a formula whose length is proportional to the sum of money obtained. Now, of two things, one: either God measures or does not measure Its blessings by the number of words. If it takes a lot of prayers, then why say little or none at all on behalf of the someone that cannot pay? This would be totally uncharitable. Conversely, if just one prayer is enough, any surplus is useless – then why make anyone pay? This would be plain prevarication.

God does not sell the blessings that It gives. Then why should anyone who is not even their dispenser, who cannot guarantee that such blessings will be obtained, can charge for a request which might yield no result? God could not possibly have subordinated an act of mercy, kindness or justice that is sought from Its mercy, to a sum of money; otherwise it would follow that if the sum is not paid, or is insufficient, then God's justice, goodness and mercy would be suspended ! Reason, common sense and logic tell us that God, which is absolute perfection, would never delegate to imperfect creatures the right to put a price tag on Its justice. God's justice is like the Sun; it is for each and every one, for the poor as well as for the rich. If it is considered immoral to traffic in things pertaining to any sovereign of the Earth, would it be more lawful to sell those pertaining to the sovereign of the Universe?

Paid prayers have another drawback, namely, that whoever buys them thinks more often than not to be exempt from praying for themselves, because they regard themselves as being quits after paying for prayers. We know that spirits are touched by the fervor of the thought of those who take an interest in them; but what can be the fervor of someone who instructs a third party to pray for him/her in exchange for paying? And what is the fervor of this third party when it delegates its mandate to another, then this one to another, and so on? Does this not reduce the effectiveness of prayer to the same value of everyday money?

VENDORS EXPELLED FROM THE TEMPLE

5. "And they come to Jerusalem: and Jesus went into the temple, and began to cast out them that sold and bought in the temple, and overthrew the tables of the moneychangers, and the seats of them that sold doves; And would not suffer that any man should carry any vessel through the temple. And he taught, saying unto them,

316

Is it not written, My house shall be called of all nations the house of prayer? but ye have made it a den of thieves. And the scribes and chief priests heard it, and sought how they might destroy him: for they feared him, because all the people was astonished at his doctrine. (MARK 11:15–18 AKJV/PCE; MATTHEW 21:12–13 ESV)."

6. Jesus expelled the vendors from the temple; thereby he condemns the traffic in holy things *in any form whatsoever.* God sells neither Its blessings, nor Its forgiveness, nor the entrance to the kingdom of heaven. Humans therefore have no right to charge for them.

MEDIUMSHIP FREE OF CHARGE

7. Modern mediums – because the apostles of old had mediumship as well – also received from God a free gift, namely, of being the interpreters of the spirits for the instruction of humans, by showing them the path to good while bringing them to faith, and disallowing them to sell words that simply do not belong to them, because they are neither *the product of their conception, nor of their study and research, nor of their personal work.* God wants light to come to everyone; It does not want the poorest to be disinherited and then say: I do not have faith, because I could not pay for it; I did not have the comfort of receiving encouragements and expressions of affection from my dearly departed, because I am poor. That is why mediumship is not a privilege but can be found everywhere – therefore, to charge for it would be to divert it from its providential goal.

8. Anyone who knows the conditions under which good spirits communicate, their repulsion for any form of selfish interest; and who knows how little it takes to chase them away; could never conceive that higher-order spirits would be at the disposal of the first comer who would call them to a mediumistic meeting. Simple common sense rejects such a thought. Would it not also be a desecration to evoke with money the beings we respect or who are dear to us? No doubt there can be spirit communications like this, but who could guarantee their sincerity? Irresponsible, frivolous, lying and mischievous spirits, and all the multitude of lower-order spirits – all quite unscrupulous – always come, and are all too ready to answer anything one asks without worrying about the truth. Anyone who wants serious spirit communications must first request them seriously, then build up on the nature of the medium's sympathies with the beings of the spiritual world. Now the first condition for gaining the benevolence of good spirits is humility, dedication, self-denial, and the most absolute *moral and material* disinterestedness.

9.   Beside the moral question, another important consideration involves the very nature of the faculty itself. Serious mediumship cannot and will never be a profession, not only because it would be morally discredited and soon associated with fortune-tellers, but also because a material obstacle is opposed to it, since it is an essentially transient, fleeting and variable faculty, on whose permanence nobody can rely. Therefore, for the operator, it would be an entirely uncertain resource, which he/she could miss when it was most needed. It would be quite another story, if it were a talent that could be acquired through study and training, and which, by this very fact, were a skill of which one could easily take advantage. But being neither an art nor a talent, mediumship cannot be turned into a profession: it only exists by the help of spirits; if such spirits are lacking, there is no more mediumship. The aptitude may remain, but its exercise is interrupted. Therefore there is not a single medium in the world that can guarantee the obtaining of a Spiritist phenomenon at a given instant. To exploit mediumship is therefore to attempt to have control over something of which one is really no master all. To affirm the contrary would be to deceive the one who pays – and what is more, it is not *of oneself* that one obtains the communication, it is from the spirits, the souls of the departed to whose assistance someone have attached a price tag. Such a thought is instinctively repulsive. It is this traffic, degenerated into abuse, and exploited through charlatanism, ignorance, gullibility and superstition, that motivated the prohibition of Moses regarding mediumship. Modern Spiritism, understanding the seriousness of the situation due to the discredit thrown upon its exploitation, has raised mediumship to the level of a mission (see Allan KARDEC, *The Mediums' Book*, Chapter XXVIII; and Allan KARDEC, *Heaven and Hell*, Chapter XII).

10.   Mediumship is a holy thing which must be practiced holily, with a religious sentiment. If there is one kind of mediumship which requires this condition even more absolutely, it is healing mediumship. Doctors give the fruit of their studies, which they carried out often at the cost of painful sacrifices; whereas magnetizers give their own fluid,[87] often even their own health: they can do it for a price. But healing mediums simply transmit the salutary fluids of good spirits, and therefore have no right to charge for it. Jesus and the apostles, though poor, never charged for the cures they operated.

Let those who have no means to provide for their own support, seek resources elsewhere other than in the exploitation of mediumship; may they devote to it, if need be, only the time that they can spare materially. The spirits will take into account their dedication and self-sacrifice, whereas they will distance themselves from those who hope to make a profit from it.

---

87 [Trans. note] About the nature and properties of fluids, see Allan KARDEC, *Genesis, Miracles and Predictions,* Part Two, Chapter XIV, "Fluids."

Chapter XXVII
Ask and it shall be given you

QUALITIES OF PRAYER

1. "'And when you pray, you must not be like the hypocrites. For they love to stand and pray in the synagogues and at the street corners, that they may be seen by others. Truly, I say to you, they have received their reward. But when you pray, go into your room and shut the door and pray to your Father who is in secret. And your Father who sees in secret will reward you.'

'And when you pray, do not heap up empty phrases as the Gentiles do, for they think that they will be heard for their many words. Do not be like them, for your Father knows what you need before you ask him' (MATTHEW 6:5–8 ESV)."

2. "'And whenever you stand praying, forgive, if you have anything against anyone, so that your Father also who is in heaven may forgive you your trespasses' (Mark 11:25 esv)."88

3. "He also told this parable to some who trusted in themselves that they were righteous, and treated others with contempt:

'Two men went up into the temple to pray, one a Pharisee and the other a tax collector. The Pharisee, standing by himself, prayed thus: 'God, I thank you that I am not like other men, extortioners, unjust, adulterers, or even like this tax collector. I fast twice a week; I give tithes of all that I get.' But the tax collector, standing far off, would not even lift up his eyes to heaven, but beat his breast, saying, 'God, be merciful to me, a sinner!' I tell you, this man went down

---

88 [Trans. note] The ESV excludes verse 26 but cites it as follows: "Some manuscripts add verse 26: *But if you do not forgive, neither will your Father who is in heaven forgive your trespasses.*"

to his house justified, rather than the other. For everyone who exalts himself will be humbled, but the one who humbles himself will be exalted' (LUKE 18:9–14 ESV)."

4. The qualities a prayer should possess are clearly defined by Jesus: When you pray, he says, do not stand out, but pray in secret; do not affect to pray much, for it is not for the multiplicity of words that you will be answered, but by their sincerity; before praying, if you have something against someone, forgive this person, because a prayer cannot be pleasing to God if it does not come from a heart purified of any feelings contrary to charity. Finally pray with humility, like that tax collector, and not with pride, like the Pharisee; examine your flaws, not your qualities, and if you compare yourself to others, look for what is wrong in you (see Chapter **X**, numbers **7** and **8** above).

EFFECTIVENESS OF PRAYER

5. "Whatever you ask in prayer, believe that you have received it, and it will be yours (MARK 11:24 ESV)."

6. There are people who dispute the effectiveness of prayer, and they rely on the principle that, God knowing our needs, it is superfluous to recite them to It. They also add that, since everything is linked in the universe by eternal laws, our wishes cannot change the decrees of God.

Undoubtedly, there are immutable laws of Nature which God cannot repeal according to each individual's whim; but from this to believe that all circumstances of life are subject to an inexorable fate, the distance is great. If it were so, humans would only be passive instruments, without free will and without own initiative. In this hypothesis, human beings would only have to bow their heads under the blow of all events, without seeking to avoid them, and not seek to deflect lightning. God did not give humans discernment and intelligence for them not to use, willpower for them not to wish and want, and the power to act for them to remain inactive. Since humans are free to act in one direction or another, their actions have consequences for themselves and for others that happen to be subordinate to what they do or do not do. Therefore, by their initiative, there are events which inevitably escape inexorable fate, and which do not destroy the harmony of universal laws, any more than the advance or the delay of a pendulum hand would destroy the law of movement on which a mechanism is established. God can therefore accede to certain requests without derogating from the immutability of the laws which govern the whole – God's assent always remaining subject to Its sovereign will.

7. It would be illogical to conclude from this maxim, "Whatever you ask in prayer, believe that you have received it, and it will be yours," that it is enough to ask in order to obtain, and unjust to accuse Providence for not acceding to any request which is made to it, because it knows better than us what is best for us. So it is with wise parents who refuse to their children things that are contrary to the interest of their offspring. Humans generally see only the present; however, if suffering is useful for someone's future happiness, God will let him or her suffer, as the surgeon lets the patient suffer from an operation which should bring about healing.

What God will grant you, if you speaks to God with confidence, is courage, patience and resignation. What God will also grant you are the means of getting yourself out of distress, with the help of the ideas which will be suggested to you by good spirits, thus leaving the merit to you. God assists those who help themselves, by following to this maxim, "Help yourself and heaven will help you,"[89] but will not help those who expect to receive everything from extraneous help without making use of their own faculties. Yet most of the time we would prefer to be rescued by a miracle without having to do anything at all (see Chapter **XXV**, no. **1** *et seq.* above).

8. Let us take an example. A man is lost in a desert; he is horribly thirsty; he feels faint, drops to the ground; he begs God to assist him, then waits; but no angel would bring him anything to drink. However, a good spirit *suggests* to him the thought of getting up and follow one of the paths that lay open before him. Then by a mechanical movement, by gathering his forces, he rises and walks on, adventuring himself. Once reaching a higher location, he discovers a stream; in the distance; at this sight he regains courage. If he has faith, he will cry out, "Thank you, dear God, for the thought that you inspired in me, and for the strength that you

---

89 [Trans. note] See footnote 84 above.

gave me. But if he does not have faith, he will say, "What a good idea *I had back there!* How *lucky* I was to take the path on the right instead of the one on the left. Chance can sometimes really help! How much I congratulate myself on *my* courage and on not letting myself down!"

But, it will be said, why did the good spirit not tell him clearly, "Follow this path, and eventually you will find what you need"? Why did it not show itself to guide him and support him in his hour of need? In this way the spirit would have convinced him of the intervention of Providence. The spirit did not show itself to the man, first of all to teach him that you have to help yourself and use your own strength. Then, through uncertainty, God tests self-confidence and submission to Its will. That man was in the same situation of a child who falls, and who, if he sees someone, shouts and waits for someone to come and pick him up; if he sees no one, he makes an effort and stands up by himself.

Likewise, if the angel that accompanied Tobit[90] had said to him: "I am sent by God to guide you on your journey and protect you from all danger," Tobit would have had no merit; by relying solely on his companion, he would not even have needed to think; this is why the angel did not become known until the return.

ACTION OF PRAYER
TRANSMISSION OF THOUGHT

9. Prayer is an invocation; by it we put ourselves in a relation of thought with the being we are addressing. It can be for a request, a gratitude-offering or a glorification. One can pray for oneself or for others, for the living or for the departed. The prayers addressed to God are heard by the spirits in charge of the execution of Its will; and those addressed to good spirits are reported to God. When we pray to beings other than God, it is only as intermediaries, intercessors, because nothing can be done without God's will.

10. Spiritism enables us to understand the action of prayer by explaining the mode of thought transmission, either by attracting the spirit prayed which answers our call, or by our thought reaching it. To realize what is happening in this circumstance, it is necessary to represent all the incarnate and discarnate beings as immersed in

---

90 [Trans. note] See footnote 85 above.

the universal fluid which occupies the universe, like here below we are immersed in the atmosphere. This fluid receives an impulsion from the will; it is the vehicle of thought, like air is the vehicle of sound, with the difference that the vibrations of air are circumscribed, while those of the universal fluid extend to infinity. Therefore when thought is directed toward any being, whether on Earth or in space, from incarnate to discarnate, or from discarnate to incarnate beings, a fluidic current is established from one to the other, transmitting the thought, like air transmits sound.

The energy of this current is proportional to the thought and will that generates it. This is how prayer is heard by the spirits wherever they are, how spirits communicate with one another, how they transmit their inspirations to us, and how relationships are established at a distance among the incarnate.

This explanation is especially geared toward those who do not understand the usefulness of purely mystical prayer. Its aim is not to materialize prayer, but to make its effect intelligible, by showing that it can exert a direct and effective action. Nonetheless it always remains subordinate to the will of God, the supreme judge of all things, and which alone can make a prayer's action effective.

11. Through prayer, humans summon the assistance of good spirits that come to support them in their good resolutions, and to inspire them with good thoughts. People thus acquire the moral strength necessary to overcome difficulties and return to the right path if they went astray from it; and thereby they can also divert from themselves the evils that they might have attracted by their own fault. So, for example, a man sees his health ruined by the excesses he has committed, and drags, until the end of his days, a life of suffering – does he have the right to complain if he does not get healed? No, because he could have found in prayer the strength to resist temptations.

12. If we make two parts of the evils of life, one made up of those which humans cannot avoid, the other of the tribulations of which we ourselves are the first cause by our carelessness and excesses (see Chapter **V**, no. **4** above), we will see that this latter part greatly outweighs the other. It is therefore quite evident that humans are the author of the greater part of their afflictions, and that they would be spared such evils if they always acted with wisdom and prudence.

It is no less certain that these miseries were the result of our breaches of God's laws, and that if we punctually observed these laws, our happiness would be perfect. If we had remained within the limits of what is necessary to satisfy our needs, we would not have the diseases which are the result of excess, and the vicissitudes which these diseases bring about. If we had put limits to our ambition, we would not fear ruin; if we did not wish to climb higher than we actually could, we would not fear falling; if we were humble, we would not suffer the disappointments of lowered pride; if we practiced the law of charity, we would not be spiteful, envious, or jealous, and we would avoid quarrels and dissensions; if we didn't hurt anyone, we would not fear revenge, and so on.

Let us admit that humans can do nothing about extraneous evils, that all prayer would be superfluous to preserve them from such evils; wouldn't it be a great achievement already for you to get rid of all the evils that come from yourself? Now, here the action of prayer can be easily conceived, because it has the effect of invoking the salutary inspiration of good spirits, of asking them for strength to resist bad thoughts whose execution can be deleterious to us. In this case, *it is not the evil that they divert, but rather ourselves that they divert from the thought which can cause the evil. They do not in any way obstruct the decrees of Divine Providence, nor do they suspend the course of the laws of Nature: it is us that they prevent from breaking these laws, by directing our free will* – but they do it without our knowledge, in a concealed way, so as not to chain our will. People then find themselves in a position of someone who seeks good advice and puts it into practice, but who is always free to follow it or not. God wants it to be so, in order that we have responsibility for our actions, and leaves us the merit of our free choice between good and evil. This is what everyone can be certain to obtain if they earnestly asks for it, and to whom these words can especially apply: "Ask and it shall be given you."

Would the effectiveness of prayer not prove immensely valuable, even if reduced to this scope? It was left for Spiritism to prove the action of prayer by revealing the relations that exist between the corporeal and the spiritual world. But that does not entail just its effects.

Prayer is recommended by all spirits; to renounce prayer is to disregard God's goodness; it is to renounce God's help toward oneself and the good that can be done toward others.

13. In acceding to the request addressed to It, God often aims at rewarding the intention, the devotion and the faith of the one who prays – this is why prayers of good persons have more merit in the eyes of God, and are always more effective, because vicious and bad individuals cannot pray with the earnestness and trust which alone can call forth a feeling of true devotion. From the heart of the selfish, of those who pray only with their lips, only words can come out, but never the outbursts of charity that give prayer all its power. We understand it so much that, by an instinctive inkling, we recommend ourselves preferably to the prayers of those whose conduct we feel must be pleasing to God, because they are better listened to.

14. If prayer exerts a kind of magnetic action, one might believe that its effect is subordinated to fluidic power. However it is not so. Since the spirits exert this action upon humans, they make up, when necessary, for the insufficiency of the one who prays, either by acting directly *on his/her behalf,* or by temporarily giving exceptional strength to them, when they are considered worthy of this favor, or when they are praying for something truly useful.

Those who think they are not good enough to exert a salutary influence should not refrain from praying for others, thinking that they are not worthy of being listened to. The awareness of one's own inferiority is a proof of humility which is always pleasing to God, and the charitable intention which animates such person will be taken into account. Earnestness and trust in God are a first step toward the return to the good path, which the good spirits are happy to encourage the one who prays. Prayers that are rejected are those of *proud individuals who have faith in their own power and merits, and believe they can replace the will of the Eternal One.*

15. The power of prayer is in the thought; it is not about words, the place, or the time we do it. We can therefore pray everywhere and at any time, whether alone or together. Influence of place or time is only due to circumstances that might favor meditation. *Prayer together with other people has a more powerful action when all* *those who pray gather with the same thought and have the same goal,* because then it is as if many plead together and in unison. Yet what does it matter to be gathered in large numbers if each person acts in isolation and for his/her personal interests! A hundred people together can pray in a selfish way, whereas just two or three, united in a common aspiration, will pray as true siblings in God's family, and their prayer will have more power than that of the hundred other people (see Chapter **XXVIII**, no. **4** and **5** below).

INTELLIGIBLE PRAYERS

16. "If I do not know the meaning of the language, I will be a foreigner to the speaker and the speaker a foreigner to me.

For if I pray in a tongue,[91] my spirit prays but my mind is unfruitful. — Otherwise, if you give thanks with your spirit, how can anyone in the position of an outsider say 'Amen' to your thanksgiving *when he does not know what you are saying?* For you may be giving thanks well enough, *but the other person is not being built up* (PAUL, ICORINTHIANS 14:11,14–17 ESV)."

17. Prayer has value only through the thought attached to it. Now, it is impossible to attach a thought to what one does not understand, because what one does not understand cannot touch the heart. For the vast majority, prayers in a unknown language are nothing but assemblages of words that say nothing to the mind. For a prayer to touch us, each word must awaken an idea, and if it is not understood, it cannot awaken any at all. It is repeated as a simple formula which supposedly is more or less effective according to the number of times it is repeated. Many pray out of duty, some even to conform to custom; this is why they think they are in good standing with God when they have said a prayer a certain number of times and in such and such an order. However, God reads in the bottom of hearts, seeing thought and sincerity – one would belittle the Divinity to think It is more sensitive to form than to substance (see Chapter **XXVIII**, no. **2** below).

PRAYING FOR THE DEPARTED AND FOR DISTRESSED SPIRITS

---

91 [Trans. note] That is, "If I pray in a language that I do not understand."

18. Prayer is needed by distressed spirits. It is useful to them because, by seeing that someone thinks of them, they feel less neglected and thus less unhappy. But prayer exerts a more direct action upon them: it raises their courage, arousing in them the desire to lift themselves up through repentance and atonement; and it can divert them from the thought of evil. It is in this sense that prayer will not only alleviate, but also shorten their suffering (see Allan KARDEC, *Heaven and Hell*, Part Two, "Examples").

19. Some people cannot accept praying for the dead, because in their belief there are only two alternatives for the soul: being saved or being condemned to eternal punishment; and that, whether in one or in the other case, prayer is useless. Without arguing about the worth or merit of this belief, let us admit for a moment the reality of eternal and inexorable sorrows, and that our prayers would be powerless to put an end to them. I ask if, in such a hypothetical case, it would be logical, charitable, and Christian, to refuse praying for the reprobate? Wouldn't these prayers, however helpless they would be to deliver them from evil, a sign of pity to them, which could ease their suffering? On Earth, when someone is sentenced to life in prison, even though there would be no hope of obtaining a pardon, is it forbidden for a charitable person to bring some comfort to the convicts in order to lighten their burden? When someone is suffering from an incurable disease, should he/she be abandoned without any relief because they offer no hope of recovery? Consider that among the reprobates may be someone dear to you, a friend, perhaps a father, mother or child, and that, because in your opinion he/she could not hope for any grace, would you refuse them a bit of water to quench their thirst, some balm to soothe their wounds? Would you not do for those spirits what you would do for a jail prisoner? Would you not give them a testimony of love and consolation? Definitely, it would not be Christian to turn them down. A belief that dries up one's heart cannot be paired with that of a God which places love of neighbor first and foremost.

The non-eternity of punishment does not imply the negation of a temporary penalty, because God, in Its sovereign justice, cannot mix up good and evil. To deny, in this case, the effectiveness of prayer would be to deny the effectiveness of consolation, encouragement and good advice; furthermore, it would be to deny the strength that we draw from the moral assistance received from those that wish us good.

20.   Others base their views on a more specious reason: the immutability of divine decrees. God, they say, cannot change Its decisions at the request of Its created beings; otherwise nothing would be stable in the universe. Therefore humans have nothing to ask of God; they must only submit to their fate and worship the Creator.

In this idea there is a false application of the immutability of God's law, or better still, an utter ignorance of the law regarding future penalties. This law is revealed by the spirits of the Lord, now that humans are mature enough to understand what, in faith, conforms to or is contrary to the divine attributes.

According to the dogma of absolute eternity of future penalties, no one is held accountable for their regrets or their repentance. For those people, any desire to improve is superfluous: they are condemned to remain in evil forever. If they are sentenced for a specific period of time, this sentence will cease when the time has expired; but who can say that then they will have been brought round to a better way of thinking? Who can say whether, like so many convicts on Earth, they will not be as wicked as before when they leave prison? In the first case, it would mean to keep someone who has been transformed to good in the suffering of punishment; in the second, it would mean to pardon someone who remained blamable. God's law is more farsighted than that; it is always fair, just and merciful; it does not set any length of sentence, whatever it may be; it can be summed up as follows:

21.   "People always suffer the consequence of their faults; there is not a single offense against the law of God that goes unpunished.

The severity of the punishment is proportional to the severity of the fault.

The duration of the punishment for any fault whatsoever is *not defined; it is subject to the guilty party's repentance and return to good;* pain lasts as long as one's obstinacy in evil; it would be perpetual if such obstinacy were perpetual; it is short-lived if there is prompt repentance.

As soon as the culprit shouts "Have mercy!" God hears and sends hope. But the simply regretting one's misdeeds is not enough: they must be atoned for. This is why the culprit has to undergo new trials in which he/she can – always by his own will – do good to make up for any evil committed.

Thus people are constantly the arbiter of their own fate: they can shorten their ordeal or extend it indefinitely; their happiness or misfortune will depend on their will to do good."

That is the law; a law *immutable* and in conformity with the goodness and justice of God.

Thus a blamable and unfortunate spirit can always save itself: the law of God tells the spirit on what condition it can do it. What the spirit most often lacks is the will, the strength, and the courage to do it. If, through our prayers, we eventually inspire it with this will; if we support and encourage it; if, through our advice, it finds the enlightenment it misses; then, *instead of asking God to derogate from Its law, we become instrumental in the execution of Its law of love and charity,* in which God thus allows us to participate by giving us a test of charity (see Allan KARDEC, *Heaven and Hell,* Part One, Chapters IV, VII and VIII).

INSTRUCTIONS FROM THE SPIRITS

WAY OF PRAYING

22.   The first duty of every human being, the first action which must signal for it the return to active life every day, should be prayer. Almost all of you pray, but how few know how to pray! What does it matter to the Lord the sentences that you mechanically link to each other, because you are used to it. That is the mere execution of a routine duty that you fulfill, and like any other fixed duty, it weighs on you.

The prayer of any Christian, of a *Spiritist* of any creed whatsoever, must be made as soon as the spirit has again taken the yoke of a fleshly body. It must rise at the feet of the Majestic One with humility, with depth, in an outburst of gratitude for all the benefits granted to date: for the night that has passed and during which it has been permitted to you – albeit without your knowledge – to return to your friends, your spirit guides, so as to draw from their contact additional strength and perseverance. It must rise humbly at the God's feet, to recommend your weakness to It, to ask for God's support, indulgence and mercy. It must be deep, because it is your soul that must rise towards the Creator, transfiguring itself like Jesus in Mount Tabor,[92] and arrive white and radiant with hope and love.

Your prayer should contain the request for the blessings you need, but these should be real needs. It is therefore useless to ask the Lord to shorten your trials and to give you joys and wealth; ask God to grant you the most precious possessions of patience, resignation and faith instead. Do not say, as many of you do, "It is not worth praying, since God does not hear me." What do you ask God most of the time? Have you often thought about asking God for your moral improvement? Oh no, not very often; but you rather think in asking God for *success in your earthly endeavors*; and then you exclaim: "God does not take care about us; if he did there would not be so much injustice." You fool! Ungrateful! If you went right to the bottom of your consciousness, you would almost always find in yourself the starting point of the evils of which you complain. Ask, above all, for your improvement, and you will see what torrent of blessings and comfort will spread over you (see Chapter **V**, no. 4 above).

You must pray constantly, without retreating into a special place of prayer or falling on your bended knees in public places. The prayer of the day is the accomplishment of your duties, of all your duties without exception, whatever they may be. Is it not an act of love toward the Lord to request assistance for your brothers and sisters in any moral or physical need? Is it not an act of gratitude to elevate your thought to God when a good thing happens to you, or an accident is avoided, even when a vexation only fleetingly strikes you, if you say in thought: *God be blessed.* Is it not an act of contrition to humble yourself before the Supreme Judge when you feel that you have failed, if only by a fleeting thought, and then say: *Forgive me, dear God, for I have sinned (by pride, by selfishness or by lack of charity); give me strength to stop failing and the courage to make amends?*

---

92 [Trans. note] *Cf.* MARK 9:2–8 and LUKE 9:28–36.

This is quite independent of the regular morning and evening prayers, and the consecrated days you may observe. As you can see, prayer can be made at all times, without interrupting your daily work – on the contrary, it thoroughly sanctifies it. And believe that only one of these thoughts coming from the heart is better heard by your Heavenly Parent, much more than any long prayers said out of habit, often without determining a cause, conventionally and mechanically reminded to you at the agreed times.

Monod[93] (Bordeaux, 1862).

THE JOY OF PRAYER

23. Come, all you who want to believe: the celestial spirits are rushing to announce great things to you. Dear children, God has opened Its treasures to give you all Its benefits. O incredulous humans! If you only knew how much good to the heart can faith do, by bringing the soul to repentance and prayer! Prayer! How touching are the words that come out of your mouths whenever you pray! Prayer is the divine dew which destroys the excessive heat of the passions. As the eldest offspring of faith, it leads us on the path which by its turn leads us to God. In inner retreat and solitude, you are with God; for you, there is no longer mystery: God is revealed to you. Apostles of thought, for you it is life; your soul is detached from matter and soars in these infinite and ethereal worlds to which poor humans are oblivious.

Walk, walk on the prayer trails, and you will hear the voices of angels. What harmony is that? It is no longer the confused noise and the garish accents of the Earth, but rather the lyres of the archangels, the soft and gentle voices of the seraphs, lighter than the morning breezes when they sound in the leaves of your large woods. In what delights will you revel! Human language would not be able to define such joy, as it will enter through all your pores, so lively and refreshing is the spring from which one drinks while praying! Sweet voices, exhilarating scents that the soul hears and savor when it soars into these unknown spheres inhabited by prayer! Without any hint of carnal desires, all aspirations are divine. And you also pray like Christ carrying his cross from Golgotha to Calvary. So carry your

---

93 [Trans. note] The spirit of Adolphe Monod (1802–1856), a French Protestant preacher.

cross, and you will feel the sweet emotions that passed through his soul, although laden with infamous wood – he was going to die, but to live a heavenly life in his Father's bosom.

St. Augustine (Paris, 1861).

Chapter XXVIII
A selection of Spiritist prayers

INTRODUCTION

1. Spirits have always said, "The form is nothing, the thought is everything. Everyone should pray according to their convictions and the manner that affects them most deeply; a good thought is better than many words with nothing from the heart within."

Spirits do not prescribe any definite formula of prayers; and when they give one, it is to help focusing the ideas, and especially to call attention to certain principles of the Spiritist tenets. They do so also to help people that are embarrassed to express ideas in their own words, because some individuals would not believe they were really praying, if their thoughts were not encased in some formula.

The selection of prayers contained in this book were chosen from messages mediumistically dictated by spirits under different circumstances – they have also dictated other prayers, using other words, appropriate to certain ideas or special cases, but the basic thought is the same, whatever the form they chose. The purpose of prayer is to elevate our souls to God; the diversity of formulas must not establish any difference among those who believe in God, and still less among followers of Spiritism, because God accepts them all without exception, when they are sincere.

We must not, therefore, consider this selection as an absolute form, but as a variety chosen among many instructions given by the spirits. It is an application of the principles of Gospel morality as developed throughout the current book, a complement to their tenets on our duties toward God and neighbor, where all the principles that it teaches are recalled.

Spiritism acknowledges as good the prayers deriving from all creeds and religions, provided they are said from the heart and not only by the lips. Spiritism imposes itself on no one, and blames no one; God is too big to repel the voice that entreats or sings Its praises,

335

one way rather than another. *Anyone who casts anathema against prayers that differ from one's own accepted form shows disregard for God's greatness.* To believe that God sticks to one formula for prayer is to try to attribute human pettiness and passions to It.

An essential condition for prayer, according to St. Paul, 1 is to be intelligible, so that it may speak to our spirit. For that reason it is not enough for it to be said in a language understood by the person who prays; there are prayers in the vernacular that do not say much more to the thought than a foreign language would, and therefore do not reach the heart – the rare ideas they contain are often suffocated under an overabundance of words and the mysticism of language.

An essential condition for prayer, according to St. Paul (see Chapter **XXVII**, no. **16** above), is to be intelligible, so that it may speak to our spirit. For that reason it is not enough for it to be said in a language understood by the person who prays; there are prayers in the vernacular that do not say much more to the thought than a foreign language would, and therefore do not reach the heart – the rare ideas they contain are often suffocated under an overabundance of words and the mysticism of language.

Being simple, concise and clear is the main quality required of a prayer, avoiding any unnecessary phraseology, or luxury of epithets, which are nothing but superfluous ornaments. Every word must have its meaning, awaken an idea, stir an inner fiber: in short, *it must make people think.* Only on this condition can prayer reach its goal, *otherwise it becomes mere noise.* Also, note the air of negligence and volubility with which they are said most of the time: we see lips moving; yet from the expression of the physiognomies to the very sound of the voices, one detects a mechanical act, purely external, to which the soul remains indifferent.

The prayers gathered in this selection are divide into five categories, namely:

1st) **General prayers**
2nd) **Prayers for oneself**
3rd) **Prayers for others (the living)**
4th) **Prayers for the departed**
5th) **Prayers for the sick and the obsessed**

In order to draw special attention to the purpose of each prayer, and to help clarify its scope, each of them are preceded by a preliminary statement or prologue, under an entry called *Introduction*.

I. GENERAL PRAYERS

THE LORD'S PRAYER

2. INTRODUCTION

Higher-order spirits have recommended placing the Lord's Prayer at the top of this selection, not only as a prayer, but as a symbol. Of all prayers, it is the one they put in the first rank, either because it comes from Jesus himself (see MATTHEW 6:9-13 ESV), or because it can make up for all prayers according to the thought attached to it. It is the most perfect model of conciseness, a truly sublime masterpiece in its simplicity. Indeed, using every word in a most economical way, it sums up all human duties toward God, toward others, and toward ourselves. It contains a profession of faith, an act of worship and submission; an entreaty for things necessary for life; and the principle of charitable love. To say it on behalf of someone is to ask for what one would ask for oneself.

However, because of its brevity, the deep meaning contained in the few words which compose it escapes most of us. That is why it is generally said without focusing its thought in the applications of each of its parts; instead it is said as a formula whose efficiency is proportional to the number of times it is repeated; or it is almost always ascribed one of three, seven or nine cabbalistic numbers, drawn from an ancient superstitious belief in the virtue of numbers, which also employs it in operations of magic.

To make up for the vagueness which this concise prayer may leave in one's thought, and following the advice and the assistance given by good spirits, a comment has been added to each proposition which develops its meaning and shows its applications. According to the circumstances and the time available, one can thus say whether a *simple* or *extended* Lord's Prayer.

3. PRAYER

[I] Our Father in heaven, hallowed be your name.

We believe in you, O Lord, because everything reveals your power and your goodness. The harmony of the universe testifies to wisdom, prudence, and foresight which far surpass all human faculties. The name of a supremely great and wise being is inscribed in all works of creation, from the blade of grass and the smallest insect to the stars moving in space, everywhere we see the proof of parental solicitude; that is why blind is the one who does not recognize you in your works, proud is the one who does not glorify you, and ungrateful is one who does not give you thanksgiving, praise and worship.

[II] Your kingdom come.

Lord, you have given humans laws full of wisdom that would make them happy if they observed them. With these laws they could make peace and justice reign among them; they would help one another, instead of hurting one another as they do. The strong would support the weak instead of crushing them; they would avoid the evils engendered by all sorts of abuses and excesses. All the miseries of this world come from the violation of Your laws, because not a single offense can escape its fatal consequences.

To the brute, you have given instincts which mark out the limit of what is necessary, conforming to it mechanically. Yet to humans, besides instincts, you have given intelligence and reason; you have also given them freedom to observe or to break these godly laws which concern them personally – that is to say, to choose between good and evil, so that humans have merit or are held responsible for their actions.

No one can pretend ignorance of your laws, for in your parental foresight you have wished that they should be engraved in the conscience of each one of us, without distinction of worship or nation. Those who violate them are the ones who do not know you.

A day will come when, according to your promise, everyone will practice them. Then unbelief will have vanished; all will acknowledge you as the sovereign Master of all things, and the reign of your laws will be your kingdom on Earth.

Deign, O Lord, to hasten your advent, giving all human beings the necessary light to lead them on the path of truth.

A day will come when, according to your promise, everyone will practice them. Then unbelief will have vanished; all will acknowledge you as the sovereign Master of all things, and the reign of your laws will be your kingdom on Earth.

Deign, O Lord, to hasten your advent, giving all human beings the necessary light to lead them on the path of truth.

[III] Your will be done, on earth as it is in heaven.

If submission is a duty of the child toward the parent, of the inferior toward the superior, how much greater should be the submission of the created being toward its Creator! To do your will, Lord, is to abide by your laws and submit, without grumbling, to your divine decrees. Humans will submit to them when they understand that you are the source of all wisdom, and that without you we cannot do anything; then we will do your will on Earth as the elect do in Heaven.

[IV] Give us this day our daily bread.

Give us food to keep our body strong and healthy; also give us the spiritual food we need to develop our spirit.

Beasts find their own food; yet, because you have created humans free, they owe it to their own activities and the resources of their intelligence.

You said to us, humans, "By the sweat of your face you shall eat bread," (GENESIS 3:19) by which you made work mandatory for us so that we can exercise our intelligence by seeking ways to provide for our needs and well-being, some by means of material work, others by means of intellectual labor. Without work we would remain stagnant and would not be able to aspire to the bliss of Higher-order spirits.

You support any individual of good will who trusts in you for basic necessities, but not those who delight in being idle and would actually like to obtain everything easily; or those who seek superfluous things (see Chapter **XXV** above).

How many of them succumb by their own fault, by their carelessness, their improvidence; or by their ambition, and because they did not want to content themselves with what had been given to them! These have been the authors of their own misfortune, and have no right to complain, for they are being punished for their sins. But even such individuals are not forsaken by you because you are infinitely merciful. You extend a helping hand to them, as soon as, like the prodigal son, they sincerely come back to you (see Chapter **V**, no. **4** above).

Before we complain of our fate, let us ask ourselves if it is not our own doing; to every misfortune that happens to us, let us ask ourselves if it would not have been up to us to avoid it. But let us also admit that God has given us intelligence to draw ourselves out of the quagmire, and that it depends on us to make good use of it.

Since the law of labor is a necessary condition for humans on Earth, give us courage and strength to perform it; give us also prudence, foresight and moderation, so that we do not end up losing the fruits of our work.

Give us, then, O Lord, our daily bread, that is to say, the means of acquiring through labor the things necessary to life, for no one has the right to claim anything superfluous.

If, for some reason, work is impossible for us, we trust in your divine providence.

If it enters into your plans to test our endurance by the severest privations, regardless of our efforts, we accept them as a just atonement for the faults we may have committed whether in this life or in a previous one. For you are just; we know that there are no unmerited sorrows, and that you never punish without a cause.

Preserve us, O God, from harboring any thoughts of jealousy and envy of those who possess what we do not have, even of those who have the superfluous, when we lack what is necessary to life. Forgive them if they forget the law of charitable love and love of neighbor that you have taught them (see Chapter **XVI**, no. **8** above). Also remove from our mind the thought of denying your justice, when witnessing the prosperity of the wicked and the misfortune that sometimes overwhelms good people. Now we know, thanks to new lights you have chosen to give us, that your justice is always fulfilled and not lacking to anyone; that the material prosperity of the wicked is as ephemeral as their corporeal existence, and that it will have terrible consequences, whereas the joy reserved for those who suffer with resignation will be eternal (see Chapter **V**, no. **7**, **9**, **12** and **18** above).

[v] Forgive us our debts, as we also have forgiven our debtors.

Each of our infractions of your laws, O Lord, is an offense to you, and a debt contracted that we will sooner or later have to pay. We ask for remission through your infinite mercy, under the promise of making an effort not to contract new ones.

You have made a specific law of charitable love; but charity does not consist only in assisting one's fellow soul in need; it is also in forgiveness and forgetfulness of offenses. By what right can we ask for your forgiveness, when we ourselves show none toward those whom we are complaining about?

Give me, God, the strength to stifle all resentment, all hatred and all grudges in my soul. *Let death not surprise me while I harbor a desire for revenge in my heart.* But if it is your will to take me to the other side, even on today, please may I be rid of all animosity when presenting myself before you, following the example of Jesus Christ, whose last words were a plea for mercy on behalf of his tormentors (see Chapter **X** above).

The acts of persecution that the wicked make us endure are part of our earthly trials and must be accepted without grumbling, like any other trials. Let us not curse those who, by their wickedness, are paving the way to our eternal happiness; for you have told us, through the mouth of Jesus, "Blessed are those who are persecuted for righteousness' sake." Therefore, let us bless the hand that strikes and humbles us, because the bruises of the body strengthen our soul, and we will be lifted up in our humbleness (see Chapter **XII**, no. **4** above).

Blessed be your name, Lord, for teaching us that our lot is not irrevocably fixed after death; that we will find in other existences the means to redeem and atone for our past faults, to accomplish in a new life what we were not able to achieve in the current one, for our advancement (see Chapters **IV**; **V**, no. **5** above).

Thus all the apparent anomalies of life are finally explained; light shed on our past and future, a striking sign of your sovereign justice and your infinite goodness.

[vi] And lead us not into temptation, but deliver us from evil.[94]

---

94 Some translations state: "And lead us not into temptation" (in Latin, *Et ne nos inducas in temptationem*). Well, this expression might suggest that temptation comes from God, which would voluntarily drive humans to evil – a blasphemous

Give us, Lord, the strength to resist suggestions by evil spirits which try to turn us away from the path of good by raising bad thoughts.

Yet we ourselves are imperfect spirits which have incarnated on this Earth to atone for past errors and improve ourselves. The first cause of evil lies in ourselves, and evil spirits will only profit from our bad inclinations, through which they can talk to us, in order to tempt us.

Each imperfection is a door open to their influence, while they are helpless and give up all attempts against perfected beings. All we attempt to do to remove them will be useless, if we do not oppose them with an unshakable will for goodness, and an absolute renunciation of evil. It is therefore toward ourselves that we must direct our efforts, and then evil spirits will naturally pull away, for it is evil that draws them, while good repels them. (See further below, "Prayers for the sick and the obsessed.")

Support our weakness, Lord. Inspire in us, through the voice of our guardian angels and good spirits, the will to correct our imperfections, in order to shut any access to our souls by impure spirits. (See below, no. **11**.)

Evil is not your work, Lord, for nothing bad can come from the source of all good. It is us who create evil by breaking your laws, and by the misuse we make of the freedom you have granted us. The day humans observe your laws, evil will disappear from the Earth, as it has already disappeared in more advanced worlds.

Evil is no one's fatal necessity, and it seems irresistible only to those who abandon themselves to it with complacency. If we have the will to do it, we can also have a will of doing good; therefore, O God, we ask your assistance and that of the good spirits to resist temptation.

[VII] Amen (So be it).[95]

May it please you, Lord, that our wishes be fulfilled! However, we bow to your infinite wisdom. On all things that we are not able

---

thought that would equate God with Satan, and could not have been what Jesus meant. Moreover, such misinterpretation would be in accordance with the popular belief in an alleged role played by demons. (See Allan KARDEC, *Heaven and Hell*, Chapter X, "... of Demons").

95 [Trans. note] In the French original, Allan Kardec makes mention of the traditional exclamation "So be it!" uttered at the end of the prayer but absent from original Gospel texts (though found in the *Authorised King James Version*).

to understand, may it be done according to your holy will, and not according to ours, because you only want our good, and you know better than us what is useful to us.

We raise this prayer to you, O God; on behalf of ourselves; we also raise it to you on behalf of all distressed souls, whether incarnate or discarnate, of our friends and our enemies as well, of all those who call for our assistance, and especially for ...[insert name].

We call for your mercy and blessings upon each and every one.

NOTE: At this point you can specify what to thank God for, and what to ask for ourselves or for others. (See below, prayers nos. **26** and **27**.)

AT SPIRITIST MEETINGS

4. "For where two or three are gathered in my name, there am I among them (MATTHEW 18:20 ESV)."

5. **INTRODUCTION**

To be assembled in the name of Jesus does not mean that it does not suffice for us to be physically gathered, but rather to be spiritually united by a communion of thought and intention for goodness. Only then will Jesus be in the midst of the congregation, either he himself or the pure spirits which represent him. Spiritism makes us under- stand how spirits can be among us. They are there in their fluidic or spiritual bodies, and bearing the appearance that would make them known should they make themselves visible. The higher they are in hierarchy, the greater their radiant power; it is thus that they possess the gift of ubiquity and that they can be found in several places simultaneously: a single ray of their thought is enough for that.

With these words, Jesus wanted to show the effect of union and loving fellowship: the greater or lesser number of people is not what draws him closer – since, instead of two or three persons, he could have said ten or twenty – but the sentiment of charitable love which animates them toward one another. Now, for that, it suffices that two people are gathered. However, if these two people pray separately from each other, although still addressing Jesus, there is no communion of thought between them, especially if they are not moved by a sentiment of mutual benevolence. If they see one another with an evil eye, with hatred, envy or jealousy, the fluidic currents of their thoughts will repel each other instead of uniting in a common outpouring of empathy – and therefore *they will not be assembled in the name of Jesus;* Jesus will thus become only the *pretext* for such a meeting, and not its true motive (see Chapter **XXVII**, no. **9** above).

This does not imply that Jesus is deaf to the voice of one person; after all has he not said, "Everyone who calls upon the name of the Lord shall be saved" (ACTS 2:21 ESV)? It is above all because he demands the love of neighbor, of which one can give more proof when together with many than in isolation; and that all selfish feelings drives him away. It follows that if, in a large assembly, only two or three persons are united in heart by a sentiment of true charitable love, while the others isolate themselves and focus in selfish or worldly thoughts, Jesus will be with the first and not with others. It is not therefore the unison of words, songs or external demonstrations that constitute a meeting in the name of Jesus, but rather a communion of thoughts in accordance with the spirit of charitable love as personified in Jesus (see Chapter **X**, nos. **7** and **8**; Chapter **XXVII**, nos. **2**, **3**, **4** above).

Such must be the character of all serious Spiritist meetings, in which the participation of good spirits is sincerely desired.

6. PRAYER
(At the beginning of the meeting)

We pray to the Lord God Almighty to send us good spirits to assist us, to keep away those which might mislead us, and to give us the necessary enlightenment to distinguish truth from falsehood.

Also, move away all malevolent spirits, incarnate or discarnate, that might try to sow disunity among us, and turn us away from charitable love and love of neighbor. If some seek to break in here, let them find no access to the heart of anyone here present.

Good spirits that deign to come and educate us, make us receptive to your advices; turn us away from all thoughts of selfishness, pride, envy, and jealousy; inspire us with indulgence and benevolence toward our present or absent fellow beings, whether friends or foes. Finally, among the sentiments

that shall animate us, please allow us to recognize your salutary influence.

Give the mediums, whom you will entrust with the task of conveying your teachings, awareness of the sacred mandate bestowed upon them, and seriousness in what they are about to perform, so that they invest it with the necessary intensity and inner retreat.

If, in the assembled group, there are people who were drawn by other feelings other than that of goodness, open their eyes to the light, and forgive them, as we ourselves forgive them for coming with bad intentions.

In particular, we pray to the Spirit ... [insert name], our Spiritual Guide, to assist and watch over us.

7.   (At the end of the meeting)

We thank the good spirits that have kindly come to communicate with us, and also ask them to help us put into practice the teachings they have conveyed to us. Please make it so that, when leaving here, each one of us feels strengthened in the practice of good and love of neighbor.

FOR MEDIUMS

8.   "And in the last days it shall be ," God declares, "that I will pour out my Spirit on all flesh, and your sons and your daughters shall prophesy, and your young men shall see visions, and your old men shall dream dreams; even on my male servants and female servants in those days I will pour out my Spirit, and they shall prophesy (ACTS 2:17–18 ESV)."

9.   INTRODUCTION

The Lord determined that light should be available to every human being, and penetrate everywhere through the voice of the spirits, so that everyone could obtain the proof of immortality. It is for this purpose that spirits manifest themselves today in all corners of the world, and mediumship; as one of the signs of the fulfillment of predicted times; is discovered in persons of all ages and walks of life, both in men and women, in children and among the elder population.

To learn the things of the visible world and to discover the secrets of material nature, God gave humans the bodily eyesight, the senses, and special instruments. With the telescope we look into deep space, and with the microscope we have discovered the world of the infinitely small. To penetrate the invisible world, God has given us mediumship.

Mediums are interpreters responsible for conveying to fellow humans the teachings of the spirits; or rather, they are the material organs by which the spirits express themselves so as to render themselves intelligible to humans. Their mission is holy because it aims at opening the horizons of eternal life.

The spirits come to educate humans about their future destinies, in order to bring us back to the path of good, and neither to spare us the material work that we all must accomplish here below for our own advancement, nor to stimulate human greed and ambition. This awareness should pervade all mediums, so that they do not misuse their faculty.

Those who understand the solemn seriousness of the mandate with which they are entrusted, perform it religiously, Their conscience would reprehend them for the sacrilegious act of deriving fun or turning into entertainment — whether for themselves or for others — a faculty bestowed upon them for a purpose so serious, which actually puts them in touch with beings beyond the grave.

As interpreters of spirit teachings, mediums should play an important role in the moral transformation that is taking place now; the services they can render are dependent on the good direction they give to their mediumistic faculties, whereas those who per- sist in wrong conduct are more harmful than helpful to the cause of Spiritism. By the bad impression they cause, they retard quite a few conversions. This is why they will be held accountable for the use they have made of a faculty which has been given to them for the good of their fellow human beings.

The mediums that want to keep the assistance of good spirits must work on their own improvement. Whoever wishes to see their mediumistic faculties grow and develop must themselves grow morally, and avoid anything that might detract from their providential purpose.

If good spirits sometimes use imperfect instruments, it is to give good advice and try to bring them back to the good path. However, if they find hardened hearts, and their advice fall in deaf ears, they retreat, leaving the field free to wicked spirits (see **XXIV**, nos. **11** and **12** above).

Experience proves that, in those who do not profit from the advice they receive from good spirits, spirit communications, after shedding some light on certain subjects for some time, gradually degenerate and fall into error, verbiage or ridicule – an indisputable sign of the absence of good spirits.

To obtain the assistance of good spirits, to banish irresponsible and lying spirits, such must be the firm goal and constant effort of all serious mediums; otherwise, mediumship turns into a sterile faculty, which can even become detrimental to those who possess it, should it degenerate into a dangerous obsession.

Mediums that understand their duty, instead of boasting of a faculty which does not belong to themselves, since it can be taken away from them, relate to God all the good things they accomplish. If their communications deserve praise, such mediums are never vain, because they know that the communications are independent of their personal merit, and instead they thank God for allowing good spirits to communicate through them. If they give rise to criticism, they do not take offence, because such messages are not the work of their own soul. Deep inside, they tell themselves that they have not been a good instrument, and that they still do not have all the necessary qualities to oppose the interference of evil spirits; that is why they seek to acquire such qualities, by asking through prayer the strength they may lack.

10. PRAYER

Almighty God, allow good spirits to assist me in the communication that I request. Preserve me from the presumption of believing that I am safe from evil spirits; from the pride that could deceive me about the worth of what I am about to obtain; and any feelings contrary to charitable love toward other mediums. If I am misled, inspire someone to warn me, and myself to be humble in accepting their criticism with gratitude, and to take firstly for myself, and not for others, the advice that the good spirits will dictate to me.

If I am tempted to abuse anything, or to take pride in the faculty that you willed to grant me, I beg you, O Lord, to withdraw it from me, rather than allow it to be diverted from its providential purpose, which is the good of each and every one, and my own moral advancement.

II. Prayers for oneself

To Guardian Angels and Protector Spirits

11. Introduction

We all have a good spirit that has been attached to us since our birth and has taken us under its protection. It fulfills with us the mission of a parent toward its child, namely, to lead us to the path of good and progress through life's trials. It is happy when we respond to its solicitude; deeply unhappy when it sees us fall.

Its name is of little relevance to us, for it may have no known name on Earth. So we invoke it as our guardian angel, our good guardian spirit. We may even invoke it under the name of any higher-order spirit with which we feel a particular affinity.

Besides our guardian angel, which is always a Higher-order Spirit, we have protector spirits that, regardless of being less elevated, are none the less good and benevolent. They usually are our deceased parents, or friends, or sometimes persons whom we have not known in our current lifetime. They assist us with their advice, and often by intervening in the acts of our life.

Sympathetic spirits[96] are those which attach themselves to humans by a certain similarity of tastes and inclinations; they may be good or bad, according to the nature of inclinations that draw them to us.

Tempting spirits strive to deduce us and divert us from the path of goodness by suggesting bad thoughts. They take advantage of all our weaknesses as open doors that give them access to our souls. There are some that go after us like prey, but *they go away when they realize they are unable to fight against our will.*

God has given us a main higher-order guide in our guardian angel, and secondary guides in our protector and familiar spirits;

---

96 [Trans. note] That is, *affinity spirits.*

however, it is a mistake to believe that we necessarily have an evil spirit placed near us to counterbalance the good influences. Evil spirits come voluntarily, according to whether they find fault with us in our weaknesses, or our negligence in following the inspirations of good spirits. It is therefore we ourselves who attract them. As a result, we are never deprived of the assistance of good spirits, and it is up to us to ward off the bad ones. By its imperfections, human beings are always the first cause of the miseries they endure; and most often they themselves are their own evil spirits (see Chapter V, no. 4 above).

A prayer to guardian angels and protector spirits should aim at appealing to them to intervene with God, to ask God the strength to resist evil suggestions; and also for assistance in coping with life's necessities.

12. Prayer

Wise and kind spirits, messengers of God, whose mission is to assist humans and to lead them in the right way, support me through my life's trials and tribulations; give me the strength to bear them without grumbling. Turn away from me any evil thoughts, and make it so that I do not grant bad spirits, which would try to induce me to evil, any access to my soul. Enlighten my conscience regarding my faults, and remove from my eyes the veil of pride that could prevent me from seeing them and confessing them to myself.

You especially, ... [insert name], my guardian angel, which especially watches over me; and you all, protector spirits, that seem to have an interest in me, make me worthy of your kindness. You know my needs, let them be satisfied according to the will of God.

13. (Another prayer)

God, allow the good spirits that surround me to come to my aid when I am in pain, and to sup- port me when I stumble. Enable them, O Lord, to inspire me with faith, hope, and charitable love. May they be for me a support, a hope and a proof of your mercy. Finally, let me find next to them the strength I lack in life's trials and, in order to resist evil suggestions, the faith that saves and the love that comforts.

14. (Another prayer)

Beloved spirits, my guardian angel, you that God in its infinite mercy allow to watch over human beings, be my protectors in the trials of my earthly life. Give me strength, courage and acceptance. Inspire me with all that is good, keep me from sliding down on the slope of evil. May your sweet influence penetrate my soul; let me feel that a devoted friend is there, near me, sharing in my joys and sorrows.

And you, my good guardian angel, never forsake me, for I need your protection to bear with faith and love the trials that God has willed to send me.

To ward off evil spirits

15. "Woe to you , scribes and Pharisees, hypocrites! For you tithe mint and dill and cumin, and have neglected the weightier matters of the law: justice and mercy and faithfulness. These you ought to have done, without neglecting the others. You blind guides, straining out a gnat and swallowing a camel! Woe to you, scribes and Pharisees, hypocrites! For you clean the outside of the cup and the plate, but inside they are full of greed and self-indulgence. Woe to you, scribes and Pharisees, hypocrites! For you are like whitewashed tombs, which outwardly appear beautiful, but within are full of dead people's bones and all uncleanness. So you also outwardly appear righteous to others, but within you are full of hypocrisy and lawlessness (MATTHEW 23:23–27 ESV)."

16. INTRODUCTION

Evil spirits go only where they can satisfy their wickedness. In order to keep them away, it is not enough to ask for them to do, or even to command them: we must take away from ourselves whatever attracts them. Evil spirits sniff the wounds of one's soul, as flies scour the wounds of one's body. Just like you cleanse the body to avoid vermin, cleanse the soul of its impurities to avoid evil spirits. As we live in a world where evil spirits abound, good qualities of the heart do not always protect you from their attempts, but they give you the strength to resist them.

17. PRAYER

In the name of Almighty God, let evil spirits depart from me, and let the good ones serve as a bulwark against them! Evil spirits that inspire human beings with bad thoughts; wicked and lying spirits that deceive them; mocking spirits, that play with human credulity, I reject you with all the strength of my soul and close my ears to your suggestions – yet I call on you the mercy of God.

Good spirits that deign to assist me, give me the strength to resist the influence of evil spirits, and the necessary lights not to be deceived by their trickery. Preserve me from pride and presumption; remove from my heart any traces of jealousy, hatred, malevolence, and all feelings contrary to charitable love, which leave as many doors open to the spirit of evil.

TO ASK FOR A FAULT TO BE CORRECTED

18. INTRODUCTION

Our bad instincts are the result of imperfections of our own spirit, and not of our physical organism, otherwise we would escape all responsibility. Our improvement depends on us: every human being who has the enjoyment of their faculties also have, in all things, the freedom of choosing to do it or not to do it – to do good, a person lacks only the will (see Chapter **XV**, no. **10**; Chapter **XIX**, no. **12** above).

19. PRAYER

You have given me, O God, the intelligence necessary to distinguish what is good from what is evil. So as long as I recognize that something is wrong, I am guilty of not trying to resist it. Preserve me from pride which could prevent me from perceiving my faults, and evil spirits which could incite me to persevere in them.

Among my imperfections, I admit that I am particularly inclined to ... [name of imperfection], and if I do not resist this practice, it is because of the acquired habit of yielding to it.

Because you are righteous, you have not created me guilty, but rather with equal abilities to do right or wrong. If I followed the wrong way, it is as a consequence of my own free will. But for the same reason that I have the freedom to do evil, I am also free to do good, therefore I have the right to change course.

My current faults are a remnant of imperfections that I have retained from my previous lives; they are my original sin, so to speak, which I can get rid of by my willpower and with the help of good spirits.

Good spirits that protect me, and especially you my guardian angel, give me the strength to resist evil suggestions, and to emerge victorious from this struggle.

Faults are like barriers that separate us from God; and every fault we overcome is a step forward in getting closer to It.

The Lord, in its infinite mercy, deigned to grant me this current lifetime for my advancement. Good spirits, help me make the most of it, so that it does not end up wasted and lost to me; and that, when it pleases God to withdraw me from it, I am better off than when I entered it. (See Chapter **V**, no. **5**; Chapter **XVII**, no. **3** above).

To ask for strength to
resist temptations

20. Introduction

Every evil thought can have two sources: one is our own imperfection coming from our soul, the other, a pernicious influence acting upon it. The latter case is always a sign of weakness which makes us vulnerable to this sort of influence, and consequently of being an imperfect soul, in such a way that the one who succumbs cannot blame the influence of an extraneous spirit, since *that spirit would not have come near that person for evildoing, if it had deemed the latter to be inaccessible to temptation.*

When a bad thought rises in us, we can imagine a malicious spirit soliciting us to evil, and to which we are equally free to yield or resist just as if it were the solicitation of a living person. At the same time, we must seek help from our guardian angel, or from a protector spirit, which, in turn, will fight the bad influence in us, looking forward to *the final decision that we are going to make.* Our hesitation in doing evil is the voice of a good spirit that our conscience is able to hear. We recognize that a thought is bad when it turns away from charitable love, which is the basis of all true morals. When instead it is rooted in pride, vanity or selfishness; when its realization may cause detriment to others; and lastly, when it asks us to do unto others what we would not have them do unto us (see section no. **15** above and Chapter **XV**, no. **10** above).

21. PRAYER

Almighty God, do not let me give way to the temptation that will make me falter. Benevolent spirits that protect me, turn this evil thought away from me, and give me the strength to resist the suggestions of evil. If I succumb, I will fully deserve to make atonement for my fault in this lifetime and in another one, because I will have acted of my own free will.

THANKSGIVING FOR HAVING OVERCOME A TEMPTATION

22. INTRODUCTION

Whoever has resisted a temptation owes it to the assistance of the good spirits whose voices he or she listened to. They must thank God and their guardian angel.

23. PRAYER

I thank you, God, for allowing me to emerge victorious from the battle I have just fought against evil; make this victory give me strength to resist new temptations.

And my guardian angel, I thank you for the assistance you gave me. May my acquiescence merit your protection again!

PRAYER FOR ASKING ADVICE

24. INTRODUCTION

When we are undecided about doing or not doing something, first we should ask ourselves the following questions:

1) Can this thing I am hesitant to do be detrimental to someone else?
2) Will it be useful to anyone?
3) Would I be glad if someone did this thing to me?

If the thing concerns only oneself, it is advisable to arrive at a balance between the sum of personal benefits and inconveniences that may arise from it.

If it concerns other people – and if by doing good to one it may harm another – one must also weigh in the sum of good and evil in order to abstain from it or to act.

Finally, even for the best things, we must still carefully consider the opportunity and the incidental circumstances, because a good thing in itself can have bad results in disqualified hands, or if it is not conducted with caution and circumspection. Before undertaking it, it is advisable to check its forces and its means of execution.

In any case, one can always ask the assistance of their Protector Spirits by keeping this wise motto in mind: "When in doubt, abstain" (see no. **38** below).

25. PRAYER

In the name of God Almighty, good Spirits that protect me, inspire me with the best resolution to make in the uncertainty where I am right now. Direct my thoughts toward goodness, and turn away the influence of those who try to mislead me.

IN LIFE'S TRIBULATIONS

26. INTRODUCTION

We can ask God for earthly favors, and God may grant them to us when they have a useful and serious purpose; but as we judge the utility of things from our point of view – and our view is limited to the current time – we do not always see the bad side of what we want. God, who sees better than us, and wants only our good, may therefore refuse to grant them to us, as a parent deny a child anything that could harm him or her. If what we ask is not granted to us, we must not feel discouraged in any way; on the contrary, we should see the deprivation of what we wish to obtain as a test or an atonement, whose reward will be proportional to the resignation with which we bear it (see Chapter **XXVII**, no. **6**; Chapter **II**, nos. **5**, **6**, **7** above).

27. PRAYER

Almighty God, you that see our miseries, deign to listen favorably to the wishes that I am expressing to you at this very moment. If my request is inconsiderate, please forgive me; but if it is deemed reasonable and useful, may the good spirits that execute your will help me fulfill it.

Whatever the outcome, my God, may your will be done. If my wishes are not answered, it is because it is in your plans to test me, and I submit without grumbling. Make me not feel discouraged, and that neither my faith nor my resignation be shaken. ... [insert request].

THANKSGIVING FOR A
FAVOR OBTAINED

28. INTRODUCTION

We should not consider only things of great importance as being worthy of celebration; often apparently trivial events and experiences are the ones that most affect our destiny. Humans easily forget good, preferring to remember grief instead. If, day by day, we recorded the benefits of which we have been the target without even asking for them, we would be constantly taken aback by their great number, which are often erased from our memory by neglect and ingratitude.

Every night, when lifting our souls to God, we must remember within ourselves all the favors It has bestowed upon us during the day, and thank It for them. It is especially at the very moment when we feel the effect of God's goodness and protection that, by a spontaneous impulsion, we must show It our gratitude. For that, it suffices to send God a thought acknowledging the benefit received, without having to turn away from one's work or activity.

God's blessings are not only in material things; we must also thank It for the good ideas and felicitous inspirations that are suggested to us. While the proud takes the merit of them, while the unbeliever attributes them to mere chance, those who have faith gives thanks to God and the good spirits. For doing that, long sentences would be useless: "Thank you, Lord, for inspiring me with a good thought" says more than too many words. The spontaneous impulsion that makes us refer to God all that happens to us testifies to a habit of being grateful and humble, which wins over the sympathy of good spirits (see Chapter XXVII, nos. 7 and 8 above).

29. Prayer

God of infinite goodness, may your name be blessed for the benefits you have bestowed upon me; I would be unworthy if I ascribed them to chance events or to my own merit.

Good spirits, you that have been the executors of God's will, and especially you, my guardian angel, I thank you all. Ward off from me any thoughts of pride, or of using these benefits for any purpose other than doing good.

Thank you especially for ... [insert favor obtained]

ACT OF SUBMISSION AND RESIGNATION

30. INTRODUCTION

When something that causes pain or suffering happens to us, once we seek its cause, we often find that it is the result of our own imprudence, our improvidence, or an earlier action – in this case, we should only blame ourselves. If we took no part whatsoever in the cause of a misfortune, then it is either a test for our current life, or an atonement for a past existence. In the latter case, the nature of the atonement can be indicative of the nature of the fault itself, since we are always punished within the scope of our wrongdoing (see Chapter V, nos. 4, 6 *et seq.* above).

In whatever afflicts us, we generally see only the current evil, and not the subsequent favorable outcomes that it may have. Good is often the result of a transient malady, since the healing of a patient is often the result of the painful means employed to obtain it. In any case, we must submit to the will of God, bear with courage all tribulations of life, if we want this to be taken into account, so that this saying by Jesus Christ is applied to us: Blessed are those who suffer (see Chapter V, no. 18 above).

31. PRAYER

God you are sovereignly just; all suffering here below must have a cause and a purpose. I accept the affliction I have just experienced as an atonement for my past faults and a test for the future.

Good spirits that protect me, give me the strength to endure without grumbling. Let it be a salutary warning for me; something that will increase my experience. Let it combat my pride, excessive ambition, foolish vanity, and selfishness, thus contributing to my advancement.

32. (Another prayer)

I feel, O God, a need to pray to you to give me the strength to bear the trials you have willed to send me. Allow the light to be bright enough in my spirit so that I can appreciate the full extent of a love that afflicts me in order to save me. I submit with resignation, O God; but alas! as your created being I feel so weak that if you do not help me I am afraid of succumbing. Do not forsake me, O Lord, for without you I cannot do anything.

33. (Another player)

I look up to you, Lord, and I feel strengthened. You are my strength, do not forsake me! I am crushed under the weight of my iniquities! Please help me. You know the weakness of the flesh, and you will not look away from me!

I am devoured by a burning thirst; do sprinkle from the spring of living water, and I will be quenched. May my lips only art to sing your praises and not to grumble in the afflictions of my life. I am weak, Lord, but your love will give me strength.

O Lord Eternal! You alone are great, you alone are the aim and objective of my life. Your name be blessed, if you strike me, for you are the master and I am your unfaithful servant; I will bend my head without a murmur, for you alone are great, you alone are the goal.

IN FACE OF IMMINENT DANGER

34. INTRODUCTION

The dangers we incur, serve as a warning of our weakness and the fragility of our existence, as reminded by God. The Lord Eternal shows us that our life is in Its hands, and that it hangs by a thread that can be broken when we least expect it. In this respect, there is no privilege for anyone, for both the mighty and the meek are subject to the same alternatives.

If one examines the nature and the consequences of a danger, it will become clear that such consequences, should they materialize, would most often be the correction for a fault committed or a neglected duty.

35. PRAYER

Almighty God, and you, my guardian angel, help me! If I must succumb, may the will of God be done. If I am spared, may the rest of my life be used to repair the harm I may have done and to repent of it.

THANKSGIVING FOR HAVING ESCAPED A DANGER

36. INTRODUCTION

By the danger we have endured, God shows us that we may from one moment to the next be called to account for the use we have made of our life. It is thus that God warns us to look within ourselves, and to amend ourselves.

37. PRAYER

God, and you, my guardian angel, I thank you for the help you sent me to deliver me from the peril that threatened me. May this danger be a warning to me, and may it enlighten me on the faults that may have attracted to me. I understand, Lord, that my life is in your hands, and that you can take it away when you please. Inspire me, through the good spirits that assist me, with the thought of constructively use the time that still remains for me to spend here below.

My guardian angel, strengthen me in my resolution to right my wrongs and do as much good as I can, so that I may arrive loaded with less imperfections in the spirit world, when it pleases God to call me back there.

When going to sleep

38. Introduction

Sleep is for resting the body, but the spirit does not need to rest. While the senses are numb, the soul emerges partially from matter, and enjoys its spirit faculties. Sleep has been given to humans for restoring organic forces and also for moral forces. While the body recovers the elements it lost through the activities of the day before, the spirit invigorates itself among other spirits – it draws from what it sees, in what it hears, and in the advice given to it. On awakening, these ideas reappear in the guise of intuition. For the spirit, sleep is the temporary return from the exile to its true homeland; like a prisoner momentarily enjoying freedom.

But it just so happens, as with the unscrupu- lous prisoner, that the spirit does not always take advantage of this moment of freedom for its own advancement. If it harbors bad instincts, instead of seeking the company of good spirits, it seeks the company of its kind, and goes to places where it can give free rein to its inclinations.

May those who have been penetrated by this truth rise their thoughts when they feel it is time to fall asleep. May they call on the advice of good spirits and those departed whose memory is dear to them. May these spirits come to those who are asleep, during the short interval granted to them; and on waking up, such persons will feel heightened strength against evil, and more courage to face adversity.

39. Prayer

My soul will be with other spirits for a moment. Let those that are good come and help me with their advice. My guardian angel, make me wake up and keep a lasting and healthy impression of these encounters.

When sensing that one's life is coming to an end

40. Introduction

Faith in the future and elevation of thought during life, toward future destinies, help the prompt release of the spirit, loosening the bonds that tie it to the fleshly body – and often bodily life is not even yet extinct that the soul, impatient, has already taken off toward the immensity. In individuals who, on the contrary, concentrate all their thoughts in material things, these bonds are more tenacious, the separation is painful and arduous, and the awakening beyond the grave is full of trouble and anxiety.

41. PRAYER

God, I believe in you and your infinite goodness; that is why I cannot conceive that you gave humans intelligence to know you and aspiration for the future only to plunge them into nothingness.

I believe that my body is only the perishable envelope of my soul, and that when it ceases to live, I will wake up in the spiritual world.

Almighty God, I feel myself breaking the bonds that unite my soul to my body, and soon I will be held accountable for the use I made of this lifetime that is now ending.

I am going to reap the consequences of both good and evil that I have done; illusions and subterfuges are no longer possible: my whole past will unfold before me, and I will be judged according to my deeds. (See Chapter **XVI**, no. **9** above.)

O merciful God, may my repentance reach you! Deign to extend to me your indulgence.

If it pleases you to prolong my existence, let the remaining time be used by me to repair as much as possible any harm I may have done. But if my hour has inexorably struck, I will take with me the comforting thought that I will be allowed to redeem myself by means of new trials, in order to merit one day the happiness of the elect.

And if it is not for me to immediately enjoy this unalloyed bliss which is the sharing only of the just par excellence, I know that hope will not be forbidden to me forever, and that with work I'll get to that goal, sooner or later, depending on my efforts.

I know that good spirits and my guardian angel will be there, near me, to receive me; in just a little time, I will see them as they see me. I know that, if I have enough merit, I will meet again those whom I have loved on Earth, while those whom I am leaving behind here will one day rejoin me, so that we are

all reunited forever in the afterlife. In the meantime, I will also be able to come to visit them on Earth.

I also know that I will meet again those whom I have offended; may they forgive whatever grievances they still have against me: my pride, my hardness of heart, my injustice; and thus not overwhelm me with shame by their presence!

I forgive all those who have done me wrong or have wished evil on me while on Earth. I hold no grudge or hatred against them, and pray to God to forgive them.

Lord, give me the strength to leave behind with- out regrets the coarse joys of this world which are nothing next to the pure joys of the world beyond which I am going to enter. Therein, for the just, there is no more torment, no more suffering, no more miseries – only the culprits suffer, but even they have hope.

Good spirits, and you, my guardian angel, do not let me fail at this supreme moment. Make the divine light shine in my eyes, in order to revive my faith should it swerve from its path.

NOTE: See below *Prayers for the sick and the obsessed.*

III. PRAYERS FOR OTHERS

FOR SOMEONE IN DISTRESS

42. INTRODUCTION

If it is in the interest of the distressed that their afflicting trials follow their course, they will not be shortened at our request; but it would be impiety on our part to feel discouraged because our demand was not granted. Besides, should there be no cessation of the trial, there is always hope of obtaining some other consolation, which attenuates the bitterness of one's situation. However, what is truly useful for those who are in pain is courage and resignation, without which what they endure have no profit for them, because they shall be obliged to go through the same trial all over again. It is therefore toward this end that we must above all direct our efforts, either by calling good spirits to our aid, or by raising the morale of the distressed through counseling and encouragement; or finally through material assistance, if at all possible. The prayer, in this case, can also have a direct effect, transmitting a fluidic current toward the person, in order to strengthen his or her morale (see Chapter **V**, nos. **5** and **27**; Chapter **XXVII**, nos. **6** and **10** above).

43. PRAYER

O God, whose goodness is infinite, deign to soften the bitterness of the current situation of ... [insert name], if that be your will.

Good spirits, in the name of God Almighty, I beg you to assist this person in distress. If, it is in his/ her interest, not to be spared this affliction, make it so, O Lord, that they understand its necessity for their own advancement. Give them confidence in God and in the future that will make them less bitter. Give them also strength not to despair, for that would make them lose the fruit of their labors, and make their future condition even more painful. Take my thoughts to this person, and may it give them courage in their time of need.

THANKSGIVING FOR A BENEFIT GRANTED TO OTHERS

44. INTRODUCTION

Those who are not dominated by selfishness rejoice in the good that comes to their neighbor, even though they had not asked it by prayer.

45. PRAYER

God, be blessed for the happiness that has happened to ... [insert name].

Good spirits, let this person see in it an effect of God's goodness. If the good that happens to this person is a test, let this person be inspired with the thought of making good use of it and not to waste it vainly, so that this good does not turn into detriment for the future.

And you, my guardian angel which protects me and wants my happiness, dismiss from my mind any feelings of envy or jealousy.

PRAYER FOR OUR ENEMIES AND THOSE
WHO WISH US EVIL

46. INTRODUCTION

Jesus said: Love even your enemies. This saying represents the sublime in Christian charity; but by this Jesus does not mean that we must have toward our enemies the sane tenderness we have for our friends. Through those words, he tells us to forgive their trespasses, to forgive the harm they done to us, and to render them good for evil. In addition to the merit which results from this attitude in the eyes of God, this serves to show true superiority in the eyes of our fellow human beings (see Chapter **XII**, nos. **3** and **4** above).

47. PRAYER

Dear God, I forgive ... [insert name] **the harm he/she did to me and the one he/she wanted to do to me, as I want you to forgive me and that they themselves forgive me the wrongs I may have done to them. If you sent it my way as a test, let your will be done.**

Turn away from me, O God, the idea of cursing him/her, and any malicious wishes against them. Make me feel no joy at the misfortunes that may come to them, nor any pain for the benefits that may be granted to them, so that I do not defile my soul with thoughts unworthy of a Christian.

May your goodness, Lord, by extending itself upon him/her, lead them back to better feelings about me!

Good spirits, inspire me with forgetfulness of all evil and the memory of good deeds. That neither hatred, nor resentment, nor the desire to render evil for evil, come into my heart, for hatred and vengeance belong only to evil spirits whether incarnate or discarnate! May I, on the contrary, be willing to extend to him/her a fraternal hand, to render him/her good for evil, and to help him/her if it is in my power!

To prove the sincerity of my words, I wish that an opportunity be given to me of being useful to him/ her; but above all, O God, guard me from pride or ostentation, and from overwhelming him/her with humiliating generosity, which would make me lose any merit of my action. Should I act this way I would fully deserve that this admonition of Jesus Christ were applied to

me: "They have received their reward." (See Chapter **XIII**, nos. 1 *et seq.* above.)

THANKSGIVING FOR THE GOOD GRANTED TO OUR ENEMIES

48. INTRODUCTION

To wish no harm to one's enemies is to be only half-hearted as far as charitable love is concerned. True charity means that we wish them well, and that we are happy with whatever good may happen to them (see Chapter **XII**, nos. 7 and **8** above).

49. PRAYER

Dear God, in your justice, you thought you ought to rejoice the heart of ... [insert name]**. I thank you on his behalf, despite the harm he has done to me or that he has sought to do to me. If he seized the opportunity to humiliate me, I would accept it as a test for my charitable love.**

Good spirits that protect me, do not allow me to regret myself for doing this; turn away all envy and jealousy from me. On the contrary, inspire me with lofty generosity. Humiliation is in evil and not in good, and we know that, sooner or later, justice will be done to each according to their works.

FOR THE ENEMIES OF SPIRITISM

50. "Blessed are those who hunger and thirst for righteousness, for they shall be satisfied. Blessed are those who are persecuted for righteousness' sake, for theirs is the kingdom of heaven. Rejoice and be glad, for your reward is great in heaven, for so they persecuted the prophets who were before you (MATTHEW 5:6,10–12 ESV)."

"And do not fear those who kill the body but cannot kill the soul. Rather fear him who can destroy both soul and body in hell (MATTHEW 10:28 ESV)."

51. INTRODUCTION

Of all freedoms, the most inviolable is that of thinking, which also includes freedom of conscience. To curse those who do not think the same as we do is to claim this freedom for oneself and to refuse it to others; it is to violate the first commandment of Jesus: charity and the love of neighbor. To persecute them for their beliefs is to attack the most sacred right of every individual to believe what is right for oneself, and to worship God as one sees fit. To constrain them to external acts similar to ours is to show that we are more interested in form than in content, more in appearances than in conviction. Forced abjuration has never resulted in faith, it can only generate hypocrisy; it is an abuse of material force that does not prove any truth. *Truth is sure of itself: it convinces instead of persecuting, because it does not need to resort to it.*

Spiritism is an opinion, a belief; even if it were a religion, why should one not have the freedom to call oneself a Spiritist like one has of saying that one is Catholic, Jewish or Protestant, a partisan of this or that philosophical doctrine, of this or that economic system? A belief will be either false or true: If it is false, it will fall of itself, because error can not prevail against truth once light is made in our intellects; if true, no persecution can make it false.

Persecution is the baptism of all new, great and righteous ideas; it grows with the size and importance of the idea. The fury and anger of the enemies of the idea is because of the fear it inspires them. It is for this reason that Christianity was once persecuted and that Spiritism is persecuted today; with the difference, however, that Christianity was persecuted by the Gentiles, whereas Spiritism is persecuted by Christians. True, the time of bloody persecution has passed, but if one no longer kills the body, one still tortures the soul. Spiritists are attacked even in their innermost feelings, in their most cherished affections. Families are divided, mother excites against daughter, wife against husband. Some even attack the body in its material needs by depriving it of its livelihood to cause starvation (see Chapter **XXIII**, nos. **9** *et seq.* above).

Spiritists, do not be distressed by the blows that come your way, for they prove that you are in the truth, otherwise you would be left alone, and you would not be struck. It is a test for your faith, for it is according to your courage, to your resignation and to your perseverance that God will recognize you among Its faithful servants, of whom he is doing the counting today, so that each one is rewarded with their due share according to their works.

Following the example left by the Early Christians, be proud to carry your cross. Believe in the word of Christ, who said, "Blessed are those who are persecuted for righteousness' sake, for theirs is the kingdom of heaven.... And do not fear those who kill the body but cannot kill the soul." He also said,"Love your enemies, do good to those who hate you,... and pray for those who persecute you." Show that you are his true disciples, and that Spiritism is good, in doing what he says and what he has done himself.

Persecution will only last for a while; wait patiently for the dawn to rise, because the morning star is already on the horizon (see Chapter **XXIV**, nos. **13** *et seq.* above).

52. PRAYER

Lord, you said through the mouth of Jesus, your Messiah: "Blessed are those who are persecuted for righteousness' sake;" forgive your enemies; "Pray for those who persecute you;" and he himself showed us how to do it by praying for his tormentors. Following his example, dear God, we ask your mercy for those who are ignorant of your divine precepts, the only ones that can assure peace in this world and in the other. Like Christ, we say to you, "Father, forgive them, for they know not what they do."

Give us the strength to endure with patience and resignation their taunts, insults, calumnies and persecutions, as trials for our faith and humility. Turn us away from any thought of retaliation, because the hour of your justice will sound for all of us, and we await it by submitting to your holy will.

FOR A NEWLY BORN CHILD

53. INTRODUCTION

Spirits reach perfection only after having under- gone the trials of corporeal life. Those who are still wandering wait for God to allow them to return to a bodily existence, which should provide them with a means of advancement, either by atonement of their past faults by means of the vicissitudes to which they are subject, or by fulfilling a mission useful to humanity. Their advancement and future happiness will be commensurate with the way they have spent their lifetime on Earth. The task of guiding their first steps, and directing them toward goodness, is entrusted to their parents, who will answer before God for the manner in which they have fulfilled their mandate. It is to facilitate its execution that God has made parental love and filial love a law of nature; a law which is never violated with impunity.

54. PRAYER

(To be said by the parents)

Spirit which has incarnated in the body of our child, welcome to our family. Almighty God be praised for sending it too us.

It is a deposit entrusted to us of which we will have to be accountable one day. If it belongs to the new generation of good spirits that must populate the Earth, thank you, dear God, for this favor! If it is an imperfect soul, our duty is to help it progress in the way of good through our counsels and good examples. If it falls into evil through our fault, we will answer for it before you for not having fulfilled our mission as this child's parents.

Lord, support us in our task, and give us strength and willpower to fulfill it. If this child turns out to be cause of hardship for us, may your will be done!

Good spirits that came to preside over this child's birth and that must accompany this child during life, please never give up. Ward off from this child any evil spirit that may try to induce evil. Give this child strength to resist such suggestions, and the courage to endure with patience and resignation any trials that may beset this child here on Earth. (See Chapter **XIV**, no. **9** above.)

55. (Another prayer)

Dear God, you have entrusted me with the fate of one of your spirits. Lord, make me worthy of the task imposed upon me; give me your protection; enlighten me, so that I may discern at an early age the tendencies of the child whom I must prepare to enter into your peace.

56. (Another prayer)

Infinitely kind God, since it has pleased you to allow the spirit of this child to reincarnate so as to undergo earthly tests intended to make it progress, give him/her the light, so that he/she gets to know you, and to love you, and to worship you. By your omnipotence, do let this soul regenerate itself at the source of your divine directives. Under the guidance of his/her guardian angel, may his/her intelligence grow and develop, and make him/her aspire to draw increasingly closer to you. May the science of Spiritism be the bright light that will illuminate this child through life's many pitfalls. Finally, may this child know how to appreciate the full extent of your love which causes us to purify ourselves.

Lord, cast a paternal look on the family to which you have entrusted this soul. May they understand the importance of their mission and make the good seeds germinate in this child until the day he/she can rise up toward you by his/her own aspirations.

Deign to answer this humble prayer, dear God, in the name and merit of the one who said: "Let the little children come to me ..., for to such belongs the kingdom of heaven."

FOR SOMEONE WHO IS DYING

57. INTRODUCTION

Death agony is a prelude to the separation of soul and body. We can say that at that moment a human being has only one foot in this world, while the other is in the world beyond. This transition is sometimes painful for those who are fond of matter and have lived more for the enjoyments of this world than for those of the world beyond; or whose conscience is tormented by regrets and remorse. Conversely, for those whose thoughts have risen to the infinite, and have detached themselves from matter, the bonds are less difficult to break, and the last moments are not at all painful, as the soul holds to the body only by a thread, while in the other condition, as described earlier, it holds to matter deep roots. In all cases, prayer exerts a powerful action over the process of separation (see farther below *Prayers for the sick*).[97]

58. PRAYER

Almighty and merciful God, here is a soul that leaves its earthly envelope to return to the spirit world, its true homeland. May it return in peace and your mercy be extended toward it.

---

97 See also A. KARDEC, *Heaven and Hell,* Part two, Chapter I, "The passage."

Good spirits who have accompanied it to Earth, do not forsake it at this supreme moment; give it the strength to endure the last suffering it must endure here below for its future advancement. Inspire it to devote the last glimmers of consciousness which remain in it, or which may momentarily return to it, to repentance for its errors.

Direct my thought, so that its action can make the process of separation less painful for this soul; and that, at the moment of leaving Earth, it may carry within it the comforts of hope.

IV. PRAYERS FOR THE DEPARTED

FOR SOMEONE WHO HAS JUST PASSED AWAY

59. INTRODUCTION

Prayers for spirits that have just left the Earth are not only intended as a a testimony of sympathy, but also have the effect of helping them disengage from the body, thereby shortening the period of disturbance which always follow a separation from the body, and make the awakening on the other side calmer. But here again, as in all other circumstances, its effectiveness depends on the sincerity of one's thought, and not on the abundance of words spoken with more or less pomp and ceremony, in which, by the way, the heart often takes no part.

The prayers that come from the heart resound around the spirit, whose ideas are still confused, like friendly voices that gently awaken one from sleep (see Chapter **XXVII**, no. **10** above).

60. PRAYER

Almighty God, may your mercy spread over the soul of ... [insert name], **whom you have just called to you. May the trials that he/she suffered on Earth be taken into account, and our prayers soften and shorten the sorrows he/she can still endure as spirit!**

Good spirits that have come to receive this soul, and you especially, its guardian angel, assist it in getting rid of its body's matter. Give it light and self-awareness to draw it from the

confusion that usually accompanies the passage from bodily life to spiritual life. Inspire it with repentance for the faults it may have committed, and with a desire to atone for them in order to hasten its advancement toward blessed, eternal life.

[Insert name] ..., you have just entered the world of spirits, and yet you are still here among us; you can see and hear us, for there is nothing between you and us than the perishable body which you have just quitted and which will soon be reduced to dust.

You have left the coarse envelope which is subject to vicissitudes and to death, and now you have retained only your ethereal envelope, which is imperishable and inaccessible to suffering. If you no longer live by the body, you live in a spirit life, which is free from the miseries that afflict humanity.

You no longer wears the veil that deprives us of the splendors of future life. Now, you will be able to contemplate new wonders while we are still plunged into material darkness.

You will roam the spiritual plane and visit worlds freely, while we crawl hard on Earth, where we still have to inhabit our material bodies, which are like a heavy burden for us to bear.

Infinity's horizon will unfold before you, and in presence of such magnificence you will understand how vain our earthly desires and worldly ambitions are, and the futile pleasures in which humans delight.

Death is only a material separation of a human from his/her fellow beings for a short while. From this place of exile in which the will of God still holds us, and besides the duties we have to fulfill here below, we will follow you with our thoughts until we are allowed to join you as you have joined those who preceded you.

If we cannot go up to you, you, on the contrary, can come to us. Come therefore amidst those who love you and that you have loved; support them during life's trials; watch over those who are dear to you. Protect them according to your power, and soften their sorrow with the thought that you are happier now, and of the comforting certainty that, one day, you are going to be reunited in a better world.

In the world where you are, all earthly resentments must disappear. May you, for the sake of your future happiness, be henceforth inaccessible to such feelings! Forgive those who may have done wrong to you, as you are forgiven the wrong you may have done to them.

NOTE: One can add to this prayer, which is generic, some specific words depending on the particular circumstances of family or relationship, and the position of the deceased.

If the deceased is a child, Spiritism teaches us that it is not a recently created spirit, but rather one that had other lives before this and can already be very advanced. If its last lifetime was short, it was only to complete a previous trial, or it was meant to be a test for the parents (see Chapter **V**, no. **21** above).

61. (Another prayer)[98]

Almighty God, may your mercy be extended to our brothers and sisters who have just left Earth! Let your light shine in their eyes, take them out of darkness, open their eyes and their ears! May your good spirits surround them and make them hear words of peace and hope!

Lord, however unworthy we are, we dare to implore your merciful indulgence on behalf of our brothers and sisters who have just been taken away from this earthly exile. Let their return to the spiritual world be like that of the prodigal son. Forget, dear God, the mistakes they made, and instead remember their good deeds. Your justice is immutable, we know it well, but your love is immense; we beg you to appease your justice with this source of kindness that flows from you.

May light surround you, my brother/sister, who have just left Earth! May the good spirits of the Lord come down to you, surround you and help you break free of your earthly chains! May you understand and see the greatness of our master; submit without grumbling to his justice, and never despair of his mercy. Brother! Sister! Let a serious return to your past open the door to the future by making you understand the mistakes you leave behind, and the work you have to do to fix them! May God forgive you, and may his good spirits give you support and encourage you! Your brothers and sisters down here on Earth will pray for you and ask you to pray for them.

---

98 This prayer was dictated to a medium in Bordeaux (France) at the moment the burial convoy of a stranger was passing right in front of the medium's window.

For those departed who were dear to us

62. Introduction

How awful is the idea of nothingness! Those are to be pitied who think that the voice of a friend who mourns his or her friend is lost in the void and finds no answering echo! They have never known pure and holy affections, those who think that everything dies with the body; that the genius which once enlightened the world with his/her vast intelligence is a play of matter which is extinguished forever, like a breath of air; or that one's dearest living being, such as a father, a mother, or a beloved child is gone forever, leaving behind just a handful of dust that time will scatter irrevocably!

How could a kind-hearted person remain indifferent to this thought? How does the idea of absolute annihilation not freeze such a person with fright and make him/her at least desire that it was not so? If up to this day his/her reason was not capable to remove their doubts, here is Spiritism, which comes to dispel any uncertainty about the future by means of material proofs that it has given of the survival of the soul and the existence of beings from beyond the grave. Everywhere these proofs are welcomed with joy, and confidence is reborn, for humans now know that earthly life is only a short passage that leads to a better life; that their labors here below are not lost to them; and that the most holy affections are not hopelessly broken (see Chapter **IV**, no. **18** and Chapter **V**, no. **21** above).

63. Prayer

Dear God, deign to receive favorably the prayer that I address to you for the spirit of ... [insert name]. **Give him/her a glimpse of your divine light, and facilitate for his/her soul the way to eternal bliss. Allow good spirits to carry my words and my thoughts to him/her.**

And you who were dear to me in this world, hear my voice calling you to offer a new pledge of my affection. God has allowed you to be the first to depart: I cannot complain without being selfish, for it would be regrettable to overwhelm you with the sorrows and sufferings of earthly life. I am therefore resignedly

awaiting the moment of our meeting again in the happier world into which you have preceded me.

I know that our separation is only momentary, and that, regardless of how long it may seem to me, its duration fades before the everlasting happiness that God has promised to Its chosen ones. May his kindness preserve me from doing anything that may delay this desired reunion, and so spare me the pain of not finding you again. at the end of my earthly captivity.

How sweet and comforting is the certainty that between us there is only a material veil that prevents me from seeing you! That you can be there, by my side, seeing me and hearing as usual, and even better than before; that you have not forgotten me as I myself have not forgotten you; that our thoughts never cease to blend; and that yours follows mine, always sustaining me.

May the peace of the Lord be with you.

For distressed souls requesting prayers for themselves

64. Introduction

To understand the relief that prayer can provide to suffering spirits, it is necessary to refer to the way it performs, as explained elsewhere (see Chapter **XXVII**, no. **9, 18** *et seq.* above). Those who are penetrated by this truth pray fervently, because they are absolutely sure that their prayers are not in vain.

65. Prayer

Merciful and forgiving God, may your kindness spread over all the spirits that recommend themselves to our prayers, and especially over the soul of ... [insert name].

Good spirits, whose goodness is your only occupation, intercede with me for the relief of these souls. Make a ray of hope shine in their eyes, and let divine light illuminate them so that they can detect the imperfections which have kept them away from the abode of the blessed. Open their hearts to repentance and the desire to purge themselves, thus hastening their advancement. Make them understand that by their efforts they can shorten the time of their trials.

May God, in Its kindness, give them the strength to persevere in their good resolutions!

May these benevolent words soften their troubles by showing them that there are beings on Earth who sympathize with them and wish them happiness.

66. (Another prayer)

We pray you, O Lord, to extend to all those who suffer, whether on the spiritual plane as wandering spirits or among us as incarnate souls, the graces of your love and your mercy. Have pity on our weaknesses. You made us fallible, but you gave us the strength to resist evil and defeat it. May your mercy be extended to all who have not been able to resist their evil inclinations, and are still dragged on a bad path. May your good spirits surround them; let your light shine before their eyes, and that, attracted by its life-giving warmth, they come humbled, repentant, and submissive, falling prostrate at your feet.

We also pray to you, merciful God, for those brothers and sisters who did not have the strength to bear their earthly trials. You give us a burden to carry, Lord, and we must not lay it down at your feet. However, our weakness is great, and we sometimes lack courage along the way. Have pity on those indolent servants who abandoned work before time; may your justice save them and allow your good spirits to bring them relief, comfort, and hope in the future. The prospect of forgiveness strengthens one's soul. Reveal it, Lord, to those guilty despairing spirits, and they, supported by this hope, will draw strength from the very enormity of their faults and sufferings, in order to redeem their past and prepare themselves to conquer the future.

FOR A DECEASED ENEMY

67. INTRODUCTION

Charity towards our enemies must follow them beyond the grave. We must think that the harm they have done to us has been a test for us that may have been useful for our advancement, if we were able to benefit from it. Such a test may even have been more profitable to us than any purely material afflictions, for having enable us to add charitable love and forgetfulness of offenses to courage and resignation (see Chapter **X**, no. **6**; Chapter **XVII**, nos. **5** and **6** above).

68. PRAYER

Lord, it has pleased you to call before me the soul of ... [insert name] **back to the spiritual world. I forgive him/her the harm he/she has done to me, and their bad intentions toward me. May he/she regret it now that he/she is no longer plagued by the illusions of this world.**

May your mercy, dear God, spread over him/ her, and remove from me any thought of rejoicing at his/her death. If I have done wrong to him/her, forgive me, just as I forgive the wrong this enemy of mine has done to me.

FOR A CRIMINAL

69. INTRODUCTION

If the effectiveness of prayers was proportional to their length, the longest should be reserved for the most culpable individuals, since they need it more than those who have lived saintly. To refuse to pray for criminals shows a lack of charitable love and a gross disregard of God's mercy. To think prayers are useless in this case, because someone has committed such or such a fault, is to prejudge the justice of the Most High (see Chapter **XI**, no. **14** above).

70. PRAYER

O Lord, merciful God, do not repel this criminal who has just left Earth. Human justice may have struck him/her, but this does not free him/her from your justice, if their heart has not been touched by remorse.

Raise the blindfold that hides the severity of their crimes. May his/her repentance find grace in your presence, and alleviate the sufferings of his/ her soul! May our prayers and the intercession of good spirits also bring him/her hope and comfort; and inspire him/her with the desire of atoning for his/her bad deeds in a new lifetime. Also give him/ her the strength not to succumb to new struggles he/she will have to face!

Lord, have mercy on him/her!

FOR SOMEONE WHO HAS COMMITTED SUICIDE

71. INTRODUCTION

No human being ever has the right to dispose of his or her own life, for only God has the right to pull one out of earthly captivity when It deems appropriate. However, divine justice can soften its severity regarding its circumstances, although it reserves all its severity for those who have tried to escape the trials of life. A suicide is like the prisoner who escapes from his prison before the expiration of his sentence, and who, when captured again, is held more severely. This is what happens to a suicide, who thinks to have escaped current miseries, only to be immersed in greater misfortunes (see Chapter **V**, nos. **14** *et seq.* above).

72. PRAYER

Dear God, we know the fate reserved for those who violate your laws by deliberately abridging their days; but we also know that your mercy has no bounds. Deign to extend it to the soul of ... [insert name]. **May our prayers and your compassion soften the bitterness of the sufferings his/her soul now endures for not having had the courage to wait the end of his/her life's trials!**

Good spirits, whose mission is to assist the unfortunate, take this soul under your protection. Inspire it with regret for its faults, and may your assistance give it strength to endure with more resignation the new trials that it will have to undergo in order to atone for them. Remove from this soul all evil spirits which could again drag it to evil and prolong its sufferings by making it lose the fruit of its labor in future trials.

As for you, whose misfortune is the subject of our prayers, may our compassion soften your bitterness and bring forth in you hope for a better future! This future is in your hands; entrust yourself to the kindness of God, which takes to its bosom all who have repented, remaining closed only to those whose hearts have hardened.

For repentant spirits

73. Introduction

It would be unfair to place in the same category of evil spirits, those suffering and repentant spirits which ask for prayers. They may have been bad in the past but have since changed their ways, and now admit their faults and sincerely regret them. They are only unhappy; some have even begun to experience some relative happiness.

74. Prayer

Merciful God, which accepts the sincere repen- tance of any incarnate or discarnate sinner, here is a spirit that had delighted in evil, but which has now acknowledged its wrongs and entered the right path. Deign, dear God, to receive this soul as a prodigal son worthy of forgiveness.

Good spirits whose voice it has misunderstood, it will listen to you henceforth. Allow it to have a glimpse of the happiness enjoyed by the elect of the Lord, so that it perseveres in the desire to purify itself in order to attain it. Support it in its good resolutions, and give it strength to resist its bad instincts.

Spirit of ... [insert name], we congratulate you on your change of mind, and we thank the good spirits that helped you!

If you formerly delighted in doing evil, it is because you did not understand how sweet the enjoyment of doing good is. You also felt too low to hope that you could attain it. But from the moment you set foot on the right path, a new light has been made for you; you have begun to taste an unknown happiness; and hope has entered your heart. It is because God always listens to the prayer of a repentant sinner; God rejects none of those who come to It. To recover God's favor completely, apply your-self from now on, not only to do no harm any more, but to do good, and especially to repair the evil that you have done. Then you will have satisfied the justice of God; every good action will erase one of your past mistakes.

The first step is done; now, the further you go, the more grati-fying and easier the path will seem. Persevere then, and one day you will have the glory of be counted among the good and the blessed spirits.

For hardened spirits

75. Introduction

Evil spirits are those not yet touched by repentance; which are fond of evil, and conceive of no regrets; which are insensitive to reproaches, reject prayer, and often blaspheme the name of God. It is these hardened souls that, after death, take revenge on humans for the sufferings they endure, and pursue with their hatred those they hated during their lifetimes, either through obsession or some fatal influence (see Chapter **X**, no. **6**; Chapter **XII**, nos. **5** and **6** above).

Among evil spirits, there are two quite distinct categories: those which are frankly bad and those which are hypocrites. The former are infinitely easier to bring back to good than the latter; this category is most often composed of often brute and coarse natures, as we see among incarnate humans, which do evil more by instinct than by calculation, and do not feign or pretend to be better than they are. In them there is a latent potential which must be awaken, which is almost always attained with perseverance, firmness, and benevolence, through counseling, reasoning, and prayer. In mediumship, the difficulty they have in writing the name of God is the sign of an instinctive fear, of an inner voice of conscience which tells them that they are unworthy of it. Those which come to Spiritist seances are on the threshold of conversion, and we can all hope for such spirits: it suffices to find the vulnerable point of their heart.

Hypocritical spirits are almost always very clever, but they have no sensitive fiber in their heart; nothing touches them. They simulate all good feelings to gain trust, and are happy when they find dupes who can accept them as holy spirits, and whom they can control as they please. The name of God, far from inspiring the slightest fear, serves them as a mask to cover their turpitude. In the invisible world, as in the visible one, hypocrites are the most dangerous beings, because they act in the shadows without raising any suspicion. They have only the appearances of faith without any sincerity.

76. Prayer

Lord, deign to cast a glance of goodness upon the imperfect Spirits that are still in the darkness of ignorance and do not know you, especially that of ... [insert name].

Good spirits, help us make it understand that by inducing humans to do evil; by obsessing and tormenting them; it prolongs its own sorrows. Make the example of the happiness you enjoy an encouragement to it.

Spirit, which still delights in practicing evil, you have just heard the prayer that we said for you. It should prove to you that we wish to do you good, even if you do wrong.

You are unhappy, for it is impossible to be happy by doing evil; then why then stay in pain when it depends on you to leave it? Observe the good spirits around you, see how happy they are, and whether it would not be more pleasant for you to enjoy the same happiness.

You will claim that it is impossible for you to do that; but nothing is impossible to those who will, for God has given you, as to all his created beings, the freedom to choose between good and evil, that is to say, between happiness and misfortune. Therefore no one is doomed to do evil. If you have the will to do it, you certainly have the one to do good and be happy.

Turn your gaze to God. Just for one moment, lift up to It in thought, and a ray of divine light will come to enlighten you. Say with us these simple words: Dear God, I repent, forgive me. Try repentance and do good instead of doing evil, and you will see that Its mercy will spread over you, and that an unknown well-being will replace the anxieties you now endure.

Once you have taken one step in the right direction, the rest of the way will seem easy. You will then understand how much time you have wasted for your happiness through your faults; but a radiant and hopeful future will unfold before you and make you forget your miserable past full of trouble and moral torture that would be hell for you if it were to last forever. One day will come that these tortures will be such that you will be willing to stop them at any cost; yet the longer you wait, the harder it will become.

Do not think that you will always remain in the state you are in. No, that would be impossible; you have two perspectives before you: either you suffer much more than you do now, or be happy like the good spirits around you. The first alternative is inevitable if you persist in your stubbornness; a simple effort of willpower on your part will be enough to get you out of the bad place where you are. Hurry up, for every day of delay is a day lost for your happiness.

Good spirits, let these words find their way into this backward spirit, so that they may help it come closer to God. We pray in the name of Jesus Christ, who had such great power over evil spirits.

---

v. For the sick and the obsessed

Prayers for the sick

77. Introduction

Illnesses are part of earthly life's trials and vicissitudes. They are inherent in the relative crudeness of our material nature and the inferiority of the world we inhabit. Passions and excesses of all kinds sow unhealthy things in our body, often hereditary. In more advanced worlds, whether physically or morally, the human organism, in more depurated and less material state, is not subject to these infirmities, and the body is not undermined by the ravages of passions (see Chapter **III**, no. **9** above). We must resign ourselves to the consequences of the environment where our inferiority has placed us, until we have deserved to move to a better one. In the meantime, this should not prevent us from doing whatever we can to improve our current condition; but if, despite all our efforts, we cannot succeed, Spiritism teaches us to bear with resignation our temporary evils.

If God had not intended that corporeal sufferings were dissipated or in some cases softened, It would not have put curative means at our disposal. God's thoughtful solicitude in this respect, in line with our instinct of self-preservation, indicates that it is our duty to seek and apply such means.

In addition to conventional medication elaborated by orthodox medicine, magnetism (mesmerism) made us aware of the power of fluidic action. Then Spiritism came and revealed another force in healing mediumship and the influence of prayer (see *Final remarks* at the end of this book).

78. PRAYER (for a sick person)

Lord, you are all righteousness; therefore I must have deserved the illness that you willed to send me, because you never strike without a cause. I rely on your infinite mercy for my healing; please restore my health, and may your holy name be blessed. But if, on the contrary, I must still suffer, let your name be blessed in the same way; I submit without grumbling to your divine decrees, for all that you do can have no other purpose than the good of all created beings.

Dear God, let this sickness be for me a salutary warning, and make me look inward. I accept it as some atonement for the past, and as a test for my faith and submission to your holy will.

(See prayer no. 40 above.)

79. PRAYER (for a sick person)

Dear Good, your designs are inscrutable, and your wisdom you have willed to strike ... [insert name] with illness. Cast, I implore you, a compassionate gaze at this person's sufferings, and deign to put an end to them.

Good spirits, ministers of the Almighty, endorse, I pray you, my desire to relieve this person. Direct my thoughts so that they may pour a salutary balm over his/her body and bring comfort to his/her soul.

Inspire him/her with patience and submission to God's will; give him/her strength to bear his/her pains with Christian resignation, so that he/she may not lose the fruit of this trial.

(See prayer no. 57 above.)

80. PRAYER (for a healing medium)

Dear God, if you deign to use me as unworthy as I am, I might cure this suffering, if that is your will, for I have faith in you. But without you I am powerless to do anything. Allow good spirits to suffuse me with their salutary fluid, so that I may transmit it to this patient; and rid my mind of any thought of pride and selfishness which could alter its purity.

Prayers for the obsessed

81. Introduction

Obsession is a persistent action exerted upon someone by an evil spirit. It presents itself in very different ways, from a mere moral influence without perceptible external signs, to a complete disturbance of one's body and mental faculties. It obliterates all mediumistic faculties; in writing mediumship (psychography), it is detected by the obstinacy of a single spirit to manifest itself to the exclusion of all others.

Evil spirits are found swarming around the earth, because of the moral inferiority of its inhabitants. Their evil action is one of the scourges to which humankind is exposed here below. Obsession, just like illnesses, and all life's tribulations, should therefore be considered as a trial or an atonement, and be accepted as such.

Just as illnesses are the result of physical imperfections which make the body accessible to pernicious external influences, an obsession is always the result of some moral blemish which opens rifts for an evil spirit. A physical cause must be countered by a physical force, whereas a moral cause can only be countered by a moral force. To avoid diseases, the body should be strengthened; to prevent obsessions one must strengthen the soul. Hence the obsessed should always work for his/her own improvement, which is usually enough to get rid of the obsessor without any extraneous help. Such help becomes necessary when an obsession degenerates into subjugation and possession, because then the patient will probably have lost all his/her willpower and free will.

The motive behind an obsession is almost always vengeance exerted by a spirit, which most often originated in a relationship that the obsessed had with the obsessor in a previous existence (see Chapter **X**, no. **6**; Chapter **XII**, nos. **5** and **6** above).

In cases of serious obsession, the obsessed is like enveloped and impregnated with a pernicious fluid that neutralizes the action of beneficial fluids by repelling them. It is this fluid that one must get rid of; but a bad fluid cannot be pushed away by another bad fluid. By an action identical to that of a healing medium in case of a disease, it is necessary to expel the bad fluid by means of a better fluid which produces something similar to the effect of a reagent. This action is mechanical, but this is not enough: it is necessary above all to act upon the intelligent being, the spirit to which one must have the right to speak with authority – and such an authority is given only to those who are morally superior. The greater the superiority, the higher the authority.

But there is still more to be done. To secure deliverance, the evil spirit must be led to renounce its evil designs, and imbued with repentance and a desire to do good, by means of deftly directed instructions, in particular evocations made for the purpose of the spirit's moral education. Thus one can finally have the double satisfaction of delivering an incarnate from an obsession and converting an imperfect Spirit.

This task is made easier when the obsessed, understanding his/her situation, adds his/her own willpower and prayers to the proceedings. That is not so when the latter, fooled by the deceiving spirit, deludes himself/herself as to the supposed qualities of the one which dominates him/ her, and delights in the error in which the spirit plunges him/her. Far from cooperating, such individuals reject all assistance. This happens in the so-called cases of fascination, which are always infinitely more rebellious than the most violent cases of subjugation (see Allan KARDEC, *The Mediums' Book,* Chapter XXIII).

In all cases of obsession, prayer is the most power- ful aid against an obsessor.

82. PRAYER (for the obsessed)

Dear God, allow good spirits to deliver me from the evil spirit which has become attached to me. If it is a vengeance that it is exerting for wrongs that I have committed against it in the past, then you have allowed this to happen as a correction, and I am suffering the consequences of my own faults. May my repentance deserve your forgiveness and my deliverance! But whatever this spirit's motive, I call your mercy on it; deign to facilitate the path of progress that will deter it from the thought of doing evil. May I, for my part, bring it to better feelings by rendering it good for evil.

But I also know, dear God, that it is my imperfections that make me accessible to the influences of Imperfect Spirits. Give

me light to recognize them. Above all, fight in me the pride that blinds me to the truth about my faults.

How unworthy I feel, to have let a malignant spirit take control of me!

Make this debacle of my vanity, dear God, serve me as a lesson in future. May it strengthen me in the resolution I now take of purifying myself through the practice of good, charitable love and humility, in order to raise a barrier against bad influences from now on.

Lord, give me strength to endure this trial with patience and resignation. I understand that, like all other trials, it will eventually help my advancement if I do not lose the fruit of my sufferings by grumbling, since it gives me an opportunity to show you my submission, and to exercise my charitable love toward an unhappy spiritual sibling, by forgiving it the harm it has done to me. (See Chapter **XII**, nos. **5** and **6** above.)

(See prayers nos. **15** *et seq.*; **46** and **47** above)

83. PRAYER (for the obsessed)

Almighty God, deign to give me the power to deliver ... [insert name] **from the spirit that is obsessing him/her. If it enters into your plans to put an end to this ordeal, grant me the grace of speaking to this spirit with authority.**

Good spirits that support me, and you, this person's guardian angel, lend me your assistance, help me get rid of the impure fluid that is wrapped around him/her.

In the name of Almighty God, I adjure the evil spirit which is tormenting this person to withdraw.

84. PRAYER (for the obsessor)

Infinitely kind God, I implore your mercy for the spirit that is obsessing ... [insert name]. **Make it catch a glimpse of the divine light, so that he can see the wrong path he has committed. Good spirits, help me make it understand that it has everything to lose by doing evil, and everything to gain by doing good.**

Spirit that enjoys tormenting ... [insert name], **listen to me, as I speak to you in the name of God.**

If you wish to reflect on it, you will understand that evil cannot prevail over good, and that there is no way you can be stronger than God and the good spirits.

They could have preserved ... [insert name] from any attack on your part. If they did not do it, it is because he/she had to undergo this trial. But when this trial is over, they will take away all influence you may have on him/her; and them the harm you have done to him/her, instead of injuring this person, will have aided his/her advancement, making him/ her feel happier. So your wickedness will have been in vain for you, and will turn against you.

God, which is all-powerful, and Higher-order Spirits are his delegates, which are more powerful than you, will be able to put an end to this obsession when they wish, and your tenacity will be broken by their supreme authority. But by the very fact that God is good, It will still leave you the merit of ceasing this obsessive process of your own will. It is a respite being granted to you; if you fail to avail yourself of this opportunity, you will suffer deplorable consequences. Great punishments and cruel sufferings await you. You will be compelled to implore God's mercy and prayers from your victim, who has already forgiven you and prays for you – which is of great merit before God, and will speed his/her deliverance.

So think while there is still time, for the righteousness of God will come upon you as on all rebellious spirits. Remember that the evil you are doing at this moment will necessarily come to an end, while, if you persist in your hardened conduct, your sufferings will incessantly grow.

When you still lived on Earth, would you not deem it foolish to sacrifice a great good for a small, fleeting satisfaction? It is the same now as spirit. What do you gain by doing this? The sad pleasure of tormenting someone, which does not prevent you from being unhappy, whatever you may say, and will make you still more miserable.

Besides, see what you have been missing: look at the good spirits around you, and see whether their fate is not better than yours. The happiness they enjoy will be yours to share when you want it. What does it take for that to happen? To implore God, and do good instead of doing evil. I know you can not transform yourself all of a sudden; but God does not ask the impossible; what It wants is goodwill. So try, and we all will help you. May we soon be able to say for you the prayer for repentant spirits, and you no longer be among evil spirits, until you can counted among the good ones.

(See prayer "For repentant spirits," no. **73** above;
and prayer no. **75**, "For hardened spirits")

Final remarks

THE CURE FOR SEVERE OBSESSIONS requires a lot of patience, perseverance and dedication. It also asks for tact and skillfulness to direct toward good this kind of spirits which are often very perverse, quite hardened and astute, besides being rebellious to the extreme. In most cases, we must be guided by the circumstances; yet, whatever the character or nature of the spirit, it is a certain fact, that one obtains nothing through constraint or threats. All influence depends solely on one's moral ascendancy. Another fact, equally ascertained by experience as well as by logic, is the complete ineffectiveness of exorcisms, formulas, sacramental words, amulets, talismans, external practices, or any material signs.

A long-term obsession can cause pathological disorders, and sometimes requires simultaneous or consecutive treatment, whether through magnetic healing or medical therapy, to restore the person"s physical health. Once the cause has been destroyed, there remain the effects to be extirpated.[99]

---

99 About obsessions, see Allan KARDEC, *The Mediums' Book,* ch. XXIII. See also *La Revue Spirite* [*The Spiritist Review*], February and March, 1864; April, 1865.

Bibliography

BOOKS BY ALLAN KARDEC

KARDEC, Allan. *Genesis, Miracles and Predictions*. Trans. H. M. Monteiro. New York: USSF, 2019.

——————. *Heaven and Hell*. Trans. D. W. Kimble, M. M. Saiz, I. Reis. 2nd ed. Brasília, DF (Brazil): ISC/Edicei, 2011.

——————. *The Mediums' Book*. D. W. Kimble and M. M. Saiz. 2nd ed. Brasília, DF (Brazil): ISC/Edicei, 2010.

——————. *The Spirits' Book*. Trans. N. Alves, J. Korngold, H. M. Monteiro. 3rd ed. New York: USSC/USSF, 2020.

——————. *Spiritist Journey in 1862*. Trans H. M. Monteiro. New York: USSF, 2019.

——————. *The Spiritist Review –1858*. Trans L. A. V. Cheim, J. Korngold. New York: USSC/USSF, 2015.

——————. *The Spiritist Review –1859*. Trans L. A. V. Cheim, J. Korngold, J. C. Madden. New York: USSC/USSF, 2015.

——————. *The Spiritist Review –1860*. Trans L. A. V. Cheim, D. Caron, J. Korngold, J. C. Madden. New York: USSC/USSF, 2016.

——————. *The Spiritist Review –1861*. Trans L. A. V. Cheim, D. Caron, J. Korngold. 2nd ed. New York: USSF, 2018.

——————. *The Spiritist Review –1862*. Trans L. A. V. Cheim, J. Korngold, J. C. Madden. 2nd ed. New York: USSF, 2019.

——————. *What is Spiritism?* Trans D. W. Kimble, M. M. Saiz and Ily Reis. Brasília, DF (Brazil): ISC/Edicei, 2010.

Note: *In 2020 and following years, the six remaining volumes of The Spiritist Review, comprising all issues from years 1863–1868, as well as The Mediums' Book and other books, are scheduled to be published in English by the USSF in New York.*

**UNITED STATES
SPIRITIST FEDERATION**
New York – USA

Book portal: https://is.gd/ussf1

Made in the USA
Columbia, SC
01 September 2020

18192677R00213